D1716600

A resource for groups and individuals:

"Try to imagine an action-oriented book on how to move from a war system to a peace system that would be equally relevant for community peace action groups and peace studies classes, filled with the best of a substantial body of knowledge about peace-building yet presented in such a fresh and lively way that even seasoned peace-builders will find their heads spinning with new ideas and new images. Well, here it is."

—Elise Boulding, Professor Emeritus of Sociology, Dartmouth College,
and Secretary General, International Peace Research Association

"Pacem in Terris in Wilmington, Delaware conducted the first study group using Bob Irwin's *Building a Peace System*. I was amazed and excited by the excellence of the book and the impact it had on the participants. In our group, which included newcomers to the peace movement as well as oldtimers, everyone found the course a stimulating experience. *Building a Peace System* helps people find the key to the 'new way of thinking' Einstein exhorted us to find. It is an invaluable tool for helping people expand their thinking, build a positive image of a peace system, and understand the steps that are needed to get there. It has the potential to move minds in a more sustained and constructive manner than *Fate of the Earth*. It is truly the right approach for the 1990's."

—Sally Milbury-Steen, Executive Director, Pacem in Terris

"Democracy requires an informed and active public, and never more urgently than now, when peace, ecology, and economic justice are survival issues. We cannot rely on experts to do our thinking for us, yet few of us have time for extensive study on our own. By offering easy access to expert thinking in a format designed for democratic discussion, this book offers the best solution I know of to that dilemma."

—Randy Kehler, former national coordinator, Nuclear Weapons Freeze Campaign

BUILDING A PEACE SYSTEM

Robert A. Irwin
Exploratory Project on the Conditions of Peace

ExPro Press
Washington, DC

Published by: ExPro Press
Exploratory Project on the Conditions of Peace
1601 Connecticut Ave., NW, 5th floor
Washington, DC 20009
U.S.A.

For more information about the Exploratory Project
on the Conditions of Peace (ExPro), write to the address above.

Distributed by The Talman Company,
150 Fifth Avenue, New York, NY 10011

Library of Congress Cataloging-in-Publication Data

Irwin, Robert A., 1950-
    Building a peace system.

    Includes bibliographical references.
    Includes index.
    1. Peace. 2. Security, International. 3. Peace—Research. 4. Peace movements.
5. Social movements. I. Title.
JX1952.I76 1989   303.6'9   89-16925
ISBN 0-936391-39-1 (paperback)

Book design and production by Rick Schwartz/Communications
First printing: November 1989

Dedication

To the women and men who do the myriad tasks, large and small, of peace activism, in gratitude for your work and the caring that motivates it.

Without you, there would be little point in writing a book like this; with you, there is hope for a better future.

Thanks for your dedication.

Table of Contents

How to Use This Book   vii

A Personal Note   viii

Acknowledgments   ix

Introduction: The Peace System Approach to Eliminating War   1

     Why think about peace?

     The concept of "the war system"

     Why "peace system"?

     What would be the elements of a peace system?

     The transition to a peace system

     The importance of a hopeful vision of the future

     No static formula

PART ONE: **THE PRESENT DEBATE—AND BEYOND**

Introduction: How the Peace Movement Shaped the Present Debate   11

Chapter 1:   Deterrence, Star Wars, and Peace   15

Chapter 2:   Arms Control: Pro and Con   19

Chapter 3:   Redefining the Issues: Aspects of the War System   25

PART TWO: **DESIGNING A PEACE SYSTEM**

Introduction: Why and How to Think About the Future   35

Chapter 4:   Envisioning and Designing a Future of Peace   41

Chapter 5:   World Governance   47

Chapter 6:   Alternative Security Policies   55

Chapter 7:   Economic Development, Ecology, and Peace   63

Chapter 8:   Psychology, Religion, Culture, and Peace   77

Table of Contents

PART THREE: **MAKING PEACE A REALITY**

Introduction: Prospects for Building a Peace System   89
Chapter 9:   The Superpowers   95
Chapter 10:   Beyond the Superpowers: Other Actors   107
Chapter 11:   Making Changes: Analyses and Approaches   119
Chapter 12:   Considering Strategies   133
Chapter 13:   Where Do We Go from Here?   151

Afterword   157

Notes   161

GROUP STUDY RESOURCES

Introduction   207
A: How to Organize a Peace System Study Group   209
B: Principles for Democratic Social Change Study Groups   223
C: How to Do a 15-session Study Group   231
D: How to Do a 7-session Study Group   237
E: How to Base a College Course on This Book   245
F: How to Order the Materials   249
G: How to Do an "Imaging a World Without War" Workshop   257
H: Evaluating Your Study Group Experience   259

INFORMATION RESOURCES

A: Recommended Periodicals   263
B: Audio, Video, and Computer Sources of News and Commentary   275
C: Annotated Bibliography   279
D: Some Peace Organizations   297

About the Exploratory Project on the Conditions of Peace (ExPro)   299
About the Author   303
Index of Names   305

How to Use This Book

This book is for anyone interested in studying the possibilities for peace and freedom in a world without nuclear weapons. It can be used in several ways. Like a Swiss Army knife, although it is called one thing, it is actually several tools compactly combined in one package.

- You can read the pages that follow as you would any book. Although without the suggested readings, this volume may be a little like a menu without the meal, it is a hearty appetizer that will serve as an introduction both to important ideas and information and to a new approach to eliminating war.

- You can use this book as a manual for organizing a 7- or 15-session study group. All you need to do is become familiar with its contents, find interested people, and order the necessary materials. At each session five members of the group provide ideas for discussion by reporting on the items they've read. This book suggests a sequence for the readings, and in addition provides a commentary on them that every group member can read. It also advises how best to make the study group serve the participants' needs and interests.

- You can use this book as the basis for undergraduate or graduate-level courses. You may wish to add or substitute other readings for some of those suggested.

- You can draw on the several parts of the book's resource section for materials useful for public events or self-education. In addition, although the text of this book is designed to be accessible to the "average peace activist," its extensive notes and annotated bibliography are intended to make it valuable for students and scholars interested in peace and global issues.

A Personal Note

When I proposed preparation of this book as an ExPro project, I was already strongly convinced that studying writings about peace would be interesting for individuals and valuable for helping to reorient the peace movement. What I didn't anticipate was how beneficial I myself would find the experience.

Few people fully realize how debilitating are the effects of operating inside the framework of deterrence and interventionism currently dominant in the U.S. Even when we reject present policies and propose alternatives, the prevailing "mainstream" debate is our frame of reference.

To begin to operate within a different framework — that a decent, warless world is possible — is liberating. The opportunity to spend even a short time immersed in books and articles that take peace seriously as a possibility has put flesh on the bones of my stubborn but previously abstract hope.

This weightier hope derives not from escapism, but from a clearer understanding of the conditions that could sustain peace and an increased knowledge of the trends working for (and against) peace. What I have learned and envisioned enables me to hear each day's news more alert to what is most significant.

That we will escape destruction and achieve peace is far from sure. But I have found my own determination to work for peace strengthened by what I have learned, and likewise my confidence that we have a chance of success.

The readings recommended in the following pages contain ideas that have now become part of me. I am pleased to have had such successful teachers. I hope that you, too, will find the best of these ideas becoming your own, and that your work for peace will be strengthened by what you learn.

Acknowledgments

Researching and writing this book were made possible by the foundations and individuals whose financial support for ExPro has provided the bulk of the funding I relied upon. Their far-sighted willingness to support a wide-ranging inquiry has enabled ExPro to clarify the factors contributing to war and peace that are deeper than the ups and downs of superpower detente and arms control talks. The renewed public awareness of global ecological issues vindicates the broader approach to peace supported by these funders through ExPro; the fruits of that support appear both in this book and in the products of ExPro's ongoing research due to follow. To all those funders I offer deep gratitude.

I owe thanks also to Christopher Mogil and Nancy Brigham for timely information and to Betsy Raasch-Gilman and Paul Halvorson of Movement for a New Society's Seed Fund for rapid provision of a grant at a crucial early stage of this work.

I owe special thanks to W. H. Ferry and Mark Sommer for their vision and their tenacity in getting ExPro started. This volume in large part results from their conviction that "We have to get people talking about peace!" As a member of ExPro since its first meeting in September 1984, I have learned a great deal from my colleagues in our thrice-yearly discussions. This book is one reflection of our desire to share that learning experience with many others and our conviction that lasting peace can only be built by the efforts of many people.

I am grateful to Randy Kehler and Beth Jacklin for their patient support, good will, and encouragement, and to Beth for help both with numerous details and with overall management of the work; to Liane Norman, whose expert and tactful editing has proved that less is more; to Kelly Flynn for assistance in obtaining permissions and materials; and to Kirkpatrick Sale and Eleanor M. LeCain for advice on various aspects of the project.

Helpful comments on an early draft of the manuscript were given by W. H. Ferry, Patricia Mische, Daniel Deudney, Beth Jacklin, Elise Boulding, Nancy Brigham, Elizabeth Richards, Dietrich Fischer, Mark Sommer, Liane Norman, and Charles Derber, and other useful suggestions by Robert Holt, Richard Smoke, Robert Johansen, and Robert C. Tucker. I am also indebted to Richard A. Falk, Saul H. Mendlovitz, and their colleagues for their work, past and present, in the World Order Models Project, and to William H. Moyer, the late Jim Nunes-Schrag, and many others who developed and refined the "macro-analysis" democratic study group model I have adapted in these pages. Sally Milbury-Steen and Donna Irwin of Delaware's ecumenical peace organization Pacem in Terris made possible the convening of the first study group to try out this book; their group's success both encouraged me and provided useful suggestions.

I wish also to acknowledge the Sociology Department of Brandeis University, which has proved to be a community supportive of scholarly work intended to be socially useful, and Gene Sharp of Harvard's Program on Nonviolent Sanctions, who has set an example of tenacious intellectual effort to eliminate war. Finally, I am grateful to Lynne Weiss, my wife, who offered invaluable advice and urged me not to work all the time. None of those named is responsible for errors of fact or judgment still present, but all deserve a share of the credit for whatever merits this book has.

It was agreed at the outset that this publication should combine inclusion of a range of readings with commentary striving toward the coherence of an individual perspective; consequently, my colleagues in ExPro should not be assumed to agree with everything in it. This book's purpose is above all to stimulate new thought, discussion, and action; it should not be misjudged as a finished proposal or strategy for how to bring about peace. Rather, what cannot be overemphasized is that at this stage the goal is less to present unassailable answers than to shift the public debate: from deterrence and arms control to the conditions of peace.

I invite study group participants and other readers to join in refining — and acting on — the best of the ideas you will find herein.

I would like to learn what you think of this book and what your own ideas about achieving peace are. Please write to me c/o Sociology Dept., Brandeis University, Waltham, MA 02254-9110.

— Robert A. Irwin
Boston
June 1989

The Peace System Approach
to Eliminating War

Though it is increasingly clear that alternatives to the arms race[1] and war are needed if human beings are to survive, there has been no widespread, systematic effort by peace activists to focus attention on peace. What does "peace" mean? What would it require? How could it be achieved?

This book is for anyone who wants to explore and critically assess the possibility that a world of peace and freedom without nuclear weapons or other means of mass killing is possible. Part One looks at familiar topics of debate on nuclear issues — such as Star Wars and arms control — and ends by redefining the issues. Part Two invites readers and study group participants to exercise their own imaginations on the subject of peace. It explores several dimensions of a world at peace: its modes of governance and security policies, and ecological, economic, psychological, and cultural factors associated with peace. Part Three examines trends that affect the prospects for peace. It addresses how to move our world toward a peace system.

This book does not focus on the U.S.-Soviet military balance, nor on claims that the Soviet Union wishes to conquer the world; these topics have been amply treated elsewhere.[2] It also gives less attention than is customary to specific arms control proposals; but both proponents and critics of arms control should find that reading *Building a Peace System* will provide a challenging new perspective from which to assess such proposals.

Why think about peace?

The Exploratory Project on the Conditions of Peace (ExPro)[3] grew from the conviction that careful investigation and widespread discussion of the problems and possibilities of a world at peace were essential to attaining such a world. ExPro co-founder Mark Sommer has written: "If we are to have peace at all, we will have to begin to design it with the same attentiveness and determination with which we now devise the strategies of war."[4]

ExPro rejected the framework of discussion, dominant among U.S. policymakers, which asserts that nuclear deterrence has "kept the peace," and that "living with nuclear weapons is our only hope."[5] This framework has virtually monopolized discussion for too long. ExPro considers all the options within that framework unacceptable. Nuclear deterrence is immoral and dangerous; nuclear war-fighting plans are senseless; defense (e.g., Star Wars) is impossible; and arms control has been a fig leaf legitimizing and obscuring arms build-ups.

In today's world even non-nuclear conventional wars in many regions are appallingly destructive. Further, such conflicts risk escalating to nuclear war. Chemical and biological warfare are also terrible possibilities. These facts point to the conclusion that war is no longer an acceptable way to conduct conflict.[6]

ExPro is not alone in feeling the need to look beyond today's immediate political options. A reader survey conducted by *Nuclear Times* in the fall of 1986 found "a high degree of reader interest in long-term strategies for disarmament and alternative security." The U.S. peace movement, the magazine concurred, "needs to define its own vision."[7] New ground is indeed being broken, as an increase in books on such topics and a proliferation of projects and discussions makes clear.[8]

ExPro's point of departure is hope for a world of peace, freedom, and well-being — not a world without conflict, risk, or adventure, but a world without nuclear weapons or war, where human life is lived free of mass killing, torture, economic misery, and the fear of human extinction. The motivation for investigating peace is not escapism, but a commitment to realism. The rationale is simple: the world has many conflicts; we cannot wish them away; we need a system for dealing with them.

How can such a system be created? ExPro believes that both study and action are necessary — both sound ideas and the human agents to put them into effect. No single group has all the wisdom needed to produce and evaluate the needed ideas. Inquiry and discussion, at all levels, are essential to mobilize the intelligence, commitment, and energy needed to solve the unprecedented problems, and realize the unprecedented potentials, of our time.

War, tyranny, and violation of human rights cannot be made to vanish merely by spreading a new way of thinking. Yet how we think about them does matter.

If we journey mentally to an imagined world of peace, looking back presents current conditions in a different perspective. How that perspective differs is best learned experientially, through the readings to which this book is a guide and its commentaries on them, and through participation in study group discussions. But in brief: if we try to imagine and to design a peaceful world, we can become less mesmerized by today's facts and by dilemmas that seem insoluble as they are now posed. Instead, we can become more aware of the missing facts of tomorrow that must be created.

The concept of "the war system"

Many people assume that there have always been wars and always will be. Actually, there have been sizable regions and eras of peace.[9] But even though wars are not happening everywhere all the time, the possibility of war has a pervasive influence; to varying degrees, countries today all prepare for war. A condition of stable peace, defined not only as the absence of war, but also as a condition in which war is not expected, seems to many no more than an idle dream.[10] The notion that the world is -- permanently — a dangerous place ruled by violence fits their experience. They regard, sadly or scornfully, those who think otherwise as naive idealists.

This image of the world has a long history. "By a necessary law of their nature [men] rule wherever they can," said the Athenians' emissaries to the Melians (whom they intended to subjugate), according to Thucydides. This was a law, they claimed (in the fifth century B.C.), that they had found existing before them and that would continue "for ever after." Consequently "the strong do what they can and the weak suffer what they must."[11] From this worldview it follows that it is best to become as "strong" as possible to prevent being subjugated by others.

According to some contemporary theorists of international relations, elements of this worldview remain correct:

> [T]he nation-state system is essentially a "war system" . . . This indeed is the premise of much of the standard international-relations literature — conservative as well as reformist. The standard view is capsulized by Kenneth Waltz:

> "With many sovereign states, with no system of law enforceable among them, with each state judging its grievances and ambitions according to the dictates of its own reason or desire — conflict, sometimes leading to war, is bound to occur."

> War, sadly, is part of the essence of international relations.[12]

According to this view, in the absence of a sovereign power, above all states, that is able to impose order and prevent violence among them, the world remains a place of constant danger. No nation can be certain another will not seek to harm it, and efforts at self-protection involve a "security dilemma": "many of the means by which a state tries to increase its security decrease the security of others."[13] With the enormous destructiveness of nuclear bombs in constant readiness, the former "balance of power" becomes the "delicate balance of terror."[14] In this view, the best that can be hoped for is stability of this balance.

We disagree with this "standard view." But presenting it should make clear that the term "war system," by which we designate the present condition of international politics, is not used simply as a term of condemnation. It describes an acknowledged situation that we want to change.[15]

It has been a long time since Thucydides. The vulnerability of all countries to missile attack has changed international politics, and some theorists recognize this: "Threats and force thus work differently from the way they did in the past."[16] Long though the "war system" image of the world has persisted, it seems that — for better (through the advent of a peace system) or for worse (through human extinction) — its time is coming to an end.

Why "peace system"?

But can peace really be possible? We think it can. Yet, since conflict is inevitable in the complex realm of human affairs, peace will not be simple.

Past efforts to end war — e.g., international treaties renouncing it, pledges by young men not to fight — have not been sufficiently sophisticated and comprehensive.[17] To be successful, an approach must be able to cope with the variety of things that can go wrong. It must be complex yet flexible, and "robust" in the sense that if one thing doesn't work, another comes into operation, and if both fail, there's something else to fall back on.

As the *Report from Iron Mountain on the Possibility and Desirability of Peace* (1967) emphasized, war and war preparations have multiple social functions.[18] Because the world is a complex whole, we can never change just one part of it. If we want to get rid of an important part or function (war), we must replace it with something else, reorganize the whole, or both.

This "systems" approach[19] is reflected in many of the readings cited in this book. We find language like "the functions of the war system," "the need for a functional substitute for war," "alternative defense," "alternative methods for international security," and so forth. Issues besides governmental military policies — matters of economics and culture, and social inequalities that influence government policies — are recognized as relevant when one uses a systemic approach.

It should be emphasized (as "realists" have long pointed out), that one cannot change the world simply by thinking up new arrangements. A systemic approach must look at the forces for change and those for stability, consider how they may be influenced, and keep in mind that we ourselves are part of the system.

What would be the elements of a peace system?

We wish to answer in two ways. First, if it is correct that the war system involves many interlocking factors, not only political but economic, social, psychological, cultural, and normative,[20] then it is reasonable to suppose that the design of a peace system must address all these areas as well. The headings for Part II of this book indicate where some of these are chiefly addressed, but the factors overlap and we have covered them only as systematically as the state of the literature and our present thinking have permitted. We have at this stage no definitive list of elements or dimensions — be they institutions, processes, policies, etc. — but rather a set of areas to explore.

Second, and doubtless more vividly, we may present the elements of a peace system in "functional" terms. Here an analogy with the proposed Star Wars defense scheme may help.[21] Star Wars is imagined as several layers of defense, each imperfect by itself, which together would prevent missiles launched by an enemy from reaching their targets. Enemy missiles would be detected and tracked during their launch and "boost" phases; some of those that got past this stage would be destroyed by laser weapons or tricked off course by decoys; finally, those (theoretically) few that might get through the earlier defense layers would be destroyed high in the air before they descended too closely toward their targets.

A peace system can likewise be conceived as involving multiple "layers" to prevent war. The *first layer*— global reforms to reduce the causes of war — is in many ways the most important: "an ounce of prevention is worth a pound of cure." It would result from two kinds of changes: a) a gradual (ultimately universal) shift to defense policies that posed no threat to others, which would reduce international insecurity, delegitimate possession of offensive forces, and lead to reduced capabilities for military aggression; b) global political, economic, ecological, and cultural change[22] efforts that would aim to reduce the number of potential war-causing grievances, minimize perception of war as a promising remedy, and increase citizens' capacity to restrain or halt aggressive acts by their own government. It should be acknowledged that b) implies an extremely ambitious program of global reform to restore ecological sustainability, reduce economic and political inequalities, and help people learn to live together without belligerence.[23] Yet nothing less seems required if we are to prevent the next layers from being overwhelmed by a multitude of stresses, and thus to enable peace with freedom to be durable.

The *second layer* would be conflict resolution. Since human beings, regardless of circumstances, are prone to feeling aggrieved,[24] institutions for conflict resolution are needed. Using methods that would become increasingly widely familiar, they would need to operate at the local, regional, national, and global levels to seek mutually acceptable[25] solutions to conflicts.

In a well-established peace system, the first layer would prevent many potential war causes from ever arising; of the many remaining, all would be successfully resolved in the second layer.[26] Over the course of several decades of decreasing violence and the development of more secure and equal economic and cultural relationships, general and complete disarmament would have taken place, and no major incentives to rearm would exist. Conflicts would occur, but none would break through to organized violence. This state of affairs could fairly be called a successful peace system.

A successful peace system would, of course, involve more than preventing military attack. Ecological and economic security for all, and the sharing of the good things in life, would also be part of it; though already important, these aspects will loom larger as the incidence of warfare diminishes. The food aid now given to areas suffering famine is a small foretaste of "common security" in the economic realm. Humanity's ability to cooperate to mitigate global warming and other ecological disasters (see Chapter 7) may determine whether humans achieve stable peace or instead suffer extinction or regression to centuries of barbarism. But, for simplicity, we concentrate in this introductory essay on security from military attack.

The transition to a peace system

From the present through the earliest stages of transition to a peace system, when some but not all of the changes discussed in this book would have been made, warfare would still exist. Severe injustices would still often generate violent conflict. Throughout this period, marked by persisting conflicts that many would believe too fundamental and acute to be settled by mutual agreement, those conflicts would be waged by violent or nonviolent means of struggle. One task for peace-makers in this period would be to substitute effective nonviolent struggle for political violence[27] to achieve freedom and justice.

During the transition, with the gradual success of efforts to build a "global civic culture,"[28] citizens would learn (and seek to further elevate) the agreed international norms of behavior for societies and states; and they would recognize their personal responsibility to secure adherence to those norms, working with, around, or against their national governments, as circumstances might require.

When conflicts, eluding resolution, threatened to erupt into military attack — or when governments refused cooperation with major supra-national decisions — grave warnings of political, economic, and other sanctions (but not of military attack) could be made by national governments, regional intergovernmental organizations, and the United Nations (to the extent internal divisions did not paralyze these bodies); and conflict resolution measures could be intensified. But let us postulate the failure of the first two layers.

If, despite warnings, a military attack occurred, it might be countered by "third party" regional, U.N., and/or nongovernmental peacekeeping forces, and/or by the defense efforts (military or nonmilitary) of the attacked country. Military attack and defense would of course be warfare. The still-immature peace system would have failed to *prevent* war at this point. Still, the attack might be rapidly halted by third party military intervention and nonmilitary sanctions. But if this *third layer* of the peace system — peacekeeping intervention — failed to operate effectively enough to halt the attack, and if the allies of the attacked country had retained no weapons capable of intervening on its behalf, it might find itself opposing aggression virtually unaided for the period that third party sanctions, diplomacy, U.N. action, etc. were ineffective.

If the attacked country's military defense were unsuccessful, or if it had already partially or com-pletely replaced military forces by civilian-based defense,[29] a policy relying on prepared nonviolent struggle by the trained civilian population, then a *fourth*[30] and final *layer* of defense by popular nonviolent resistance (preferably prepared but at worst improvised), would remain available against any attack short of outright annihilation.[31] Victory is not guaranteed (nor is it in war); but the determined resistance of a country's people is indeed the ultimate sanction that will remain to them if all else fails.[32]

The importance of a hopeful vision of the future

This discussion of the early stages of a peace system, before it is well established, will dismay anyone expecting a magic formula for international security. The foregoing was a worst-case scenario in which nearly everything goes wrong. In this case, the worst outcomes could be as bad for the unluckiest victims as is now the case in war. This should not be disheartening; it follows from the realism of our approach.

What is important to keep in mind is that *if any parts* of the peace system *work as intended*, the outcomes will be *better* than the suffering now taken for granted as normal. Increasing redeployment of the immense human resources now devoted to the war system should help the peace system to work; and, over time, social learning should enable it to work still better.

Just as a sick person is more vulnerable to additional illnesses than a person in robust health, the emerging elements of a peace system face their most difficult challenges when they are least able to cope with them: this is, regrettably but unavoidably, the nature of such a transition period.

During the difficult transition it will be essential, we believe, to sustain our courage and motivation by cherishing a vivid vision of a world at peace — one with a well-established peace system. As will be discussed in Part Three, building a peace system includes a number of activities already under way. But the adoption of a peace-system orientation by the U.S. peace movement and allied forces in other countries — which is what ExPro advocates — will make possible new unity and purposefulness. Recognizing what is necessary to build a peace system can focus energy and create synergy among efforts now seen as unrelated or contradictory (e.g., nonviolent struggle and world law).

No static formula

Finally, we wish to emphasize that the peace system concept does not imply something totally formalized or imposed by an authority. We envision a peace system as growing from multiple initiatives, at many locales and levels. The term "system" is meant in its unpretentious meaning of how things work together in practice. For us the phrase "peace system" also evokes the complexity, stability, and resilience of natural, ecological systems. A peace system would be

> an integrated and mutually supporting network of processes, institutions, attitudes, and trends. . . . A wisely structured political peace system makes allowance for misfortune and mischief and builds redundancy into itself. Rather than depending on any single institution or group, it seeks to broaden and decentralize responsibilities so particular components may fail for periods of time without paralyzing the functions of the larger system.[33]

We do not offer here a finished formula for a peace system, much less a blueprint; perhaps not even all the needed components are identified in readings cited herein, though many of them surely are. What we affirm, above all, is the importance of the effort to create one; and we call on you — reader, thinker, planetary citizen, and activist — to join in mobilizing the collective creativity, wisdom, and energy needed to discover and make real the conditions of peace.

Part I
The Present Debate
—and Beyond

Introduction: How the Peace Movement Shaped the Present Debate

Chapter 1: Deterrence, Star Wars, and Peace

Chapter 2: Arms Control: Pro and Con

Chapter 3: Redefining the Issues: Aspects of the War System

Introduction:
How the Peace Movement
Shaped the Present Debate

In a society whose mass media focus on government officials more than on grassroots leaders who may be dealing far more creatively with society's problems, awareness of how major change begins is frequently obscured. That a shift in the orientation of the U.S. peace movement could be important for achieving world peace might at first seem unlikely. Even many activists lack perspective on the history and cumulative impact of the efforts of their own and kindred movements.[1]

Consider, for example, how the repressive political climate of the McCarthy era began to be changed in the mid-1950s. Pacifists protested against nuclear testing by sailing boats into nuclear test zones and doing acts of civil disobedience at missile bases. Black Americans created the civil rights movement that became widely visible in the Montgomery, Alabama bus boycott of 1955-56 (in which both black and white pacifists played important roles as mass black militance found its strategic path in nonviolent struggle). These events made principled dissent from Cold War attitudes, civil disobedience, and mass nonviolent resistance more familiar as ways to change government policies.[2]

A brief review of what was accomplished by the U.S. peace movement in the decade after 1975, the year the Vietnam War ended, can both help us understand how political change takes place in the U.S., and provide some useful perspective for considering what might realistically be accomplished in the decades ahead.

A recent book on the Nuclear Freeze campaign states that after the Vietnam war the U.S. peace movement was "dormant," with no national peace initiatives until the Freeze.[3] In reality, although the struggle to end the Vietnam War had been long and exhausting, within months of the war's end the staff of the War Resisters League (WRL) began organizing a "Continental Walk for Disarmament and Social Justice." Walkers crossed the U.S., leafleting and speaking out, from January to October of 1976.

In 1975, working with SANE, Women Strike for Peace, and others, Sidney Lens (a labor union official and intellectual) sought to catalyze new peace activity focused on the dangers of the nuclear arms race.[4] In February 1976 *The Progressive* magazine devoted most of its issue to a long article by Lens entitled "The Doomsday Strategy." It found a receptive audience, soon becoming the second-most requested reprint in the magazine's history. Lens and allies from several peace organizations organized a series of meetings to explore the formation of a new coalition against nuclear dangers. By the end of 1977, with a sense of new possibilities growing from the antinuclear power plant actions at Seabrook, New Hampshire, Lens and WRL's Norma Becker called a meeting that led to the founding of Mobilization for Survival. Its four slogans were: zero nuclear weapons, ban nuclear power, stop the arms race, and fund human needs.

Meanwhile Helen Caldicott was revitalizing Physicians for Social Responsibility and stirring thousands with her impassioned speeches on the threat of nuclear war. In the summer of 1979 the (Quaker) American Friends Service Committee called for a U.S. nuclear moratorium. National peace and church-related organizations responded encouragingly to peace researcher Randall Forsberg's proposal for a bilateral, verifiable U.S.-Soviet nuclear weapons freeze. By December 1979, when Forsberg presented her proposal at the Mobilization for Survival's annual national conference, the emerging movement was growing ready to coalesce around a new strategic focus.

The launching of a European Nuclear Disarmament movement (END) in April 1980 in response to NATO's 1979 decision to deploy cruise and Pershing II missiles gave further prominence to nuclear issues. The two-to-one victory in November 1980 of a Freeze referendum organized by Randy Kehler and others in Western Massachusetts showed that Reagan's election was no mandate for the arms race; peace proposals could win victories.[5]

By December 1979, when Forsberg presented her proposal at the Mobilization for Survival's annual national conference, the emerging movement was growing ready to coalesce around a new strategic focus.

The national Freeze campaign did not merely propose what the superpower governments should do (bilaterally halt production, deployment, and testing of nuclear weapons); it is a mistake to assess the Freeze simply as another arms control proposal. Essential to it was that it also recommended what ordinary people should do. They were urged to seek endorsements for the Freeze through referenda, local governments, and all manner of organizations. Local organizations were encouraged to get their national counterparts to endorse the Freeze. National groups (religious, professional, activist) were encouraged to get their chapters to do the same. The education and organizing efforts required to win referenda and endorsements — for a position contrary to the incumbent administration's policies — provided people with a meaningful outlet for their concerns.

The decade after 1975 was also distinguished by tenacious efforts to prevent or halt U.S. military interventions abroad, most conspicuously in Central America. The "anti-intervention movement," although not focused on nuclear war, has arguably been of great importance to preventing it because of a "deadly connection" between Third World conflicts and nuclear crises. (See Chapter 3's readings on this connection.)

This incomplete sketch is meant to suggest how the interaction of individual initiatives, governmental decisions, religious and political organizations, publications, grassroots organizing, actions in different countries, and wise strategy brought the U.S. peace movement to the point where it became visible to the Congress, television, and the press. Key ingredients in the development of the Freeze movement included: determined activists; intellectuals with a sense of responsibility and the chutzpah to put forth bold ideas; demand for, or receptivity to, new ideas; small, dedicated organizations; thoughtful and creative funders; and most of all, the public's concern and desire for peace, shown in its readiness to respond to ideas and programs of action that offer hope for fundamental changes for the better.[6]

Bucking the powerful tide of a late-1970s shift to the right by elite circles in the U.S. — often erroneously attributed to the whole population[7] — the peace movement gained political strength. In the 1982 elections, voters where the Freeze was on the ballot supported it by 60% to 40% — a "landslide" victory, in standard political terms. As a result, political rhetoric changed, and within months a new policy initiative came from the federal government. In his March 1983 Star Wars speech the President echoed the peace movement's condemnation of nuclear deterrence as immoral and presented his own plan to prevent nuclear holocaust. Star Wars was acknowledged by White House staff (in a leaked memo) as an attempt to recapture the "moral high ground" from the peace movement.

Here we end this account, attempting no assessment of the experience of the peace movement from 1982 on.[8] Suffice it to say that its seeming death after the 1984 election was, in Mark Twain's phrase, "greatly exaggerated." In 1986 there continued to be, according to Randy Kehler, a grass-roots peace movement that was not smaller but, "if anything, larger" than at the height of the Freeze.[9] Innovative work by many local and national groups continues. Efforts to restructure and thereby strengthen the U.S. peace movement — including the laboriously negotiated 1987 merger of SANE (the peace group with the most individual members) and the Freeze (the peace group with the most local groups) — should, despite initial difficulties, create new possibilities. Only time will tell if a new organizational configuration and new strategies will result in effectiveness exceeding anything we have yet seen.

Any simple conclusions risk misleading. The U.S. and other peace movements developed not only from their own initiatives but in reaction to terrible and alarming government policy moves. In important ways the situation has worsened since 1975. Still, in less than eight years, a movement starting from a few people's efforts grew to the point of altering the public agenda and compelling responses from the top.

Whether the goal of "building a peace system" will become the predominant orientation for the U.S. and other peace movements, and whether major progress toward a peace system will be made in the years ahead, no one can be sure. Yet, building on what has already been accomplished, on the many people who have been educated, activated, and organized thus far, we can have realistic hopes to make larger changes in the future. What happens will surely depend in part on what you, the reader of these pages, decide to do.

Chapter 1:
Deterrence, Star Wars, and Peace

In the early 1980s nuclear weapons once again had become controversial. *Living With Nuclear Weapons* (1983) was written by the Harvard Nuclear Study Group (Albert Carnesale, Paul Doty, Stanley Hoffmann, Samuel P. Huntington, Joseph S. Nye, Jr., and Scott Sagan) at the request of Harvard President Derek Bok. Prompted by "the growing nuclear arms debate," it aims, writes Bok, "to supply the public as a whole with an objective account of the basic facts about nuclear arms control" and "to present fairly all the significant arguments on all sides of every important issue" (pp. xiii, xvi). Note that Bok assumes that arms control is the solution to the problem of nuclear weapons — undercutting the claim of objectivity. How the war problem is to be defined receives particular attention in this and the following two chapters' readings.

Four of the six members of the Harvard group have worked for the U.S. government. They give minimal attention to those active on the peace movement side of the debate, though it was the growth of that movement that led to the writing of the book. Helen Caldicott and E. P. Thompson, for example, are never mentioned. In fact, except for George Kennan, Michael Howard (a critic of the peace movement), and Randall Forsberg (in one footnote), not one of the dozens of writers represented in the book in your hands — some of them scholars who have been publishing for decades — appears in the Harvard book. So much for fairness!

The Harvard Nuclear Study Group's book shows little interest in alternatives to nuclear deterrence. Already on page 18, for example, the idea that world government might be a solution is judged a "dream for the distant future." "Balance of power" politics is "inevitable" and "a nation's only way of self-protection" (p. 25). The notion that nuclear weapons can be eliminated is labeled a symptom of "discouragement" — because "humanity has no alternative but . . . to learn how to live with nuclear weapons" (p. 19). In setting out to explore alternatives to the war system, it is worthwhile to begin with these reminders of the views of those who have been aptly termed "activists for the status quo."[1]

Richard Smoke, a professor of political science and Research Director of the Center for Foreign Policy Development at Brown University, begins his analytic survey of possible *Paths to Peace* by examining the most "paradoxical" of them: pre-emptive attacks "to remove a threat to peace" and deterrence to prevent attack by posing a counter-threat.

Smoke observes that when it became possible for bombers and missiles to "inflict intolerably severe destruction on the aggressor's homeland . . . punishment became effectively disconnected from military 'victory' and 'defeat' in the traditional sense of the terms" (p. 12). Millions of people, and most of the authors discussed in this book, have understood this and concluded that nuclear war cannot be won and that human beings had better find alternatives to nuclear deterrence.[2]

Readings: for study group use

A. Harvard Nuclear Study Group, *Living With Nuclear Weapons* (1983; pp. 3-20, 22-44, 111-113). Total = 41 pp.

B. Richard Smoke, "Traditional Paths to Coping with Conflict" in *Paths to Peace* (1987; pp. 7-16);

   Colin Gray & Keith Payne, "Victory is Possible," from *Foreign Policy* (Summer 1980; 14 pp.).

   Total = 23 pp.

C. Patricia Mische, *Star Wars and the State of Our Souls: Deciding the Future of Planet Earth* (1985; pp. v-viii, 1-53). Total = 57 pp.

D. McGeorge Bundy et al., "The President's Choice" (1984); Don Carlson, "Breaking the Trance" (1986); both in *Securing Our Planet*, pp. 194-209 and 9-16;

   "An Interview with Michael Howard: Peace Movements and the Meaning of Peace," from *Peace and Security* (1987; 2 pp.).

   Total = 24 pp.

E. Kirkpatrick Sale, "August is the Sanest Month";

   Robert R. Holt, "The Necessary First Step toward Peace and Survival";

   Eleanor M. LeCain, "Shaping Foreign Policy to Meet Emerging Realities";

   Mark Sommer, "The Real Enemy is War Itself";

   W. H. Ferry, "The Choice: Non-violence";

   Dietrich Fischer, "An Active Peace Policy."

   Total=18 pp., all from *The ExPro Papers* #1, "Steps Toward a Peaceful World" (1986); it is suggested these be read in this order, not their order in the booklet.

Colin Gray and Keith Payne, in contrast, were in 1980 still seeking "victory." Their article "Victory is Possible" illustrates what is called the nuclear "war-fighting" perspective. The authors coolly contemplate a nuclear war involving millions of deaths. Confronting the perpetual stalemate of deterrence, and what has been termed "the illogic of American nuclear strategy"[3] — making threats that would be suicidal to carry out — they attempt a rational approach to the use of nuclear weapons. Their views were representative of a major current in Reagan administration thinking; Gray, for example, was appointed to the General Advisory Committee on Arms Control and Disarmament.

The selection from Patricia M. Mische's book on *Star Wars and the State of Our Souls* presents the various arguments of proponents and critics of the policy President Reagan first presented in his March 23, 1983 speech. Unlike critics who focus solely on the technical infeasibility of a Star Wars defense or on its political dangers (combined with offensive weapons, Star Wars would make a U.S. first strike more thinkable), Mische also considers the psychological and spiritual significance of humankind's relation to space and to the earth.

"The President's Choice" presents a critique of Star Wars by McGeorge Bundy, George F. Kennan, Robert S. McNamara, and Gerard Smith, four eminent "establishment" figures. They assert that Mr. Reagan's objective, to shield the U.S. from nuclear attack, "cannot be achieved," and that pursuit of it is too costly and jeopardizes what might be accomplished in arms control. The wisdom of present "defense" policies is so doubtful that it has moved people who might not ordinarily be expected to think critically about them — like successful businessman Don Carlson, who favors a "strong, realistic military" — to become actively involved in trying to "Break the Trance" in which such policies seem to be continued.

> *Millions of people have concluded that nuclear war cannot be won and that human beings had better find alternatives to nuclear deterrence.*

Historian of war Michael Howard criticizes "the peace movement" for failing to come to grips with the requirement to use power — necessarily military, he believes — to protect one's society. "If you don't like the answers [present policy-makers] come up with, then it is your job to try to think of other answers. And this is my exasperation with the peace movement. On the whole, they don't." His criticism poses a challenge that in recent years has been increasingly taken up by peace movement proponents of "alternative security" ideas.

The half-dozen short articles by ExPro authors offer perspectives on why the present situation is unsatisfactory and what kind of "other answers" should be sought. Kirkpatrick Sale succinctly summarizes the premises shared by the ExPro writers:

> Fighting a nuclear war is plainly insane. Building a defense against nuclear weapons is impossible. . . . [The] deterrence system we now suffer with is extremely risky, not to say immoral. Arms [control] negotiations have failed to achieve peace and, worse, have in fact increased armaments. Even disarmament, nuclear or conventional, would not be adequate to keep the peace unless some sort of system permitted nations to settle their differences without wars. And so the job is to figure out what that peace system would look like and persuade citizens and their governments that it's worth giving it a chance.

Chapter 2:
Arms Control: Pro and Con

In this chapter on "arms control," the critique of arms control deemed most interesting is not that of right-wingers who erroneously allege wholesale cheating by the Soviets (see Patricia Mische's discussion of such charges). It is that even when agreements are adhered to by both sides, arms control does little good. Rather, it legitimizes and encourages arms build-ups to the agreed ceilings as well as the creation of new weapons systems as "bargaining chips" (which are then never wholly bargained away).

A range of positions exists among those authors discussed in this chapter who share a critique of arms control as inadequate. George Rathjens, William Schwartz, and Charles Derber are more critical of arms control as a focus for peace movement efforts, while Patricia Mische and Robert Johansen defend it against right-wing opposition as a step toward a global security system.

Another debate, only partially represented by the readings, concerns whether it is not the nuclear *weapons* they have stockpiled but instead the superpowers' *relationship* to each other that is most important. Some argue that it is not the weapons themselves, or knowledge of how to make them, that poses a threat. For example, the U.S. does not worry about British nuclear weapons because we have a friendly relationship with Britain.

In response, it has been argued that, given the possibility that they can be used, *any* nuclear weapons do pose threats, and measures to eliminate them cannot simply be set aside while efforts to build trust (whether at the elite or grassroots level) are undertaken.

It may, however, be a mistake to contrast the weapons and the relationship. The two nuclear arsenals can be considered as one major *indicator* of the superpower relationship's quality. We *would* worry about British missiles, and would conclude (even in the absence of any other indications) that U.S.-British relations had somehow drastically deteriorated, if tomorrow we learned that the British had retargeted their missiles from the U.S.S.R. to the U.S. The soundest position would seem to be to seek a better superpower relationship, while including efforts to eliminate threatening weapons as part of that work.[1]

In the fall and winter of 1987-88, there was much talk of U.S.-Soviet intermediate nuclear forces (INF) and strategic arms reduction agreements. The INF treaty was hailed as an important step: for the first time, agreement had been reached to dismantle a whole class of weapons. Extensive new inspection arrangements were worked out for mutual on-site verification of treaty compliance. U.S. and Soviet personnel began hosting each other around previously sealed-off and sacrosanct weapons facilities, cooperating in a common task serving the security of both sides.

Such events tend to encourage a less hostile and more hopeful outlook; to the degree that this happens, the signing, ratification, and implementation of such agreements can be applauded. Outside the U.S. administration, peace movement pressure is widely credited with having contributed to President Reagan's and Mr. Gorbachev's willingness to negotiate; there is important symbol-

Readings: for study group use

A. Harvard Nuclear Study Group, "Arms Control and Disarmament: What Can and Can't Be Done," pp. 188-213 in *Living With Nuclear Weapons*;

Richard Smoke, "Traditional Paths to Preventing Conflict," pp. 17-30 in *Paths to Peace* (1987).

Total= 40 pp.

B. George Kennan, "Deep Cuts" (1982), pp. 285-292 in *Securing Our Planet* (8 pp.);

Gar Alperovitz, "Naked NATO: America's Europe Problem," from *The New Republic* (September 29, 1986; 3 pp.);

Daniel Yankelovich & John Doble, "The Public Mood: Nuclear Weapons and the USSR," from *Foreign Affairs* (Fall 1984; 15 pp.).

Total = 26 pp.

C. Graham Allison et al., "Introduction" and "Analytic Conclusions," pp. 3-22, 206-246, in *Hawks, Doves, and Owls: An Agenda for Avoiding Nuclear War* (1985);

George Rathjens and Jack Ruina, "The Real Issue in the Geneva Talks"; and George Rathjens, "Reducing the Risk of Nuclear War: SDI and Alternatives," in *The ExPro Papers* #1 (1986; 6 pp.).

Total= 67 pp.

D. George Rathjens, "First Thoughts on Problems Facing ExPro," *The ExPro Papers* #5 (1986; 23 pp.);

William A. Schwartz and Charles Derber, "Arms Control: Misplaced Focus," from *Bulletin of Atomic Scientists* (March 1986; 6 pp.).

Total= 29 pp.)

E. Patricia Mische, "Why Arms Control is Needed," "Compliance: Won't the Russians Cheat?" and "Doing It Better: Planning for Success," pp. 58-81 in *Star Wars and the State of Our Souls* (1985);

Robert C. Johansen, "The Future of Arms Control," from *World Policy Journal* (Spring 1985; 34 pp.).

Total= 57 pp.)

ism in the elimination of nuclear missiles; and even the most modest victories are worth celebrating for people engaged in a long-term struggle to transform a system.

But such deals also need debunking. It was widely noted that the INF treaty would eliminate less than 4 per cent of existing missiles. Much less noted was that the U.S. government does not lack plans to adjust to the withdrawal of the Pershing II and ground-launched cruise missiles. According to a CBS report (September 17, 1987):

> The U.S. will almost certainly be putting in new nuclear weapons that could attack targets which now only the Pershing and ground-launched cruise missiles can reach. . . .Under consideration: moving F-111 bombers now based in England forward to the Continent, closer to targets behind enemy lines; deploying ships and submarines armed with sea-launched cruise missiles which have a range of 1,500 miles; modifying B-52 bombers to carry long-range missiles armed with powerful new conventional warheads; and fielding a longer-range version of the Lance surface-to-surface [missile]. . . .When it's all done, defense officials say it is conceivable there actually could be more nuclear weapons assigned to the defense of Europe than there are now.[2]

Further, as Green activist and West German parliament member Petra Kelly has pointed out, contrary to most people's impression, the INF treaty does not destroy a single nuclear warhead: "a provision. . .allows nuclear warheads and missile guidance mechanisms to be reused."[3] As this fact and the CBS report indicate, an arms control deal premised on continuation of the war system has limits that are painfully evident. What the superpowers have been willing to agree on so far — and this would be true even of a 50% cut in strategic nuclear arsenals, though it too would be desirable — are only very limited steps toward peace, with which no one should rest content.

The chapter "Arms Control and Disarmament: What Can and Can't Be Done" from *Living With Nuclear Weapons* disposes of world government and disarmament in four pages and explains why "'arms control' has replaced 'disarmament' in the specialist's vocabulary" (p. 191). In evaluating "those freezes [sic] that have produced such large public followings" (pp. 207-8), the Harvard Nuclear Study Group portrays the negotiations necessary for an agreement as extremely complex, requiring a "hundredfold or more" increase in arms control negotiations budgets and more than a few years. This assertion, made without any reference to expert testimony on the feasibility of the Freeze, continues a tradition of exaggerated and dismissive elite responses to proposals for change.[4] Why a hundredfold increase in the arms control negotiations budget would be prohibitive, given the other larger expenditures the authors approve without blinking, is not explained. The intent, however, seems plainly to be to discredit the Freeze and reinforce the status quo.

In part of *Paths to Peace* Richard Smoke explores preventive diplomacy, arms control, and disarmament. He finds that although "it is impossible to be sure how often preventive diplomacy has succeeded in preventing war," it probably succeeds "often enough to make imaginative efforts to extend it and employ it well worthwhile." Regarding disarmament talks, "on the whole we cannot expect too much." Progress has usually occurred only after crises or wars; even though "future crises are only too likely," one would not want to rely on such events to produce progress. Smoke suggests, however, that a sound arms control and disarmament program "might be an essential ingredient in a more inclusive approach to creating a sustainable peace."

George F. Kennan — diplomat, former U.S. ambassador to Moscow, historian, and, in recent years, an eloquent spokesman for reducing the danger of nuclear holocaust — argues for "Deep Cuts" in nuclear arsenals. He suggests reducing them by 50% to start with, followed shortly by two-thirds cuts of what remains. He advocates such action as an alternative to the typical arms negotiations

> in which each side is obsessed with the chimera of relative advantage and strives only to retain a maximum of the weaponry for itself while putting its opponent to the maximum disadvantage. . . [S]uch negotiations . . . are not a way of escape from the weapons race; they are an integral part of it.

Gar Alperovitz, whose *Atomic Diplomacy: Hiroshima and Potsdam* (1965; revised edition, 1985) was a pioneering study of the use of nuclear weapons for political influence, here shows the erosion of established rationales for deterrence and the maintenance of costly U.S. forces in Europe. Like the call for reduced arsenals by Kennan, an architect of the Cold War "containment" policy, the statements Alperovitz quotes from former top officials critical of the status quo in Europe lay the groundwork for policy change. U.S. spending for NATO is estimated at roughly half of the Pentagon's total budget. Alperovitz suggests that legislation for a phased reduction of U.S. troop levels in Europe "could have a strong populist appeal . . . if it specified that funds saved would be allocated to domestic use, tax reduction, and/or deficit reduction."

The existence of the peace movement shows that readiness for change is not confined to elites. But many within that movement, frustrated and anguished over defeats at the policy level, are unaware of the extent to which their efforts during the early 1980s succeeded in transforming U.S. public consciousness. According to polling experts Daniel Yankelovich and John Doble, by 1984 overwhelming percentages had come to disagree with government spokespersons and agree with the peace movement that (by an 89% to 9% margin) all-out nuclear war is unwinnable, that (by 83% to 14%) nuclear war might end life on earth, and that (92%) the arms race cannot be won. The pollsters conclude that "the American electorate is now psychologically prepared to take a giant step toward real arms reductions" because "the public finds the long-term risks of continuing the way we are going to be simply unacceptable."

The portrait by Yankelovich and Doble of four general groups in the electorate is thought-provoking and a valuable supplement to the impressionistic speculation underlying most political strategy discussions. Their conclusions about the kinds of policy changes that would be acceptable to the public should be kept in mind by those working for peace. Perhaps the most pertinent of these is that the public has "not yet thought through the strategic and policy implications" of the unusability of nuclear weapons, but is "prepared — somewhat nervously — to take certain risks for peace."

The three editors of *Hawks, Doves, and Owls: An Agenda for Avoiding Nuclear War* (1985), two of whom also co-authored *Living With Nuclear Weapons*, argue that the views of both "hawks" and "doves" are inadequate to meet the hazards of the nuclear age. They argue for a new, more sophisticated, position, that of "owls," who hold that loss of control leading to accidental war may be as great a danger as those they believe lie in hawkish provocation or dovish appeasement.

Unfortunately, as many people know, owls are predators undeserving of their reputation for wisdom. Although the Harvard owls' ten-point agenda includes two each of items they consider hawkish and dovish, their commitment to nuclear deterrence and opposition even to moderate reforms like a "no-first-use" policy places them squarely in the policy camp of the hawks. It would be understandable if some considered their undertaking to be an agenda for continuing to threaten nuclear attack with impunity.

The owls' call for "humility . . . in exploring the realm of ideas beyond deterrence," however, is praiseworthy. Although they think that a world without nuclear weapons is a possibility only "over the very long term" (p. 245), they state that

> the search for less conventional, more imaginative alternatives for the long run must begin. Bold, creative approaches to the subject must be stimulated, nurtured, and rewarded. In particular, the community of defense and foreign policy specialists must resist cynicism toward nontraditional concepts, misplaced confidence that all of the important ideas have been examined, and condescension to newcomers from other fields.

It is a mistake to think that "particular kinds of reductions must be avoided so as to maintain 'strategic stability'"; even a fraction of current arsenals is enough to deter a nuclear attack.

This expression of open-mindedness, if lived up to in practice, might enable the owls to contribute something to exploring the problems of building a peace system. Unfortunately, the record is not encouraging.[5]

M.I.T. professors George Rathjens and Jack Ruina argue (contrary to the main emphasis of the owls) that it is a mistake to think that "particular kinds of reductions must be avoided so as to maintain 'strategic stability'"; even a fraction of current arsenals is enough to deter a nuclear attack. "Within very broad limits," Rathjens suggests, "the nuclear postures of the superpowers hardly matter."

In his "First Thoughts on Problems Facing ExPro," Rathjens examines thirteen proposed steps toward international security — from Star Wars to a comprehensive test ban to nuclear-free zones to "general and complete" disarmament to "abolition of the war system."

Rathjens thinks that focusing on constraining development of weapons rather than on "the reasons nations want to acquire weapons" (p. 15), has proved generally unsuccessful. Efforts to develop superpower "rules of behavior" in relation to world trouble spots out of which nuclear crises might grow seem more important to Rathjens than tinkering with the weapons balance. Over the longer term, some combination of alleviating grievances and creating a global police authority, aiming to eliminate the desire and prevent the possibility of using nuclear weapons, seems necessary, he concludes — but that conclusion raises further questions, with which he closes.

William A. Schwartz and Charles Derber, authors of "Arms Control: Misplaced Focus," are (with Gordon Fellman, William Gamson, and Morris Schwartz) members of the Boston Nuclear Study Group (their forthcoming book is entitled *The Nuclear Seduction*). The Boston group believes that successive peace movement campaigns against particular weapons systems (B-1 bomber, anti-ballistic missiles, neutron bombs, cruise and Pershing missiles, M-X, Trident, etc., etc.) amount to a mistake they call "weaponitis." Like Rathjens, they believe that nuclear arsenal reductions of less than 90% would do little to improve the prospects of human survival. They state that "under current political conditions it is unclear whether such reductions would increase or decrease the likelihood of [a nuclear] exchange."

Anticipating some of the readings in Chapter 3, Schwartz and Derber contend that the greatest danger of nuclear war is caused by the "endemic conventional violence from which nuclear war can always escalate," and thus "the essential problem is. . . conventional militarism . . . . Making basic changes in the foreign policies which enflame regional conflicts and bring about crises in the first place is much more important [than] campaigns around weapons."

Patricia Mische presents a case for the value of the limited past achievements of arms control and its future importance in preventing further militarization of space. Her review of Soviet treaty compliance rebuts widely publicized allegations of Soviet cheating. She ends by suggesting ways that future arms control could be more successful while we move to create a global alternative security system.

Robert C. Johansen, in "The Future of Arms Control" (1985), traces opportunities lost because the Reagan administration lacked interest in negotiating anything that might constrain its own ability to develop arms with which it could hope to "prevail" in a "prolonged" nuclear war (p. 204). He advocates a new approach going beyond arms control to "conflict control" (pp. 213ff) and seeking to develop a superpower code of conduct that elevates "the goal of war prevention far above the struggle for geopolitical advantages." He suggests both general guidelines and specific measures for Congress and the public to press for, including an internationally-controlled system of satellites and other means that could monitor U.S. and Soviet military capabilities, thus providing a more impartial opinion about compliance with arms control treaties. In remarkable contrast to "Peace through Strength" thinking, he concludes that in the nuclear age "'bargaining from strength' is a weak, self-deceiving approach": "the U.S. cannot have both military superiority and security."

Chapter 3:
Redefining the Issues:
Aspects of the War System

Readings discussed in the preceding chapters addressed the issues of U.S. security primarily as defined by the dominant circles and journals of the country: nuclear war-fighting, deterrence, Star Wars, and arms control. Although many of the readings challenged the prevailing positions on those issues, and to some degree the very nature of the debate, most were nevertheless primarily addressed *to* those prevailing positions.

Each of the readings in *this* chapter redefines the problems of war and security in some way.

It is common to characterize our era as "the nuclear age." But consider how in the 1930s the bombing of Ethiopians and the aerial attack on Guernica during the Spanish Civil War horrified the world. Less than a decade after Guernica, the Allies had firebombed whole cities such as Dresden and Tokyo — acts that were overshadowed by the bombings of Hiroshima and Nagasaki, but should not be forgotten. It was the widespread acceptance of such acts that led some pacifists to say that though Hitler lost World War II, Hitlerism won. Perhaps the distinctive characteristic of our era is not its nuclear bombs but the acceptance of mass killing of civilians, and of preparation for such killing.[1]

> *Heightened self-reliance would remove one present-day cause of political tensions.*

If benevolent flying saucer people magically altered the physics of matter on Earth so that nuclear fission and fusion became impossible, human survival would still not be guaranteed. Nonnuclear incendiary warheads, launched in sufficient numbers, might trigger "'nuclear' winter" phenomena. And this is not the only nonnuclear threat: those who write about nuclear weapons would do well to emulate the late Alva Myrdal[2] in taking chemical and biological warfare into account as well.

Kirkpatrick Sale, a decentralist and author of *Human Scale* (1980), a comprehensive survey of thinking on the relevance of scale to human affairs, is actively involved with the stirrings of political activity that are variously termed bioregional, ecological, or "Green." His paper "Centrifugal Force" argues that war is a phenomenon generated by large-scale mass society and that decentralization to a world of smaller societies, with accompanying changes toward an ecologically sound lifestyle, is the necessary and sufficient solution to the problem of war. Sale contributes to an important tradition of writers who have argued that "from bigness comes impersonality, insensitivity, and a lust to concentrate abstract power."[3]

Decentralized societies need not be inward-looking or entirely self-reliant, but heightened self-reliance would remove one present-day cause of political tensions. Hal Harvey, a founder of the computer network PeaceNet,[4] is director of the Security Program of the Rocky Mountain Institute, whose research director Amory Lovins is well known for his advocacy of "soft energy paths" (emphasizing conservation and renewable sources) that meet energy needs more cheaply than new nuclear or fossil fuel plants or imported oil.[5] Harvey's article suggests that energy self-reliance and

Readings: for study group use

A. Kirkpatrick Sale, "Centrifugal Force: Making the World Safe from Mass Society" *The ExPro Papers* #2 (1986; 10 pp.); Hal Harvey, "The Best Defense is Dealing With the Roots of Conflict," *New Options* newsletter (April 30, 1987; 2 pp.); Gernot Kohler, "Global Apartheid," *World Order Models Project Working Paper* #7 (1978; 13 pp.);

Ethel Jensen, "How Feminists View Peace and Conflict," from "Feminism and Peace" (1982), pp. 11-19.

Total= 34 pp.

B. Joseph Gerson, "Introduction" and "What is the Deadly Connection?" (pp. 2-21);

Randall Forsberg, "Behind the Facade: Nuclear War and Third World Intervention" (pp. 24-35);

Daniel Ellsberg, "Call to Mutiny" (pp. 36-59); Noam Chomsky, "Patterns of Intervention" (pp. 60-68); Michael Klare, "Conventional Arms, Military Doctrine, and Nuclear War: The Vanishing Firebreak" (pp. 98-109); Stuart Schaar, "The Dangers of Nuclear Proliferation and War in the Middle East" (pp. 162-164); and

Gerson et al., "The United States in the Middle East" (pp. 167-183); all in Joseph Gerson, ed., *The Deadly Connection: Nuclear War and U.S. Intervention* (1986). Total= 91 pp.

C. Noam Chomsky, "Planning for Global Hegemony," "The Rule of Law and the Rule of Force," "Cold War Realities," pp. 1-2, 39-58, 63-72, 78-95, 217-219 (read or skim additional material as desired) in *Turning the Tide: U.S. Intervention in Central America and the Struggle for Peace* (1985);

George Scialabba, "Watergate and Contragate: The Essential Continuity," from *The Activist Review* (1987; 2 pp.).

Total= 55 pp.

D. Joanna Macy, "Foreword"; and

George Lakey, "Introduction" and "Empowering Ourselves for Peace," pp. vi-x, xiii-xxvi, 7-27 in *Powerful Peacemaking: A Strategy for a Living Revolution* (1987);

Gerald Mische, "A Tale of Two Tables: The Link Between Economic and Military Security" from *Breakthrough* (1985; 5 pp.).

Total= 44 pp.

E. Daniel Deudney, "Whole Earth Security: A Geopolitics of Peace," *Worldwatch Paper* #55 (1983; 64 pp.). Total= 64 pp.

new technologies could reduce U.S. dependence on both foreign oil and the so-called "strategic minerals" that are often invoked as the reason the U.S. must ally itself with Saudi Arabia, South Africa, and other internally-repressive regimes. "Reducing the economic and political roots of conflict" is one part of Harvey's "three-part alternative security agenda." (The other two are: "stronger international rules and better conflict resolution" and "nonprovocative defense." About these, more in later chapters.)

Gernot Kohler makes vivid the severity of present-day political and economic inequality, a major source of conflict, by his characterization of it as "global apartheid." He writes that "the possibility of a future nuclear war between the United States and the Soviet Union [has] so much occupied the minds of some of us in the affluent countries that we fail to see that actual international violence (resulting from international wars and intervention) and actual civil violence (from revolutions, riots, massacres, etc.) and actual structural violence (from miserable socioeconomic conditions) are all related to global apartheid" (pp. 6-7).

> *"The roots of violence and war lie in the patriarchy itself, in systems of dominance and submission, the most basic of which is that between men and women."*

"Structural violence," a term closely associated with peace researcher Johan Galtung,[6] refers to

> violence exerted by situations, institutions, social, political, and economic structures. Thus, when a person dies because he/she has no access to food, the effect is violent as far as that person is concerned, yet there is no individual actor who could be identified as the source of this violence. It is the system of food production and distribution that is to blame. The violence is thus exerted by an anonymous "structure" (p. 7).

But such violence is certainly real and can even (as Kohler explains) be measured.

Ten years from now, many more of the readings used in study groups on peace will include an awareness of the pervasive way that masculine or patriarchal domination affects not only everyday life but the deepest assumptions of political theory and practice. Increasingly we recognize that the very concepts we use are "gendered."[7] In her lecture "How Feminists View Peace and Conflict," Ethel Jensen, President of the Jane Addams Peace Association, surveys a number of feminist books and papers and speaks candidly of the emotional impact of confronting feminist writings about war and violence. The "message was that the roots of violence and war lie in the patriarchy itself, in systems of dominance and submission, the most basic of which is that between men and women. It was very hard for me to accept this, but in the end, I did."

Some people work on the problem of nuclear war, some on opposing U.S. military intervention in other countries. Since 1982 an increasing number of people have become aware of a "deadly connection" between these two issues. Joseph Gerson has been a pioneer in spreading the awareness that most nuclear crises have arisen not from U.S.-Soviet confrontation in Europe, where NATO and Warsaw Pact forces face each other, but from U.S. and Soviet involvement in Third World conflicts. Randall Forsberg argues that the arms race, far from being chiefly a way to deter and defend against Soviet nuclear and conventional threats, "has nothing to do with defense" and "little to do with deterrence, except in the sense of deterring their interventions while permitting our own." The experience she recounts of studying with a top Pentagon consultant at M.I.T. illustrates the taboo nature of the straightforward question, "Which of our forces are for defense and which of our forces are for intervention?"

Former RAND Corporation and Pentagon analyst Daniel Ellsberg, best known for leaking the secret "Pentagon Papers" on U.S. policy toward Vietnam, describes the known U.S. nuclear threats and their function in relation to foreign policy objectives. M.I.T. linguist Noam Chomsky's brief overview of U.S. "patterns of intervention" argues that, because of the deadly connection, "there could be no greater contribution to world peace and . . . human survival" than action to halt U.S. interventionism.

Not only does the lethal potential of chemical and biological weapons challenge the common assumption that nuclear weapons are the core of humanity's predicament in "the nuclear age," but, as Michael Klare shows in his article on "The Vanishing Firebreak," the distinction between nuclear weapons and "conventional" weapons is rapidly eroding: nuclear weapons are getting smaller and conventional weapons are getting more accurate and destructive. Finally, two articles discuss the dangers of nuclear war in the Middle East, which many analysts believe is the likeliest point of origin for a global nuclear holocaust.

These "deadly connection" analyses have a very important implication. They suggest strongly that the viewpoint of politicians who (along with some arms control organizations) combine support for decreased nuclear deployments with calls for increased conventional military spending would, if put into effect, actually increase the chances of nuclear holocaust.[8]

"In all American history, no one's writings are more unsettling than Noam Chomsky's," writes the editor of a recent anthology of his writings.[9] Chomsky's *Turning the Tide: U.S. Intervention in Central America and the Struggle for Peace* (1985) makes shocking reading for anyone accustomed to thinking that the United States's role in the world is basically benevolent. Chomsky marshals massive and irrefutable evidence of horrifying crimes by regimes effectively controlled from the U.S., or by U.S. forces themselves, and documents pervasive media bias that prevents most of the U.S. public from learning of this evidence. He traces current U.S. policies to planning for global domination done in the closing years of World War II and carried out since with moderate success. His careful use of evidence and logic and his relentless juxtaposition of ascertainable facts with hypocritical pronouncements give his books (of which this is only one of the more recent) exceptional power.

In places Chomsky's tone recalls Brecht's words that "Even anger against injustice makes the voice grow harsh." After more than twenty years of documenting in numerous essays and books facts about violence supported or carried out by the U.S. government, Chomsky sometimes describes as "cynical" behavior that is more plausibly attributed to self-deception, moral laziness, and ideologically-produced blindness and confusion.[10] How the mentalities of policy-makers, journalists, and ideologues are best to be interpreted, however, should not divert attention from the painful evidence adduced by Chomsky about U.S. policy, policy-makers' stated views, and the degree of domestic change required to alter U.S. global policies.

George Scialabba's "Watergate and Contragate: The Essential Continuity" (1987) reminds us that both scandals erupted over crimes that were much less heinous than the crimes of ongoing government policies: money for the *contras* has cost many lives, regardless of whether Congress authorized it or was illegally bypassed. But "unlike the World Court or the victims of American foreign policy, Congress [or in the case of Watergate, the Democratic Party] is sufficiently powerful to insist that its prerogatives be respected. That the rights of the powerful are vindicated — this is the precise sense in which, as we were assured again and again after Watergate . . .'the system works.'"

Joanna Macy's eloquent "Foreword" to George Lakey's *Powerful Peacemaking* emphasizes the importance of four ingredients in a strategy capable of leading to peace:
1) "willingness to face the crisis";
2) "a capacity to see and think systematically and holistically";
3) a changed view of power;
4) and "an awakening to the meaning and necessity of nonviolence."
Her stress on a holistic, "systems" view of the world and how change occurs has enabled her to help people understand the linkages between their own lives and emotions and the lives of others who share the fate of the planet. These linkages can be discovered experientially in Macy's highly regarded workshops on acknowledging and working through despair about the world's prospects as a route to personal empowerment.[11]

Lakey, for seven years director of Pennsylvania's Jobs With Peace Campaign, begins his book by recounting his personal struggle to overcome cancer. He vividly explains six principles he used that pertain to humanity's struggle to overcome social ills. In his next chapter he describes an early failure to recognize kinship — despite his own working-class background — between his moral peace protesting and the concerns of Boeing helicopter factory workers. A successful strategy to overcome the war system, he believes, must recognize and provide substitutes for that system's defense, economic, and identity-providing functions. Looking at the needs met (however destructively) by the present system is key to identifying who is hurt by it. All its victims are potential allies in work for change. Later parts of his book address how to develop the power — including nonviolent "coercive force" (p. xxiv) — to change social systems.

Gerald Mische's *Toward a Human World Order* (1977; co-authored with Patricia Mische) was a pioneering effort to view humanity's multiple crises systemically rather than as separate problems. In "A Tale of Two Tables" he points out that

> arms negotiators assume that nations are still territorially sovereign, that territories can still be impenetrable, and that national legislation and institutions are adequate for providing security for their peoples. [But] most persons sitting around the table of monetary and trade negotiations . . . recognize that a radically new world has come into being . . . a world that is economically, monetarily and environmentally interdependent [and in which] nations are *no longer* fully sovereign.

Mische concludes that "the need now is to develop international institutions that — while preserving basic sovereignty and cultural diversity — would have the functional authority needed to cope with those global problems which nations cannot handle, thereby providing a structural framework for nations to achieve security." Security, according to Mische, is both political and economic.

Now, nations must "secure themselves against what they have always relied upon for security — their weapons."

The crises we face involve many persisting factors: economic inequality, political insecurity, domination. In addition, changing technology alters the relations of the elements of national power. Daniel Deudney's *Whole Earth Security* (1983) applies "geopolitical" analysis — usually associated with conservative, even militarist, outlooks — to the implications of recent technologies. Satellite surveillance using high-resolution optics has produced a "transparency revolution" of considerable importance for peace, since decisions to make war have often resulted from secrecy and uncertainty about an opponent's capabilities.

Space has become the new "high ground" for gaining earthly advantage. "Throughout history," Deudney writes, "changes in the securable terrain have driven former warring neighbors into common cause against a new, bigger threat." But now, nations must "secure themselves against what they have always relied upon for security — their weapons."

New technology, it should be added, is affecting economic as well as military security. The spread of "electronic teller" bank machines is the everyday counterpart to the growing rapidity, and hence possible volatility, of electronic funds transfers on a global scale. According to a former strategic planner for a major multinational corporation, annual global foreign exchange transactions reached $65 trillion in 1985 — "another doubling since last year, and twenty times the annual U.S. Gross National Product [— also] several times the world GNP." For corporations with billions on hand, fractional interest rate differences between Paris and Tokyo can mean millions in easy profit for money shifts of a few hours' duration. "The movement of money itself has become the game . . . [resulting in] an extremely difficult and unstable system to manage . . . . What is absolutely clear to me is that it is a system out of control. Nobody really understands it."[12]

As with the increasing role of computer-programmed investment strategies, executing automatic reactions to stock price changes, the potential of computerized funds transfers to cause (or possibly to prevent) global economic collapse appears not to be reliably known.[13] If economies can be ruined in hours — or milliseconds — then major changes would appear required to make possible a world of stable peace.

Part II
Designing a Peace System

Introduction: Why and How to Think about the Future
Chapter 4: Envisioning and Designing a Future of Peace
Chapter 5: World Governance
Chapter 6: Alternative Security Policies
Chapter 7: Economic Development, Ecology, and Peace
Chapter 8: Psychology, Religion, Culture, and Peace

Introduction:
Why and How
to Think about the Future

If the problem of "denial" is to be overcome, it is necessary to do more than merely scare people with horrendous pictures of the possible future. Indeed, the more horrendous the picture which is drawn, the more it is likely to result in denial and pathological inactivity. . . . It is hard for people to visualize the nature of the system change which is necessary for survival. This, then, is one of the major tasks today of the political scientist, the philosopher, the journalist, and the prophet: to give the people an image of changes in the international system which seem small enough to be feasible yet large enough to be successful.

–Kenneth E. Boulding[1]

The book *Visions of a Warless World* (1986) begins by quoting the Book of Proverbs — "Where there is no vision the people perish" — and then continues:

> The idea for this study was born when it became apparent that many citizens have no real hope that humankind can create a world without war. . . . Without some sustaining vision of a more hopeful future and a sense of next steps to reach it, many people will remain discouraged and apathetic.

There seem to be at least three important reasons for devoting time and energy to envisioning the future. First (as countless volumes on planning, management, and self-help insist), clarity about our goals is essential to enable us to work toward them effectively. To the degree that the goal is unclear, we do not know what we are working for when we seek to bring about peace.

Second, the more vivid our goal, the more it will inspire us, motivate us, and sustain our morale over the time required to accomplish it. This is true even though the goal we actually achieve will doubtless differ from our original vision.

Finally, as proponents of a better world order have written, "Envisioning new institutions, whether they be self-reliant communities, appropriate technology industries, human service organizations, or global mechanisms of accountability, poses a challenge to existing institutions . . . . It is thus a form of struggle as well."[2]

Vision work, therefore, is not merely the creation of comforting daydreams, but an activity of practical importance as a benchmark and tool for use in guiding change efforts, as a source of psychological fortitude and perseverance, and as an element in making change.

Envisioning and designing

It seems useful to distinguish two types of activity which we can term "envisioning" and "designing."

Envisioning (or imaging, or imagining) is using our imagination, drawing on our knowledge, fantasies, and dreams — what is inside us (including our values, ethical or religious). Readings by Elise Boulding discussed in Chapter 4 describe a deliberate way of engaging in this process. (See "Image Before Action" and "The Social Imagination and the Crisis of Human Futures.") You are encouraged to try "Imaging a World Without War." (See later in this book.)

Vision work is not merely the creation of comforting daydreams, but an activity of practical importance.

"Designing" can be our term for a more systematic and formal effort aiming to determine what structures, processes, etc. can realize and sustain the values and conditions we have envisioned as desirable. Designing seems to be a better label for sustained intellectual work that can test putative solutions to global problems against the evidence of history and scrutinize them for internal consistency. It seems sensible to do envisioning first, and then designing; but one can repeat either process as often as desired.

The contrast between envisioning and designing should not, however, be exaggerated. The imaging workshops described by Elise Boulding use "the strongest critical judgment" as well as free (but focused) imaging. (See her explicit cautions about undisciplined fantasy quoted in Chapter 4.)

The notion of designing a better future has had a rather bad name. Thinkers like Fourier who specified their ideal future society down to the layout and dimensions of the buildings made "utopian" susceptible to becoming an epithet of dismissal. As Karl Marx's colleague Friedrich Engels (who respected Fourier as a forerunner) wrote: "the more completely [the new social systems] were worked out in detail, the more they could not avoid drifting off into pure fantasies."[3]

Such an approach is in trouble if it encounters unpredicted situations. Robert Boguslaw contrasts it with design "that uses principles to provide guides for action. It is not bound by preconceptions about the situations the system will encounter. Its principles provide action guides even in the face of completely unanticipated situations."[4] (See Hanna Newcombe's *Design for a Better World*, discussed in Chapter 4, for an excellent discussion and application of design principles.)

Two more aspects of designing a better world concern how "utopian" to be and the time span under consideration.

How utopian to be?

By "how utopian" is meant the degree of likelihood of the imagined future's becoming reality. Arthur Waskow advocates a way of imagining the future that is neither utopian in the sense of disregarding probabilities nor resigned to the continuation of present trends. He suggests

> an examination of the seriously *possible* rather than the most likely. Instead of being a prediction — that is, the author's best judgment as to what present trends are likely to produce — it is what might be called a *possidiction* — that is, the author's projection of how certain seeds of change that exist already might be made to flourish, given certain kinds of political action. The possidiction describes worlds that are, say, 30% likely — as against either worlds that are only 1% likely or those that are 60% likely. There is a serious chance they can be brought into being, but it will take a lot of doing. And the possidiction acts as an incitement to the necessary action. . . .
>
> The whole process . . . looks like this: one develops a notion of possible social change and from that a vision of a desirable practicable future. One works out as vividly and in as much detail as possible, the way in which that practicable desirable future would work . . . And then one works backward from that, in a kind of retroprojection, to see what kinds of change in detail would be necessary in order to get to that stage. In a sense this is a method of successive approximations, in which one could move from analysis of change to an image of the future and back again, back and forth as many times as you like, getting more and more detailed each time.[5]

What time span should be considered?

It is natural to focus on dates by which one can expect or at least hope that one's goal, or some significant step toward it, can be accomplished. How soon you can possibly imagine getting the kind of world you want depends on how much power you have. In 1974 the Council on Foreign Relations, a group dominated by New York bankers, corporate executives, and other elite figures who move in and out of top government policy-making positions, announced its "1980's Project" — "an attempt to analyze the characteristics of the kind of international system that would be suited to deal with the conditions and problems of the upcoming decade."[6] In contrast, the World Order Models Project (WOMP) of the Institute for World Order, a far less powerful group, was begun in 1968 (six years earlier) yet defined the distinguished models it produced as "Preferred Worlds for the 1990s."[7]

Another approach to the future is to enlarge our sense of "the present," as exemplified by Elise Boulding's "200-year present," which involves looking both toward the past and the future 100 years, or about the span of the longest human lives.[8]

Analysis, vision, and strategy

The terms *analysis, vision,* and *strategy* constitute a framework many people find useful. Analysis is usually of what presently exists. Vision suggests what could come to exist in the future. Strategy is about the process of getting from the present to a desired future, and implies planning of efforts and overcoming obstacles.

Each of these, to be explored with any thoroughness, requires attention to the other two.[9] What presently exists is really understood only by comparison with what might be. Knowledge of what could come to exist in the future is based on understanding and assumptions about how existing forces and factors interrelate. And for strategy to link the present forces to the future vision, attention must be paid to both.

> *Analysis is usually of what presently exists. Vision suggests what could come to exist in the future. Strategy is about the process of getting from the present to a desired future, and implies planning of efforts and overcoming obstacles.*

A useful tool is the *scenario.* Ideas of the future can be static — an unchanging image, possibly of something conceived as perfect. Scenarios represent a vision extended in duration, enabling it to incorporate the dynamics of change — the interplay of forces over time. Scenarios are thus about transition, and can be excellent stimuli to thinking about strategies for making envisioned goals into realities. We have included several brief scenarios among the readings discussed in this book.

Perhaps the best social change scenario written in recent years is Ernest Callenbach's novel *Ecotopia Emerging,* a "prequel" to his popular *Ecotopia* and a good source of information and practical ideas as well as inspiration.[10] Unfortunately, those books are not global in scope (they portray how the U.S. Pacific Northwest becomes an independent, ecologically responsible country). A novel of the creation of a peace system, whether by Callenbach or someone else — several such books would not be too many — would be an enormous contribution to peace.

In this book Part I corresponds best to analysis (of the war system), Part II to vision, and Part III to strategy — but each includes elements of the others.[11]

Implementing what has been designed

Analyses are usually partly wrong, and visions can be vague or harbor latent contradictions. The advice for organizational problem-solving given by the scholars who edited a two-volume *Handbook of Organizational Design* — relevant because global society can be conceived as a big organization — can be summarized (in paraphrase) as "try several solutions simultaneously, and expect that some won't work (or will create new problems); keep trying; and keep paying attention to what happens." Their concluding words about organizations apply equally well to global redesign: "A well designed organization is not a stable solution to achieve, but a developmental process to keep active."[12]

A quotation from Rene Dubos nicely combines the notions of system design and problem-solving over time:

> If we model ourselves . . . on our ecological systems, we find, surely, that we do not achieve balance by any one line or solution but by a careful interweaving of a great variety of partial solutions which added together give us the possibility of proceeding without disaster: correcting, reconsidering, backtracking, advancing, observing, and inventing as we go.[13]

We don't need a perfect design for a peace system in order to bring about peace. Even if we thought we had one, chances are we'd be wrong. What we need is enough understanding of what it takes to design and create one to know with some confidence what direction to head in, and enough wisdom (enough humility, courage, and willingness to learn) and perseverance to keep trying and reevaluating our experience "as we go."

Chapter 4:
Envisioning and Designing a Future of Peace

In contrast to those who argued that "living with nuclear weapons is our only hope," in the readings discussed in this chapter we meet people with other hopes.

Walden Bello's *Visions of a Warless World*, prepared in collaboration with the Friends Committee on National Legislation (a Quaker lobbying group), is an "effort to understand visions of peace in different religious and intellectual traditions and to explore the ways these perspectives might complement one another in the urgent endeavor to bring about a state of genuine peace." The book's premise is that "each . . . has a unique contribution to make in the effort to formulate and forge a lasting peace." In the first half of the book Bello reviews major religious perspectives and conservative, liberal, and Marxist intellectual traditions. (In the second half he explores psychological, feminist, Third World, and nonviolent perspectives.)

Kermit D. Johnson, retired Chief of Chaplains of the U.S. Army (with rank of major general), briefly reviews Jewish and Christian conceptions of peace found in the Bible. He then presents fifteen propositions of his own on the meaning of peace as a basis for discussion. The last of these may be especially apt to quote in this chapter that begins the study of readings on the rational designing of peace: "Since peace involves a mix of persons and structure/systems, both the rationality of ordered planning and the inspiration of persons who incarnate peace in their lives are to be valued."

Sociologist Elise Boulding has been a pioneer in the fields of futurism, peace research, and women's history. Her one-page article "Image Before Action" explains the origin and nature of the workshops conducted by the "Imaging a World Without Weapons Project." These workshops, which "can be done in a mini-version of three hours, or a full-length version of two and a half days," invite people to draw on fantasy as well as analysis to create an image of a future "in which one's wishes for society have been realized."

> What do people see when they step into the future? A more localist world, where problems of scale, size and complexity are handled differently than in the present. Computer networking keeps local communities connected. It is a world without age and gender segregation, a "clean green" world which gives much attention to sharing of resources and management of conflicts. People look happier, are more relaxed. These themes are common, although the specifics . . . vary as much as the individuals engaged in imaging.

In "The Social Imagination and the Crisis of Human Futures: A North American Perspective" (1983), Elise Boulding suggests there is a circular relationship among "image literacy, technological dependence, and feelings of collective and personal helplessness." She proposes "the cultivation of the capacity for social imaging as a way out" of this trap, and describes in detail a method for this cultivation.

Readings: for study group use

A. Walden Bello, "Religion and the Vision of Peace" and "Envisioning Peace in Three Intellectual-Ethical Traditions," pp. v-vi, 1-62 in *Visions of a Warless World* (1986; 59 pp.). Total= 59 pp.

B. Kermit Johnson, "What is Peace? Judeo-Christian Insights," *The ExPro Papers* #4 (1987; 9 pp.);

Elise Boulding, "Image Before Action" from *Peace and Freedom* (June 1987) (1 p.); and

Elise Boulding, "The Social Imagination and the Crisis of Human Futures: A North American Perspective," from *Forum for Correspondence and Contact*, 13:2 (February 1983), pp. 43-44, 49-56 (small print, equivalent to ca 18 pp.).

Total= 28 pp.

C. Hanna Newcombe, *Design for a Better World* (1983), pp. 1-26;

Michael Marien, "Sixty Paths to U.S. and Global Security" from *Future Survey Annual 1984* (2 pp.);

Richard Smoke, "What is Peace?" and "Nine Paths to Peace," pp. 1-5 in *Paths to Peace* (1987).

Total= 33 pp.

D. Kenneth Boulding, "Research for Peace" (1978), pp. 158-169 in Stephenson, ed., *Alternative Methods for International Security* (1982);

Carolyn Stephenson, "A Research Agenda on the Conditions of Peace," *The ExPro Papers* #7 (1987; 22 pp.).

Total= 34 pp.

E. Dietrich Fischer, "Introduction," pp. 1-10 in *Preventing War in the Nuclear Age* (1984);

Kenneth Boulding, "Foreword," and

Mark Sommer, "Alternative Futurism: Toward More Practical Utopias," pp. iii-vi, x-xiii, 111-135, in *Beyond the Bomb* (1986; 31 pp.).

Total= 41 pp.

Boulding is also explicit about the limits of imaging and imaging workshops. Her workshops include critical judgment about the images. They

> are physically exhausting to the participants . . . because the two approaches of allowing a free (yet focussed) flow of imagery and then directing the powers of the intellect to that imagery are very difficult to harness together in the same enterprise. There is always the danger that in other, less disciplined settings people will indulge in fantasy-type imagery and persuade themselves they are thereby creating the future or that charismatic leaders will "sell" fantasy images to people longing for instant social transformation (p. 56).

Hanna Newcombe, author of *Design for a Better World* (1983), is a long-time world federalist who is co-director of the Peace Research Institute in Dundas, Ontario, and editor since 1962 of *Peace Research Abstracts Journal.*[1] This editorial work has given her an exceptionally broad overview of peace research and related ideas, and her book has been described as a valuable synthesis of much world government and world federalist thinking of recent decades.

> **Any structures planned should be "flexible enough to provide for future peaceful orderly change."**

In introducing her effort to design a "better" — not ideal or perfect — world, Newcombe argues for seven general guidelines: first, the importance of not presenting a single "static, rigid" design, but rather giving, "at various points, several alternatives, or even a continuous range of alternatives." Any structures planned should be "flexible enough to provide for future peaceful orderly change." Second, one should "build in . . . nonviolence, order, and justice" as the three components of peace.

Third, she advises, "pay attention to stages": change takes time, and priorities must be chosen. Like the editors of the *Handbook of Organizational Design*, she recognizes the importance of "proceeding experimentally, . . . evaluating successes and failures along the way, so that corrections may be introduced" (pp. 12, 14). Her concept of "planned gradualism"—involving social mechanisms pre-programmed to produce a set result over time without requiring further negotiation (pp. 14-15, 18) — deserves special notice.

Fourth, "pay attention to comprehensiveness and integration of planning." Fifth, "pay attention to levels." Newcombe advocates "the principle of subsidiarity: any activity should be carried out at the lowest levels . . . consistent with the efficient performance of the task."

Sixth is the requirement of getting "in equilibrium with nature" — "almost" in equilibrium is not good enough, for it will lead to disaster eventually. Last, "maximize both the acceptability and the effectiveness of the plan." Since these two goals tend to relate in opposite ways to the degree of change involved in a plan, a dilemma tends to exist in choosing strategy, one compounded by the many uncertainties involved. Newcombe's advice for strategy is for different groups to push different plans that vary in how modest or far-reaching they are. This is preferable to single-minded insistence on a particular plan or strategy (p. 28), which may after all turn out to be inadequate. Her advice thus echoes that of the organization design scholars mentioned earlier, who advocate combining "multiple, simultaneous . . . solution attempts."[2]

Some people, absorbed with one or more ideas they cherish, make little effort to learn about or evaluate the "solution attempts" being undertaken by others. Michael Marien, editor of the valuable monthly *Future Survey*,[3] shares with Hanna Newcombe the unsung virtue of paying careful attention to the work of others. A chart he has prepared, entitled "Sixty Paths to U.S. and Global Security," part of the introductory material to his *Future Survey Annual 1984*, may be helpful to anyone seeking order in a complex field; it provides one way of categorizing a large number of approaches (including many discussed in this book).

Marien has written that the most important issue of our time is how to curb the costly global arms race, reduce the risk of nuclear war, and attain national security.

> There are many answers, or alternative futures. Many of these answers are proposed singly as the best, most important, or initial approach to take. Unfortunately, we do not have individuals and institutions disposed to debating, digesting, refining, and combining these answers. Until we do, we may very well continue along the path to greater insecurity.[4]

The increase in recent years in alternative security thinking suggests that the situation Marien laments may be changing for the better. As a reader of this book (and even more if you are a study group participant), you are part of the kind of learning process he considers essential for human survival.

Another categorization of peace approaches is found in the introduction to Richard Smoke's *Paths to Peace*. Smoke lists nine proposed paths that he will examine: preemptive attack to remove a threat, deterrence, diplomacy for peace, disarmament and arms control, eliminating the fundamental causes of war, alternative defense, nonviolent resistance, alternative conflict resolution, and changing attitudes and perceptions. He also defines three peace goals, differing in degree: abolishing the threat of a global nuclear holocaust, "operational peace" (in which war has been delegitimized and peaceful conflict resolution is fairly consistently used by nations), and "complete peace" ("a state of nonviolence, and even low conflict, among peoples").

Kenneth Boulding, a founder of the field of peace research, outlines its rationale in "Research for Peace" (an excerpt from his 1978 book *Stable Peace*). He defines peace research as "an intellectual movement, mainly within the social sciences, to apply methods of science to problems of conflict, to war and peace." He notes (p. 165) that there has been important controversy within the peace research community between those who emphasize "negative peace" (absence of war) and those who emphasize "positive peace" (including social justice and related well-being).

Political scientist Carolyn M. Stephenson has long been concerned with synthesizing what is known about "alternative methods for international security" (the title of her book on that topic). In "A Research Agenda on the Conditions of Peace" (1987) she discusses some of the problems facing peace research, outlines the process used by ExPro's Research Agenda Committee, and presents its results. A propos of the negative peace / positive peace debate, she suggests that "whether one's goal is social justice or the abolition of nuclear weapons, one is eventually led to the conclusion that both must be addressed together" (p. 8). Her article and its appendices present a host of specific questions and topics worthy of exploration.[5]

In contrast to many recent books about nuclear war, Dietrich Fischer's main emphasis in his *Preventing War in the Nuclear Age* (1984) is not on the *dangers* of nuclear war but on "the exploration of *solutions* to the problem" (p. 1). In contrast to the advocacy of complex and protracted negotiations characteristic of arms controllers, Fischer highlights unilateral measures that increase a country's security whether they are reciprocated or not. Fischer has a gift for apt and vivid analogies. His approach is based on a few sensible and relatively simple principles; yet present policies are so counter-productive for security that persistent application of these "common sense" principles impresses ever more forcefully on the reader the irrationality of the present threat system[6] of deterrence. Common sense, Fischer shows, prescribes pursuing common security as the goal in our own best interest.

> *"Whether one's goal is social justice or the abolition of nuclear weapons, one is eventually led to the conclusion that both must be addressed together."*

Beyond the Bomb: A Field Guide to Alternative Strategies for Building a Stable Peace, by writer, farmer, and visionary Mark Sommer, was the first work commissioned by ExPro to map out what territory an "exploratory project" might explore. His chapter on "Alternative Futurism" eloquently outlines and assesses a number of approaches, from Fred Polak's work on "the image of the future"[7] to imaging, scenario-writing, "possidiction," political science fiction, and utopia creation.

Chapter 5:
World Governance

"Governance," rather than "government," is used in the title of this chapter because the function denoted need not be delegated totally to an institution called a government. How the functions of governance would best be apportioned among human institutions and groups should be a topic for exploration, not settled in advance by choice of terminology. But let us begin this exploration by examining the idea of world government.

A remarkable range of people, from politicians (including U.S. presidents) to scientists, writers, and religious leaders, have remarked that the ultimate solution to the problem of war has to be establishment of world government.[1] But most of these, to the frustration of world government advocates, seem to see this idea as for "later" and of little immediate relevance. (Cf. Fischer: "If we were to wait for the establishment of a global body with the power to enforce international law in order to prevent a nuclear holocaust, the hopes for human survival might be slim.")

The advocates of world government (hereafter referred to as "world federalists," for reasons of brevity and because most desire a "federal" government above national governments, not the abolition of the latter) believe that if world law enforced by world government is the "ultimate" solution to war, we had better get working on it now.

> *How the functions of governance would best be apportioned among human institutions and groups should be a topic for exploration.*

The world government arguments are simple and plausible to most people at some level. As President Harry Truman said: "When Kansas and Colorado have a quarrel over the water in the Arkansas River they don't call out the National Guard in each state and go to war over it. They bring suit in the Supreme Court of the United States and abide by the decision. There isn't a reason in the world why we cannot do that internationally."[2] World federalists point to the adoption of the U.S. Constitution by the thirteen colonies and the resulting benefits as a model and as proof of the feasibility of their goal.

But world federalists seem to ignore the inconvenient fact of the U.S. civil war.[3] What is its implication for world federalism? Hundreds of thousands died in a struggle for supremacy of a federal government over a group of its constituent states. Law—even "enforceable law"—is not, as world federalists seem to think, a cure-all even when it prevails. President Lincoln did succeed, after all, in enforcing the inviolability of the Union (and, as an explicitly secondary goal, in eliminating slavery). But is so destructive a war an acceptable byproduct of federalism in the late twentieth century?

When world federalist Lawrence Abbott suggests that ever-larger governmental units are desirable because history shows that "the broadening of government reduced the arena of warfare,"[4] he does not consider the points Kirkpatrick Sale raised in his article "Centrifugal Force" (see Chapter 3 of this book). "The broadening of government" has coincided with ever-larger wars, and Abbott's comment that, whatever civil wars may erupt, they will at least not be "intergovernmental," is scant reassurance.[5]

Readings: for study group use

A. Benjamin Ferencz with Ken Keyes, Jr., *PlanetHood* (1988), pp. 25-110;

Emery Reves, "Why Waste Time Discussing Disarmament?" (1961; 3 pp.);

World Federalist Association, "We the People of the World" and "Getting from Here to There: Creative Solutions to Meet Six Current Crises" (brochures).

Total=82 pp.; some of Ferencz and Keyes is fast reading.

B. Ronald J. Glossop, "Institutional Aspects of the Contemporary Situation" and "Legal Aspects of the Contemporary Situation," pp. 178-203, 204-216 from *Confronting War* (1987; 39 pp.);

Robert C. Johansen & Saul H. Mendlovitz, "The Role of Enforcement of Law in the Establishment of a New International Order: A Proposal for a Transnational Police Force," pp. 307-337 in *Alternatives: A Journal of World Policy* (1980).

Total= 69 pp.

C. Hanna Newcombe, *Design for a Better World* (1983), pp. 27-126. (Because this reading contains many tables, its length is more like 70-80 pages than 100 of prose. The formulas and graphs should not trouble most readers, but anyone allergic is hereby warned.);

Mark Satin, "Reforming the U.N.," from *New Options* (Dec. 29, 1986; 3 pp.).

Total= 80 pp.

D. Richard Falk, *Future Worlds* (1976), pp. 3-60 (58 pp., including twelve diagrams);

Patricia Mische, "Re-Visioning National Security: Toward a Viable World Security System" (1981), pp. 71-84 in Stephenson, *Alternative Methods for International Security.*

Total= 60 pp.

E. Mark Sommer, "Alternative Security," "World Order," and "Peace Research," "Negotiation," and "Game Theory," pp. 27-47, 87-95, 101-109 in *Beyond the Bomb* (1986);

Dietrich Fischer, "Conflict Resolution," pp. 171-186 in *Preventing War in the Nuclear Age* (1984);

Richard Smoke, "The Path of Alternative Conflict Resolution," pp. 55-62 in *Paths to Peace* (1987).

Total= 49 pp.

What is plausible in the world federalists' case is that laws and government indeed provide advantages (as well as some disadvantages) over *ad hoc* approaches to regulation of behavior and resolution of conflict.

What is inadequate in a legal-governmental approach is perhaps at first less easy to see. Benjamin Ferencz defines adequate government as requiring three elements:

1) "elected representatives to make laws";
2) "an executive branch with police to enforce the laws"; and
3) "courts to fairly resolve disputes, decide who's innocent, who's broken the law, and what their punishment will be";

in brief: laws, enforcement, and courts.[6]

But also crucially involved in the functioning of a system of law are four other elements:

1) the tensions (seeds of future overt conflict) inherent in its social makeup;
2) the perceived legitimacy of the legal system and the consequent willingness of various social actors to (in Truman's words) "abide by the decision" rendered in a given situation by that system;
3) the conflict resolution methods known and used to deal with problems before they reach an acute stage; and
4) the means used for enforcement when conflict has not been mutually resolved and laws are being broken.

At present global institutions such as the United Nations and international law confront a world in which:

1) tensions are superabundant;
2) legal decisions are flouted by powerful nations (the U.S. government disregards the World Court's judgment against its actions in Nicaragua; the Soviet government for nearly ten years waged a war in Afghanistan condemned by U.N. votes);
3) known conflict resolution methods are under-utilized by parties who calculate unilateral actions to be more advantageous for gaining objectives vis a vis adversaries; and
4) the use of violence to enforce decisions, given current technology, risks enormous destruction.

These well-known contemporary conditions constitute major obstacles to a satisfactory global legal order. Overcoming them is no simple matter. Awareness of these difficulties, and of the absence of an adequate strategy for confronting them, may account for the slow progress of world federalists' advocacy, despite their hard work and the undoubted merits of their ideas.

The preceding analysis suggests that achievement of the world federalist ideal will require, at a minimum:

1) changes to reduce the generation of conflicts to within the capacity of conflict resolu-

tion and law enforcement mechanisms to deal with them;
2) greater willingness of various social actors to abide by — and contribute to enforcement of — legal decisions;
3) increased development and use of conflict resolution methods;
4) ways that are effective, yet less destructive and costly than warfare, for restraining powerful lawbreaking countries (or other actors).

Many of the remaining readings discussed in this book can be understood as addressing, directly or indirectly, these elements and needs inadequately handled by world federalist thinking.

• • •

Except among some lawyers and peace activists, international law seems little known to most Americans not professionally involved with it for business or other reasons. And even those peace activists who may invoke "the Nuremberg principles"[7] to justify civil disobedience or nonpayment of "war taxes" generally have little idea of the history or present scope of international law. "[Before this trial] I thought it was just something vague like the Golden Rule," confessed a juror in a civil disobedience case.[8] But international law is far more definite, and its progress more significant, than most in the U.S. are aware.

Benjamin B. Ferencz, Chief Prosecutor for the U.S. at the Nuremberg war crimes trial of Nazi extermination squads and author of three two-volume studies on *Defining International Aggression, An International Criminal Court,* and *Enforcing International Law,*[9] is a scholar well qualified to discuss the potential and problems of law. In *A Common Sense Guide to World Peace* (1985) he outlined the growth of world law. Perhaps surprisingly, the period since 1945 has been a time of great progress in codifying legal and human rights principles and in establishing regional and functional courts. In *PlanetHood* (1988), Ferencz has collaborated with a prolific author of "personal growth" books, Ken Keyes, Jr., to give an easily readable argument for seeking world peace through the enforcement of legal settlement of disputes under the auspices of a strengthened United Nations.

That Emery Reves's world federalist book *The Anatomy of Peace* (1945) was a bestseller, serialized in *Reader's Digest,* and the focus of 23,000 study groups, tells us that movements for world peace have had their ups and downs before now, and that there are no guarantees of success.[10] (It can also encourage us to imagine that a huge public discussion of peace might again be possible.) In his 1961 article "Why Waste Time Discussing Disarmament?" Reves denounces the disarmament talk of the big-power leaders of that era as mere repetitions of such talk in the 1930s. Like the members of the Boston Nuclear Study Group (see Chapter 2), he argues that weapons are not the problem — people in New York State are not afraid of weapons made in Tennessee — but rather it lies in the nature of the relations between groups. His solution — "a sovereign power set up over and above the clashing social units" — is open to the objections indicated earlier; but his article is of interest for its forceful argument that disarmament is not a crucial first step toward peace, but rather essentially irrelevant.[11]

Finally, the brochures "We the People" and "Getting from Here to There" give the flavor of contemporary world federalist argumentation. The latter does an excellent job of presenting specific federalist positions on current issues that could garner wide support while strengthening the groundwork for further progress toward a satisfactory global legal order.

The first chapter to be read from Ronald J. Glossop's *Confronting War* (1987) capably sketches the history, components, peacekeeping efforts, and accomplishments of the United Nations, including some of its functional organizations (such as the World Health Organization and International Labor Organization). Glossop also outlines the roles of regional intergovernmental institutions (such as the Organization of African Unity) and international nongovernmental organizations. The United Nations, though in need of improvement and long out of fashion in the U.S., has fulfilled a number of functions successfully, including providing a forum for diplomacy facilitating peaceful resolution of disputes, serving as a focal point for organizing a variety of activities in the global human interest (e.g., conferences on food, the environment, women, and disarmament), and providing assistance of several kinds to poorer nations. In 1988 the U.N. enjoyed a modest revival of effectiveness and prestige as it played important roles in resolving regional conflicts (Iran-Iraq; Afghanistan; Angola) and as financial strains were eased by Soviet and U.S. decisions to pay monies long withheld because of political objections to certain U.N. operations. The 1988 Nobel Peace Prize was awarded to the United Nations peacekeeping forces.

> *How can international law, and the decisions of the present World Court, or of whatever other global authorities might be established, be enforced?*

The second chapter by Glossop reviews the nature of international law. Unlike national law, which is largely derived from legislation, international law is derived from a complex combination of treaties, behaviors recognized as traditional and customary, past decisions of international (or sometimes also national) courts, general principles common to all major legal systems, consensus (when it exists) of expert opinion about international law, and unanimous U.N. General Assembly resolutions.

How can international law, and the decisions of the present World Court, or of whatever other global authorities might be established, be enforced? We shall return to this question in Chapters 6 and 12. One important element might be a transnational police force as envisaged by Robert C. Johansen and Saul H. Mendlovitz of the World Policy Institute in their "The Role of Enforcement of Law in the Establishment of a New International Order: A Proposal for a Transnational Police Force" (1980). Their inquiry into the types of situations in which such a force could be useful, and into its make-up, training, funding, etc., illustrates the kind of detailed analysis such questions merit, but too rarely receive.

Building a Peace System

The authors recognize that what they advocate is as much political as legal. Pending progress at the governmental level, they suggest that a peacemaking force, operating with strict adherence to nonviolence, could get started on a private, nongovernmental basis, and speed the process of mobilizing suport for a public transnational police force. Since their article was written, two groups — Peace Brigades International and Witness for Peace — have been created that engage in nonviolent intervention in conflict situations. The former has provided bodyguards for Guatemalans active on behalf of those "disappeared" by their government, while the latter has provided a force of U.S. citizens whose presence on the Nicaragua-Honduras border has helped prevent contra attacks in some areas.[12]

Hanna Newcombe's *Design for a Better World* begins (after her discussion of design principles) by examining "weighted voting" plans that could be used either by a reformed United Nations or a new world government. This seemingly dry topic in fact involves such fundamental matters as assessing the proper role of ideal principles vs. accommodation to power realities, and recognizing the unintended incentives that may be implicit in different plans (e.g., voting strength proportional to population is democratic, but provides an anti-ecological incentive for leaders to increase population). Newcombe's comparative evaluation of different voting formulas includes a computerized study of the effects they would have had on past vote outcomes, taking into account East-West and North-South balances and nine voting blocs of nations.

Scholarly studies that reduce uncertainty— and thus reduce unfounded fears, a barrier to reform— can increase the likelihood of major positive changes.

Such detailed and technical inquiries might seem to epitomize the irrelevantly "academic." In reality, however, such work may have very practical significance. During Law of the Sea Treaty negotiations the availability of an M.I.T. computer model able to simulate the effects of various alternative schemes for apportioning mining rights and profits played an important role.[13] In any proposed major reform of international governance, each actor is likely to be most concerned to know "How will this affect our country's interests?" Scholarly studies that reduce uncertainty — and thus reduce unfounded fears, a barrier to reform — can increase the likelihood of major positive changes. It is thus potentially of great value "to have the information on the political implication[s] of reform proposals ready and laid out for detailed inspection by those who might in the future be called upon to choose between alternative plans" (p. 89).

Apropos of voting plans, in the short article "Reforming the U.N." (1986) political journalist Mark Satin interviews several persons long concerned with global governance — including Saul Mendlovitz – about a weighted voting scheme that can be compared with those assessed by Newcombe. Called the "Binding Triad," it was originated by Richard Hudson and mandates that for a resolution to pass in the U.N. General Assembly, the favorable votes must represent over two-thirds of 1) the total number of nations, 2) the world's population, and 3) contributions to the U.N. budget.

The remaining part of the selection from Newcombe's book presents a plan for a "guaranteed annual income." While the notion of "development aid" is a very simplified approach to "development" problems, which have important systemic dynamics of their own (see Chapter 7), Newcombe's discussion does serve to show that relatively small transfers of wealth from the rich countries could make a very big difference for the poorest countries, and that redistribution is far from being a "zero-sum game": the poor countries would gain more from it than the rich countries would lose (pp. 108-9).

Although Newcombe uses GNP (Gross National Product) figures, it is important to recognize, as anyone with ecological or "green" political sympathies should be quick to point out, that GNP is severely flawed as a measure of well-being (even economic well-being), and therefore devising and popularizing other measures and assembling a pertinent global data base is an important intellectual task for world reform.[14]

Richard A. Falk is one of the foremost advocates of the "world order" approach to global reform. In part an outgrowth of world government thinking, the world order approach pioneered by Falk and his World Policy Institute colleague Saul Mendlovitz seeks to maximize the four values of peace, economic well-being, social and political justice, and ecological balance (later reformulated as five values — see Mische, below). Falk's book *A Study of Future Worlds* (1975), for which the booklet *Future Worlds* (1976) can serve as an appetizer, was described in 1976 by Michael Marien, in a unique survey of over one thousand books and articles on "societal directions and alternatives," as "perhaps the best work yet on thinking about alternative futures of any sort."[15]

Falk's booklet offers diagrams (which may serve to aid understanding) that depict different world order models: the present world order, ones with greater corporate influence, one with a greater role for international regional institutions, one with world government, a world empire, and his own preferred model, in which specialized global institutions cooperate to serve coordination and "central guidance" functions within a network of checks and balances and there is a minimum of coercion and bureaucratization at all levels of social organization. Falk states that although the most likely direction of global evolution may be toward intensified inter-state conflict ending in abrupt global collapse, there is a possibility of bringing his preferred model into being sometime "early in the next century" (p. 39). That model would not be an end point, but a point of departure for the continuing evolution of human social arrangements.

Patricia Mische's essay on "Re-Visioning National Security: Toward a Viable World Security System" (1981) argues that "global structures and mechanisms related to law, adjudication, verification, and compliance" are needed if security for nations is to be attained. Also needed are: 1) education to develop the will to create such institutions, and 2) a strategy for bringing about a transition to them. She outlines the chief global structures that seem essential, including a world representative body, world constitution, and tax revenue and satellite monitoring systems. While Mische's peace system would cost more than the present U.N., it would cost much less than the world now spends on unilateral efforts at national security and might permit overall lessening of taxation.

While some peace advocates believe economic development and social justice concerns must be subordinated to peace and disarmament, without which the former cannot be achieved, Mische and her Global Education Associates concur with Falk and Mendlovitz in believing that the key world order values (peace, economic equity, social justice, ecological balance, and participation in decision-making) must be pursued in tandem. This approach, as far as it can be translated into practice, puts U.S. disarmament advocates and Third World countries into alliance with each other.

Mische notes that reason alone rarely moves people; to effect change, a more holistic approach must be used to engage people at the levels of personal meaning like art, religion, and the imagination.

> *Reason alone rarely moves people; a more holistic approach must be used.*

Mark Sommer's chapters on "Alternative Security," "World Order," and "Peace Research" survey conceptions of the elements of an alternative security system capable of providing for the "common defense," where this phrase from the U.S. Constitution must now be understood, in a smaller world, to apply to all countries. He also describes the origins of the world order approach and some contributions of peace research to designing a "peace system": "a synthesis of mutually reinforcing elements blended into an integrated system in which the machinery of war is gradually supplanted by the coordinated mechanisms of international peacekeeping and a complex web of less formal arrangements" (p. 91). His brief chapters on negotiation and game theory suggest approaches to conflict and its resolution that lead to mutually beneficial outcomes.

Dietrich Fischer's chapter on "Conflict Resolution" discusses negotiation, gives encouraging examples of successful handling of the grievances of minorities, and offers a simple yet widely applicable method for the fair and mutually acceptable sharing of disputed resources.

Richard Smoke briefly examines several kinds of conflict resolution, ranging from mediation to international law, some forms of nonviolent struggle, and unofficial peacekeeping. His analysis illuminates the pros and cons of each: for example, mediation may be more attractive to conflicting parties than recourse to international law because whereas recourse to law ultimately turns the decision over to a court (a third party), "mediation tends to create confidence that each party can retain enough control to ensure that it will not be forced to accept a disadvantageous outcome." The building of a peace system will require sophisticated understanding of the incentives and dynamics associated with a large repertoire of conflict resolution methods.

Chapter 6:
Alternative Security Policies

It is a widely held and seldom questioned assumption among many theorists of international relations that there exists a "security dilemma." In the words of Kenneth Waltz:

> If each state . . . strove only for its own security and had no designs on its neighbors, all states would nevertheless remain insecure; for the means of security for one state are, in their very existence, the means by which other states are threatened.[1]

This axiom of international relations theory, if true, would render the creation of a peace system extraordinarily difficult (though not impossible). Collective agreement to create a world government would be required among states whose relations were unavoidably ones of mutual threat.

Fortunately, the axiom is false. The readings discussed in this chapter show that there are means of defense that do not threaten others; they involve no significant[2] attack capability.

Dietrich Fischer's *Preventing War in the Nuclear Age* offers a powerful intellectual framework for thinking about security policies. Fischer shows that two very different kinds of "strength" are typically blurred together in discussions of defense policy: the ability to defend one's own country and the ability to attack others. Only the former contributes to international security. The latter detracts from it.

The distinction between defensive and offensive weaponry, though not clear-cut in every case, is a useful one. Weapons in fixed locations (like fortresses, minefields, and antiaircraft emplacements) and weapons useful only within or near one's own territory (like short-range aircraft) are more purely defensive. Aircraft carriers, and long-range missiles and bombers, all suited for attacking people far from the home country, are more purely offensive. But weapons must also be evaluated in their larger context. Defensive arms combined with offensive arms can be like a shield held by an attacking warrior; "the entire combination of weapons and other defense preparations of a country must be considered in order to decide whether the whole system is predominantly offensive or defensive" (p. 61).

Fischer argues that it is in every country's interest not to pose threats to others. Protestations that one's intentions are purely defensive are inadequate; they should be combined with a weapons posture and other measures that make the claims credible. And to rely for security upon defense alone — even non-threatening defense — would be the equivalent of a one-crop economy; security can be increased by using a variety of measures. "Nonmilitary defense," as defined by Fischer, should involve incentives for peaceful, friendly behavior from potentially hostile neighbors as well as provision for defense against attack.

Fischer's model of defense is not hypothetical; he draws on the history and current policies of neutral, nonaligned Sweden and Switzerland. Though those countries have been criticized for abstaining from the fight against Hitler, Fischer suggests that their experience in staying out of war

Readings: for study group use

A. Dietrich Fischer, "The Dual Meaning of 'Strength,'" "Defensive vs. Offensive Arms," "Does Balance of Power Promote Security?" "Transarmament Before Disarmament," "Nonmilitary Defense," "Entangling Alliances," and "General Defense" pp. 29-53, 61-62, 102-141, 154-163 in *Preventing War in the Nuclear Age*. Total= 74 pp.

B. Audio cassette: "A Modern Alternative to War" (Common Ground interview with Gene Sharp, June 1983; 29 minutes);

Gene Sharp, "National Security Through Civilian-Based Defense," "Ten Points about Civilian-Based Defense," "Questions about the Applicability of CBD," "Steps in Consideration of CBD," and "Key Definitions," in *National Security Through Civilian-Based Defense* (1985), pp. 9-10, 13-52;

Theodore B. Taylor, review of Sharp, *Making Europe Unconquerable: The Potential of Civilian-based Deterrence and Defense* (1985, 1986), from *Bulletin of the Atomic Scientists* (January-February 1987; 1 p.).

Total= 41 pp.

C. Mark Sommer, "Alternative Defense" and "Nonviolence," pp. 3-25, 67-85 in *Beyond the Bomb* (1986; 40 pp.);

Richard Smoke, "Alternative Paths to Coping with Conflict" (alternative defense, civilian-based defense), pp. 39-54 in *Paths to Peace* (1987).

Total= 55 pp.

D. Liane Norman, "Defending America Without War: A Guide for Thought and Discussion" (1987), 4 pp.;

Robert Irwin, "Civilian-Based Defense" (1987; 7 pp.);

Gene Sharp, postscripts to "Gandhi's Defense Policy" and to "Gandhi as a National Defense Strategist" from *Gandhi as a Political Strategist* (1979), pp. 161-164, 191-195;

Brian Martin, "Social Defence: Elite Reform or Grassroots Initiative?" in *Civilian-based Defense: News & Opinion*, Vol. 4, No. 1 (June 1987), pp. 1-5.

Total= 24 pp.

E. George Lakey, section on Czechoslovakia 1968 and "Counter-Institutions for World Community" in *Powerful Peacemaking* (1987), pp. 180-196;

Hanna Newcombe, "Collective Security, Common Security, and Alternative Security: A Conceptual Comparison" (1986; 10 pp.);

Robert Irwin, "Coercion, Force, and Nonviolent Sanctions: Their Place in a Peace System," *The ExPro Papers* #3 (1986; 17 pp.).
Total= 43 pp.

is highly relevant for all nations now that preventing war is essential. (He also notes that a more equitable settlement after World War I would probably have prevented Hitler's becoming a major threat.)

Readers curious about the everyday reality of Switzerland's defense policy may wish to read *New Yorker* writer John McPhee's short and entertaining *La Place de la Concorde Suisse*.[3] (Despite its title, the book is in English.) McPhee gives a vivid, ironic portrait of an army of highly competent part-time soldiers who enjoy fine wine and chocolate in breaks between dangerous, deadly serious military maneuvers. Though vastly different in tone, nothing in his account undermines the defense logic Fischer explicates; rather, McPhee's book serves to illustrate that it requires neither a utopia nor a nation of peace activists to carry out a strictly defensive defense policy.

Gene Sharp directs the Program on Nonviolent Sanctions in Conflict and Defense established in 1983 at Harvard University's Center for International Affairs. He has worked since the 1950s to develop solutions to the problems of war, dictatorship, genocide, and social oppression by increasing our understanding of how nonviolent struggle can be used to combat violence and provide a substitute political technique that can be used in place of it in acute conflicts.[4] His book *The Politics of Nonviolent Action* (1973) is universally regarded as a classic, and no one has done more to encourage research in the field of nonviolent struggle.

Sharp believes that "World government is either unrealizable, or if achieved would itself be likely to produce a world civil war, become tyrannical, and be used to impose or perpetuate injustice."[5] He has looked instead for a way that societies could defend themselves against aggression without the enormously destructive and potentially suicidal use of war.

In *National Security Through Civilian-Based Defense* (1985), Sharp offers a concept that extends the logic of non-threatening defense still further. "CBD" (for short) is "a defense policy against foreign invasions and internal take-overs relying on prepared noncooperation and defiance by the trained civilian population and their institutions to deny the attacker's objectives and make lasting control impossible."[6] Through strikes and other forms of noncooperation tailored to frustrate the particular goals — economic, political, or other — of potential invaders, suitably prepared CBD could, Sharp argues, make invasion fruitless and compel withdrawal. The perception that such would be the result of invasion could also effectively deter attack. Besides its title essay, Sharp's book includes questions for discussion, suggestions of the steps to be taken to explore the policy's potential for meeting the security needs of various countries, and an essay outlining issues about CBD that need further research.

A national defense policy relying on the technique of nonviolent struggle has received increasing attention in recent years. It has become part of the political platforms of at least half a dozen parties in Western Europe,[7] including members of NATO, and has received discussion in Australia and New Zealand. Austria's defense minister has stated that nonviolent civilian resistance is already part of his country's defense policy, as a back-up to military defense, and to some degree this may be true of Switzerland and Yugoslavia as well, though planning and training of the population for it falls far short of what Sharp and other CBD proponents advocate.

Through strikes and other forms of non-cooperation tailored to frustrate the particular goals—economic, political, or other—of potential invaders, suitably prepared CBD could, Sharp argues, make invasion fruitless and compel withdrawal.

CBD is also gaining growing attention in the U.S. The Stanley Foundation's two half-hour radio interviews with Gene Sharp in 1983-84 proved to be among the most popular programs their "Common Ground" public affairs series had ever broadcast. They provide, via cassette, an opportunity to hear CBD explained by Sharp himself. In early 1986 George Kennan's highly favorable review of Sharp's book *Making Europe Unconquerable: The Potential of Civilian-Based Deterrence and Defense* was featured on the cover of *The New York Review of Books.*[8]

Kennan was not alone in his interest in CBD. Theodore Taylor, a physicist and prominent former designer of nuclear weapons,[9] reviewed Sharp's book for the *Bulletin of the Atomic Scientists.* Taylor notes the "largely improvised frustration, for eight months, of the Soviet takeover of Czechoslovakia in 1968-69" as an example of effective (though in this case — lacking advance planning, training, and strategy — ultimately unsuccessful) use of nonviolent resistance. He also cites movement toward partial dependence on CBD in Switzerland, Finland, Yugoslavia, Sweden, and Austria, which "are not maintaining significant offensive military forces for use beyond their borders. Thus, they can be thought of as in a state of 'transarmament,' which may or may not eventually lead to complete dependence on nonviolent resistance to aggression."

Thinking about defense has become so warped during the decades of nuclear "deterrence" ("defense" by threat of counter-attack) that it has become necessary to coin the awkward term "defensive defense" and its synonyms "non-offensive defense," "alternative defense," and the like.[10] In two chapters of *Beyond the Bomb*, Mark Sommer first surveys the ideas that go under these rubrics, with special attention to alternative defense proposals that have been prepared for Britain and the U.S. He then assesses the possibility of civilian-based defense and gives special attention to the problem of "nuclear blackmail" raised by some in connection with CBD. When we step away from the misleading ideology of deterrence, the problem of nuclear threats can be seen more clearly as not peculiar to non-nuclear or nonviolent defenses. There is no defense against nuclear weapons (Star Wars fantasies notwithstanding). As George Kennan points out, the only prudent response to nuclear threats is defiance.[11]

The third chapter of Richard Smoke's *Paths to Peace* likewise examines both military "alternative defense" and "defense by nonviolent resistance" (CBD). He points out that none of the alternative defense ideas can be definitively evaluated given the lack of historical experience with them, but does examine the implications of the wars in Vietnam and Afghanistan for the idea of decentralized military resistance, and suggests it may be most relevant in Western Europe. Concerning nonviolent action, he states that it "is not 'pacifism,' if pacifism is interpreted to mean the rejection of all force or coercion; many nonviolent actions are coercive (for example, going on strike or blockading roads with human bodies)."

While raising questions about the utility of nonviolent defense against certain kinds of attacks — those with genocidal intent, or ones intended chiefly to gravely weaken a society by external bombardment — Smoke suggests that it may be most useful in combination with other measures, such as arms agreements eliminating the kind of offensive weaponry capable of such bombardment.

For the future, he observes that "Improvised military defenses have rarely succeeded . . . . Why, then, should it be surprising that improvised nonviolent actions also have rarely succeeded?" Recognizing nonviolent struggle as "an approach that has scored notable successes even in primitive applications, one can only conclude that this path deserves much greater development."

For anyone who has considered even a little the logistical difficulties of a Soviet invasion of a country as large and distant as the U.S., it is remarkable that any U.S. citizens can imagine a Soviet occupation as plausible. Nevertheless, such films as "Red Dawn" have been made, and in winter 1987 ABC broadcast the television series "Amerika," which had already stirred a storm of controversy. In response to "Amerika," Liane Ellison Norman and the Civilian-Based Defense Association (formerly the Association for Transarmament Studies) produced "Defending America Without War: A Guide for Thought and Discussion."

Norman, founder of the Pittsburgh Peace Institute[12] and co-editor of *Civilian-Based Defense: News and Opinion*,[13] poses more than a dozen questions about war and conquest, power, civilian-based defense, and preparation for it — all of them designed to make our thinking less paranoid and more realistic, concrete, down-to-earth.

If invasion is not a realistic danger for the U.S., is civilian-based defense really worth discussing here? Robert Irwin's article "Civilian-Based Defense" suggests that it is, for three reasons. First, if it can be developed to a level of effectiveness such that the U.S.'s NATO allies would adopt it, that would eliminate the rationale for the large U.S. expenditures on troops in Europe. Second, talking about CBD breaks through the lingering Cold War assumptions that totalitarian regimes can be defeated only through war, and redirects defense discussion away from counter-attack threats (nuclear deterrence) to genuine defense. Third:

> CBD has an often neglected aspect that is important even for people who do not share a critique of U.S. foreign policy or of war: its role as a defense against internal take-overs. In the waning months of Watergate in 1974, as Richard Nixon grew more desperate in his desire to retain power, Defense Secretary James Schlesinger (according to an account by Seymour Hersh in *The Atlantic Monthly*) made discreet inquiries into what troops would be available to Nixon should he decide (for example) to take military action against the Supreme Court or the Congress to prevent his removal from office. To counter the possibility of a presidential coup, Schlesinger ordered the Joint Chiefs of Staff to insure that any unusual White House orders concerning troops in the Washington area be routed through his own office.

> No coup attempt occurred in this case. But the integrity shown by the hawkish Schlesinger should not be assumed in all his successors. The episode points up the absence of a national plan for nonviolent resistance and defense of Constitutional government against an executive take-over attempt. Such a plan could be highly legitimate and would strengthen the U.S. public's capacity to resist in any future crisis.

The time to work on such a plan is not in periods of acute conflict when concerns about a coup might be harbored — that would likely be too late, and then even to voice concerns would seem to be taking sides in the immediate conflict. It should be worked on in a non-crisis time when U.S. society's traditional consensus on preferring constitutional democracy to executive dictatorship can most easily be tapped. Irwin concludes: "How to bring such a plan into existence should become a question on the agenda of the U.S. peace movement."

Gene Sharp, in excerpts from his 1979 book *Gandhi as a Political Strategist*, and Brian Martin, in his 1987 article "Social Defence: Elite Reform or Grassroots Initiative?", express differing positions on the best way to advance CBD. Sharp sees research as most crucial: it "will not receive serious consideration, much less be adopted by any country, until its practical operation has been worked out carefully and in considerable detail." Sharp sees introducing a new defense policy — which must be acceptable to conservative and military elements if it is to be adopted — as a prerequisite for "basic social change," not as something that can only follow it.[14] Martin argues that what he terms "social defense" is a radical idea that should be linked with other movements opposing the status quo, and that "activists cannot afford to wait for research and action from the top." Despite these disagreements on strategy, both agree that more public attention should be directed to the potential of civilian-based defense.

George Lakey's *Powerful Peacemaking* presents a short, vivid account of the dramatic 1968-69 Czechoslovakian resistance to Soviet and Warsaw Pact invasion, analyzing the dilemmas it faced as an unplanned defense effort in a geopolitically difficult situation. Among his conclusions are that the methods of nonviolent struggle, "although unable magically to overcome all odds, can mobilize considerable power."

Lakey then undertakes a pioneering discussion (first published in 1973) of how decentralism, world institutions, socialist revolution, and nonviolent struggle could work together to create a new world community. Lakey notes that a world government could bring a risk of world tyranny. Although he believes that at a later stage in the change process "world referenda and a legislature are needed," Lakey suggests that the concerns of both the world government and decentralist camps and the needs for global problem-solving and coordination could begin to be met by increased use of global commissions "organized by function — for the seabeds, space, air pollution, world trade, currency, and so on."

These commissions would rely for enforcement (when necessary) of their decisions on "people's enforcement": campaigns by concerned voluntary associations to secure compliance, possibly using nonviolent action (e.g., a boycott) if persuasion failed. The activities of Amnesty International and Greenpeace's nonviolent direct action voyages combating nuclear testing might be considered examples of Lakey's conception beginning to become a reality.

> *The methods of nonviolent struggle, "although unable magically to overcome all odds, can mobilize considerable power."*

Hanna Newcombe's article "Collective Security, Common Security, and Alternative Security: A Conceptual Comparison" defines the presently predominant concept of security as "unilateral competitive national military sovereignty." Collective security, theoretically enshrined in the League of Nations and United Nations plans, means a system in which an aggressor state is to be punished by the collective action of all the other states. Difficulties in gaining agreement on what is aggression and in responding with concerted action have been some of the weak points of this approach.

Newcombe considers "common security" to be "a basket of ideas . . . centered on war avoidance." In recent decades increased national military power for most nations has proven counter-productive for the security of most. What approaches might work better? Newcombe presents several lists of specific measures from recent Canadian security discussion, including an International Satellite Monitoring Agency, a permanent U.N. Commission on Mediation, weighted voting at the U.N., a comprehensive test ban treaty, a standing U.N. peacekeeping force, an International Criminal Court, and creation of a second U.N. Assembly for non-governmental representatives.

Newcombe applies "alternative security" first to non-provocative military or nonviolent civilian defense policies, and second to mean "the permanent, long-term replacement for unilateral competitive military national security" — the replacement ExPro has been terming a "peace system." Like Lakey, Newcombe recognizes that "some of the adherents of each approach [a world federal government and principled nonviolence] might consider them divergent, even antagonistic." But she sees them potentially contributing to a balance between order and justice.

Irwin's "Coercion, Force, and Nonviolent Sanctions: Their Place in a Peace System" is concerned chiefly to establish that coercion and force are not to be equated with violence. He follows Sharp in contending that some sanctions are needed in any social system, certainly including a global one, but that human suffering can be reduced by substituting nonviolent for violent sanctions. Irwin shows how the reality of the possibility of nonviolent coercion invalidates commonly accepted beliefs about the dynamics of conflict; and he refutes a much-acclaimed notion put forth in Andrew Schmookler's *The Parable of the Tribes* (1984).

The readings discussed in this chapter show that there are policies societies can adopt unilaterally, without waiting for anyone else, that increase their security without decreasing anyone else's. The same policies, prudently implemented, also contribute to making the whole international system more stable, peaceful, and secure.[15]

Coercion and force are not to be equated with violence.

Chapter 7:
Economic Development, Ecology, and Peace

The previous chapter was called "alternative security policies," but this one equally well merits that title. Insecurity comes not only from dangers of attack; it can be ecological and economic in origin. The reliable provision of food, water, shelter, and the ecological conditions on which life depends can be jeopardized by such factors as crop failure, pollution, climate change, or ozone depletion, and by the defects of national socio-economic systems or the workings of global economic forces.

Ecological jeopardy

We cannot live in peace if we destroy the ecological basis for living at all. The Worldwatch Institute reports that "the earth's forests are shrinking, its deserts expanding, and its soils eroding — all at record rates."[1] Thermal pollution and increased carbon dioxide levels, associated with industrial activity and worsened by inefficient energy use, are also serious problems. They are portrayed in the fascinating "future history" *The Third Millennium*[2] as leading (by way of the "greenhouse effect") to rising sea levels and devastating effects on coastal towns and cities by 2120.

> *We cannot live in peace if we destroy the ecological basis for living at all.*

The latest scientific findings suggest this fictional projection may be much too optimistic. In reality (according to a March 1988 report), depletion of the atmosphere's protective ozone layer and related changes "are taking place faster, and they are more severe than the [computer] models had predicted. . . . Scientists also worry that ozone depletion and the greenhouse effect could feed on each other, making things go from bad to worse more quickly."[3] Climatic change could mean that the weather most conducive to agriculture shifts away from where farms are, decimating human food production capabilities. Other possible consequences are impairment of photosynthesis, "a devastating effect on the marine food chain," and weakening of humans' abilities to fight off certain infectious diseases. Without a change of course, "industrial summer" might approach "nuclear winter" in its disruption of human life. We do not reliably know. Yet growth in Gross National Product (GNP) is still mindlessly reported as good news.

Below we will sketch three criteria for an economic order consistent with peace. But with regard to the ecology underlying economic life, the need is less to envision a utopia than to become aware of the "utopia" (in the negative sense of an illusory condition) that we are currently living in. As ecologists have been teaching for two decades, our current way of life "is not sustainable. Its termination within the lifetime of someone born today [1972] is inevitable."[4] If the record-breaking heat of the summer of 1988 proves to be a catalyst for serious attention to the changes required, it will have been a very lucky occurrence.

How unsustainable our way of life is, and how soon it will terminate, we do not know because of the very complexity of the ecosystems we depend on, including time lags before effects are perceptible.[5] Because we are so ignorant, currently recognized problems may be less or more

Readings: for study group use

A. Dietrich Fischer, "Reducing Economic Vulnerability," pp. 147-151 in *Preventing War in the Nuclear Age* (1984);

   Richard Smoke, "The Path of Removing Fundamental Causes of War," pp. 31-37 (on global economic inequality as a cause of war) in *Paths to Peace* (1987);

   Andre Carothers, "Small Wonders: The Energy Efficiency Revolution," pp. 11-17 in *Greenpeace Magazine* (March-April 1988);

   Rocky Mountain Institute, "America's Stake in Soviet Energy Efficiency" (and related stories), pp. 1-4 in *RMI Newsletter* (November 1987);

   General Assembly of the United Nations, "Universal Declaration of Human Rights" (1948; brochure);

   United Nations Environment Program, "World Charter for Nature"; (no date; 4 pp.).

   Total= 32 pp.

B. Gar Alperovitz & Jeff Faux, "A Community-Sustaining Economics"; "Productivity and Stability"; and "Toward Democratic Planning"; in *Rebuilding America: A Blueprint for the New Economy* (1984), pp. 71-111, 257-270.

   Total = 53 pp.

C. Guy Gran, "Preface" and "Development, the World-System, and Human Potential," from *Development by People* (1983), pp. xiii-xvi, 1-24;

   Robert Gilman, "Mondragon: The Remarkable Achievement," from *In Context* (Spring 1983; 3 pp.);

   Guy Gran, "Mondragon," from *Learning from Development Success* (1983; 3 pp.);

   Jeremy Brecher & Tim Costello, "Labor Internationalism," from *Zeta Magazine* (November 1988; 7 pp.).

   Total= 41 pp.

D. Lisa Leghorn, "The Economic Roots of the Violent Male Culture," pp. 195-199 from Pam McAllister, ed., *Reweaving the Web of Life: Feminism and Nonviolence* (1982; 5 pp.);

   Women's International League for Peace and Freedom, *The Women's Budget* (2nd edn., 1987; 40 pp.).

   Total= 45 pp.

E. Elise Boulding, "Learning to Learn: North's Response to the New International Economic Order" from *Alternatives: A Journal of World Policy*, Vol. IV, No. 4 (1979; 26 pp.);

Arjun Makhijani and Robert S. Browne, "Restructuring the International Monetary System," *World Policy Journal* (Winter 1985-86; 21 pp.).

Total= 47 pp.

serious than we now think. What we do know for sure is that conventional economic measures like GNP take literally no account of major environmental damage, and thus misrepresent economic reality. Any social change program that does not address issues of ecology risks becoming irrelevant in the face of massive new crises.[6]

Although the global economy now operates as a machine that is destroying its ecological base at an accelerating rate, with appropriate redirection of effort we could ally ourselves with the earth's self-renewing processes. In one estimate, "steps to reverse the physical deterioration of the earth and restore economic progress worldwide will cost an estimated $150 billion per year" by the early 1990s — a large figure but "only one-sixth of the global military budget."[7]

Beyond capitalism and communism

Most people desire economic security and, beyond ensured subsistence, to better their condition; this force for change is a potential source of conflict. Capitalism, dominated by giant profit-seeking corporations, and communism, dominated by authoritarian bureaucracies, are not the only two options human intelligence has devised. Alternatives exist in theory and, more than is generally realized in the U.S., in practice.

The world's two dominant economic systems will not continue as they are unchanged. Both are experiencing severe problems. The pursuit of (unlimited) economic growth, accepted as a goal and in fact virtually equated with "the common good" by both capitalist and communist ideologies, is colliding with the natural limits of the ecological processes on which human life depends. Nuclear power plants have proved a source of bankruptcies and disasters, not the cheap solution to energy needs they were once touted as. The inequality generated by the dynamics of capitalist development has reached a global extremity known as "the debt crisis," which threatens to trigger a collapse of the whole system.[8] The Soviet Union and China have each recognized that their economic systems need major changes.

Even economic "success" has become problematic. Though far more people are poor, there are also millions of people with more money than they know what to do with (despite constant advertising to create new "needs"). Both toxic and non-toxic wastes pose serious problems. U.S. cities are running out of landfill space for garbage and planning pollution-causing incinerators that are provoking citizen opposition.

What economic and ecological conditions are consistent with building and maintaining a global peace system? The subject is in one sense highly complex, but it is contended here that the most important requirements are simple and interrelated. In the following section one formulation is offered.

The economics of a lasting peace system should be secure, sustainable, and satisfying.

The different changes needed importantly depend on each other. This might seem an insuperable obstacle to system transformation, but — arguably — in the process of change many of the factors will tend to reinforce one another; and each of them (to some extent, despite currently dominant counter-trends) is already occurring.

Toward an economics of peace

The economics of a lasting peace system should be *secure, sustainable,* and *satisfying.* Why these three requirements? 1) Insecurity can be a motivation to wage war, as people use military means in an effort to "secure" things in other countries they rely on (including natural resources, markets, and opportunities for investment); more self-reliant economic security must become prevalent. 2) A economy that is not sustainable will, by definition, not last. 3) Only a system in which people are reasonably satisfied will be stable.

A secure economy. People are economically secure if they have uninterrupted access to the food, shelter, water, clothing, health care, etc. needed to support healthful life. (They may not be *satisfied* with subsistence levels of these goods; we turn to that subject below.) Although a very few people (in percentage terms) are economically secure because they have enough wealth safely invested to live off the income, and some people live as subsistence farmers without selling much of their produce on the market, most people depend for subsistence on their own income from work, or are supported by someone else who works for money. Those receiving government social benefits financed by taxes levied on those working are also ultimately dependent on the global economy; inflation or benefit cutbacks may result if a country's economy produces inadequate government revenue.

In a world economy where most capital is moved around in pursuit of profit, and in which people using computers and telecommunications make transactions across the globe almost instantaneously, global "market forces" will be not only changeable but volatile and to a degree unpredictable. That may be fine in some respects — life involves change and novelty — but it should not be permitted to wreck people's chances for a decent life.

"Tightly coupled" is the term that has been applied to systems whose different parts strongly and immediately affect each other.[9] When a tightly coupled system is complex, it is accident-prone. Much of the world economy is moderately tightly coupled: for example, irresponsibly large deficits or high interest rates in the U.S. have damaged economies elsewhere. Economic downturns tend to result in lay-offs, plant closings, disruption of lives, misery, and desperation. To support global peace, security of decent economic subsistence should be "uncoupled" as much as possible from the fluctuations of market economics.[10]

In a few countries — Austria, Switzerland, and the Scandinavian countries — domestic social and economic policies have, on the whole, successfully protected their populations, providing security and a measure of prosperity despite ripples from the larger global economy.[11] In these countries (except Switzerland, a special case) strong labor movements and social-democratic governments supported by labor combine to represent the interests of most of the population.

> *To support global peace, security of decent economic subsistence should be "uncoupled" as much as possible from the fluctuations of market economics.*

In the U.S. organized labor has an image among many people of rigidity and inefficiency. Where labor is strong enough to influence the government and bargain with the owners of business on a more equal footing, it has been possible to create flexible work rules and introduce more efficient technology with labor cooperation because workers know they can get retraining at government expense for other jobs if they are laid off.[12] This means that the personal security of workers is less threatened by economic change, and hence they and their unions need not resist modernization of production technology. And it means that for the society as a whole, it can act with sufficient unity to respond to global market forces or other adverse circumstances by improving economic efficiency or making a collective (not imposed from above) decision to tighten belts.

What is an economically secure society like? Consider the Swedes. They are prosperous (even though they spend substantial money on their military forces — safeguarding their right to independence and a non-aligned foreign policy), they get longer paid vacations than U.S. workers (and far longer than those the Japanese get), and they give more foreign aid than most countries to the Third World. It is reasonable to expect societies to be less war-prone and more generous to the extent they replace misery, desperation, and insecurity with reliable subsistence for all.

A sustainable economy. Although ecological concerns seem to go in and out of fashion in the media, their importance persists. There are indeed limits to economic growth on a finite planet. Those limits need not condemn humankind to misery; with efficient use of resources, wise management of public goods, and non-wasteful cultural practices, they would permit a decent life for all the world's people. A sustainable economy can be one of "biophysical equilibrium and moral growth," in Herman Daly's fine formulation.[13] But as long as some consume far more than their fair share (that is, far more than the earth could sustain if everyone did likewise), others will likely feel they have an equal right to adopt the same version of "the good life."[14] Consequently, as Paul and Anne Ehrlich have written, "the issue of creating a sustainable society cannot be separated from the issue of social justice."[15]

A satisfying economy. Capitalism has held out a vision of limitless "economic growth" equated with unending progress. Marxism has held the vision of "socialist accumulation" leading finally to communism, a society in which scarcity has been overcome and all can have as much as they

> *"The issue of creating a sustainable society cannot be separated from the issue of social justice."*

"need" (want). Both ideologies have erred in regarding scarcity and abundance as matters of amounts of material goods. Scarcity and abundance are relational concepts; they describe the relation between what people want and what they can have or get.[16] Yet many films, songs, and plays, as well as books by social critics and currents within all cultural traditions, say that satisfaction is not found through pursuit or possession of commodities.

Nearly twenty years before the MIT study *The Limits to Growth* (1972), Samuel H. Ordway, Jr. wrote in *Resources and the American Dream* that resource use would eventually reach "the limit of growth." Sounding like a contemporary ecofeminist Green activist, he wrote that our mass media "would profit [humankind] more by sustained emphasis on the values of self-reliance, relaxation, and the nurture, not the exploitation, of natural and spiritual resources."[17] What is distinctive about those values, of course, is that they can be pursued with little or no damage to nature. One strolls through the meadow instead of building a luxury casino on the site. The challenge of creating a more satisfying way of modern life, long posed by critics of industrial society, is being accepted in practical terms by increasing numbers of people in industrial capitalist countries.[18]

Those who live in the United States, with its enormous global cultural as well as economic influence, have a special role in the struggle to create a secure, sustainable, and satisfying global economy. A program for changing the U.S. economy cannot be elaborated here,[19] but it should be recognized that if the U.S., still the world's largest economy, could be transformed, it could help the entire world move toward an economic system that serves, rather than crushes, human potential, and that operates in harmony with nature.

• • •

The section on "Reducing Economic Vulnerability" from Dietrich Fischer's *Preventing War in the Nuclear Age* provides helpful comments on the concepts of self-reliance and interdependence. A country that wants to be invulnerable to any cut-off of commodities it normally imports can stockpile reserve supplies, arrange stand-by domestic production facilities (where feasible), explore possible substitutes, and prepare plans for reduced consumption in emergencies. Self-reliance doesn't mean autarky. "Someone is self-reliant who keeps candles in case the electricity is interrupted. Autarky would be practiced by someone who refused to use electricity out of fear that it might be cut off." Such preparations are not exorbitantly expensive; Sweden's "economic defense" stockpiles cost only 2 to 3% of its total defense budget. Potential self-sufficiency in vital areas is the objective.

"Interdependence" can work either for or against war, in Fischer's view. His recommendation is "to strengthen mutually beneficial relations in trade and many other areas, but not to make oneself or others so vitally dependent on those relations that they would risk war to restore or preserve them."

> *"Interdependence" can work either for or against war.*

Fischer's discussion seems most relevant to countries prosperous enough to maintain an adequate defense against military attack and also set aside resources for economic security. What about the poorer countries who have little economic security to begin with? In a selection from *Paths to Peace* Richard Smoke states that "It is difficult to find wars that were directly caused by poverty," but "it is hard to escape a conviction that the seeds of future wars already lie incubating" in widespread destitution. One might add to Smoke's comments the observation that where people are extremely poor they are unfavorably situated to exert informed, democratic control over demagogic leaders who may draw their countries into war in part to submerge domestic conflicts.

"Small Wonders: The Energy Efficiency Revolution" (1988), drawing on research by Amory Lovins and his colleagues at the Rocky Mountain Institute, reveals such facts as that "if the United States spent as much to make buildings heat-tight as it does in one year protecting the flow of oil through the Persian Gulf, the U.S. would not need any of the oil imported from the Middle East." Such a changed approach to energy security, it should be emphasized, has nothing to do with deprivation ("freezing in the dark"); it is about eliminating waste and putting money where it brings the largest return (from the viewpoint of society as a whole). Using less energy to get the same benefits as now would reduce pollution, consumption of irreplaceable fossil fuel, and global warming. Greater efficiency would permit a higher proportion of present uses to be met by renewable sources, and thus ease shifting the U.S. economy toward ecological sustainability and away from its (perceived) "need" to control the politics of foreign countries. Such change would be consistent with the self-reliance Fischer advocates.

The "common security" notion that we are all in the same boat is exemplified by the Rocky Mountain Institute's analysis of "America's Stake in Soviet Energy Efficiency." RMI staff traveled to the

U.S.S.R. in 1987 to arrange a joint book exploring new developments in energy efficiency and their relationship to security. They explain that while it might seem that "a more efficient and hence economically stronger Soviet Union could threaten a variety of U.S. interests . . . closer study reveals that helping the Soviets in this sphere" can benefit the U.S. If Gorbachev's "restructuring" (*perestroika*) of the Soviet system leads to faster economic growth, it will increase Soviet energy demand. If their energy efficiency is not simultaneously improved, that will lead them either to build more nuclear plants (two, three, many Chernobyls?), burn more coal (increasing global air pollution) or increase oil consumption (driving up world oil prices). It is for such reasons, RMI reports, that its mission to the U.S.S.R. received informal prior approval from Reagan Administration officials. Such insightful and persuasive analysis is RMI's specialty,[20] and its ideas are increasingly influential with U.S. utility regulators, utility corporations, and Soviet and Chinese policymakers.

The "World Charter for Nature" issued by the United Nations Environment Program outlines 24 principles for safeguarding global ecological processes.

The "Universal Declaration of Human Rights" adopted by the General Assembly of the United Nations in 1948 is a document with which relatively few in the U.S. are familiar. (We might have a better world if it were in everyone's possession.) The aspirations it expresses are relevant to every chapter in this book, but it is appropriate to mention here because of the several articles pertaining to economic rights.

That so many of the rights declared are so widely violated, and that some may be interpreted as conflicting with others, does not, it may be argued, make the document useless. In a world of diverse cultures and social systems the very existence of such a document is a useful source of ideological support for groups struggling to win the rights it proclaims; and to the extent the rights may conflict — and the notion of "rights in conflict" is not unfamiliar in U.S. politics — the Declaration presents us with a common, global agenda for conflict resolution. Perhaps the Declaration will need revision; or perhaps future developments toward global community will enable certain rights to be interpreted and reconciled in creative ways we do not yet imagine.[21]

So much for human rights — what about nature? The "World Charter for Nature" issued by the United Nations Environment Program outlines 24 principles for safeguarding global ecological processes. Short on rhetorical grandeur ("Nature shall be respected"; "due account shall be taken of . . . natural beauty"), they are highly reasonable, yet far-reaching in their implications because so little heeded. "Living resources shall not be utilized in excess of their natural capacity for regeneration" (#10a). "The productivity of soils shall be maintained or enhanced . . ." (#10b). "Activities which are likely to pose a significant risk to nature shall be preceded by an exhaustive examination; their proponents shall demonstrate that expected benefits outweigh potential damage to nature, and where potential adverse effects are not fully understood, the activities should not proceed" (#11b).

Responsibility for implementation of these principles is given not only to states and international organizations, but (#21) to other public authorities (e.g., local governments) and groups. "Each person has a duty to . . . strive to ensure that the objectives and requirements of the present Charter are met" (#24). The "World Charter for Nature" provides a sensible standard by which the policies and practices of any locality or organization can be investigated, evaluated, and corrected. Like the Universal Declaration of Human Rights, its prescriptions need elaboration and refinement, but it likewise aids the creation of global norms that should eventually gain binding force to insure human decision-making consistent with the common good.

The focus of *Rebuilding America: A Blueprint for the New Economy* (1984) by Gar Alperovitz and Jeff Faux is on the U.S. in the 1980s, but it is appropriate reading not only because the U.S. is so important to the world economy, but because their discussion concentrates on basic principles, some of which are equally applicable on a global scale. Their fundamental concerns are to sustain decent communities and enhance personal freedom and democracy. Unlike some localists who disregard national-level policy-making, considering it inherently bureaucratic, unresponsive, and oppressive, Alperovitz and Faux seek to define national policies that will support rather than undermine local communities and individual choice.

As codirectors of the National Center for Economic Alternatives, the two economists have for several years been formulating specific proposals, some of which have gained significant Congressional support, that are intended to serve the interests of the majority of the U.S. population. In 1984 presidential candidate Rev. Jesse Jackson described their book as "the economic platform of the Rainbow Coalition."

Rebuilding America is a thoughtful effort to confront frankly whatever trade-offs may exist between fulfillment of different values; the authors advocate making our social choices explicit. But they argue vigorously against some alleged trade-offs that are not necessary: they contend that "the traditional trade-off between unemployment and inflation can be resolved in favor of high employment and stable prices."

Alperovitz and Faux advocate democratic "strategic planning for national economic stability, combined with an emphasis on radical decentralization and local development." It is a book that should be considered as a possible source for analogous policy ideas to promote global economic stability and development of the world's poorer countries.

Economic development is often portrayed as a technical problem to be solved by expert-advised policymaking or, more recently, as a moral challenge to be met by huge charitable ("but it is in our own self-interest to avoid global instability") transfers of money from "developed" countries. In *Development by People* (1983) Guy Gran defines its essence as the creation of citizens who can democratize the power concentrations that constitute the present system of gross inequality, oppression, and war. Through his ambitious book Gran aims to encourage people to be "development catalysts" who can help themselves and other people become such citizens.

Major parts of his book present a critique of current unsuccessful "development" efforts in the Third World, and a contrasting model for participatory development. Gran believes it is desirable that the "First and Second Worlds" also democratize their economies through participatory development.[22] Gran advocates a "paradigm shift for all of human development," but emphasizes the importance of translating such grand phrases into down-to-earth "operational" action steps. "Each citizen in the North or South [who reads the book] should as a result have a clear idea what to do next" (p. xiii). Naturally maximum insight can only be gained from reading the whole book, whose strength is in its embrace of details in a systematic framework.

To eliminate poverty and enable all people to develop their human potential, the poor and relatively powerless must be organized so they can better defend their interests against the external forces that keep them in poverty.

Gran's opening chapter provides an overview of the book's basic approach. To eliminate poverty and enable all people to develop their human potential, the poor and relatively powerless must be organized so they can better defend their interests against the external forces of the world system that keep them in poverty. He sees local development efforts as frustrated by what (following Peter Evans) he terms "the triple alliance — local capital, the state, and international capital" (p. 84).

Top-down projects, even when well-intentioned, too often tend to perpetuate or worsen power inequalities. For Gran, participatory processes are not a "frill," but essential to learning that is empowering — that is, that can help people act effectively on their own behalf.

Gran asserts that development must precede achievement of peace. Prior to many countries' becoming economically and politically democratic, he contends,

> the world is simply organizationally and politically unprepared to deal with [problems like the Cold War and the arms race] in any substantive fashion. . . . With great political pressure for the authentically developmental use of social resources would come applied creativity for ending the Cold War (pp. 350-351).

The overall strategic perspective expressed in Part III of this book differs from Gran's view: it suggests that much can be done to move toward peace short of complete (that is, concurrent with partial) global development and democratization; it shows that various elements of a potential peace system are now being built by different social groups. But the difference with Gran may be chiefly one of emphasis. The participatory development he advocates, plainly desirable in itself, would certainly aid humanity's capacity to create and maintain a peace system.

Most who are dissatisfied with both corporate capitalism and communism are unaware that there is another economic model better suited to serve the common good than either of the two dominant systems. What Cornell economist Jaroslav Vanek terms "the participatory economy" offers a kind of market socialism or collectivized capitalism in which firms democratically managed by their workers compete in the global market. (They may also coordinate their activities through institutions controlled by representatives of the firms or be regulated by governments.)

Some might conceive worker management as an interesting but risky idea — all right to experiment with in wealthy countries that can afford inefficiency in return for more humane working conditions, but irrelevant or a luxury for poor countries that "must" industrialize rapidly to overcome poverty. Contrary to this reasoning, Vanek has argued[23] that the participatory economy is particularly suited to the development of poor countries whose chief underutilized resource is their people's labor; and that such a system has shown greater economic efficiency than capitalism or communism.

> *There is another economic model better suited to serve the common good than either communism or capitalism.*

Powerful evidence for Vanek's approach has subsequently emerged into economic discussion: above all, the example of Mondragon. This previously impoverished region in northern Spain is regarded by many observers as the world's most successful economic development model. Gran, in his "Learning from Development Success," calls it "probably the most impressive and hopeful experiment in worker-management in the world." Robert Gilman's concise 1983 account of Mondragon's significance traces its growth from one propane stove cooperative in 1956 to a remarkable complex comprising — at latest report[24] — over 100 worker cooperatives and supporting organizations that employs nearly 20,000 people. Although many new businesses anywhere fail in their first several years, 97% of the coops established at Mondragon have continued to operate successfully. The firms, making products such as refrigerators and machine tools and supplying services such as education, industrial research, and banking, compete successfully in the global marketplace while providing democratic working conditions for their employees, who elect a council of representatives that chooses managers.

In contrast to industrialization that typically drastically increases economic inequality, no manager earns more than four and a half times the lowest-paid worker's pay. Mondragon's ingenious financial structure, devised for the first of the coops by the brilliant Catholic priest Father Jose Maria Arizmendi, balances individual and group interests, facilitates reinvestment and ever-more efficient production, and promotes social solidarity. Educational institutions to produce trained workers and managers, a savings bank that invests capital to create jobs through new cooperative firms in the community, and market and other research to insure continual adaptation to changing technology and market conditions are all essential parts of the Mondragon model. Social conscience and maximum freedom of choice are two cherished principles.[25]

Widespread participatory economic development[26] could potentially support global peace in three different ways:

1) by speeding economic progress out of poverty, enabling people to become informed citizens with leisure to pay attention to global problems, scrutinize and control leaders, and resist manipulation into war;

2) by preserving the global environment through increasing democratic local control over economic life (one need not be a romantic populist to believe that management controlled by a local workforce is less likely to pollute the local environment than a distant corporate headquarters or government planning bureau);

3) by increasing people's competence and desire to participate in decision-making (research has shown that people who have a say at work are more likely to become politically active as well).[27]

"Just as various U.N. declarations and agreements provide standards for human rights, so the covenants of the U.N.'s International Labor Organization (ILO) provide standards for labor rights."

Although Mondragon is very important as a successful and expanding model (as well as improving the lives of tens of thousands), far more workers at present are employed by large corporations whose aim is profit for owners, or by government officials who place their own interests ahead of workers' welfare. Progress towards participation and democracy involves defense of these workers' fundamental rights against those who now often violate them. In "Labor Internationalism" Jeremy Brecher and Tim Costello present an encouraging survey of ways workers are cooperating across national boundaries by sharing information about corporation practices through a new computer network, establishing "sister locals" (modeled on "sister cities") between workers in Massachusetts and El Salvador and between Wisconsin and the Philippines, refusing to unload ships that have violated work rules elsewhere, and fighting for the safety and freedom of unionists menaced by death squads or apartheid.[28]

"The new labor internationalism," Brecher and Costello explain, "is marked by close ties with religious, human rights, women's, development, and other movements, often drawing on their far more extensive international networks." Recognizing that "just as various U.N. declarations and agreements provide standards for human rights, so the covenants of the U.N.'s International Labor Organization (ILO) provide standards for labor rights," the new movement uses publicity and "public mobilization [to] build pressure for enforcement — both on the perpetrators and on other countries and institutions that can affect them." Such efforts both draw on and advance a vision of global solidarity and cooperation to create economic conditions worthy of human beings.

Lisa Leghorn, co-author with Katherine Parker of *Woman's Worth: Sexual Economics and the World of Women* (1981), is one of those who has increased recognition of women's key role in the global economy. Women's work, she writes, "from housework and childcare to subsistence agriculture and fishing" and much else, has usually been unpaid and omitted from economic statistics. A 1980 U.N. report concluded that women "perform two-thirds of the world's work hours yet only receive 10% of the world's income and own less than 1% of the world's property."

Although the present economic exploitation of women is conducive to a violent male culture that produces war, Leghorn believes that women have also developed "the qualities of empathy and sensitivity, the skills in administration, cooperation and arbitration, and an alternative worldview which, if used on a policy level in the world around them, would provide exactly what's needed to redirect the world from its destructive path."

The *Women's Budget*, produced by the Women's International League for Peace and Freedom (WILPF), is explicitly offered as "a document to aid in envisioning a reversal in U.S. budget priorities." It challenges rising military spending and an interventionist foreign policy and proposes in very concrete terms a "re-ordering of national priorities so that all people will have basic human needs met and will live in a world of peace." In ten sections (including jobs and income security, housing, education, environmental protection, special women's programs, and international relations), the *Women's Budget* presents alternative programs and their budgetary costs. WILPF proposes cutting $146 billion from military spending, a savings figure that is to be generated primarily by instituting a nuclear freeze and eliminating forces for foreign intervention, and is based on alternative budgets introduced in recent years by the Congressional Black Caucus.

In "Learning to Learn: North's Response to the New International Economic Order" (1979), Elise Boulding (a former chairperson of WILPF) explores not only the immediate issues generated by the demand from the less-developed countries for a "New International Economic Order," but also considers the historical and psychological factors conditioning North-South relations. She believes that there is a great need for dialogue and two-way social learning to promote shared goals for global economic development.

Among the factors hindering social learning by the North is the North's having lived, since the beginning of the colonial era, in a condition of "social autism" — "the condition in which one communicates only with oneself and takes in no information about the outside world except what already fits the inward image." One-way communication has obscured (for the North) the North's interdependence with the South.

Boulding uses the device of the "200-year present" (in this case, the span from 1875 to 2075) to provide historical perspective on the scope of change to be expected as the global economic order evolves. She offers a brief, positive vision of 2075, "the year when global zero population growth has been achieved," but warns (writing in 1979) that "The North is entering a prolonged transitional period of intense crises . . . that will both hinder and help its responses to the new global order."

"Restructuring the International Monetary System," the topic addressed by Arjun Makhijani and

Robert S. Browne, is one whose very name suggests to most people something too abstract, complicated, and technical to touch with a ten-foot pole. These authors, however, offer some ideas that address the issues of labor and subsistence for the world's poor as well as the issues more often found in the business pages.

They contend that the present monetary system "artificially lowers relative wages in the Third World" and argue that a more equitable system would ease the debt crisis and thus benefit the richer countries as well as the poorer by stabilizing the global economy.

Makhijani and Browne propose that "exchange rates of currencies should be determined according to the relative prices of basic consumer goods in each country," so as to better reflect labor productivity, and that "each country would set aside certain stocks of commodities whose monetary value would be proportional to that of the country's foreign trade."

The present monetary system "artificially lowers relative wages in the Third World"; a more equitable system would ease the debt crisis.

Further, they propose creation of an International Currency Unit that would replace the dollar's dual role as the U.S. national currency and the global reserve currency, which means that U.S. economic policies have an unwarranted effect on the rest of the world. (The disadvantages of this system have become even more evident since their article was written.)

The authors recognize that rethinking the international monetary system will take time; but they believe that, in the long run, implementation of their proposal would benefit everyone throughout the global economy.

Chapter 8:
Psychology, Religion, Culture, and Peace

The legendary ancient law-giver Solon was reportedly once asked when justice would be achieved on earth. He replied: "When each man feels a wrong done to another as keenly as one done to himself." Much the same might be said about peace and the doing of violence to others. Short of a sudden change in the nature of the human nervous system — an idea that has been unforgettably explored in Damon Knight's science fiction story "Rule Golden"[1] — Solon's solution can only be approximated through individual and social learning that result in the evolution of increased intercultural and interpersonal empathy; in plainer words, when we learn to understand others better and to care more about them.[2]

That war and peace have psychological dimensions, few would deny; but the conclusions to be drawn from this premise are uncertain. Although UNESCO's founding document states that "wars begin in the minds of men," human minds are not autonomous first causes. Minds are shaped by culture and religion, which also shape and are shaped by economics, politics, and history. Without assuming causal primacy for any one dimension, we can nevertheless gain insight by using each of them as a lens.

The authors in this chapter do not postulate or predict a sudden, sweeping change in culture, religion, or the human psyche as the path to peace. Rather, most discuss aspects of present reality and suggest the kinds of changes in culture, religion, thought, or sensibility required for us to move toward a peaceful world.

• • •

In "Nuclear Nonsense" (1985) psychologist Steven Kull analyzes what he terms a "perception theory" that is used to justify continuing U.S. nuclear build-ups even though arms proponents often concede that the weapons bring no military advantage. The build-up proponents argue that others — such as leaders of other countries, or the public at home and abroad — erroneously perceive the U.S.-Soviet nuclear weapons balance as indicating meaningful superiority for one side, and that such perceptions affect political decisions and thus the real power balance. Therefore, to maintain its world position, the U.S. must build the weapons that will create the (false) perception of meaningful U.S. nuclear superiority.

Kull points out numerous contradictions within this strategy — for example, that the arms proponents must each year offer convincing evidence of U.S. weakness to Congress and the public so as to get increased military spending that is intended to convince everyone else the U.S. is militarily strong. Why, he asks, spend billions to cater to false perceptions (assuming they do exist), rather than seek vigorously to dispel such misperceptions? One possible answer, dismissed too hastily (p. 50) by Kull, is that senseless military spending satisfies influential economic and political interests. The "iron triangle" of military contractors, Congressional representatives voting appropriations for their districts, and Pentagon officials, has been well analyzed by many authors.[3]

Readings: for study group use

A. Steven Kull, "Nuclear Nonsense," pp. 28-52 from *Foreign Policy* (Spring 1985);

Elizabeth Richards, "Moving Heaven and Earth Together," (1987), from Deborah Gorham and Janice Williamson, eds., *Up and Doing: Canadian Women and Peace* (1988; 5 pp.);

Richard Smoke, "The Power of Understanding the Psyche," pp. 82-87 in *Paths to Peace*.

Total= ca 36 pp.

B. Mark Sommer, "Epilogue: The Bomb Has Already Fallen," pp. 145-168 in *Beyond the Bomb* (1986; 23 pp.);

Elise Boulding, "Two Cultures of Religion as Obstacles to Peace," from *Zygon* (December 1986); 17 pp.

Total= 40 pp.

C. Walden Bello, "Understanding War: The Psychological Perspective" and "Understanding War: The Feminist Perspective," pp. 63-71, 73-79 in *Visions of a Warless World* (1986);

Carol Cohn, "Slick'ems, Glick'ems, Christmas Trees and Cookie Cutters: Nuclear Language and How We Learned to Pat the Bomb," from *Bulletin of the Atomic Scientists* (June 1987; 7 pp.);

Ethel Jensen, "Could Feminism Save the World?" from "Feminism and Peace" (1982), pp. 20-27;

Patricia Mische, "Women, Power and Alternative Futures" (1978; two parts: "Women and World Order" and "Women and Power"; 16 pp.).

Total= 47 pp.

D. Robert R. Holt, "Converting the War System to a Peace System: Some Contributions from Psychology and Other Social Sciences" (1987; 63 double-spaced pages= ca 40 pp.);

Paul Wachtel, "Economic Growth — or Human Growth?" and

Herman Daly, "Economic Growth — or Moral Growth?" from *New Options* (November 30, 1987; 3 pp.).

Total= ca 43 pp.

E. Elise Boulding, "Learning Peace," from Raimo Vayrynen et al., eds., *The Quest for Peace* (1987; 11 pp.);

Lloyd Etheredge, "Introduction," "Operation MONGOOSE," and "Dual-Track Decision Making and the American Foreign Policy System," pp. viii-x, 78-87, 141-162 from *Can Governments Learn? American Foreign Policy and Central American Revolutions* (1985).

Total= 45 pp.

Instead, Kull suggests (and he may be partly right about many policymakers and others even if he is wrong in assuming, over-simply, that "the country as a whole continues to support the arms race") that people in the U.S. seek relief in illusion from the terrifying and perplexing reality that they are threatened by nuclear weapons in a way that no unilateral measures can remedy. "What is required," he believes, "is no less than a reconsideration of the role of force in international relations." Though "there are no simple solutions," recognition of our vulnerability may at least free us from some of the self-deception involved in present policies.

Let us turn from the psychology of nuclear weapons proponents to that of peace activists. Elizabeth Richards, a journalist and former staff person for the Canadian Institute for International Peace and Security, describes in "Moving Heaven and Earth Together" (1987) how her initial realization of the danger posed by nuclear arsenals led her to work on "various disarmament campaigns for the rest of the year in a state of perpetual panic that afforded little time for reflection." When the arsenal that had built up inside her from focusing constantly on nuclear war finally exploded in a dream, it was a step toward the realization that it was essential for her to direct her energies "towards peace, not war" — a shift possibly occurring in others as well.

With wit and candor, Richards notes that "too often those who preach tolerance and flexibility practice the opposite," showing that internalization of the values of peace and feminism in our behavior is not automatic. She suggests that we regard peace not as "a condition or state of being — the end of a process" — but as itself a process.

In "The Power of Understanding the Psyche," Richard Smoke outlines (pp. 82-83) research findings on when and how people are prone to oversimplify and misperceive reality, permitting cycles of hostility to develop and persist.[4] He also summarizes speculations on unconscious motives and the effects of "unconscious programming" that may perpetuate obsolete or destructive beliefs, expectations, and images of reality.

In his "Epilogue: The Bomb Has Already Fallen," Mark Sommer sounds a number of psychological and cultural themes. He cites evidence of a division of attitudes in the U.S. concerning nuclear weapons: experts generally accept them, not only for deterrence but also for a "broad range of supplementary functions"; the general public is "less accepting of continuing dependence on nuclear weapons." He follows Robert Coles in recognizing that so-called "psychic numbing" in the face of the nuclear threat may for many people be a consequence of preoccupation with "a half-dozen more intimate and inescapable threats. . . . [W]e may not be able to understand why others appear numbed to the nuclear threat until we become aware of our own numbness to their more immediate sources of anguish."

Some people interpret humankind's nuclear predicament as the effect of an unconscious collective death wish. Sommer believes that any such tendencies are less "central a motive force [than] the ancient and perennial fear of the enemy . . . masterfully orchestrated by politicians and publicists in both superpowers." He considers that "virtually nothing has been written on the psychology of peace" — "those attitudes and emotions which foster peace at both individual and social levels." He ends his book by asking: "Can we imagine and evoke a culture of peace . . ? And more importantly, can we create a culture and myth sufficiently compelling and attractive [to generate] the will to make peace"?

"(W)e may not be able to understand why others appear numbed to the nuclear threat until we become aware of our own numbness to their more immediate sources of anguish."

The effort to create a culture of peace need not begin from nothing, although our heritage is certainly mixed. Of this we are reminded by Elise Boulding's "Two Cultures of Religion as Obstacles to Peace" (1986). She finds

two contrasting cultures in every religious tradition, the holy war and peaceable garden cultures. Conflict is basic to human existence, stemming from the uniqueness of human individuals and their groups. Churches, instead of helping their societies develop the middle-ground skills of negotiation and mediation, have insisted on a choice between two extreme behaviors: unitive love or destruction of the enemy. In international affairs this has led to the identification of the church with the state in wartime and kept it from claiming the important middle ground of peacemaking. Institutionalized religion can pick up its missed opportunities.

Boulding looks at the holy war and peace cultures in Judaism, Islam, and Christianity "in terms of the sociopolitical outcomes for the societies in question," including the codes of conduct, norms of governance, and types of role models available for the socialization of women and men.

From the perspective of nonviolent struggle, it might be added that the "middle ground" between war and cooperation is not exhausted by negotiation and mediation. Gene Sharp has frequently argued that some struggles on fundamental issues (independence, freedom, racial equality) must be vigorously waged before negotiated agreements are either possible or desirable.[5] Nonviolent struggle, especially when conducted with an explicit ideology of respect for life,[6] offers an alternative way of forcefully confronting injustices or other conflicts that often result in war — a way that differs both from "armed liberation struggles" or holy war and from submission to a destructive (perhaps ostensibly "peaceful") status quo.

Walden Bello, in a chapter presenting a psychological perspective on war from his *Visions of a Warless World,* briefly discusses the ideas of Freud, Jung, Robert Jay Lifton, Jonathan Schell, and Joanna Rogers Macy. Drawing on Macy's innovative "social psychotherapy designed to empower people in the face of the nuclear threat," Bello concludes that "Individual psychic liberation from nuclear repression . . . goes hand in hand with a process of communal politicization or 'conscientization' — of becoming aware of our collective, democratic power to regain our future."

An increasing number of persons are coming to regard peace and feminism as profoundly linked. In her article on the two cultures of religion Elise Boulding wrote that "the template of patriarchy as a social institution continues to mold generation after generation, . . . continuing the practice of warfare and the subjection of women." Feminist Cynthia Adcock writes that militarism "is primarily a male phenomenon, and the ultimate power of patriarchy is the organized, legitimized violence of the nation-state."[7] In his chapter on feminist perspectives on war, Bello cites the thoughts of Carol Gilligan, Marilyn French, and others. A feminist ethic of caring and concern for life seems an essential element both for a peace system and for the effort to bring it into existence.

> *A feminist ethic of caring and concern for life seems an essential element both for a peace system and for the effort to bring it into existence.*

Carol Cohn's essay on the "nuclear language" and apparent sexual imagery used by "defense intellectuals" (who are virtually all men) is thought-provoking even if the meaning of the language she cites is not so "transparent" as she asserts. (Some seems more related to strength and toughness than to sex as such.) She suggests that some of the imagery and metaphors used ("Little Boy," "footprint," "cookie cutter") serve to "domesticate" weapons and render them more safe and familiar and less terrifying. Her article helps to illuminate the subculture in which the national security planning officials and their academic counterparts operate. As Cohn later observes, "'Peace' is not a part of this discourse. . . . To speak the word is to immediately brand oneself as a soft-headed activist instead of a professional to be taken seriously" (p. 22). Yet, as Kull, Cohn, and an increasing number of writers have demonstrated, the war planners' claim to "hard-headed" rationality is fraudulent.[8]

The idea that women are different from men has long been used by men to justify denial of equal rights to women; this idea has been countered by assertions of women's equality. The idea of gender differences has also been used by suffragists and some contemporary feminists to argue that a greater role for women in politics will serve to make politics more ethical and humane. Ethel Jensen's "Can Feminism Save the World?" presents an array of writers she interprets as representing three positions on these matters: "getting out of the [war] system; getting into the system; transcending the system."

Patricia Mische's two-part article on "Women, Power and Alternative Futures" (1978) is a pioneering contribution to the topic Jensen explores, a complex discussion now involving a sizable number of writers.[9] Rather than conceiving patriarchy as producing war in a linear cause-and-effect fashion, Mische regards patriarchy as in part a result of societal insecurity: "because 'masculine' values [related to physical combat by men to defend the tribe through war] were considered more essential to group survival they came to be more highly esteemed along with the men embodying them most fully." Her viewpoint seems consistent with the insights of a systems understanding of the world — in which causation is more often circular or reciprocal than one-way — and also with anthropological scholarship.[10]

> *Rather than conceiving patriarchy as producing war in a linear cause-and-effect fashion, Mische regards patriarchy as in part a result of societal insecurity.*

One hopeful implication of a systems view may be that, contrary to what some believe, the creation of a more feminist world may not depend exclusively on a very gradual development over generations, emanating outward from a handful of feminist women (and men) raising children through more equally shared nurturant parenting. Rather, progress toward greater gender equality and a more caring, life-nurturing public value system may be significantly hastened by whatever is achieved within the next few decades toward a world of greater security and less violence. A systems approach suggests a multidimensional strategy for change.

The importance of a systems perspective is the starting point of psychologist Robert R. Holt's essay "Converting the War System to a Peace System" (1987). Holt briefly refutes the notion that something in human nature (like an instinct) makes war inevitable, and presents a short cross-cultural overview of war and peace. He then proceeds to examine the relative valuation put by U.S. culture on two contrasting patterns of values he terms (following David Bakan) "agency" (achievement orientation or power-seeking, and more war-prone) and "communion" ("an orientation toward the forces that bind people together in larger social units or communities").

Holt concludes that whatever the ideal balance between these should be, "there can be little doubt that our present culture is tipped way over toward exaggerated agency." But "there are some good reasons to believe . . . that we can build a society in which there is . . . more love and less aggression, more care and less competition, autonomy tempered by responsibility, and more integrated human beings." Not only would such change be possible; such a society would be even "more congruent with human nature than the one we have."

How to make such a change? Holt looks at the history of violence in the U.S., its role in the mass media and U.S. culture (including the present prevalence of violence on television) and considers the effects on our sociocultural dispositions toward violence or peacefulness. In the last part of his paper, "Toward Solutions," he focuses on "what changes are needed in our sociocultural system and some ideas about how to start working toward them."

Holt's thoughtful and concise proposals for a host of changes in people, institutions, economy, culture, values, etc. defy easy summary, but include some quite manageable projects that could be undertaken by individuals without delay. One example: concerning popular culture and the entertainment world, Holt proposes production of "a writer's handbook on how to introduce conflict, drama, and attention-catchers without the easy recourse to assault, murder, weapons, treachery," etc., "on the model of the guides to nonsexist language now becoming widely used." Holt's paper offers a remarkable combination of visionary aspirations, a sense of the dynamism of culture and personality, and a practical awareness that even those changes that are relatively feasible in the short run require hard, intelligent work to bring them about.

> *"There are some good reasons to believe . . . that we can build a society in which there is . . . more love and less aggression."*

In his 1983 book *The Poverty of Affluence*, Paul Wachtel offered "a psychological portrait of the American way of life." Although advocates of capitalism have long hailed its record of providing economic growth, Wachtel (represented here by a 1987 speech excerpted in *New Options*) offers a very different assessment.

> We *are* destroying our environment. But I think the way [critics of economic growth have] tried to communicate this has been faulty. Very often, the message that seems to be coming through is that we've got to tighten our belts; we've got to give up a lot . . . .
>
> As long as your message is that people's standard of living has got to go down, people are going to be powerfully motivated not to hear that message. People don't want to live worse — and that's very understandable.
>
> But I think that's an erroneous message. Because . . . it leaves out . . . all the ways our present way of life *doesn't work*. . . . It doesn't bring us the kinds of satisfactions we assume it brings.

The capitalist way of life, Wachtel suggests, involves geographic uprooting, disruption of traditions, and weakening of family ties which have traditionally brought life's greatest satisfactions. Yet "when you say to your kids, 'Don't bother me now! I'm working,' you then have to work even harder. Because every time you undermine your more gratifying ties, your need to compensate with material goods becomes greater. And the circle keeps on generating itself." The rationale that economic growth is needed to eliminate poverty is unpersuasive, Wachtel believes: given major inequality, "being low man on the totem pole is painful no matter how high the totem pole is." He recommends we create a way of life involving greater "equality and sharing and intimacy."

Herman Daly, in a companion speech, suggests that "growth" and "development" should be distinguished, the first being quantitative, the second qualitative. "An economy therefore can develop without growing — or grow without developing." To be sustainable, our economy must be a "steady-state" one — "that does not grow, but is free to develop." Daly acknowledges that

> If you stop growing in a growth economy, you're in trouble! It's like an airplane that's designed for forward motion. If it stops still in the air, it's going to crash. It just wasn't meant to do that. It doesn't mean there's no such thing as a helicopter — which can stay still in the air; but you can't do it with an airplane.

To convert the growth airplane into a steady-state helicopter, Daly finds three changes essential: limitation of population; limitation of "throughput," that is, production of artifacts (perhaps by taxing depletion of basic resources); and establishing "minimum and maximum limits on income," with the maximum perhaps ten times the minimum. Community, Daly suggests, "really cannot tolerate unlimited inequality. And without justice and community there can be no steady-state."

Community "really cannot tolerate unlimited inequality."

Elise Boulding's "Learning Peace" is reproduced from *The Quest for Peace* (1987), a volume prepared at the initiative of the International Social Science Council in cooperation with several United Nations bodies. In contrast to fantasies of harmony, Boulding assumes that "conflict of interest exists, in however small a degree, whenever two human beings come together." But, unlike many writers on international relations, she does not infer from this an eternal Hobbesian "war of all against all." Rather, Boulding emphasizes that while conflict is ubiquitous, conflict resolution is almost equally ubiquitous, in the sense that "negotiation," often unconscious and nearly imperceptible, takes place continuously.[11] This viewpoint can enlarge our sense of society's peace-making capacities and alter our conception of everyday social life, thereby changing our image of the world and its possibilities.

Another scholar of global relations has proclaimed "the attainment of some system of mutual accommodation" as the essential international political need of our time.[12] Although negotiation under conditions of unequal power may serve to ratify oppression, "negotiation" and "accommodation" in these senses need not entail capitulation to injustice. As Boulding notes elsewhere, the dominated can wield "the power of non-compliance."[13]

Boulding points out that, despite negative influences (e.g., the global distribution of violence-oriented U.S. television), grassroots efforts for peace and better understanding like those by international nongovernmental organizations (INGOs) provide a framework within which social learning appropriate for making a more peaceful world can take place.[14] "These groups," she writes, "are forming a whole new set of global structures which will become increasingly important as the nation-state moves toward obsolescence."

In the meantime, we face the challenge of surviving despite the behavior of institutions and official leaders and others who have not yet "learned peace." Lloyd S. Etheredge's book *Can Governments Learn? American Foreign Policy and Central American Revolutions* (1985) is important for at least two reasons. The first is that Etheredge provides a concise account of a momentous but little-known episode of U.S. history. Operation MONGOOSE, a U.S. government anti-Castro campaign, was kept secret from the U.S. public for over ten years. Initiated in frustration and anger over the failure of the April 1961 Bay of Pigs invasion intended to overthrow Castro, MONGOOSE included multiple assassination attempts, commando raids and sabotage to destroy factories and crops (at one point 10 to 20 thousand tons of sugar cane were burned per week), bombings, worldwide efforts to disrupt all Cuban international trade, and "dozens and perhaps hundreds of people killed."[15]

This campaign was not conducted by out-of-control renegade intelligence agents. It took place at President Kennedy's orders and under Robert Kennedy's personal supervision, lasting from early fall of 1961 until the October 1962 discovery that the Soviets (seeking to deter an expected second invasion) were placing nuclear missiles in Cuba. Etheredge's account, based mainly on neglected publicly available sources, would seem to show definitively that the Cuban Missile Crisis, perhaps our closest brush with nuclear annihilation, resulted from the Soviet Union's effort to defend an ally against a vicious and protracted attack by U.S. policymakers "hysterical" (Robert McNamara's word) at the continued survival of a Third World revolution in their sphere of influence.

Etheredge observes that "The American press, public, and most members of Congress, unaware of MONGOOSE's ferocity, faced a mystery and were led to believe the nuclear missiles were unjustified, solely introduced by Khrushchev to threaten America and change the global balance of power."[16] Twenty-five years later most Americans have still never heard of MONGOOSE,[17] and the Harvard scholars who wrote *Living with Nuclear Weapons* perpetuate the "mystery" by beginning their account of the Cuban Missile Crisis with the Soviets' action, as if nothing relevant preceded it.[18]

Etheredge's second contribution is his major theme: the nature of government learning. He identifies a "'hardball politics' imagination system" characteristic of how "ambitious men experience the nature of power." This imagination system (including overconfidence, fear, "defective ethics," "cold" aggression, and scorn of weakness) handicaps or overrides rational analysis and blocks learning, producing characteristic policies, policy-making behavior, and faulty judgments. The result is "dual-track decision-making," in which strong emotions play a large and dangerous part precisely because the men involved typically deny that emotional factors influence them.

Although Etheredge believes the foreign policy process could work better with men of greater maturity and stronger character, he stresses that "there is a system-level logic involved." Power issues crucially affected learning: the "learning rate . . . was a function of motivation, itself an effect of the issues of power at stake."[19] U.S. policy-makers thought hard when Soviet nuclear missiles became involved; they proceeded unreflectively while victimizing a weaker country with impunity.

Part III
Making Peace a Reality

Introduction: Prospects for Building a Peace System
Chapter 9: The Superpowers
Chapter 10: Beyond the Superpowers: Other Actors
Chapter 11: Making Changes: Analyses and
                 Approaches
Chapter 12: Considering Strategies
Chapter 13: Where Do We Go from Here?

Introduction:
Prospects for Building
a Peace System

Early conceptions of global reform tended to ignore the problem of transition. Some reform-oriented authors placed their faith in rationality, expecting the persuasiveness of their proposals to generate by itself a politics of acceptance. Their approach was to design a better system of world order and then argue for its adoption. . . .

An adequate conception of transition . . . must be grounded in political reality. It must connect analysis of what is projected as preferred with an inquiry into the actors and social forces that might make such an outcome materialize within a certain historical context.

—Richard Falk, Samuel S. Kim, and Saul H. Mendlovitz, *Toward a Just World Order*[1]

What are the prospects for a peace system becoming reality? Who could make it happen? How?

The essay at the beginning of this book proposed a peace system as the solution to the problem of nuclear weapons and war. Part II explored processes, ideas, and issues involved in envisioning and designing a peace system. In Part III we inquire into what actors, social forces, actions, and strategies "might make such an outcome materialize."

Chapters 9 and 10 focus primarily on governmental actors: first the superpowers, then other governments. Chapter 11 examines a wider variety of agents of change, forms of action, and strategies. Chapter 12 continues the examination of strategies and begins the transition to Chapter 13's focus on how individuals can work with others in a sustained way to create a peace system.

This introduction provides an overview of some trends potentially supportive of change from the war system to a peace system; it thereby offers a context for the readings in the chapters that follow.

Unlike some reformers, we do not look to persuade top policy-makers — or "everyone"[2] — to cooperate in a plan of action that will bring a sweeping reorganization of the planet's governance. Ambitious schemes that require many antagonistic actors to agree with a preconceived plan are rarely adopted.[3] Further, it is possible that a comprehensive, fairly rapid change would be unwise even if it could be made:

> A complex system that works is invariably found to have evolved from a simple system that worked. The parallel proposition also appears to be true: a complex system designed from scratch never works and cannot be made to work.[4]

Whatever might be desirable, it only seems feasible to build gradually most of the elements of a peace system.[5] What we conceive as relevant for making peace is not simply adding a world government on top of the present war system; the relevant factors are the whole complex system of interactions generating the world's present mixture of war and peace. Our task is to "evolve" in the direction of a lesser "output" of war and more of peace (including ecological soundness, reduced economic inequality, increased freedom and democracy) from the global system in which we now live.

Building a Peace System

As we review certain evolving trends in this Introduction, the United States is sometimes the chief reference point, even though a theme of Part III is that U.S. peace activists should become more aware of the rest of the world. The reason is that people in the U.S. are likely to understand the U.S. world role less well than many in other countries understand it; and, for better or worse, no other society has so much influence on world affairs. To understand the world better, U.S. activists must come to understand their own country's role more realistically.

There are plenty of negative trends: multiple ecological perils (ozone depletion, global warming, overpopulation, scarcity of usable water, pollution), increasingly destructive weaponry, desperate poverty, massive waste by the "affluent," the global "debt crisis," and increase of scientific knowledge faster than the wisdom to use it well. These important trends, which are not the focus of this book, do provide the occasion for peoples often historically at odds to work for common solutions. And indeed, some of the trends of our time are encouraging.

> To understand the world better, U.S. activists must come to understand their own country's role more realistically.

The delegitimation of war and violence. A full decade before the 1980s' upsurge of peace activism, sociologist Egon Bittner wrote of:

the rise of the sustained, and thus far not abandoned, aspiration of Western society to abolish violence and install peace as a stable and permanent condition of everyday life. [Despite the overwhelming violence that has marked the period,] there can be no doubt that during the past one-hundred-fifty years the awareness of the moral and practical necessity of peace took hold of the minds of virtually all people. The advocacy of warfare and violence did not disappear entirely, but it grew progressively less frank and it keeps losing ground to arguments that condemn it. . . . The trend towards the achievement of peace is basically new in Western history, even as we admit that it is continuously in danger of being overwhelmed by counter-tendencies.[6]

The growth of international law. Benjamin Ferencz's *A Common Sense Guide to World Peace* reminds us that the past forty years have seen greatly increased codification of international law and recognition of human rights agreements. Even though the violators may dispute the applicability of the principles to their behavior, we now have non-arbitrary standards that can be invoked when we say that such policies as preparing to use nuclear weapons (i.e., nuclear deterrence) are crimes.[7]

The decline of U.S.-Soviet dominance. The U.S.S.R. has maintained its grip on territory the Red Army occupied in World War II, but at the price of much reduced influence over Communist parties elsewhere as a result of its invasions of Hungary, Czechoslovakia, and most recently, Afghanistan. The Soviet Union now exerts little appeal as a model; it struggles to remedy internal problems and has taken steps to disengage from costly foreign commitments. The Vietnam War, other U.S. military interventions, and the economic decline caused by decades of stupendous military spending have all combined to lower U.S. prestige and power worldwide. As the price of Reagan's passion for "standing tall" has come to be recognized, "morning in America" has become "the morning after," and elite discussion has turned to the topic of whether further decline is inevitable.[8] Even countries long allied with the U.S. have distanced themselves from its policies and actions of recent years.[9] The weakening of the superpowers has reduced world polarization, permitting some increase in independence for other countries.

The declining utility of military force. Concerning nuclear arsenals, many have quoted Henry Kissinger's lament asking what one can *do* with nuclear superiority. Superpower defeats or stalemates in Vietnam and Afghanistan and the overthrow of heavily armed regimes in Iran and the Philippines have also highlighted for government elites the limits of military force for achieving political objectives.

The rising influence of the Non-aligned Movement. As we shall see in a reading for Chapter 10, the number of nations adhering to the Non-aligned Movement (a movement proclaiming the principles of peace and disarmament, economic and cultural equality, and support for the United Nations) has increased. That movement has taken important initiatives for peace.

> *The weakening of the superpowers has reduced world polarization, permitting some increase in independence for other countries.*

Steps toward demilitarization in some countries. "China has reduced the share of its GNP used for military purposes by nearly half over the last decade. . . . [It] is shifting resources toward environmental restoration, family planning, technological advancement, and overall economic development," reports Lester Brown of the Worldwatch Institute, and he adds that Argentina has made a similar shift even faster.[10]

An increased emphasis on economic well-being. Related to the preceding trends is recognition that even military power must rest on economic strength, including a labor force increasingly educated to be able to handle modern jobs. The growing economic power of Japan and its newly industrializing neighbors in East Asia have contributed to proclamation of the "rise of the trading state."[11] Despite the anti-ecological effects of conventional economic growth and the dangerous political tensions engendered by competition, the economic focus is still (at least temporarily) a step forward from military threats and conquest.[12]

The increasing use of nonviolent struggle. The twentieth-century rise of nonviolent struggle as a factor in world politics is a kind of counterpart to the declining utility of political violence. More than just protest is involved. The role of nonviolent struggle in regime changes in Iran, Poland, and the Philippines has been widely recognized; and not only the frequency but also the sophistication of nonviolent struggle has grown.[13]

The growth of international nongovernmental organizations. Elise Boulding has written that "the rise of people's associations as distinct from governmental organizations and activities represents a major shift in the nature of the international system [and is] one of the most striking phenomena of the twentieth century."[14] Now 18,000 in number, international nongovernmental organizations ("INGOs") include such groups as service clubs, chambers of commerce, churches, YWCA's and YMCA's, and associations of farmers, teachers, doctors, and scientists as well as explicitly peace-oriented associations. INGOs, free to act in ways that nation-states are not, link all continents and, at their best, promote global understanding and provide a continuing lobby, more stable than social movements, for constructive international policies.

Let us look now more specifically at the U.S.

"The rise of people's associations is one of the most striking phenomena of the twentieth century."

The women's liberation movement. The women's liberation movement, to a considerable degree a global phenomenon,[15] has encouraged political mobilization of women and increased respect for values of caring and nurturance largely antithetical to war, threats, and violence. Its influence has augmented female leadership for peace and provided a source of both nonviolent direct action against military facilities — exemplified by the women's peace encampments at Greenham Common (U.K.), Seneca Falls (N.Y.), and elsewhere[16] — and efforts to evolve a participatory democratic and peaceful form of human relations — illustrated by the women's peacemaking initiative known as the Great Peace Journey.[17]

The lesbian and gay liberation movement. Like the women's movement, gay and lesbian liberation has encouraged questioning of rigid ideals of masculinity and femininity that perpetuate the war system.[18] Both movements, by focusing on the realities of people's lives, have served to reduce mindless acquiescence to crusades against official enemies.

Resistance to government aggression. In the United States, top leaders and the media rarely question the idea[19] that they are entitled to pass judgment on smaller countries' governments (especially those "in our own backyard" — the Caribbean, Latin America) and invade, subvert, or overthrow them; and they see no inconsistency in condemning Soviet leaders for the same attitudes toward *their* "backyard" (Eastern Europe, Afghanistan).

But much of the U.S. public learned from the Vietnam War that fighting wars to preserve the status quo in other countries was costly in lives and dollars as well as morally unacceptable. The aftermath has been a heightened dislike for and outright resistance to the government's war-making abroad, sometimes known as "the Vietnam Syndrome." In addition to the hundreds of groups acting in solidarity with Central American countries and the tens of thousands who joined the "Pledge of Resistance" to prevent an invasion of Nicaragua, public sentiments have been reflected in seven state governors' refusal to send National Guard troops to Latin America.[20]

Citizen peacemaking initiatives. The effort to reassert popular control over foreign policy in the wake of Congress's and the executive branch's refusal to follow the democratic will of the U.S. public on war and peace has not been limited to resistance. Active "citizen diplomacy" and "municipal foreign policy" are becoming familiar, supplementing earlier efforts for international exchange and understanding.[21]

Efforts to organize progressive forces. Built in large measure on an organizational base of issue-oriented activism across the country, Rev. Jesse Jackson's 1988 campaign for the presidency both inspired people by its eloqence and impressed them with the sizable voter percentages it won. Despite the difficulties of breaking through the Tweedledum-Tweedledee two-party politics dominant in the U.S. (see Cohen and Rogers in Chapter 11), the extensive support Jackson's Rainbow Coalition won has encouraged activists to believe that political action in the interests of peace and justice can be more than marginal and to seek to strengthen that Coalition as a vehicle for future change efforts.

> *"Citizen diplomacy" and "municipal foreign policy" are becoming familiar.*

Recognition of these trends (combined with what can be learned from the readings discussed in Part III) leads to a surprising and important conclusion:

The U.S. peace movement is part of a majority movement. Massive majorities of the U.S. public — 70 and 80% — agree with main positions of the peace movement: the desirability of a Freeze and of a no-first-use nuclear weapons policy.[22] Internationally the U.S. peace movement has very powerful allies. The peace movements of Western Europe, Australia, New Zealand, and Japan are significant forces that limit their countries' cooperation with U.S. government military plans (while of course also refusing alliance with the Soviets). A majority of the countries in the world, active through the Non-aligned Movement, give a measure of support to principles of peace, disarmament, and international law and constitute a source of constructive pressure on the U.S. and U.S.S.R. The heads of state of India, Sweden, Tanzania, Argentina, Mexico, and Greece have jointly called on the superpowers to freeze, reduce, and eliminate their nuclear arsenals and to redirect resources to social and economic development.

The prospects for peace have also been bolstered by the advent in the U.S.S.R. of a leadership beginning to articulate the ideas of common security and non-provocative defense and to recognize that "concessions" serve its own security interests better than hard-line intransigence. The Soviets' unilateral 19-month halt to nuclear testing, followed in December 1988 by announcement of unilateral troop reductions in Europe, exemplified their new willingness to take bold steps for peace.

Building a Peace System

But for people inside the U.S., the picture has often appeared bleak. The 1984 and 1988 election results, the U.S. refusal to reciprocate Gorbachev's testing halt, social decay in U.S. cities and towns, and the continuing bloodshed in Central America were discouraging factors hardly compensated by the INF Treaty's small forward steps.

Since its rise to world dominance after World War II, the U.S. government has become unusually backward on the world scene, often in a tiny minority or even completely alone (as in its vote against reform of infant formula marketing and its rejection of the laboriously-negotiated Law of the Sea Treaty). The U.S. government's extremism is largely kept from U.S. public awareness by the unwillingness or inability of U.S. news media to convey consistently how far our government is from international norms on many issues. The extent of both domestic and foreign opposition to the U.S. policies of "low-intensity warfare" (El Salvador), invasions (Grenada), bombings (Libya), and flouting of international judicial decisions (the World Court's judgment on the "covert" U.S. *contra* war against Nicaragua) is underreported and consequently often underestimated even by those involved in the opposition.

The U.S. government has become unusually backward on the world scene.

The discouragement that results, the sense that there is no realistic hope for world peace, creates tendencies toward desperate actions, apocalyptic pronouncements ("By 1985, after deployment X, it will be too late!"), and eventual burn-out and withdrawal from activism. Counteracting the debilitating influences of the U.S. government, corporate culture, and mass media requires that we supplement and sustain our awareness of the encouraging trends and facts outlined above by systematically altering the mix of information we and our associates receive. This costs some money, but is a crucial investment in mental and political health. For specific suggestions, see this book's sections on periodicals and audio and video information sources.

When forces for change combine, the effects can be large. Writing in 1979, Rajni Kothari emphasized "the necessity for a grand global coalition in which progressive governments of the Third World join activist reformers and radical social movements in the North."[23] Such a coalition, he wrote, was "emergent but by no means already there, as yet more potential than real."[24] By now, though, a million U.S. peace activists have experienced this coalition. On June 12, 1982 the largest demonstration in U.S. history occurred as peace activists marched through New York in response to the United Nations Special Session on Disarmament. That session, and the resulting boost to U.S. peace activism, would not have occurred without Third World governments' initiatives.

The effort in this book is to steer a course between two extremes: despair and shallow hopes. Converting friendly opinion into policy changes, and organizing favorable forces to carry through an effective strategy, is not simple. But there is a real basis for informed hope.[25] The forces for peace and justice are far stronger than we ordinarily realize. Building a peace system is a global project; and in the efforts of people around the world, it is already underway.

Chapter 9:
The Superpowers

Just before the December 1987 Reagan-Gorbachev meeting, the *Boston Globe* began its front-page pre-summit coverage thus:

> For most of the world's 5 billion people . . . superpower summits have become an accepted secular rite, symbolically as important to survival as were the ceremonies of primitive man to assure the rising of the sun. So great is the destructive capability of the superpowers that an awed and helpless world looks to these face-to-face encounters as the best chance for the triumph of reason over brutish emotions, light over dark, life over death, and the continuation of civilization.[1]

This portrayal uncritically accepts and reinforces an appalling portrait of humanity as "helpless" dependents gazing passively upward at god-like potentates. The governments of the United States and the Union of Soviet Socialist Republics are plainly the top-ranking organizations in the world when one reckons destructive power. But where they rank in capacity to achieve peace — or even to maintain their own survival—is much less certain. Prudence dictates exploring whether humanity's "best chance" lies in other hands.

A sizable part of the U.S. peace movement conceives the problem it is addressing as primarily one of fear, distrust, and hostility between the two superpowers. This book has already offered reasons for conceiving today's war dangers quite differently. (Recall Chapter 3's readings on "the deadly connection" between Third World conflict and nuclear war, and Chapter 8's on Operation MONGOOSE and the 1962 Cuban Missile Crisis.) As has been suggested in the Introduction to Part Three, a much broader range of actors than the superpower governments are relevant to the prospects for peace. But the superpowers are undeniably important, and this chapter focuses on them.

• • •

John F. Kennedy's American University speech of June 1963 marked one of the high points of U.S. government wisdom and initiative in the post-World War II era. Speaking eight months after the Cuban Missile Crisis, Kennedy announced a halt to U.S. atmospheric nuclear testing and proposed a bilateral treaty banning it (but allowing underground testing) which was promptly negotiated and signed in September 1963. Kennedy proclaimed that the U.S. and U.S.S.R. were "both caught up in a vicious and dangerous cycle with suspicion on one side breeding suspicion on the other, and new weapons begetting counter-weapons" and that both sides had "a mutually deep interest in a just and genuine peace and in halting the arms race." Anyone who would rejoice to hear such language from the White House today should consider the limits of what followed then.

In his 1967 article "The Kennedy Experiment," sociologist Amitai Etzioni analyzed Kennedy's policy initiatives, and the apparent Soviet counter-moves, as exemplifying the strategy of "Graduated and Reciprocated Initiatives in Tension-reduction" (GRIT) advocated by psychologist Charles Osgood. As Mark Sommer states, "Whether Kennedy was acting with Osgood's strategy in mind is still not clear. McGeorge Bundy reports that as Kennedy's national security adviser, he knew nothing of

Readings: for study group use

A. John F. Kennedy, "A Strategy of Peace" (1963), pp. 31-39;

Amitai Etzioni, "The Kennedy Experiment" (1967), pp. 40-50;

(Optional: Charles Osgood, "The Way GRIT Works" [1986], pp. 24-30); all in *Securing Our Planet* (1986);

Mark Sommer, "Independent Initiatives: GRIT" (and following sections), pp. 58-65 in *Beyond the Bomb* (1986; 7 pp.);

Mark Sommer, "The Gorbachev Experiment" *The ExPro Papers* #1 (1986; 3 pp.);

Mikhail Gorbachev, "Address to the United Nations" (December 7, 1988; 23 pp.).

Total= 52 pp.

B. Noam Chomsky, "The Race to Destruction," pp. 171-219 (especially pp. 172-173, 177-178, 188-198, 202-204, "The Roots of the Pentagon System," pp. 207-217, and "Cold War Realities," pp. 217-219) in *Turning the Tide: U.S. Intervention in Central America and the Struggle for Peace* (1985). Total= 49 pp.

C. Harvard Nuclear Study Group, "Military Power and Political Purpose: What Do We Want from Nuclear Weapons?" pp. 133-159 in *Living With Nuclear Weapons* (1983);

Robert Irwin, "Redefining the 'National Interest'" (1982; 6 pp.); and "Changing U.S. Foreign and Defense Policy" (1982; 15 pp.).

Total= 47 pp.

D. Robert C. Tucker, "Where is the Soviet Union Headed?" *World Policy Journal* (Spring 1987), pp. 199-204;

Robert C. Johansen, "The Reagan Administration and the U.N.: The Costs of Unilateralism," *World Policy Journal* (Fall 1986); 39 pp.;

George Perkovitch, "New Soviet Thinking," in *Nuclear Times* (May/June 1987); 3 pp.;

Joergen Dragsdahl, "Are the Soviets Really Serious?" from *Nuclear Times* (May/June 1988); 3 pp.

Total= 51 pp.

E. Robert C. Tucker, "Keeping Peace Between the Superpowers: Toward a Cooperative Regime of War Prevention" (1985; 7 pp.);

Dietrich Fischer, "Peace 2010" scenario, pp. 121-128 from Earl Foell and Richard Nenneman, eds. *How Peace Came to the World* (1986; 7 pp.);

Robert C. Johansen, "Toward National Security Without Nuclear Deterrence," *The ExPro Papers* #8 (1987; 38 pp.);

Michael T. Klare, "Policing the Third World: A Blueprint for Endless Intervention," from *The Nation* July 30/August 6, 1988, 4 pp.

Total= 56 pp.

GRIT while in office." But in any case, the experiment worked to ease tensions and produced a lasting arms control agreement.

Why did the process stop? Etzioni says "the reasons were many." Osgood notes that the moves "slowed down with deepening involvement in Vietnam." Whatever the precise set of explanatory factors, it seems reasonable to conclude that reducing superpower tensions was less important to U.S. leaders than other political objectives, such as escalating the war in Vietnam.

> *Reducing superpower tensions was less important to U.S. leaders than escalating the war in Vietnam.*

Sommer suggests the problem may have been that the initiatives "worked too well." As Etzioni writes, there was an unanticipated "danger" [sic]: "the Russians responded not just by reciprocating American initiatives but by offering initiatives of their own, in the spirit of the detente. Washington was put on the spot: it had to reciprocate if it were not to weaken the new spirit, but it could lose control of the experiment." "Hopes and expectations" began "running too high." The U.S. had difficulty (in Etzioni's judgment) making "a good case for its objection to a non-aggression pact" between NATO and the Warsaw Pact.

In "The Gorbachev Experiment" (1986) Mark Sommer compares Soviet leader Mikhail Gorbachev's August 6, 1985 halt to nuclear testing with the "Kennedy experiment." Sommer judges it a bolder move than Kennedy's: Kennedy "enjoyed an overwhelming strategic advantage," whereas the Soviets have only a "hard-won position of parity." Noting that "despite a consistently hostile response from the Reagan Administration, the Soviets . . . thrice extended the deadline of their unilateral moratorium," renouncing testing for well over a year, Sommer wrote that their action was a rare opportunity, not to be missed, for the U.S. However, in the absence of U.S. reciprocation, the Soviets eventually ended their unilateral halt.

Joining and making permanent Gorbachev's testing moratorium would certainly have been in the interest of the United States. The decline in reliability of both arsenals in the absence of periodic testing of stockpiled weapons (presented as a disadvantage by U.S. opponents of a test ban) would lower the chances that either side could confidently contemplate a first strike. But a review of the relevant history suggests that a rational interest in long-term survival has seldom been an overriding motivation for U.S. policymakers, a point elaborated in the reading from Noam Chomsky discussed below.

In the judgment of many, the most encouraging actions from either superpower since the token reductions of the December 1987 Intermediate Nuclear Forces (INF) Treaty were the decisions announced in Mikhail Gorbachev's December 1988 speech to the United Nations General Assembly. Gorbachev, like countless previous UN speakers, expressed opposition to "the threat or use of force"; unlike them, he announced a unilateral reduction of his country's armed forces — by 500,000 troops. In addition, and perhaps of equal or greater importance, he announced that all Soviet divisions remaining in the territory of its Eastern European allies were being "reorganized" so that "their structure will be different" and "will become clearly defensive" (p. 19).

> *A rational interest in long-term survival has seldom been an overriding motivation for U.S. policymakers.*

Gorbachev's proclamation of a principle of "reasonable defense sufficiency" and "a new model of ensuring security — not through the buildup of arms" (p. 18) may prove to be, if consistently followed through, of epoch-making significance as a breakthrough at the superpower level toward the "defensive" or "non-provocative" defense policies advocated in several of Chapter 6's readings. (On the origins of this Soviet policy shift, see the article by Dragsdahl discussed later in this chapter.) At this writing, similar reductions by several Soviet allies have been announced, and the Soviet withdrawal from its aggression in Afghanistan has been completed despite continuing U.S. aid to the anti-Soviet forces in violation of the withdrawal agreement.

Gorbachev's speech, though in places "diplomatically" abstract and vague, contains other elements of interest such as forthright acknowledgment that continued "traditional-type industrialization" will mean "environmental catastrophe" (p. 3); statements of commitment to freedom of choice, tolerance, and the rule of law — and tacit admission of past Soviet deficiencies indicated by announcing cessation of jamming foreign radio broadcasts and work on new laws to "improve [Soviet] domestic conditions for respecting and protecting the rights of its own citizens" (p. 16); and a pervasive desire for better relations indicated by avoidance of "recriminations" concerning matters of U.S.-Soviet conflict, praise for Reagan and Shultz, and calls for many-sided dialogue and movement "toward a nuclear-weapon-free and nonviolent world" (p. 22).

In the chapter "The Race to Destruction" in *Turning the Tide*, Noam Chomsky suggests a disturbing answer to why U.S. leaders generally seem little interested in reducing tensions with the Soviet Union; he offers an analysis of the Cold War rarely (if ever) encountered in the U.S. mass media. Chomsky argues that the Cold War has been a tacit partnership in global management . . . in which each superpower exploits the threat of [the other] to mobilize its own population and often recalcitrant allies to support brutal and violent measures in its own domain. The Cold War long ago came to have a certain functional utility for the superpowers, one reason why it persists. . . .

The picture becomes relatively clear, writes Chomsky, "if we consider the actual events of the Cold War, putting the rhetoric aside":

> The typical event of the Cold War is an act of aggression or subversion by one of the superpowers against an enemy within its own domains: East Germany, Hungary, Czechoslovakia, Poland, Afghanistan — Greece, the Philippines, Iran, Guatemala, the Congo, Indonesia, the Dominican Republic, Chile, El Salvador — and all too many others.[2]

The superpower conflict is also real, Chomsky recognizes: "each superpower provides barriers to the ambitions of the other." But more fundamentally, "For us, the Cold War has been a war against much of the Third World, while for the USSR, it has been a war against their subject populations."

Chomsky offers no easy optimism:

> The system has a certain inner rationality in the short term . . . . In the longer term, it is a system of mutual suicide, but it is far from easy to see how we can extricate ourselves from it, because core institutional factors are involved.

Nevertheless, Chomsky emphasizes the importance of action — action "to try to protect people who are being viciously oppressed," as well as (p. 253) "honest search for understanding, education, organization, action that raises the cost of state violence for its perpetrators [Chomsky has repeatedly advocated and engaged in nonviolent resistance] or that lays the basis for institutional change."

In "Military Power and Political Purpose," a chapter from *Living With Nuclear Weapons*, the Harvard Nuclear Study Group discusses "What Do We Want from Nuclear Weapons?" Although deterrence of a Soviet attack on the U.S. or its allies is probably what the average person assumes U.S. weapons are for, the Harvard group offer a list of purposes for nuclear weapons including to "support U.S. foreign policy in peacetime and prevent nuclear coercion of the U.S. and its allies."

What this means in practice is left rather obscure. Although the Harvard group notes that the U.S. government has been "much more reluctant to use nuclear threats" since the Soviet Union achieved strategic (i.e., nuclear) parity, they decline to spell out the nature of 19 incidents from 1945 to 1973 in which the U.S. used nuclear threats because "it felt major interests to be at stake." One can, however, find details in Daniel Ellsberg's article in Joseph Gerson's volume *The Deadly Connection*. As Gerson summarizes the matter: "Our commanders in chief have repeatedly threatened to use nuclear weapons against the Soviet Union and Third World nations to retain U.S. control over the

'Grand Area,' the sphere of influence won as a result of World War II which extends from our shores to the borders of the Soviet Union and China."[3]

The desirability of alternative defense policies or of a global peace system will presumably be evaluated at least in part by people in each country according to how they well they think their country's interests will be protected. In "Redefining the 'National Interest,'" Robert Irwin inquires into the varying conceptions of "the national interest" used in the United States. He reports (citing several writers who express surprise) that no official statement of U.S. security interests exists, but analyzes a relatively authoritative statement by former presidential advisor General Maxwell Taylor. In an introduction to the book *American National Security* Taylor asserts that:

> National security is not only the protection of our people and territory from physical assault but also the protection by a variety of means of vital economic and political interests . . . . As the richest nation in the world, we have many valuables to safeguard . . . . Abroad, we must be ready to protect thousands of nationals, allies, scores of public and private investments, military forces, bases, and markets [and also] a favorable balance of power, freedom of the seas, and our international reputation. . . . To maintain an adequate level of productivity, the economy must have uninterrupted access to raw materials, located mostly in four regions: Latin America, the Middle East, parts of Africa, and the Southwest Pacific . . . [4]

Taylor's version of the interests of the United States, with its various elastic elements (markets, a favorable balance of power, reputation, raw materials) is expansive enough to justify efforts at U.S. control over virtually any part of the world. By Taylor's standard, any country that chooses (as all Communist countries do) to limit or deny U.S. corporations' freedom to do business as they wish may be regarded as acting aggressively against U.S. national security.

Needless to say, this notion of national interest does not allow other countries much room for freely defining their own national interests. (As Phil Ochs once sang, "You are living in the Free World, in the Free World you must stay.") And any Soviet move may threaten (immediately or potentially) to limit the scope of such U.S. freedom to operate. Such a conception of the national interest requires endless military spending and, in a changing world, many wars. Global peace, Irwin contends, will require a conception of the U.S. national interest that will be more conducive to the safety and well-being of the U.S., which he briefly sketches.

Why does the U.S. government support regimes that mistreat, torture, and kill their people?[5] In "Changing U.S. Foreign and Defense Policy," Irwin finds the explanation in the predominant influence on policymaking of a small sector of the U.S. population whose financial interest in a "favorable investment climate" far exceeds their concern for the well-being of other people. A favorable investment climate correlates positively with repressive attacks on or wholesale suppression of political opposition, trade unions, human rights, etc. While the influence of this sector is predominant, anti-interventionist public opinion and the diligent efforts of concerned citizens have put some limits on the ability of the U.S. government to destroy governments it dislikes (as in

Nicaragua). The humanitarian concerns of the U.S. public consequently remain a real (even though distinctly secondary) factor in policy determination; the forcefulness with which those concerns are acted on makes a life-or-death difference to people abroad.

Robert C. Tucker, a distinguished scholar of Soviet affairs and author of a psychologically sophisticated biography of Stalin, examines "Where is the Soviet Union Headed?" in a Spring 1987 article adapted from a forthcoming book on *Political Culture and Leadership in Soviet Russia.* Any examination of fast-changing current developments risks becoming in some respects outdated, but Tucker's eloquent closing pages are of more than topical interest. Besides his domestic reform aspirations, Gorbachev also appears to Tucker to be a "would-be reform leader in world affairs." Aided by Lenin's having bequeathed no doctrine on nuclear weapons, Gorbachev is free in the international realm to address what he has termed "the real tasks and demands of our time." These are, Tucker writes, "historically unprecedented" and include saving humankind from "nuclear self-annihilation and from global environmental, demographic, and other ills."

Of greatest long-term significance may be "a final consideration":

Anti-interventionist public opinion and the diligent efforts of concerned citizens have put some limits on the ability of the U.S. government to destroy governments it dislikes.

> When the government of a great power has come to recognize that its country faces an internal crisis situation calling for thoroughgoing reform, . . . that government loses the need it had in the past to conjure up for its citizens the image of a relatively intractable external enemy — a danger on which energy and attention need to be focused as a matter of highest priority, normally by continually increasing the country's military strength. When a government is willing to openly confront the existence of profound internal problems, it becomes free to take a less combative and more co-operative stance in external relations.

Tucker believes that under Gorbachev "there have been many signs of such a shift in the regime's outlook." A reformed, more open and pluralist Soviet Union will, Tucker concludes, "be abler and readier to work with other states [to deal] effectively with global problems." And for other states, "the time to start on a new path of cooperation with a willing Soviet Union is now."

Regrettably, the U.S. government under Reagan has been less inclined to cooperate with anybody than any U.S. administration since World War II. Although in the closing months of 1987 the crisis-battered Reagan administration reached out (like Nixon during Watergate) to the Soviet Union to generate some favorable publicity, the predominant stance of the U.S. government in the 1980s has been isolated defiance. One computer analysis of U.S. votes in the U.N. shows the U.S. "increasingly isolated not only from Third World countries, but also from Japan and other western countries . . . [to the point of] sharing the 'most isolated' position with Israel and South Africa. . . .

Because U.S. policies have become isolated from those of the rest of the world, the U.S. perceives the rest of the world as anti-American."[6]

In "The Reagan Administration and the U.N.: The Costs of Unilateralism," Robert Johansen provides an informative review of recent U.S. behavior in the United Nations. Johansen finds that "If there has been anything for us to learn from the failure of America's militarized, go-it-alone approach to world policy, it is that real security can be achieved only through international cooperation — through multilateral processes of goal setting, coordination, and dispute settlement." In contrast to U.S. behavior,

> A growing number of governments have come to recognize the need for the United Nations to play an increased role in promoting common security. Middle-range powers, like Australia, Canada, and Sweden, have long supported a stronger United Nations. A U.N. voting majority, including many nonaligned Third World countries, has also consistently supported Charter norms governing the use of force. And some have begun looking to world institutions for protection against great-power intervention — consider, for example, Nicaragua's submission of its dispute with Washington to the World Court. Even the Soviet Union under Gorbachev has become more receptive to the collective-security functions of the organization, such as international monitoring and peacekeeping. Moscow has accepted IAEA inspection of its civilian nuclear reactors, has for the first time supported the renewal of the UNIFIL peacekeeping force in Lebanon, and has sought U.N. cooperation for the control of international terrorism. All this suggests a modest but nonetheless real opening for internationalism.

Johansen concludes that "what is sadly missing" is U.S. support. With such support, "the U.N. system could evolve into the cornerstone of world security that many of its founders envisioned." Alternatively, the U.S. "will face a more hostile world at a time when its influence has declined."

George Perkovitch of *Nuclear Times* canvasses (in the May-June 1987 issue) the opinions of U.S. experts on whether the apparent "New Soviet Thinking" marks a genuine change. Their consensus is that the change is real. Veteran analyst Raymond Garthoff concludes that "The Soviets are prepared to go a long, long way towards far-reaching arms reductions, . . . even to take steps that are less than fair to them." Indeed, the December 1987 INF agreement marked Soviet acceptance of "the very proposal that [had been criticized in 1982 as] too advantageous to the United States for the Soviets to take seriously."

While the Soviets' new position has been interpreted by the Reagan Administration as a triumph vindicating its years of hard-line policy, it may instead represent a changed assessment by the Soviets of their security interests: higher valuing of arms reductions, lower valuing of parity in mutual overkill capacity. Consistent with the latter interpretation, scholar Robert Legvold says that "Gorbachev is the first Soviet leader [who] has explored the link between national security and common security — that idea that one's own security is related to the security of others and that the other guy's loss is not necessarily your gain." The Soviets' decision in late 1987 to pay up their past debts to the U.N. (while the U.S. continued to withhold a portion of its share) also offered evidence that the Soviets were putting their money where their mouths were.

A May-June 1988 *Nuclear Times* article reports genuine ferment and even confusion among Soviet defense experts as new ideas compete with old ones. One study at the U.S.A.-Canada Institute "prompted by Gorbachev's proposal for a world without nuclear weapons by the year 2000 . . . concluded that Soviet influence would be dramatically diminished in such a world." Commented a Soviet expert ("dryly"): "We will be killing our influence as a superpower by making the world safer."

But whatever the mixed feelings, on key points there seems clear progress. In February 1988 Defense Minister Yazov declared that "it is becoming obvious" that not only nuclear but conventional war would be difficult to win. Specialists have argued that a minimal nuclear deterrent, less than numerical parity, would be sufficient. And Soviets have been studying what in the West is called "defensive" or "non-provocative" defense, with the evident result that Gorbachev, in a September 1987 article in *Pravda*, defined military sufficiency as "a structure of a state's armed forces which is enough to repulse any possible aggression, but which is inadequate for the conduct of offensive actions." Thus, as Dragsdahl appraises matters, for the Soviets "Non-offensive defense has grown from an embryonic idea to an officially endorsed ideal" — and since December 1988, to a policy that is being acted on.

For the Soviets "Non-offensive defense has grown from an embryonic idea to an officially endorsed ideal" — and since December 1988, to a policy that is being acted on.

In "Keeping Peace Between the Superpowers: Toward a Cooperative Regime of War Prevention" (1985), Robert C. Tucker noted the long-standing dominance in superpower relations of what he termed the "security-through-superior-strength" axiom. He cited evidence of a new outlook in remarks by the then recently deceased Soviet leader Yuri Andropov that war was "a common foe" of the two countries and in Gorbachev's assertion that what was to be decided was "whether we are prepared to switch our mentality and our mode of acting from a warlike to a peaceful track." What it might mean concretely to do that — from establishment of "risk-reduction centers" for preventing war through misunderstanding to the development of new understandings to minimize interventions in the Third World, reduce arms sales, and curb nuclear proliferation — is explored in Tucker's article.

In 1984 the *Christian Science Monitor* sponsored a contest entitled "Peace 2010." Readers were invited to submit essays of 3000 words or less that assumed peace to have been achieved by 2010 and then looked "back over the intervening quarter-century [to explain] how the world had achieved peace in that period."[7] Excerpts from some of the more than 1300 essays received, along with editorial comments, were published in 1986 in Earl Foell and Richard Nenneman, eds., *How*

Peace Came to the World. They reveal "how extraordinary a storehouse of 'peace energy' lies beneath the surface of our society."[8]

The instructions for the contest implied, as the editors acknowledge, "that peace between the superpowers was paramount."[9] Within that framework, Dietrich Fischer offers a scenario in which a U.S.-Soviet crisis that takes the world to the brink of all-out nuclear war but is resolved by a timely U.N. proposal, provides a catalyst for development of a peace system. (After the shock of the near-catastrophe, "the world was suddenly willing, even eager, to listen to proposals for alternative world orders. . . .")

Fischer's model of a peace system has four layers: "greater efforts to eliminate the causes of war"; international conflict resolution procedures (in cases of negotiations proving unsuccessful, mandatory jurisdiction by the World Court, which would deploy both incentives for compliance with its decisions and "an international police force to stop offenders"); dissuasion from aggression by making peace more attractive than war; and defense against aggression, assisted by a new U.N. Agency for Transarmament.

Peace scenarios counter-balance the "worst-case" planning that has served to rationalize a continual arms build-up.

Readers who find such scenarios implausible should consider why "best-case" scenarios can be worth generating. They counter-balance the "worst-case" planning that has served to rationalize a continual arms build-up, and they also provide rationales to undergird peace initiatives and creative negotiation.

A shorter-term approach than Fischer's, containing a range of specific proposals, is presented in Robert Johansen's "Toward National Security Without Nuclear Deterrence" (1987). He points out how the October 1986 Reykjavik superpower summit talks revealed that U.S. policymakers were "ill prepared for major changes in security policy and for moving toward a denuclearized and demilitarized world."

Johansen examines "what immediate steps can be taken to replace nuclear deterrence with a more reliable global security system," outlining measures for halting the arms buildup, reducing capabilities for superpower military intervention, establishing "zones of peace," and strengthening international peacekeeping, among others. Johansen's proposals for actions the U.S. government could and should take provide important material available to any Presidential candidate or Congressional figure interested in accepting the challenge of promoting a foreign policy platform for peace.

Peace, however, hardly seems on the minds either of most presidential candidates[10] or of top policymakers. Michael Klare finds that those policymakers regard the U.S. as facing "a vast and growing threat from social and political disorders in the Third World." What is termed "low-intensity conflict" (see Chapter 10 for discussion of this very intense kind of warfare) represents, in the words of Defense Secretary Frank Carlucci, "the principal form of conflict in the world today." In this situation, concluded the elite U.S. Commission on Integrated Long-Range Strategy in its January 1988 report *Discriminate Deterrence*, the U.S. needs a conventional force buildup to strengthen its armed intervention capabilities.

From this nationalist viewpoint, intent on maintaining a grip on overseas resources, investments, military bases, and markets, whatever detente can exist with Gorbachev's U.S.S.R. is no reason to expect peace. And indeed, Klare concludes, the Third World military interventions U.S. policy-makers expect to make "could escalate rapidly and inadvertently" to a nuclear confrontation with the Soviets.

Chapter 10:
Beyond the Superpowers:
Other Actors

There are many actors in world politics besides the superpowers and many problem areas that pose challenges for those who want to build a peace system. (The Middle East, the most likely place of origin of a nuclear holocaust because of the superpowers' alliances with hostile parties, was briefly examined in Chapter 3.) Though none can be explored in detail here, we will look in this chapter at developments involving a large number of countries and several regions of the world — the Non-aligned Movement, the Pacific, Japan, Western Europe, southern Africa, and Central America.[1] Emphasis has been given to two topics whose importance people in the U.S. are likely to be inadequately aware of: rising U.S.-Japanese tensions and the U.S. military doctrine of "low-intensity conflict." Each reading discussed serves either to inform readers about events and social actors that tend toward creation of a peace system, or about problems that will have to be coped with if peace is to be established.

• • •

Non-alignment in an Age of Alignments (1986) by A. W. Singham and Shirley Hune provides an excellent introduction to a political grouping about which most in the U.S. understand very little. The Non-aligned Movement:

> is a coalition of small and middle-sized states, mostly former colonies and developing countries, from the Third World. It was formed in 1961 with 25 states and has grown to more than 100 members [out of about 160 countries in the world]. Non-aligned countries have developed a flexible organizational structure and meet from time to time in their different regions of the world to coalesce around specific issues and to promote their objectives. . . . aiming to change existing global structures and create a more just, equal and peaceful world order.

The NAM was founded through the efforts of Nehru (India), Tito (Yugoslavia), Soekarno (Indonesia), Nkrumah (Ghana), and Nasser (Egypt). Having escaped European colonial domination (in Tito's case, Soviet domination), and resistant to incorporation into either a "Free World" (that included former colonial masters) or a "socialist bloc" that subjected its members to strict Moscow control, the countries of the Non-aligned Movement sought to pursue common interests and ideals. Singham and Hune identify and explicate (pp. 14-30) five principles of the movement: 1) peace and disarmament; 2) independence; 3) economic equality; 4) cultural equality; 5) universalism and multilateralism through strong support for the United Nations system.

Singham and Hune, professors of political science and social science, respectively, at Brooklyn College and Medgar Evers College of the City University of New York, have imaginatively characterized the NAM as an "international social movement." Since social movements (such as the women's movement or ecology movement) are usually conceived as by definition nongovernmental, it is surprising to read the contention that the NAM "encompasses the quality of a social movement within the framework of state structures" (p. 61; cf. pp. 2-3).

Readings: for study group use

A. A.W. Singham and Shirley Hune, "Introduction," "Principles of Non-alignment," "Structure and Organization," and "Non-alignment: Retrospects and Prospects Within a Global Context," pp. 1-56 (especially 1-3, 13-35, 42-47) and 364-376 from *Non-alignment in an Age of Alignments* (1986). Total= 39-65 pp.

B. Walden Bello, "Third World Visions of a Warless World," pp. 81-93 in *Visions of a Warless World* (1986);

"The Delhi Declaration" (1985) from *Securing Our Planet*, pp. 281-284;

Parliamentarians Global Action, "Ending the Deadlock: The Political Challenge of the Nuclear Age," pp. i-ii, 1-12, 15-16 (1985; 16 pp.);

"Parliamentarians Global Action: for Disarmament, Development and World Reform" (no date; 8 pp.);

Elise Boulding, "The Rise of INGOs: New Leadership for a Planet in Transition," from *Breakthrough* (Fall '87 / Spring '88), pp. 14-17.

Total= 44 pp.

C. Lyuba Zarsky et al., "Brinksmanship in the Pacific" from *Nuclear Times* (May/June 1987), pp. 17-23;

Andre Carothers, "Loose Cannons: The Nuclear Navies and the Next War," *Greenpeace Examiner* (Oct.-Dec. 1987), pp. 7-10;

Gordon Bennett, "Is a Nuclear-Free Pacific Possible?" from *The New Abolitionists: The Story of Nuclear-Free Zones* (1987), pp. 137-161;

Carolyn M. Stephenson, "Hiroshima, the Rainbow Warrior, Chernobyl, and Beyond Chernobyl?" *The ExPro Papers* #1 (1986; 3 pp.).

Total= 37 pp.

D. John W. Dower, "America's Japan: The End of Innocence," from *The Nation* (September 12, 1987; 3 pp.);

(skim:) Karel G. van Wolferen, "The Japan Problem," from *Foreign Affairs* (Winter 1986-87; 16 pp.);

E. P. Thompson, "Beyond I.N.F.: The Peace Movement's Next Task" from *The Nation* (December 12, 1987); 2 pp.;

Richard Falk and Mary Kaldor, "Introduction," pp. 1-27 from Kaldor and Falk, eds., *Dealignment: A New Foreign Policy Perspective* (1987).

Total= 47 pp.

E. Sara Miles, "The Real War: Low Intensity Conflict in Central America" *NACLA Report on the Americas* (April-May 1986), pp. 17-46 (especially 17-25, 40-46);

David Freedman, "Low-Intensity Warfare," *The Nonviolent Activist* (October-November 1988), pp. 11-13;

Noam Chomsky, "Is Peace at Hand?" from *Zeta Magazine* (January 1988), pp. 6-14;

Carole Collins, "Voices from Apartheid's Other War," (American Friends Service Committee, 1987; 14 pp.).

Total= 39-52 pp.

Yet Singham and Hune show the NAM does resemble more typical social movements in significant respects: its "non-hierarchical, rotational, and inclusive" administrative style ("providing all member states regardless of size and importance with an opportunity to participate in global decision-making") and its use of consensus decision-making at its periodic summit conferences.[2]

Because it provides a unique setting in which small and middle-sized countries can unite around common interests, the NAM's make-up has broadened so that it now includes pro-West "dependent capitalist" and Marxist-Leninist states as well as those that originally composed it. This diversity has made for political strains that have required adept management, sometimes by deferral of overly controversial issues in the cause of maintaining unity. The NAM should certainly not be idealized; anyone searching for the less attractive aspects of political dealing can certainly find them in it. But the NAM has exercised needed leadership in efforts to reduce global inequality and promote peace; for example, its members were "primarily responsible for calling the two [1978 and 1982 U.N.] Special Sessions on Disarmament" (p. 28).

In the final section of their book Singham and Hune assess the past and future of the Non-aligned Movement and other global actors. They do not conceive the NAM as confronting a unified hostile antagonist in the industrialized countries. Noting the positions of the U.S.'s Rainbow Coalition, the Scandinavian countries, the Western European peace movements, and others, Singham and Hune see "the potential of a coalition emerging of progressive forces within the U.S. and Europe to develop a new policy towards the non-aligned and the Third World."

The evolution of the Non-aligned Movement, traced in greater detail in the whole of Singham and Hune's book, affords an intriguing foretaste of genuine global politics; it reflects the real complexities of a diverse world in ways that make the two-sided Cold War seem not only dangerous but boring.

Building a Peace System

Walden Bello, in his chapter on "Third World Visions of a Warless World," summarizes the principles of the Non-aligned Movement and quotes from statements of the Special Sessions on Disarmament endorsing the establishment of "nuclear-free zones" in Africa, the Middle East, and South Asia, and "zones of peace" in Southeast Asia and the Indian Ocean. Bello, a citizen of the Philippines, also criticizes the NAM's support for nuclear energy and the way a majority of the non-aligned countries use the greater evil of the nuclear arms race as an excuse to justify their own national conventional arms build-ups. He praises, by way of contrast, the tiny Micronesian nation of Palau, which ("while disarmament and peace were being bureaucratized in NAM and U.N. councils") adopted a constitution rejecting nuclear weapons and other specified "harmful substances." Without the "sense of wonder and respect for nature" that Bello finds in the Palauans, an indigenous people with a culture and economy that cooperate with nature, he believes "the movement for peace will stand on fragile foundations."[3]

The evolution of the Non-aligned Movement affords an intriguing foretaste of genuine global politics.

The "Delhi Declaration," signed on January 28, 1985, calls for an "all-embracing halt to the testing, production and deployment of nuclear weapons, . . . [to] be immediately followed by substantial reductions in nuclear forces" and eventually by their complete elimination. Issued by the heads of state of India, Argentina, Mexico, Tanzania, Greece, and Sweden (acting as "the Five Continent Peace Initiative"), and directed to the nuclear weapons states, the Declaration urges the transfer of resources from arms spending to social and economic development, expresses "determination to facilitate agreement among the nuclear weapons states," and advocates "general and complete disarmament," the strengthening of the U.N., and the pursuit of "common security." The six leaders further assert that "Progress in disarmament can only be achieved with an informed public applying strong pressure on governments. Only then will governments summon the necessary political will to overcome the many obstacles which lie in the path of peace."

The Delhi statement was prepared at the initiative of Parliamentarians Global Action, a group of more than 600 legislators from 36 countries, "representing the full spectrum of political parties," who have formed a worldwide network to "press for an end to the arms race and to help build a more just and secure international system." The group, founded in 1980 as Parliamentarians for World Order, advocates creation of a "system of world institutions to guarantee disarmament, prevent international aggression, protect the 'global commons' and ensure a sufficient transfer of resources between the rich and poor nations to abolish hunger once and for all."

The Five Continent Peace Initiative and the other actions of the Parliamentarians represent efforts to organize parts of the generally unorganized global constituency for peace. The Parliamentarians have circulated a "Call for Global Survival," signed so far by over a thousand parliamentarians in 55 countries on behalf of over 50 million constituents, that calls for a "world peace force" and other measures. Proposals taken from the Call have been introduced into the parliaments of Australia,

Canada, Iceland, India, Jamaica, Kenya, New Zealand, Nigeria, the United Kingdom, the United States, and the European Parliament. According to the group, "this was the first time legislators have stood up simultaneously around the world to introduce common proposals for peace." By creating a new vehicle for coordinated political action, the Parliamentarians group has opened up new possibilities; for example, U.S. citizens could urge their Congressional representatives to become active participants in the group, as at least three U.S. Congresspersons already have.

As indicated in the introduction to Part Three of this book, Elise Boulding has identified the twentieth-century expansion of international nongovernmental organizations (INGOs) as representing "a major shift in the nature of the international system." In "The Rise of INGOs," excerpted from her *Building a Global Civic Culture* (1988), she writes that though "small and poor compared to nation-states," these "people's associations" have "a lot of human know-how," whether they are service clubs, professional associations, peace groups, or religious bodies. The newer INGOs tend to be

> *U.S. citizens could urge their Congressional representatives to become active participants in Parliamentarians Global Action.*

> less hierarchically organized and more aware of local needs . . . emphasizing skill and information sharing and local-global coordination. . . . They are by nature future-oriented . . . and have some vision, however modest, of a world community. . . . [Since 1972] INGOs have been playing an increasingly important role at each major U.N. special-topic conference [including those on the environment, population, hunger, technology, the status of women, and disarmament].

INGOs now link indigenous peoples, consumer movements, and self-help community development efforts on all continents; INGOs in the social and natural sciences and humanities have increased understanding of

> the linkages between development, environmental conservation, cultural autonomy, free two-way information flows, and disarmament. . . . By maintaining vigilance, facilitating discourse and enabling people to work together, the international people's organizations are playing a vital role in the shaping of our global future.

"The United States has entered the Pacific Age. Since 1978 more American trade has crossed the Pacific Ocean than the Atlantic: after more than 350 years, the Atlantic Age is coming to an end." Thus began a 1984 article in *World Policy Journal.*[4] While trade figures need not dictate how we define our reality, this statement does highlight a shift in the balance of world economic power toward East Asia, one more fully recognized by the business press than by peace activists.

Despite the bitter fighting in the Pacific theater during World War II and the major impact of the Korean and Vietnam wars, three related factors — the United States's history as a country mainly populated by people of European and African descent, the language "barriers" to easy communication with East Asian societies, and the traditionally dominant role in U.S. society played by the people of its northeastern, Atlantic-facing coast — all incline the U.S. to be more attuned to Europe than to Asia and the Pacific. Although this imbalance is beginning to diminish because of economic and demographic changes — consider California and Hawaii, with their large Asian-American populations — most U.S. peace activists, if asked to name a symbol of the Cold War, would be more likely to name the Berlin Wall than the Korean Demilitarized Zone.

Yet, as Lyuba Zarsky, Peter Hayes, and Walden Bello point out in "Brinksmanship in the Pacific," an excerpt from their book *American Lake*,[5] South Korea contains "the only American soldiers in the world who remain on a war footing 24 hours a day." In the Pacific Ocean itself, U.S. and Soviet nuclear-armed ships and submarines trail each other, and although the Soviet Union is distinctly in second place in its abilities to wage conventional war — it has no aircraft carriers, for example, compared to the six the U.S. has there — both sides have enormous nuclear firepower. The world's nuclear navies, which because of the difficulty of long-range underwater communication are necessarily under less strict control than land-based nuclear weapons, are considered by some analysts (as a *Greenpeace Examiner* article reports) as the most likely sources of World War III.

The world's nuclear navies are considered by some analysts as the most likely sources of World War III.

All this means that people concerned to build a peace system must not ignore the Pacific Basin. In *The New Abolitionists: The Story of Nuclear-Free Zones*, Gordon Bennett asks "Is a Nuclear-Free Pacific Possible?" He recounts the efforts of people throughout the Pacific, including New Zealand, Japan, the South Pacific Forum (an alliance of governments), and the Nuclear Free and Independent Pacific Network, to eliminate nuclear weapons from their region.

Nuclear testing by the U.S., Britain, and France, with its immediate and delayed health effects, has been a growing concern since the 1950s. "In 1973," Bennett reports, "New Zealand took France to the World Court on the nuclear testing issue and won [but] the French kept on testing," posing the problem of enforcement we have noted earlier in this book. Only as a result of continued protests, often involving nonviolent direct action by Greenpeace and others, did the French stop their atmospheric testing. This provides an example of tenacious popular action supplementing the present inadequacy of established global legal institutions.

Carolyn Stephenson, a professor of political science at the University of Hawaii and active in Pacific peace efforts, writes in "Hiroshima, the Rainbow Warrior, Chernobyl, and Beyond Chernobyl?" about the implications of those three events, spelling out concisely an array of minimal steps that should be taken toward greater security.

Japan, the economic superpower of East Asia, is too often thought of only in economic terms. But U.S.-Japanese relations are unavoidably political for both countries as well.

Over the past decade, friction in the trade relationship between the United States and Japan has increasingly been accepted as an economic fact of life. But a closer look at the situation suggests that a crisis of vast proportions is brewing. A [September 1986] symposium titled "America and Japan: A Collision Course" painted a picture so grim that the moderator . . . apologized for delivering such bad news . . . . The conclusion . . . is inescapable: pressures are building toward a rupture between the United States and Japan. [The stakes are high because] the American and Japanese economies are the most powerful and dynamic in the world and are critically intertwined. There is great potential for misunderstanding and antagonism between the two nations, whose post-World War II friendship is still young and occasionally awkward. . . . A recently published research project [by] more than thirty scholars . . . suggests that structural factors, highly resistant to change, are driving the United States and Japan toward collision.[6]

It is to be hoped that these fears are exaggerated. Nevertheless, articles have already appeared in the U.S. that complain of Japanese export policies toward the U.S. as "an economic Pearl Harbor"; they suggest the potential for rekindled U.S. hostility.

The Japanese government, after prolonged U.S. pressure to spend more on "defense," has broken through the 1% (of GNP) ceiling on military spending that had long been considered inviolate. While Japan's decades of living with a peace constitution and the strength of its peace organizations and anti-nuclear sentiment may be sufficient to prevent major Japanese remilitarization in response to outside pressures, the breaching of the 1% barrier was a warning sign, and militarist possibilities cannot be entirely discounted.[7]

John Dower's award-winning *War Without Mercy: Race and Power in the Pacific War* (1986) detailed how racism on both sides prolonged and intensified World War II combat in the Pacific. In "America's Japan: The Loss of Innocence," Dower notes that "the continued existence of positive American attitudes toward Japan deserves emphasis." But he summarizes recent discussions of "Japan's Troubled Future" and the "trade crisis" from *Fortune, Newsweek,* and the *Journal of Japanese Studies* that suggest the Japanese will find it "difficult if not impossible to restructure their domestic economy in ways that seriously contribute to rectifying trade and investment imbalances." Many Japanese, not surprisingly, feel that "rectification" is not their responsibility; they "maintain that Americans are simply making scapegoats of the Japanese for problems of their own making" (a position with important truth in it). Such feelings have contributed to "a rising tide of neonationalism and outright racial arrogance" that in turn elicit resentment from some in the U.S.

"Such a situation," Dower concludes, "in which seemingly intractable material problems have become so intertwined with national pride and visceral emotions, offers little room for optimism." Dutch journalist Karel G. van Wolferen presents a lengthier discussion of "The Japan Problem" to the elite readers of *Foreign Affairs.* The accuracy of his analysis and the merits of his prescription (a tougher U.S. policy stance toward Japan) are less significant than two other aspects of his article. First, he underscores the concern that

The relationship between the world's two greatest economic powers is in serious trouble. With a frightening momentum economic disputes between Japan and the United States are growing into a political conflict. . . . [that could lead to U.S. trade legislation that could produce] uncontrollable consequences in Japan, including political instability and a xenophobic reaction.

Second, the article serves as a sample of the kinds of non-military problems likely to be more typical in the future during the period before full transition to a peace system with a stabler, less crisis-prone (and eventually steady-state) economy.

The articles discussed here serve to highlight a troubled relationship presently receiving minimal attention from the U.S. peace movement. Part of building a peace system is identifying and addressing developing conflicts before they get to the point of war. (Though it is admittedly difficult to imagine U.S.-Japan conflict leading to war — and this difficulty is itself a positive sign — economic conflict involving those two countries might have its worst effects in indirectly generating suffering and war in third countries.)

Part of building a peace system is identifying and addressing developing conflicts before they get to the point of war.

The U.S. peace movement has come to understand the value of "sister cities" and other links with people in the Soviet Union and Central America. Similar links with people in Japan might now be an important new step.[8] Stronger connections with the Japanese peace movement itself, involving dialogue on the economic and cultural changes both countries need to make to function harmoniously in a stable, ecologically-sound world economy, would be highly desirable.[9] Destructive conflict is not inevitable. Each country has much to teach the other, and much to learn from the rest of the world about the conditions of peace.

Divided Europe has long been the chief symbol and reference point of the Cold War. The European peace movements that gained prominence in the early 1980s helped limit military spending increases, spawned a great deal of creative thinking about security, helped inspire peace activity in the U.S., and influenced the strategies of the superpowers.

In "Beyond I.N.F.: The Peace Movement's Next Task" British historian E. P. Thompson points out that the superpowers have now begun discussing peace movement proposals dismissed until recently as "impractical and extremist"; consequently, "this is a moment to enlarge our demands." Thompson, a founder of European Nuclear Disarmament and a principal author of its April 1980 Appeal, reflects that a similar appeal today would put more emphasis on conventional weapons and on the relation of European concerns to global nonaligned strategies. He believes that "The European and North American peace movements can realize their objectives only as partners within a global shift to nonalignment."

Although he praises the Soviets' lengthy unilateral moratorium on nuclear testing, Thompson considers that the superpowers have so far achieved less toward peace than Palau and nuclear-free New Zealand. Cold war ideologues may yet engineer the destruction of civilization. But it nevertheless seems clear that "We have come to the end of the cold war epoch . . . . The transition . . . from global, bipolar confrontation through polycentric diplomacies to cooperation will entail moments of heightened tension . . . . There is going to be work enough for peace movements to do." But, he concludes (with pride), "Human consciousness has changed and we have helped to change it. This has redrawn and enlarged the limits of the politically possible. Everywhere, and on both sides, people know that a profound change is about to come."

By 1986 there had developed a substantial discussion among Europeans on ways "to denuclearize European defense policies (East and West) and make them visibly defensive and non-threatening to neighboring states." The Alternative Defence Commission (a British group that was one of the chief inspirations for ExPro, and whose 1983 book *Defence Without the Bomb* had a major influence on the defense and security position adopted by the Labour Party in 1984) expressed the view that possibly "world peace will be better served by a 'de-aligned' Europe that stands outside the superpower bipolar confrontation and acts as a moderating and reconciling force."[10]

In their Introduction to *Dealignment: A New Foreign Policy Perspective* (1987), a book that grew out of a 1983 conference on "Dealignment for Western Europe?" Richard Falk and Mary Kaldor (the latter a British scholar active with European Nuclear Disarmament) discuss the prospects for "letting go of the rigid postwar alliance arrangements . . . [and] gradually building a new consensus around respect for pluralism and tolerance for a variety of social experiments." They make their conception of dealignment more concrete by specifying five dimensions of it: denuclearization, demilitarization, depolarization, democratization, and development. Even though they feel it is "probably true to say that a geo-political shift has been taking place from Europe to the Pacific, [nevertheless Europe] still retains a pivotal psychological importance as a theatre of war and a source of ideological conflict."

Some European countries, including not only the Scandinavian countries but also such members (respectively) of NATO and the Warsaw Pact as Greece and Romania, have shown interest in closer ties to the Non-aligned Movement. In their contribution to the Kaldor/Falk volume, Singham and Hune, while acknowledging that "it could be important to develop a new framework to foster dealignment and non-alignment globally," suggest "an alternative strategy [that] would be to develop links between transnational social movements within both the developed and the underdeveloped world. Such transnational movements could insist on a new concept of national and global security" and link the peace movement with movements for social justice. They conclude that "while the political success of such a movement seems far away, the process has certainly begun."[11]

Building a Peace System

Lest we too hastily shift our thinking toward a better future as if it already existed and gloss over ugly facts that must be dealt with here and now, Sara Miles's report on "The Real War: Low Intensity Conflict in Central America" describes how the doctrine of "low-intensity conflict" ("LIC") has been developed as "a new instrument for establishing U.S. political control in the Third World." In some respects like the "counter-insurgency" doctrine with which the U.S. approached the Vietnam War, LIC combines military with non-military measures, subordinating the former to the latter (at least in theory). It involves use of economic aid, training of officials, and "civic development" in a kind of integrated "psychological warfare" that blurs the distinction between military and civilian activity.[12] Attempting not only to beat guerrillas at their own game but to seize the offensive, it is, Miles writes, "a science of warfare whose goal of controlling the qualitative aspects of human life merits the term 'totalitarian.'"

Superpower detente continually risks foundering in the Third World.

Miles shows that "humanitarian" or "non-lethal" aid functions just like military aid in serving the larger purposes of low-intensity conflict strategy: the waging of "total war at the grassroots level," in the words of one advocate. Although low-intensity conflict derives its name from not involving all-out effort by the country applying it, there is nothing low about its intensity for the victims.

Two major points should be made about low-intensity conflict. First, such warfare is anticommunist ideology at the operational level, defined as a permanent war against communism. It has been said that the U.S. and Soviets really have no important conflicts. But the perennial determination of those who predominantly shape U.S. foreign policy to prevent change with a major — or even a scarcely detectible — Communist element is a continual source of conflict whenever the forces under attack turn to the Soviet Union or Soviet-allied governments (e.g., Cuba) for aid — or even if they don't. For the most impassioned U.S. crusaders, world politics is a zero-sum game: our loss is automatically a Soviet gain. If the Soviet Union isn't actually involved, it might as well be, from this perspective, and hence some may feel little compunction about suggesting that (as Harvard political scientist Samuel Huntington has put it) "you may have to . . . create the misimpression that it is the Soviet Union that you are fighting."[13] Superpower detente continually risks foundering in the Third World.

Second, the crusade against any social change in the Third World that could threaten U.S. corporate prerogatives, either immediately or ultimately, is necessarily linked with a campaign at home to win the hearts and minds of the U.S. public to fanatical anti-communism. Efforts to organize "private sector" "humanitarian" aid for the Nicaraguan *contras* and anti-Communist guerrillas from Angola to Afghanistan are a way of developing a climate of support for war in the Third World, seeking to give such wars a more morally acceptable face. Such domestic support is being sought by right-wingers to counteract the sizable opposition to wars in Central America and elsewhere from "the peace movement, anti-intervention and solidarity activists, sectors of the churches and the human rights community." As David Freedman reminds us in his concise article "Low-Intensity

Warfare," the LIW/LIC doctrine has corollaries at home: gathering of intelligence on peace activists by police forces and (since authorization by Reagan in December 1984) by CIA, Defense Department, and military intelligence units. CIA domestic psychological warfare also includes use of public relations firms to influence U.S. opinion, along with creation of phony "incidents" ("Nicaragua Invades Honduras"; "Soviet MIGS Shipped to Nicaragua") timed to sway Congressional votes.

Although LIC strategy calls for ruthless assassination and bombing where they are useful, it attempts "to *avoid* high levels of violence." As Miles observes, "It is much harder to oppose U.S. efforts to control Third World societies if they involve non-military tactics, or forms of warfare that claim to promote economic development." More sophistication is needed from the U.S. public if we are to be able to carry out our responsibility to compel our government to let other societies make their own choices about how they are organized — in peace.

The need for such sophistication runs headfirst into the subservience of the U.S. mass media to the U.S. government's definition of issues. Appearing in the left-wing monthly *Zeta Magazine*, Noam Chomsky's "Is Peace At Hand?" compares U.S. press coverage of the Central America ("Arias") Peace Plan with the realities of that region. Chomsky shows that for the U.S. press the chief issue has been whether Nicaragua is complying with the plan's terms, even though the Sandinista government has complied much more fully than the U.S. or the regimes it backs in El Salvador or Honduras.

Far less familiar than Central America for many in the U.S. are the conditions in southern Africa. "Voices from Apartheid's Other War," by Carole Collins of the American Friends Service Committee, provides a brief overview of "South Africa's aggression against its neighbors" Namibia, Mozambique, Angola, Botswana, and Zambia. Apartheid is often thought of as a problem in one country; but Collins's report illustrates how one unsolved conflict can spread to hurt people in a larger area. The report's photograph of a man whose ear and nose were cut off by the South Africa-backed RENAMO forces — we will not quote here from even more horrifying verbal accounts — can serve to remind us of the brutality and suffering emanating from a regime still backed by the U.S. and British governments. The U.S.-supported "freedom fighters" of UNITA, laying mines in Angolan fields, have not produced freedom, but their efforts do not lack for results: Angola has the largest number of amputees per capita in the world.

Proponents of peace cannot be satisfied with progress toward U.S.-Soviet detente; while desirable, it is no substitute for ending wanton destruction of human life in other parts of the world.

Chapter 11:
Making Changes:
Analyses and Approaches

Johan Galtung has observed that "Typically proposals for transition focus on what should be done and why it should be done — but not on who should do it, how and when and where. What is missing is the actor-designation (whether of *actual* or *potential* actors); a clear image of the *transition path,* including the first steps; and some idea of the *concrete context.*" Galtung does not mean "that proposals that fall short of these criteria are worthless, even when the receiver remains anonymous and 'somebody should do something' is the whole message. A proposal of that kind is like a cry, . . . incomplete rather than wrong."[1]

We have tried in this book to go beyond saying "somebody should build a peace system." Chapters 3, 9, and 10 (and to varying degrees, many of the others) of this book have sought to indicate the concrete context from which efforts to build a peace system must proceed. More context is added in this and the other chapters remaining in Part Three. The most immediate audience and actor to which we address our peace system approach is the U.S. peace movement — which we define broadly[2] — and through it, everyone we can reach who is concerned about peace. Many of the needed steps are already being taken, as the following pages show.

• • •

Anyone wanting to build a global peace system will hope that the U.S. government could come to play a more positive role. Yet the experience of seeing that government fail to implement the overwhelmingly supported Nuclear Freeze must raise questions in anyone's mind about the workings of democracy in the U.S.

Why is it so hard to change government policies in this society? In their concise booklet *Rules of the Game,* Joshua Cohen and Joel Rogers offer a clear, enlightening explanation of three kinds of obstacles to majority rule in the U.S.: historical factors, the nature of the electoral and party system, and recent changes in the party system. By historical factors are meant long-time features of American life that tend to fragment society's capacity to act together, including the Constitution's checks and balances (designed to temper majority rule that might threaten the propertied); the enormous size of the country and consequent differences in regional interests; racial, ethnic, and religious diversity; and government repression of groups seeking change.

The second obstacle is the electoral and party system. The U.S. system of presidential elections and winner-take-all elections based on states and districts leads to a system with two parties (only one more than the Soviet Union, Europeans have commented) "that attempt to blur their differences in order to win the voters in the middle."[3] By way of contrast, with proportional representation as in West Germany, if 5 per cent or more of the public support a party (like the Greens), candidates on their slate get 5 per cent of the seats in the parliament. In the U.S., they get nothing. Third parties in the U.S. — over a thousand have been started[4] — rarely elect anyone and consequently millions of people have no one in Congress adequately representing their views. That's the way the system works.

Readings: for study group use

A. Joshua Cohen and Joel Rogers, *Rules of the Game: American Politics and the Central America Movement* (1986), pp. 1-43;

Rick Jahnkow, "Electoral Politics: Progress or Pitfall?" from *The Nonviolent Activist* (March 1987); 2 pp.

Total= 45 pp.

B. Paula Rayman, "Labor and Disarmament: The Meeting of Social Movements," pp. 188-204; and

Jack O'Dell, "Racism: Fuel for the War Machine," pp. 120-121, 127-8, 135-141, 144-153; (21 pp.); both in Michael Albert and David Dellinger, eds., *Beyond Survival: New Directions for the Disarmament Movement* (1983);

Jobs with Peace Campaign, "A National Budget for Jobs with Peace" and "Jobs with Peace: A Healthy Economy in a Peaceful World" (1987; ca 6 pp.);

Cong. Ronald V. Dellums, "Dellums Defense Alternative" budget, *Congressional Record* (May 5, 1987); 4 pp.

Total= 47 pp.

C. Daniel Deudney, "Forging Missiles into Spaceships," *World Policy Journal* (Spring 1985), pp. 271-303; and exchange with Marcy Darnovsky, *World Policy Journal* (Fall 1985; 6 pp.). Total= 39 pp.

D. Jeb Brugmann and Michael Shuman, "Thinking Globally, Acting Locally" in *Nuclear Times* (May-June 1987; 3 pp.);

"New Partnership Forged in Nevada Desert," *Bulletin of Municipal Foreign Policy*, II:1 (Winter 1987-88); 2 pp.);

Alan and Hanna Newcombe, "Mundialization: World Community at the Doorstep: Citizen Taxes for the U.N., Mundialization, and Town-Twinning as a Way to Peace" from Israel Charny, ed., *Strategies Against Violence: Design for Nonviolent Social Change* (1978; 17 pp.);

The New Abolitionist: sample issue and other items from Nuclear Free America.

Total= 22 pp. plus additional material.

E. Liane Norman, "The 'Politics of Love' in the Cause of Peace" from *The Center Magazine* (March/April 1984; 11 pp.);

"The Nonviolent Alternative: An Interview with Liane Norman" from *The Center Magazine* (January/February 1987; 6 pp.);

Paul Goodman, "A. J. Muste and People in Power" from *Liberation* (November 1967; 5 pp.);

Daniel Ellsberg, affidavit prepared for *U.S. v. David Biviano et al.* (October 11, 1986; 11 pp.);

John Swomley, "Stopping Nuclear War with Little Boats" from *The Christian Century* (September 24, 1986; 2 pp.).

Total= 35 pp.

With viable campaigns limited to those that get major financial support (which comes overwhelmingly from the wealthier strata of society), candidates of both parties have an incentive to compete to serve the priorities of the wealthy. But don't the voters ultimately decide?

In the U.S. relatively few people vote. A comparison with 19 other industrialized democracies shows that over half have turnouts ranging between 81 and 94 per cent of the voting age population; the laggards range from 78 down to 62 per cent. The U.S. is in a class by itself at 52.6 per cent — there is more of a gap between it and the second lowest than between any of the others.[5]

Voting in the U.S. is class-skewed: the wealthier are more likely to vote. And thus "the most natural constituency for democratic change [those who are poor and thus benefit least from the status quo] is least active" (p. 2). "In terms of electoral participation the U.S. was far more democratic—both on its own terms, and in comparison to Europe—in the 19th century than it is today" (p. 24). Laws passed in the 1890s reduced voter participation, and further decline has been occurring more recently.

One analyst finds "a growing inability of the political system to represent . . . the interests of the bottom three-fifths of society." Why so few in the U.S. vote may be illuminated by "A 1984 *Times/ CBS* poll [that] showed that 49% of the public thought the government was run 'by a few big interests looking out for themselves,' while 40% believed that government is run for the benefit of all the people." This suggests that about half the population holds views usually considered "left-wing" or "cynical."[6]

With Franklin Roosevelt's New Deal came an increase in voter participation, and his electoral coalition inaugurated what can be called a "center-left party system"; but "the past few years have seen the emergence of a center-right one." Why this change? Despite thousands of articles during the 1980s on "America's turn to the right," Cohen and Rogers contend that

> There is no evidence in opinion surveys that the public endorses social welfare cuts of the sort that have been put through in the past few years, or regressive tax changes, or rollbacks in environmental or health and safety legislation enforcement, or a military buildup on the scale that has been achieved, or increased U.S. intervention abroad.
>
> Rather, . . . the shift to the right was precipitated by a realignment of American business elites in the face of a changing international environment. Such figures comprise the most powerful forces in both parties . . . . [7]

An influential school of thought in political science[8] has defined democracy crudely in yes-or-no terms: are there periodic elections in which voters can choose between competing candidates? A sounder view of democracy is that it is a matter of degree; and, as industrialized democracies go, the United States isn't very democratic.

Democracy is a matter of degree; and as industrialized democracies go, the United States isn't very democratic.

Rick Jahnkow's "Electoral Politics: Progress or Pitfall?" gives a refreshingly undogmatic discussion of the often-debated question of how political activists should best relate to elections. Jahnkow reminds us that there is a range of options larger than either working for candidates or trying to ignore elections while doing grassroots education and agitation. He argues that candidates' positions, and election winners' behavior in office, are mainly influenced by the balance of forces in society, and therefore that (in Michael Albert's words) "electoral gains can be promoted most effectively as by-products of more general consciousness raising, demonstrating, direct actions, organization building, etc., rather than by making [electoral gains] our primary focus." Jahnkow concludes that electoral activity should not be ruled out, but may be effective chiefly in citizen-initiated referenda or some local elections.

The difficulty of achieving objectives through electoral politics helps to explain why so many "movements" have developed — often using unorthodox strategies and tactics — in U.S. politics. In "Labor and Disarmament: The Meeting of Social Movements," sociologist Paula Rayman discusses some of the problems and potentials involved in collaboration between different movements. The dominant organization of the U.S. labor movement, the AFL-CIO, has been committed to Cold War politics and unwilling to challenge corporate priorities in foreign affairs.[9] Peace movement organizations have been predominantly middle class in their membership and not readily sensitive to the issues confronting either labor unions and their members or working class people more generally.

Yet if either workers or middle-class peace activists want to win their objectives in a political system that poses obstacles, it makes sense for them to seek ways of forming alliances. Rayman suggests that common ground can be found in pursuit of "economic conversion — the transfer of machinery, skills, labor power and resources from military production to production [for] civilian needs"; the latter is less prone to the boom-and-bust cycles of weapons production and thus a more reliable source of employment. Rayman describes "conversion projects" from several parts of the country that are exploring alternative uses for military production facilities.[10]

A second approach to alliance — combining the predominantly middle-class orientation to "human rights" with U.S. workers' concern to avoid losing jobs to underpaid foreign workers — is represented by recent efforts to attach "workers' rights" provisions to trade-related federal legislation. Rather than U.S. workers giving up established rights and benefits to keep their jobs, a bill such as the Omnibus Trade Act of 1988 aids foreign workers in gaining comparable rights and benefits by defining as an "unfair trading practice" any competitive advantage gained by a country through denying internationally recognized workers' rights to organize, bargain, improve working conditions, etc. The legislation "directs the president to make it a primary U.S. objective to negotiate an agreement . . . that keeps denial of workers' rights from being used to gain a competitive advantage."[11] Pressure from middle-class activists to see that such mandates are carried out could help U.S. working people gain the breathing space they need in order to attend more to the changes needed for global peace.

Local chapters of Jobs With Peace seek to unite labor unions, peace groups, low-income groups and civil rights organizations around a common agenda.

The National Jobs With Peace Campaign works "to redirect federal funds from military spending towards pressing domestic needs, such as jobs in health care, housing, education, transportation and other civilian industries," toward the goal of "A Healthy Economy in a Peaceful World." Its local chapters seek to unite labor unions, peace groups, low-income groups and civil rights organizations around a common agenda. Over 2 million people in 86 cities and towns have voted "yes" in its referenda favoring cuts in the military budget and more spending on human needs. Its brochure "A National Budget for Jobs With Peace" spells out specifically what military spending the Campaign considers unnecesary and why, and lists sixteen alternative domestic programs on which it proposes the money saved be spent.

A photograph of Jobs With Peace's Coordinating Committee and national staff shows it has developed a more multiracial organization than most peace organizations, presumably as a result of its deliberate efforts to carry out a strategy oriented to perceived common interests that cross racial divisions. In "Racism: Fuel for the War Machine," Jack O'Dell, Director of International Affairs for Operation PUSH (founded by Jesse Jackson) and one of the staff organizers for the huge June 12, 1982 peace demonstration in New York City, discusses a host of related themes. He observes that some white peace movement leaders express "apprehension that really involving the Afro-American and Latin communities in building the bridge between peace and human needs concerns would cause the traditional peace organizations to 'lose control' or 'be taken over' by these 'militant' constituencies. While such attitudes expressed by white peace activists are not always motivated by racism, the organizational results are the same as if they were."

O'Dell surveys the U.S. history of oppressive treatment of racial minority groups at home[12] and of similar racist policies toward colonized people abroad, as in the Philippines, the Panama Canal Zone, and Puerto Rico. In his section on "'Master Race' Politics in the Atomic Age," he notes the U.S. vetoes of U.N. resolutions for independence for African colonies, and the U.S. partnership with South Africa. Outlining the extensive and growing involvement of black organizations in foreign policy issues, he also affirms the need for a "synthesis of peace and human needs issues" because "The goals of the human needs movement will not be met short of drastic reduction in the military budget, and the goals of the disarmament movement will require the massive involvement of those constituencies involved in struggle for the various human needs issues. . . . Such unity serves mutual self-interest" (p. 145).

If the Black Caucus's positions were to prevail, U.S. foreign and defense policy would be distinctly more peaceful.

Congressman Ronald V. Dellums of California, a member of the House Armed Services Committee and of the Congressional Black Caucus, has annually since 1982 (in 1986 with fellow Armed Services member Patricia Schroeder of Colorado) introduced an alternative defense budget into Congress.[13] The bill has provided a useful point of reference (it is drawn on both in the Women's International League for Peace and Freedom's *Women's Budget* and by Jobs With Peace). In 1987 Dellums deplored the absence of serious defense debate in Congress and, declining to submit a full alternative budget for vote, instead submitted a short statement outlining the goals of his alternative approach, including reducing the risk of nuclear war, cutting forces committed to Third World intervention, reducing the number of U.S. troops abroad, and establishing new programs for economic conversion and military toxic waste cleanup.

While Dellums's work on defense is particularly noteworthy, the public stands and voting records of the Congressional Black Caucus as a whole are similarly preferable to those of Congress's white majority. Most white peace activists are too little aware that if the Black Caucus's positions were to prevail, U.S. foreign and defense policy would be distinctly more peaceful.

A different sort of "economic conversion" is represented by Daniel Deudney's "Forging Missiles into Spaceships." Deudney proposes that the peace movement and other progressives advocate U.S.-Soviet space cooperation as a way of channeling technical energies and bureaucratic inertia away from military projects like Star Wars and toward something beneficial. Deudney suggests a two-part program of 1) deep-space pioneering and 2) global habitability studies and information security. The former, including a joint moon base and trips to Mars, would be "expensive, bold, and visible" yet benign: "Star Trek instead of Star Wars." Global habitability research would expand knowledge of climate, weather, pollution, earthquake warning, etc. Information security projects would extend the peace-enhancing functions of present satellites that serve to verify compliance with international agreements and aid crisis communications.

Deudney notes that space expenditures have in the 1970s and 1980s been generally viewed by the peace movement as wasting money that is needed for human needs. Yet he argues that lack of a progressive agenda for space has ceded it to the right-wingers who thought up Star Wars, and that "large-scale [U.S.-Soviet space] cooperation could create its own momentum and exploit, rather than futilely resist, the advance of technology."

Deudney acknowledges that eradicating "nuclearism" will take moral fervor; but argues that a post-nuclear vision of a positive role for advanced technology is needed. A "highly visible . . . cooperative enterprise in space could create a counterweight to the endless self-fulfilling expectations of inevitable conflict."

Many issues are inherent in the assumptions and logic of Deudney's proposal, and an exchange of letters between Marcy Darnovsky and Deudney serves to clarify them. The space cooperation proposal leaves intact and unchallenged many aspects of the war system, targeting just one — superpower antagonism — for remedy; precisely for this reason, it is one peace-related proposal that might conceivably be undertaken by a U.S. President in the near-term future.

Local governments have begun to have a growing impact on U.S. foreign policy.

Jeb Brugmann is field coordinator for Local Elected Officials for Social Responsibility and former director of the Cambridge (Mass.) Peace Commission; Michael Shuman is President of the Center for Innovative Diplomacy. In their article "Thinking Globally, Acting Locally," they write that "'Municipal foreign policies,' once dismissed as trivial, symbolic initiatives coming from a few radical towns, have become increasingly mainstream." Whether they are offering sanctuary to Central American refugees, refusing to participate in nuclear "crisis relocation planning," or divesting from firms doing business in South Africa, local governments have begun to have a growing impact on U.S. foreign policy.

Although many of the actions are undertaken on an issue by issue basis, Brugmann and Shuman suggest the potential that could be realized by creating permanent local government institutions for dealing with foreign affairs. They describe how the environmental movement of the 1950s and 1960s has become partly institutionalized in the national Environmental Protection Agency and counterpart commissions at state and local levels.

> Now private environmental groups are in the position of lobbying agencies that have somewhat sympathetic agendas, rather than having to create policies from scratch against wholly unsympathetic national policymakers. Municipal foreign policies hold the promise of similarly transforming the U.S. peace movement into a network of thousands of institutions, employing tens of thousands of Americans dedicated to peace.

Although that may sound improbable, in fact there are already successes to report (e.g., Chicago's City Council has created a nuclear-free zone and a conversion commission within the city's Department of Economic Development), enough that the Center for Innovative Diplomacy now publishes a sizable (the Autumn 1987 issue was 68 pages) quarterly *Bulletin of Municipal Foreign Policy*. In it one can learn that "Some 55 American cities are now forming relationships with Soviet cities (up from one in 1980), and 87 American cities are sending economic assistance to sisters in Nicaragua (double the number from four months earlier)," that over 900 cities, towns, and counties passed resolutions supporting a nuclear freeze, and that nearly 100 cities have divested from firms doing business with South Africa.[14]

In "New Partnership Forged in Nevada Desert," the Winter 1987-88 *Bulletin* describes "the coming together of local elected offficials and peace and justice activists" to commit civil disobedience at the Nevada Nuclear Weapons Test Site in December 1987. At that action Oakland Councilmember Wilson Riles, Jr. emphasized the connection between military spending and homelessness, poverty, and joblessness in U.S. cities. The "Nevada Declaration," signed by over 700 local elected officials, eloquently asserts the right and duty of cities to play a role in making foreign policy and calls for an end to all nuclear weapons testing and negotiation of a Comprehensive Test Ban Treaty. These activities offer another example of how people, blocked from achieving major policy changes through electoral politics, have found other means of action.

The creation of nuclear-free zones has been described as "the largest anti-nuclear movement in the world." Each issue of *The New Abolitionist*, the newsletter of Baltimore-based Nuclear Free America, reports on the progress of the movement (3,607 nuclear-free zone communities in 24 countries as of May 1987). In a wise recognition that two tactics are better than one (what do you do next after your locale becomes a nuclear-free zone?), NFA's Campaign for a Nuclear-Free America includes a pledge to boycott investment in and business with the Top 50 Nuclear Weapons Contractors and, as first steps, to boycott Morton Salt (made by Morton Thiokol, maker of MX, Pershing, and Trident rocket boosters) and long-distance phone companies that profit from nuclear weapons.[15]

An individual taking such actions is not alone. INFACT, now conducting a campaign to stop General Electric's production of nuclear weapons, reported in 1987 that "2 million Americans are now boycotting GE products and that 13.5 million people are aware of the campaign."[16] (INFACT is the organization that challenged Nestle's lethal infant formula marketing policies through a global boycott.) Economic tactics like these can infuse the routine actions of daily life (phoning, shopping) with small but significant peace-promoting effects on both one's own consciousness and major actors in the war system.

In "Mundialization: World Community at the Doorstep," Alan and Hanna Newcombe, peace researchers and long-time World Federalists, report on a cluster of ideas that, using an approach different from "municipal foreign policy," can likewise produce "local and early success." In "mundialization," a movement begun by Hiroshima survivors in 1945 and independently in France about the same time, a locale declares itself a "world city" and by ordinance declares its desire "to live in peace with other communities in the world under a World Government or a system of World Law or other synonym." In 1966 the Newcombes pondered how to adapt the Japanese experience of mundialization (which by 1965 had embraced localities representing 54 million people) to Canada. They hit on combining mundialization with decisions to: 1) fly the United Nations flag daily beside the national flag at City Hall; 2) raise each year, by voluntary means, a sum of money, equal to 0.01 per cent of the total taxes raised by the city, to be given to the United Nations Special Account; and 3) to "twin" (form a "sister city" relationship) with another community in another country which was mundialized on the original Japanese model or willing to become so. These measures were adopted by the Newcombes' home town, Dundas, Ontario, and have since spread to other Canadian towns.

Describing the effects of town-twinning for Dundas (its twin is Kaga, Japan), the Newcombes report a variety of small changes of behavior and attitude on the part of people who are not involved in ambitious plans to save the world but who attend Kaga-Dundas Day events, taste foreign foods, and learn that Japanese children have

Mundialization appeals to the centrist majority of the population.

snowball fights, though under different rules. Among by-products of the twinning, local "divisions between Catholics and Protestants or Christians and Jews are minimized when one is dealing with a sister city whose inhabitants do not belong to the Judaic-Christian tradition." The small changes, repeated many millions of times over, would constitute an enormous shift toward the ideal expressed in the phrase "world community." The latter half of their article analyzes experiences with mundialization, with an eye to evaluating its potential. They find that the extreme right abhors the idea; and the extreme left finds it

> too bland and mild, [for it] does not "attack" social "evils," [it] is not sufficiently "against" anything. The moderate left and centre is perhaps the most enthusiastic. The moderate right (conservatives) is usually somewhat reservedly willing to go along, and then discover to their surprise that they *are* different from the far-out conservatives who are opposed — who they previously felt were the same type of people as themselves.

The authors conclude that the "associative, unifying, integrationist, participatory type of activity associated with mundialization" (in contrast to "demonstrations and other forms of confrontation politics") appeals to the centrist majority of the population who need influencing if really profound social changes are to be made.

Liane Ellison Norman, essayist and co-director of the Pittsburgh Peace Institute, is an advocate and practitioner of nonviolence "as both a tactic and a principle." In "The 'Politics of Love' in the Cause of Peace" she describes her experience of arrest for blocking the entrance to Rockwell International, a manufacturer of components for first-strike weapons systems. With other members of the River City Nonviolent Resistance Campaign, she sought to "break through the psychological and moral numbness" that people create to shield themselves from awareness of the deadly implications of "every day's lethal business-as-usual," the preparation of atrocities beyond anything in prior human history.

Like many practitioners of nonviolent struggle, Norman cites the Nuremberg principles derived from trials of Nazi war criminals, which declared individuals morally responsible for their complicity in such matters as crimes against peace (which include the planning of war crimes such as indiscriminate mass killing). But she also cites this suggestive Pennsylvania law:

> "A person who knowingly or recklessly fails to take reasonable measures to prevent or mitigate a catastrophe, when he can do so without substantial risk to himself, commits a misdemeanor of the second degree if: (1) he knows that he is under . . . [a] legal duty to take such measures; or (2) he did or assented to the act causing or threatening the catastrophe." In other words, since we knew what we knew about both international law and the state of first-strike weapons preparation, we had a positive duty to act in accordance with that knowledge [and to spread the duty to Rockwell employees by sharing the knowledge].

As Norman recounts her experience: "Why, one of the policemen asked, do you do this? . . . We explained. One of them shook his head and said it wouldn't do any good. Over and over we encountered this hopelessness. You — we — are powerless. Objecting to nuclear weapons is useless. There was deep despair, resignation . . ."

Norman describes her group's communications with Rockwell officials, her experience of arrest and jail, and the varied reactions (support, unease, fury) of other members of her family. She reflects on the power she felt kneeling at Rockwell's doors:

> It is as if this power, once glimpsed, terrifies because it compels and thus threatens real disruptions in many daily lives. If one person can use that power, others can, too; and it scares many people to realize that they can act. . . . The problem with such small acts [as the one Norman describes] is that the civil disobedient will get into trouble . . . . My response is that we are already in trouble . . . . Living at the brink of planetary cremation is living in trouble.

In the wide-ranging interview "The Nonviolent Alternative" Liane Norman explains her views of power and defense, her political evolution, and more about the activities in which she has been involved and their consequences.

Paul Goodman (1911-1972) was one of the United States's greatest social critics. His writings (of which the best-known is *Growing Up Absurd*) were a major influence on the New Left of the 1960's. His eulogy "A. J. Muste and People in Power" (1967) is a neglected classic exposition of the logic of nonviolence.[17]

People in power, busy with their own goals, . . . tend to act in a self-centered delusion that other people do not really exist, with needs and aspirations of their own. . . . They then act out their parochial interpretation of the world without imagining that their "policy" is having flesh-and-blood consequences. . . and they deceive themselves with rationalizations about what they are doing. . . . The worst form of self-deception is not to notice altogether, to deny the existence of problems and realities.

Without confrontation, it is impossible to reason, create, solve. Things inevitably go from bad to worse. Thus, it is good for everyone if those who are hurt but shut out of attention demand attention and redress. . . . The revolt of the oppressed is salutary also for the powerful, for it shatters their illusory self-centeredness and brings them, too, back into humanity.

[Muste] did not shun conflict but sought it out. [Muste's nonviolence] was both rational and feelingful, tactical yet religious, revolutionary yet mediating. . . . In a conflict itself, nonviolence has great moral advantages. . . . For those in revolt, nonviolence prevents the spiral into brutality. It awakens not only physical but moral courage. It diminishes vindictiveness and makes future reconciliation possible. That is, nonviolent conflict is both tactical and educative.

But the chief advantage of active nonviolence is that it personalizes the conflict. It gets away from the mechanical and passional bondage of armies and strategy, mobs, castes, and classes; thus it releases fraternal feelings and creative ideas.

In the fairly short run it is the only realistic position, for the combatants are indeed brothers and will have to live together in some community or other. How? In what community? We do not know, but nonviolent conflict is the way to discover and invent it.

Although Gene Sharp, George Lakey, and others have analyzed the political efficacy of nonviolent struggle, individual or small-scale group actions are often disparaged as "merely symbolic." Paul Goodman cogently wrote that "the distinction between what is 'symbolic' and what is 'real' is a spurious one; the correct distinction is between what leads further and what does not (and to what it does lead)."[18]

The next reading addresses directly the question of the efficacy of actions as "symbolic" as one person resisting the draft. Daniel Ellsberg, a former high government official, is best known for his 1971 release of the secret Pentagon Papers to the public, exposing government lies and undermining support for the Vietnam War. In recent years he has frequently engaged in civil disobedience on nuclear issues. His October 1986 affidavit, submitted on behalf of the defense at the trial at which Amy Carter, Abbie Hoffman, and their co-defendants were acquitted for blocking CIA campus recruiting, states that

It was the specific example of Randall Kehler, whom I met in August 1969 as he prepared to go to prison for two years for refusing to cooperate with his draft board, that put in my head the question: "What can I do — non-violently, truthfully — to help end this war, if I am willing to go to jail for it?" And that question found its answer within weeks, at which point I began to copy the documentary evidence in my safe of governmental deception and law-breaking. Only a person speaking from Kehler's position, on his way to prison for choosing to confront a government evil as powerfully as he could, could have been heard by me so consequentially.

What I heard was a challenge to action that Kehler had hoped someone would hear. My reaction was precisely what most people undertaking such a course hope and intend to help cause. I learned then the power of committed, risk-taking, conscientious, non-violent direct action, because I felt its power on my own life. It is a lesson, and an effect, that I seek to pass on when I take part in such actions. I do them, and accept the costs that sometimes follow for me, because I know they can work. They worked on me.

Nor was Kehler's example the only one to have a direct role . . . . [Most people are] unaware of facts of personal experience, of the sort I have reported here, that have empirically linked actions commonly perceived as "symbolic acts of conscience" to other actions more easily recognized as socially and politically efficacious. . . . To a degree and for reasons that many judges seem not to have appreciated, symbolic acts that risk trial and imprisonment are often chosen — and properly so — for their unique and essential *efficacy.*

The deeds of nonviolent resistance mentioned by Ellsberg continue their influence when you read about them. In a 1979 interview Ellsberg spoke of how civil disobedience can alert people to the need to act to reduce the risk of nuclear war:

How does one communicate to other people the fact that they must change their lives or take risks or act? . . . It seems to take a personal example to make a very strong point: the example of someone who is changing their life or risking and acting in some committed way.

That is why I come back to the notion that to get people to do the work of publication; to get people to read it; . . . it's very useful to have this other ingredient that might seem quite unrelated; the example of committed actions of various kinds, whether they are risky disclosures by people, people risking their jobs, or civil disobedience and people going to jail. Because that motivates other people; it awakens their conscience . . . it confronts them with the fact that perhaps their values need reexamination.[19]

Nonviolent struggle is not limited to influencing the consciousness and actions of individuals. Among the effects of some campaigns, as is indicated by John M. Swomley, Jr.'s "Stopping Nuclear War with Little Boats," can be changes in national government policy. Swomley describes protests in New Zealand's Auckland harbor, beginning in 1976, which helped expand public opposition to U.S. nuclear navy visits to the point that by 1983 the incoming Labour Party "was firmly committed to nuclear-free harbors. Party officials had been involved in nonleadership roles in the boat resistance. As a lawyer, David Lange, the new Labour prime minister, had defended some of those arrested in the boat protests." One can only speculate on the extent to which first-hand witnessing of the risky harbor protests encouraged Lange and other party officials to adhere to their campaign promises to refuse future nuclear visits, rather than abandon them as do many politicians once in office.

Chapter 12:
Considering Strategies

People concerned to bring about global peace have developed a variety of distinct, though often complementary, approaches. Keeping abreast of how these approaches are being tried out, debated, and modified requires attention to an ongoing flow of reports, articles, and reviews; to the extent there is real progress, any discussion in a book eventually becomes outdated. What follows should be read with that in mind and, if possible, supplemented by the latest available readings.[1]

"A Step-by-Step Approach" by Randall Forsberg, a prime initiator of the Nuclear Freeze movement and Director of the Institute for Defense and Disarmament Studies, is excerpted from her "Confining the Military to Defense as a Strategy for Disarmament" (*World Policy Journal*, Winter 1984). She outlines seven steps leading ultimately to a world without war or national armed forces. The first step is a U.S.-Soviet bilateral nuclear freeze shutting down nuclear weapon production facilities; the second, an end to large-scale military intervention by industrialized countries (including military bases as well as use of troops or air and naval forces) in the "developing" countries. Next would come a fifty-percent cut in both nuclear and conventional NATO and Warsaw Pact forces, and in those of China and Japan.

Each step "is aimed at eliminating the least defensive, most aggressive, escalatory, and provocative aspects of the military forces and policies that remain in existence at each stage of the process." Each step is designed to be "desirable in its own right, regardless of when or even whether any of the subsequent steps are taken," and to "create a plateau of stability which can be maintained for an extended period." Forsberg's later steps include a shift to purely defensive military postures and, finally, elimination of all national armed forces and their replacement by "international peacekeeping forces."

Forsberg's remarkable vision is carefully conceived and well argued. It was out of this vision (already formulated, in its essentials, by 1979) that the massive Freeze campaign grew. The changes she outlines should surely form an important part of the transition to a peace system.

However, in the interests of developing the most effective possible strategy for peace, it is worthwhile to look for weaknesses as well as strengths in this approach. One weakness, arguably, is that six of the seven steps chiefly prescribe what someone should *stop* doing. (The exception is Step 4, calling for Third World economic development, promotion of civil liberties, and improvement of "international institutions for negotiation and peacekeeping.") Second, the initial steps are addressed to the major military powers (who "account for nearly 70% of world military spending"). Yet it is unclear what might motivate them to significantly change long-established behaviors.

Forsberg's plan brilliantly focuses on those actors at the heart of the *problem* of war, and how they should change. But it may be precisely the actors she does not focus on — the non-aligned countries, the U.N., other international institutions and associations, citizens taking various initiatives for international understanding, groups oppressed by the status quo struggling for a fair share of power, and practitioners of nonviolent direct action such as Greenpeace — to whose actions we must look for the *solution* to war.

Readings: for study group use

A. Randall Forsberg, "A Step-by-Step Approach" (1984), pp. 360-367 in *Securing Our Planet*;

Mark Sommer, "Constructing Peace as a Whole System," from *Whole Earth Review* #51 (1986; 8 pp.);

Richard Falk, Samuel S. Kim, and Saul H. Mendlovitz, "General Introduction" and introduction to "Section 9: Orientations to Transition," pp. 1-9, 559-564 from idem, eds., *Toward a Just World Order* (1982);

Rob Leavitt, "Vision Quest," *Defense and Disarmament News* (Aug.-Sept. 1987; 1 p.);

Bruce Birchard and Rob Leavitt, "A New Agenda: Common Security is the First Step on the Road to Disarmament," *Nuclear Times* (November-December 1987; 3 pp.);

Committee on Common Security, "Common Security and Our Common Future: A Call to Action" (1989; 3 pp.);

Bruce Auster, "A New Foreign Policy? Program at the Institute for Policy Studies Gives 'Security' a New Meaning," *Nuclear Times* (November-December 1987; 2 pp.).

Total= 38 pp.

B. Michael Klare, "Road Map for the Peace Movement: Getting from Here to There," from *The Nation* (June 29, 1985; 4 pp.);

Mark Satin, "Visioning Our Way Out of Here," from *New Options* (November 30, 1987; 2 pp.);

Andrea Ayvazian and Michael Klare, "Decision Time for the American Peace Movement," from *Fellowship* (September 1986; 3 pp.);

Patricia Mische, "The Soul of the Universe," pp. 113-130 in *Star Wars and the State of Our Souls* (1985);

Michael Nagler, scenario for Peace 2010 contest, from Earl Foell and Richard Nenneman, eds., *How Peace Came to the World* (1986), pp. 151-159.

Total= 35 pp.

C. Walden Bello, "Toward a Warless World," pp. 107-115 in *Visions of a Warless World* (1986);

Richard Smoke (with Willis Harman), sections on "the delegitimation of war" and "changing attitudes," plus "Recapitulation," "Some Elements of an Image," "The Plausibility of Transformative Change," "The Shape of the Next Age," "Reassessing the Possibility of Peace," and "Conclusion," pp. 62-71, 78-80, 87-99 in *Paths to Peace* (1987);

Tom Greening, "Introduction" (1986; 2 pp.);

Michael Marien, "The Transformation as Sandbox Syndrome" (1983; 8 pp.);

Marilyn Ferguson, "Transformation as Rough Draft" (1983; 2 pp.); and

Michael Marien, "Further Thoughts on the Two Paths to Transformation: A Reply to Ferguson" (1983; 8 pp.); all from Tom Greening, ed., *Politics and Innocence: A Humanistic Debate* (1986), pp. 43-45, 52-59, 59-61, 61-69;

Mark Satin, "Harman: Best and Worst of the New Age" (review of Willis Harman, *Global Mind Change*), from *New Options* (December 28, 1987; 1 p.).

Total= 53 pp.

D. William H. Moyer, "The Movement Action Plan: A Strategic Framework Describing the Eight Stages of Successful Social Movements" (2nd ed., 1987; 16 tabloid-size pp.);

Robert Irwin, "Nonviolent Struggle and Democracy in American History," from *Freeze Focus* (September 1984; 2 pp.);

David Dellinger, "Introduction" to *Por Amor al Pueblo: Not Guilty! The Trial of the Winooski 44* (1986; 5 pp.);

National War Tax Resistance Coordinating Committee, brochures on war tax resistance;

Eileen Sauvageau, Karl Meyer, speeches; Nancy Brigham, interview by Lynne Weiss in *Life and Taxes* #3 (1988; 8 pp.);

World Federalist Association, "Will Uncle Sam Remain an International Outlaw?" (1987; brochure);

Robert Irwin, "Nonviolent Direct Law Enforcement" (1989; 11 pp.).

Total= 43+ pp.; counting brochures and the larger pages of the Moyer article, allow time as if reading 55-60 pp.)

E. Randall Kehler, "Thoughts on War and Patriotism," in *The ExPro Papers* #1 (1986; 5 pp.);

Mark Sommer, "Ten Strategies in Search of a Movement," *ExPro Paper* #6 (1987; 15 pp.);

"Peace is Life Work of Scarsdale Man [W. H. Ferry]" (*New York Times*, February 1, 1987; 1 p.);

Petra Kelly, "New Forms of Power: The Green Feminist View," from *Breakthrough* (Summer 1986; 1 p.);

Building a Peace System

Thirty-five authors (Pat Farren, ed.), "Movement-Building: Challenge and Opportunity," *Peacework* special issue (1986; 24 pp.);

Elvia Alvarado, "Don't be Afraid, Gringo," from *Don't Be Afraid, Gringo: A Honduran Woman Speaks from the Heart* (1987), excerpted from *Toward Freedom: Report on Non-alignment and the Developing Countries* (Oct. 1987; 1 p.).

Total= 47 pp.

Efforts to change the policies of the most militarily powerful governments through means such as education, lobbying, electoral politics, and diplomacy should not be neglected. But the success of those efforts may depend on a variety of initiatives that "outflank" those governments at the transnational (e.g., international law and institutions) and subnational (e.g., municipal) levels in order to force changes. Programs of action that move toward (and publicize) what we're in favor of as well as plans that target what we're against seem essential for mobilizing the political power needed for change.

Forsberg's more recent work,[2] seeking to shift peace movement attention to "alternative defense," is consistent with the peace system approach suggested in this book; the efforts complement each other. Forsberg's original framework can and should remain a point of reference, as she suggests, to "plan and evaluate" campaigns.

Mark Sommer's "Constructing Peace as a Whole System" grew out of a decade of "looking for a way to think about peace." Sommer begins by speaking of many "peace systems," meaning processes of interaction ranging from city traffic to local government that can include conflict "without being consumed by it." The down-to-earth dilemmas of defending garden crops from porcupines on Sommer's rural homestead suggest to him that "despite one's best intentions, there is inevitably some violence in any system of human design." But he remains convinced that "If war can be planned and organized as a system to produce harm, peace can also be planned and designed as a system to produce harmony."

Returning to the more limited usage of "peace system" adopted in this book — one global system to eliminate war permanently — Sommer offers a "sketch, necessarily very incomplete, as a means of initiating the design process." It includes four "dimensions": 1) "military transarmament" to "*mutually* protective" defenses; 2) "political integration" through a global legal system; 3) "economic conversion" away from military spending; 4) "cultural adaptation" (shifts in attitude and behavior to support coexistence among different societies). These dimensions provide a way to think about a peace system that is distinct from but overlapping with the "functional" image outlined at the beginning of this book.[3] The peace system concept is not a dogmatic formula but a still-developing idea and approach.

In their "General Introduction" to the important anthology *Toward a Just World Order* (1982), Richard Falk, Samuel Kim, and Saul Mendlovitz review three stages in the evolution of their approach to attaining a just world order. The first stage they identify with Grenville Clark and Louis Sohn's *World Peace Through World Law* (initially published in 1958 and twice revised). Clark and Sohn aimed to win the support of world leaders for a carefully conceived modification of the United Nations.

In the second stage the World Order Models Project (WOMP), with which Falk and Mendlovitz were associated from its beginning in 1968, published a series of books by scholars from different countries envisioning "Preferred Worlds for the 1990s." WOMP hoped to influence academics (and thoughtful people in "public affairs") to recognize the desirability of transforming the present world order to one that would better satisfy the values of peace, economic well-being, social justice, and ecological balance.

> *"If war can be planned and organized as a system to produce harm, peace can also be planned and designed as a system to produce harmony."*

Falk et al. describe the World Order Models Project as moving since 1978 to a third stage[4] that aims to correct their previously inadequate attention to what social forces could bring about the transition to a better world order. They have shifted their emphasis away from formal organizations, states, and international institutions and toward a "world order populism" that seeks to listen to "the voices of the oppressed" and attend more to "movements and grassroots initiatives." Their candid but unapologetic self-criticism provides ideas and criteria useful for assessing and guiding all current efforts to bring about a better world.

ExPro's efforts, particularly as presented in this book, can be seen as a further development of third-stage world order work. Some possibly distinctive elements are that: 1) its study groups are designed to encourage grassroots participation in developing visions of the future and strategies for change; 2) its study groups include experiential exercises alongside study of readings so as to tap more varied abilities and energies; 3) its efforts are beginning at a riper historical moment, introducing important new thinking from varied sources at a time when many activists are rethinking their long-term goals and strategy; and 4) it aims (with the help of study group participants) to go beyond education to developing a grassroots strategy and approach consistent with its outlook.[5]

In the introduction to the section of their book on "Orientations to Transition," Falk et al. emphasize that "an adequate conception of transition . . . must connect analysis of what is projected as preferred [i.e., a better future world] with an inquiry into the actors and social forces that might make such an outcome materialize." They summarize several strategic conceptions consistent with their approach, including: Rajni Kothari's advocacy of a "grand coalition" of progressive Third World governments and social movements in the industrialized countries; Johan Galtung's case for becoming more autonomous or "self-reliant" as a general approach to positive change at all levels; and George Lakey's five-stage model for fundamental system change (elaborated in his book *Powerful Peacemaking*). The "Questions for Discussion and Reflection" with which their introduction concludes are indeed worth discussing.

"The search for a vision to re-energize the peace movement began three years ago, just after the 1984 election," Bruce Birchard of the American Friends Service Committee and Robert Leavitt of the Institute for Defense and Disarmament Studies write in the November-December 1987 issue of *Nuclear Times*. "Resistance and protest, although essential, will not be enough." Birchard and Leavitt outline seven elements of a "common security" policy, including "strengthened international and regional institutions of peacekeeping," shifts to defensive military orientations, and other provisions consistent with the ideas of Forsberg, Sommer, and others.

Birchard and Leavitt's article, the first in a regular "alternative security" section of *Nuclear Times* inaugurated in response to reader interest, serves to illustrate the spreading belief that the peace movement would benefit from clarifying its goals. (Leavitt's article "Vision Quest," citing explorations and rethinking by a host of groups, shows how widespread that belief has become.) They suggest that to "focus on the creation of a just, demilitarized global security system could help unite a broad range of peace and justice organizations and many new constituencies . . . [and] move us away from a bipolar, U.S.-Soviet conception of the world."

"Common Security and Our Common Future: A Call to Action" (1989) states that "The fundamental principle of Common Security is that no nation can ensure its own security at the expense of another." Issued by the Committee for Common Security (initiated by Pam Solo and Paul Walker, co-directors of the Institute for Peace and International Security), this document argues that "transformation of international political life away from militarism and toward cooperative problem-solving is essential for the survival of human civilization." Echoing the titles of two major international reports, the Palme Commission's *Common Security* (1982) and the report of the World Commission on Environment and Development (Brundtland Commission), *Our Common Future* (1987), this call aims to outline policies and principles that can replace the premises of the Cold War with a visionary yet practical strategy appropriate for the world of today, and thereby "give voice to a new consensus among the American people."

Writer Bruce Auster reports on the "Real Security" program of the Institute for Policy Studies. According to IPS co-founder Richard J. Barnet, U.S. policy since World War II has rested on four security principles: 1) nuclear deterrence of Soviet aggression; 2) a system of anti-communist alliances; 3) intervention, especially in the Third World, to prevent the spread of communism; and 4) "a liberal international economic system established at Bretton Woods in 1944." Because the world has changed over four decades, Barnet believes these principles are outmoded and must be replaced. Barnet, who served as an official in the Kennedy administration, advocates a "new coherent vision" and a more comprehensive notion of security that considers the economic effects of security policies on the domestic economy's international competitiveness.

Like the World Policy Institute's Security Project,[6] IPS's Real Security program has addressed itself less to the peace movement than to Democratic presidential candidates and other politicians, hoping to influence election-year public debate. It remains to be seen whether even very moderate and "reasonable" proposals for a less belligerent U.S. world role — ones that take as given many questionable elements of the status quo — can affect government policy through the electoral process. Such proposals may, however, provide images, slogans, or concepts that can facilitate policy shifts when political developments create opportunities for change.

Michael Klare's 1985 article, "Road Map for the Peace Movement: Getting from Here to There," was written, like Birchard and Leavitt's, with the view that the peace movement needs a new approach after the setback of the 1984 presidential election. Rather than a single overarching concept like "common security," Klare (Five College Professor of Peace and World Security Studies at Hampshire College) proposed "an interim strategy for the peace movement" based on five elements: persuading people deterrence doesn't work; exposing the "deadly connection" between conventional wars and nuclear war; criticizing Soviet policies by the same standard used to judge U.S. policies; building alliances with minorities, labor, the elderly, and the religious community; and projecting "an aura of hope and unity."

> To "focus on the creation of a just, demilitarized global security system could help unite a broad range of peace and justice organizations."

Klare's article suggests the peace movement should aim at four objectives: war prevention (conventional as well as nuclear); diminished U.S.-Soviet antagonism; peace action and education (Klare specifies several priority topics); and "charting a path to peace" (outlining "near-term, midterm, and long-term steps" to a "stable, just and disarmed world"). Klare's short but comprehensive article provides a checklist of ideas a peace group could use to assess whether it is making the most of its opportunities.

Andrea Ayvazian, Director of the Peace Development Fund's Exchange Project,[7] and Michael Klare suggest in their 1986 article "Decision Time for the American Peace Movement" that the peace movement needs "a broad political concept that incorporates a long-term vision, a way of both explaining and responding to complex phenomena, and a general strategic approach." Without it, the effort to address a widening range of issues risks creating a scattered "movement that has grown a mile wide and an inch deep." They propose thinking of the U.S. as facing a "Choice": between the "Fortress America" future laid out by the right wing, and a "Life-Centered/Global Cooperation" choice they advocate.

Ayvazian and Klare suggest that the peace movement should adopt a greater emphasis on values, a positive and well-defined vision of the future, and a respect for the best of American history and tradition (including the tradition of protecting dissenters); and should recognize that "the entire spectrum of violence is our enemy" (including violence within families, not just wars or nuclear weapons), should return from a focus on votes in Washington to the "unglamorous, hard work of creative organizing on the community level," and should confront racism ("one of the essential roots of violence and war"). Ayvazian and Klare suggest that the themes of valuing all life and seeking to solve problems cooperatively can "link together in a coherent pattern all of the disparate issues we have focused on in recent years" and enable us to "advance a view of America that maximizes freedom, equality and justice and present ourselves strongly as *for* something."

The peace movement needs "a broad political concept that incorporates a long-term vision."

"The Soul of the Universe," the final chapter of Patricia Mische's *Star Wars and the State of Our Souls*, also presents a strong and eloquent emphasis on "choice." Mische sees the most fundamental conflict of our time not as between the U.S. and U.S.S.R. or capitalism and communism, but as between "a mechanistic, atomistic vision of the earth, with its corresponding belief in human dominance over the earth and over each other" and "a vision rooted in attunement to the creative life processes of the earth/universe as primary educator, healer, inventor, and the human as continuation of those processes." As human beings prepare to move into space, the militarization of space threatens to destroy humanity and all that has evolved on the earth. The future depends on whether we can find a "creative resolution for present earth-threatening conflicts. . . . We will survive and our lives will be enhanced to the degree that we can sustain a high degree of diversity within an interacting, cooperative, whole earth community."

In "Visioning Our Way Out of Here," from *New Options* (November 30, 1987), Mark Satin reports that "In study groups, forums, and workshops across the U.S. . . . thousands of professionals, independent activists, and ordinary citizens" are exploring alternative directions for the future. Satin describes five "dramatically different" visioning processes ranging from the Domestic Policy Association's "National Issues Forums" to Sarah Pirtle's Interhelp workshops (an example is found later in this book) and projects based in Montana, Maine, and Virginia. "The phenomenon would be hailed as a major new 'movement' if it were easier to type; if there were one spokesperson or organization bringing people together. But there are dozens." The proliferation of "visioning" suggests a growing awareness that there are indeed choices to be made.

Berkeley professor and peace activist Michael Nagler's remarkable scenario for the *Christian Science Monitor*'s "Peace 2010" contest portrays the transition to a world that has decisively turned toward peace. In the spirit of this book and WOMP's "stage three" world order thinking, Nagler builds on actual events and current efforts, and extends them seamlessly into a transformed future.[8] Beginning with Mrs. Degranfenried (a rural Tennessee woman who in 1984 "disarmed" a gun-wielding escaped convict with the words "Put that gun down, young man; we don't allow no violence around here") and the work of Witness for Peace and Peace Brigades International, he finds the origins of future peace in projects "undertaken without official sanction" and the "dogged work of ordinary people." After those efforts and the related ones Nagler imagines bear fruit (the West German Greens begin organizing civilian-based defense in 1990, inspiring a successful later defense by Poland against a Soviet invasion), breakthroughs occur and human extinction ceases to be in prospect. "Popular pressure [forces] key governments to give the International Court of Justice binding power." The world still has problems in 2010. "But the point is that we now have ways to tackle them."

In the final chapter of his *Visions of a Warless World*, Walden Bello notes signs of the delegitimation of war: the absence of open glorification of war and the rarity of pro-war songs. Although the positive character of various trends should not be overestimated (antiwar public opinion has sometimes vanished rapidly), he finds that some building blocks for eventual world peace now exist, including the 1963 atmospheric nuclear test ban, U.N. covenants on economic, social, and other rights, the development of U.N. agencies, and the Non-Aligned Movement and Third World regional bodies. Another example is the Law of the Sea treaty, "painfully negotiated over a decade, [which] shows that nations *can* make far-reaching peace-enhancing agreements for mutual advantage."

Important as are various social processes tending toward peace, "they are not as crucial today as conscious, deliberate strategies." Bello finds that "The role peacemakers are being called upon to fill is indeed a complex and creative one [requiring] orchestrating vision and strategy, short-term diplomacy and long-term social processes, governmental efforts and a multiplicity of non-governmental, mass movement initiatives . . . all around one theme, one goal: the achievement of disarmament and a lasting peace."[9]

In the final portions of *Paths to Peace*, Richard Smoke (with Willis Harman) recapitulates the book's assessment of nine paths, suggests how they could fit together in a process leading to peace, notes (like Bello) trends toward the delegitimation of war, and stresses the importance of belief in the possibility of peace.

Writers looking for positive trends court the danger of wishful thinking, from which Smoke and Harman do not altogether escape.[10] The notion that "As more and more people truly believe in peace, the belief will make itself true" (p. 98) is misleading, containing grains of falsity as well as of truth. To present only one objection: it takes no account of power differences among people and the significance of who holds which beliefs.[11] Comparing widespread beliefs — e.g., a majority of the U.S. public has for years supported a nuclear freeze and opposed aid to the *contras* — with the policies actually implemented suggests that some beliefs do *not* "make themselves true."

Given the number of people who have been led by fundamentalist preachers to believe in an inevitable nuclear Armageddon, it may be lucky that beliefs do not automatically become reality. But these critical comments notwithstanding, some of the psychological dynamics discussed by Smoke and Harman may indeed contribute to peace, and deserve thoughtful attention.

Thoughtful and critical attention to ideas, whether "New Age" or conventional, is *Future Survey* editor Michael Marien's specialty. The weaknesses of "New Age" or "transformational" thinking are analyzed in Marien's "The Transformation as Sandbox Syndrome." Marien believes that:

> Although a transformation in values, perceptions, and institutions is desirable, it is far from inevitable. Despite an urgent need, change in a humanly desirable direction may not be taking place at all, or may be taking place at such a miniscule pace as to be irrelevant.
> Indeed, I strongly suspect that the widespread belief in a transformation that is happening in fact keeps it from happening . . . [by] deflect[ing] energies away from the hard work that must be done.

The Law of the Sea treaty "shows that nations can make far-reaching, peace-enhancing agreements."

Marien finds a "widespread tendency [which, as a sympathizer, he deplores] of the [New Age or transformation] movement . . . to render itself politically impotent." His witty nine-point prescription for political irrelevance ("Confuse Goals and Results"; "Don't Criticize"; "Promote Your Own Dialect"; "Ignore Power"; etc.) has generated controversy as well as entertained, as the related readings by Tom Greening and Marilyn Ferguson show.[12]

But far more important are Marien's contrasting guidelines for effective social change work, among which are: Develop "indicators that describe both successes and failures"; "Be constructively critical: Point to good work and how it can be improved — and also to work that is useless or damaging"; "Seek to debate opponents and learn from them"; "Invite hard questions"; "Insist on measures of performance"; "Use your intuition as one of many learning tools"; engage in both cooperation and struggle. There are few, if any, peace and social change organizations that could not benefit from posting pages 56-59 on their bulletin boards.[13]

The "human potential" movement and the proponents of "New Age" or "Aquarian" thinking have challenged old assumptions about human limitations, and have inspired and enabled many individuals to alter their lives for the better. Such worthy contributions, however, neither replace the need for system change, nor provide a sound strategy. Marien makes an analogy with solar energy, which could potentially satisfy the world's energy needs, but doesn't yet: "The energy for . . . social change is abundant and widespread, but we have yet to harness it effectively."

Mark Satin, editor of *New Options* newsletter and like Marien a friendly but frank critic, responds to Willis Harman's *Global Mind Change* (1988) by asserting that Harman "fails to prove [his] central thesis" that a better world "may well be inevitable" by virtue of a "shift in prevailing metaphysical assumptions." "Many of [Harman's] arguments go to show not that we *are* changing, but that we *could* or *should* change." But in that case, Satin suggests, it is our task "to help *create* the 'forces of historical change' and not just act as if they're already in place."[14]

If Michael Marien is right that lack of indicators for measuring a movement's successes and failures is a handicap, what can be done about it? Bill Moyer's "Movement Action Plan" ("MAP") is one answer. Moyer, active for over 25 years as an organizer and strategist in the civil rights, antinuclear, anti-intervention, and other movements, has produced "A strategic framework describing the eight stages of successful social movements." Moyer had observed that, lacking an understanding of the stages movements go through, significant numbers of activists have frequently felt discouraged and given up "even when movements were actually progressing reasonably well along the normal path taken by past successful social movements!" Parents don't criticize a child for not graduating after completing two years of college with straight A's; they know that getting a college degree is a four-year process. A social movement, therefore, "should be judged not by whether it has won yet, but by how well it is progressing along the road of success."

> *Activists have frequently felt discouraged "even when movements were actually progressing reasonably well."*

For each stage, Moyer suggests the appropriate activities and goals for activists, the responses they can expect from their opponents, the amount of public support that is typical, and the pitfalls to be avoided in order to advance toward success for the movement's ultimate goal. For example, Moyer suggests that movements that have reached Stage Four, Movement Take-Off (big demonstrations, proliferation of growing organizations, rapid progress toward majority support) should not merely seek more of the same, but shift instead to a strategy that combines continuation of (more selectively used) rallies, demonstrations, and occasional civil disobedience with renewed use of mainstream political and social institutions such as local and state government, widespread local educational efforts, and creation of new means of grassroots citizen involvement. (Nuclear-free zones, sister cities, and citizen diplomacy are good elements for such a broader strategy in the case of the peace movement).

Different components of a large movement, such as efforts to change U.S. policies in Europe, Central America, and the Middle East, may be at different stages, as may different parts of an organization's program. Moyer's well-organized and detailed "MAP" of social movement stages, distilling much hard-won experience, has already proven itself in workshops around the U.S. to be a valuable tool with which groups and individuals can make better sense of the complicated task of social change work.[15]

One of the modes of action discussed by Bill Moyer as part of the repertoire of social movements — nonviolent struggle — is often controversial, especially when involving behavior judged illegal. For many people the forms of nonviolent struggle[16] grouped under the label "civil disobedience" (loosely definable as nonviolent struggle that deliberately and openly breaks a law) do not seem legitimate "in a democracy." Actually, as Robert Irwin's brief article "Nonviolent Struggle and Democracy in American History" shows, without nonviolent struggle we would not have gained the degree of democracy we have. Noncooperation and defiance of abusive government authority were important, but until recently under-appreciated, parts of the American Revolution.[17] Women and blacks both found it necessary to use nonviolent struggle to secure the right to vote. In our time, Irwin suggests, defense of the human rights to "life, liberty, and the pursuit of happiness" again requires the use of nonviolent struggle.

What may seem a disproportionate emphasis on nonviolent struggle in these readings (and those of Chapter 11) is not intended to elevate one political approach above all others. The emphasis partly reflects a judgment about what can be effective in a political system that is inadequately democratic (see Cohen and Rogers in Chapter 11); but it has also been chosen to redress an imbalance of knowledge. Although how voting and lobbying work (or are supposed to work) is taught in high school civics and reinforced in daily news reports, the functioning of nonviolent struggle is far less often taught or understood. Even those who find civil disobedience objectionable should benefit from understanding better its relation to more widely accepted political activities.

A corresponding word to enthusiasts of civil disobedience is also in order. Bill Moyer writes that movements are only as powerful as the power of their grassroots support: "All that national offices in Washington, D.C. can do is 'cash in' on the social and political gains created at the community level all over the country" (which is not to deny that the quality of those offices' work makes a difference as to how much is in fact gained). There may be a rough corollary: that civil disobedience can only ultimately win as much as has been earned through persistent public education. Competence and creativity in nonviolent struggle can make a big difference; but no method is a magic shortcut to success.

Education and nonviolent struggle should not, however, be crudely contrasted. At its best — as in the civil rights movement — nonviolent struggle can be a powerful educational tool at the same time that it fights for victories (cf. the quotations from Goodman and Ellsberg in Chapter 11). Efforts directly to stop crime and bloodshed cannot wait until education is "finished."

There is evidently more than one way to lobby politicians. David Dellinger, a long-time practitioner of nonviolent struggle, tells in his introduction to *Por Amor al Pueblo: Not Guilty! The Trial of the Winooski 44* (1986) about a three-day sit-in in Vermont Senator Robert Stafford's office for which 44 persons were tried in November 1984. The group was part of a larger body requesting that the Senator stop voting for military aid to Central America and also hold a public meeting on the issue. Stafford initially refused these requests; but after the sit-in he changed his voting pattern to accord with the protesters' position.

The defendants called witnesses who presented first-hand knowledge of the killings and brutalities that result from U.S. backing of repressive forces in Central America. The defendants invoked the "necessity defense," arguing that their actions were justified as a response to a life-threatening emergency.[18] Despite the prosecution's contentions that "a clearer case of unlawful trespass is not to be found" and that "the place to determine the foreign policy of the United States is in the ballot box, not the courtroom," the jury accepted the defendants' argument and found them "Not Guilty."

The acquittal, writes Dellinger, "confirmed our hypothesis that the carefully planned and explained conscientious actions of a few ordinary citizens can open the eyes and hearts of other ordinary citizens" and overcome "the media-trumpeted lies of the government." Apparently, Dellinger finds, "the truth really does make people free." It can free a jury "from their illusions about the government's role in Central America and from their prejudices against people who sit in at the offices of a duly-elected official." And "when people become free, they begin to act from their deepest impulses of human unity, of love and caring."

At its best nonviolent struggle can be a powerful educational tool at the same time that it fights for victories.

Although it is a difficult thing for Washington-based peace lobbyists to stay aware of, the approaches of lobbying and electoral work on the one hand, and nonviolent direct action and the raising of demands that go beyond short-term political "realism" on the other, are complementary. (This is so even though not infrequently their methods and ethos are deemed — by people on both "sides" — antagonistic.) The relation of the two approaches has been well summarized as follows:

> Both play critical roles in changing public policy, but their roles are very different. Whereas an effective Congressional lobby must shape its strategy according to the near-term prospects on Capitol Hill, a successful citizens movement has to hold out for more radical changes. The lobbyists have to work within the parameters of what is possible today. A citizens movement that sets its sights on the bigger picture today will move back the parameters of what is possible tomorrow.[19]

Alexander Haig is said to have remarked "Let them march all they want, as long as they continue to pay their taxes." A similar judgment about what is crucial to continuing the war system is shared by the thousands who have engaged in war tax resistance: refusal to pay all or part of their federal taxes in order to protest and noncooperate with the deadly uses to which tax money is predominantly put. Resisters often place the withheld taxes in an escrow fund from which loans or grants to purposes they consider socially beneficial can be made.

War tax resistance is little publicized or even prosecuted — at least in part because the entire income tax system depends on voluntary compliance. The Internal Revenue Service strives mightily through public statements about powerful computer technology to create the impression that non-payment will be detected and punished. If more people realized how rarely war tax resisters have money seized by the IRS, let alone suffer imprisonment, the amount of resistance might increase even further beyond the IRS's enforcement capability. Increased budgets for enforcement and heightened penalties are always a possibility; but confrontations between resisters and the IRS — probably the least popular federal agency — risk providing forums for further Winooski-type conversions of ordinary citizens to the belief that the future of the U.S. is "in good hands" if entrusted to conscientious resisters rather than to the government.[20]

In a 1987 talk Karl Meyer, a long-time (and once imprisoned) war tax resister, reports a strategy developed in Chicago that prevents tax withholding from paychecks and has prevented IRS tax collection from resisters there since 1980, enabling the resisters to donate thousands of dollars of refused taxes to peace and justice work. On a national scale a coordinating office and network of counselors experienced with IRS behavior functions to provide mutual aid to resisters old and new.[21] A way for those who may not choose to be resisters themselves to support the movement is provided through a War Tax Resisters Penalty Fund whose members spread the cost of any penalties IRS collects over more than five hundred people.[22]

Meyer and war tax resisters Eileen Sauvageau and Nancy Brigham speak candidly about effectiveness, inner security, fearlessness, and fear as well as the practicalities of resistance. Brigham suggests — and her view is supported by the Winooski prosecutor's argument that war in Central America is "too far removed" to be a legitimate emergency for Vermonters — that the U.S. government's strategy

> has been to continue to keep these interventions all very distant from us and to keep us
> from feeling that we are responsible for them. It's really important to counter that sense of
> distance and lack of responsibility.

In principle, the human community now has institutions — the International Court of Justice (the "World Court") and the United Nations Security Council — which have global responsibility to prevent war by adjudicating conflicts and responding to threats to peace. On June 27, 1986, in the case *Nicaragua vs. United States*, the World Court determined by a vote of 14 to 1 that U.S. mining of Nicaraguan harbors violated international law and pertinent treaty obligations. By a 12 to 3 vote the Court held: that the U.S. had violated international law by interfering, through the use of force, in the internal affairs of a sovereign nation; that U.S. actions in training and supplying the *contra* forces violated international law; and that the U.S. was under a duty to "cease" and "refrain" from such activities. The U.S. had contested the Court's jurisdiction (after decades of saying all nations should accept it) and refused to participate in the case during the 19 months before a decision was rendered. The Court had unanimously rejected the U.S. contention that the suit was not admissible because of the existence of an armed conflict.

The U.N. Charter authorizes the Security Council to decide how to "give effect" to World Court judgments. Eleven nations, including U.S. allies Australia and Denmark, voted for "full and immediate" U.S. compliance with the Court decision. France, the U.K., and Thailand abstained. No nation voted against — except the United States, which vetoed the call for compliance.

This account comes from the World Federalist Association's brochure "Will Uncle Sam Remain an International Outlaw?" The W.F.A. and a group of co-plaintiffs (including Benjamin Linder, subsequently killed by the *contras*) filed suit in September 1986 to enforce the World Court judgment through U.S. courts. "The suit is based on Article 94 of the U.N. Charter which obligates every U.N. member to 'comply with' the decisions of the World Court and on Article VI of the U.S. Constitution which makes all treaties (including the U.N. Charter) part of the 'supreme law of the land.'"

In response, the U.S. Attorney General's office contended that *contra* aid legislation had overridden the provisions of the U.N. Charter, that the plaintiffs lacked standing to sue, and that the matter was a "political question" reserved for Congress and the President and not "justiciable" by the courts. A February 1987 District Court judge dismissed the suit on grounds it raised essentially political ques-tions which the Court "dare not interfere with" and declined to rule on the merits of the case. The W.F.A. appealed the ruling.

> *In principle, the human community now has institutions which have global responsibility to prevent war.*

This sequence of events renders vivid the issues of world governance treated in Chapter 5. World federalist Lawrence Abbott and legal scholar Benjamin Ferencz agree that an effective legal system requires three elements: law, courts, and enforcement. Which of the three is lacking in this case is unmistakable. It is worth asking what the future victims of aggression should be told. Is it this? "Sorry. The U.S. is democratic (even if the government is acting contrary to majority opinion) and its people are therefore obedient to lower laws even when their government flouts supreme ones at the cost of your lives. Maybe in the next election a government will be elected that stops waging war against you. In the meantime, good luck! We sympathize with your plight." Or can we do better?

In "Nonviolent Direct Law Enforcement," Robert Irwin offers a strategic concept that could help to bridge the gap between nonviolent direct action campaigns against nuclear weapons and overseas military interventions and the visions of a lawful, peaceful world held by world federalists and many others. He argues that heightened public concern over government law violations (the Iran-*contra* scandal and *contra*-related drug dealings, among others), and wide recognition of Congress's ineffectuality at exercising even moderate control of the executive branch's covert wars, have created conditions ripe for an effort by peace activists to shift legitimacy from government leaders' decisions to the rule of law.

Despite its limitations, existing international law against aggression and preparing to do mass killing of civilians would, if enforced, make for a much better world. Political activists in the U.S. are showing increased awareness of international law. Presidential candidate Rev. Jesse Jackson made respect for international law a major plank of his foreign policy platform.[23] Many practitioners of nonviolent direct action, either against arms shipments to Central America, nuclear weapon manufacture, or CIA covert warfare, have already begun calling their deeds "Nuremberg actions" instead of "civil disobedience." [24] Irwin suggests that planning and presenting future such actions as "civil resistance to crime" or "law enforcement" could link them to other issues and to a vision of a lawful global order, further educate the public, and gain new allies in moderate circles for fundamental policy changes.

Irwin quotes the great Afro-American scholar W. E. B. DuBois, who argued that the immensely

> **Conditions are ripe for an effort by peace activists to shift legitimacy from government leaders' decisions to the rule of law.**

destructive Civil War would have been prevented and much social evil before and after it avoided had the people of the U.S. had the sense of enlightened self-interest and moral courage simply to enforce the law prohibiting the slave trade placed on the books in 1807. The importance today of preventing a final war of annihilation can hardly be exaggerated, and there is no reason for delay in bringing aggressive wars to an end. DuBois concluded that "it behooves nations as well as [people] to do things at the very moment when they ought to be done."[25]

The first readings for this chapter began with strategic orientations for the U.S. peace movement; the final ones present voices that in part represent social forces contributing to peace, and equally much symbolize the importance of committed individuals who persevere through a long struggle to make change. The many contributors to the symposia and articles in the *Peacework* collection on "Movement-Building" address some of the personal issues of motivation and perspective that may get lost in high-flown strategic debate.

Randy Kehler's "Thoughts on War and Patriotism" describes his thoughts as he and his young daughter and her friends attend the Memorial Day celebration in their small Massachusetts town. Unwillingness to flee his country despite deep disagreement with the Vietnam War led Kehler to two years in federal prison for draft resistance. Patriotism, Kehler believes, today compels recognition that war itself now threatens our country. "In place of war, and the militarized system that feeds it, we must begin to establish a global 'peace system,' a system based upon procedures and institutions for resolving conflicts non-violently."

W. H. Ferry, "a 76-year-old philanthropist, essayist, and self-described 'peace activist'" (in the words of a February 1987 newspaper story), was profoundly affected by the dropping of the atomic bomb on Hiroshima. "I realized that the world had changed and that it would never be the same again. I felt like I ought to apologize to somebody or do something. Since that day this feeling has never left me." One "something" Ferry has managed to do is start ExPro, in order "to shift attention away from developing a war system and toward the necesssary conditions for a peace system." Inspired by the idea of nonviolence and by such individuals as his friend, the late Trappist monk and author Thomas Merton, Ferry has felt it essential to develop changed relationships among nations. "Imagine what the world will be like in 20 years if present policies continue," Ferry says. "Clearly, a different vision must come into play. And prevail."

Mark Sommer's "Ten Strategies in Search of a Movement" (1987) offers not a "catalogue of specific policy options . . . [but] instead a set of general working principles within which particular [alternative] policies would logically fit," intended as "mutually supporting elements" in a peace system. These include renouncing threats to others, reducing our own vulnerability, undertaking shared ventures with our adversaries, fostering peace initiatives, and related ideas.

That Sommer concludes his article with an account of how ExPro originated also makes this a fitting reading to place near the end of this book. "It has never been ExPro's intention," he writes, "to remain an insular debating society," but rather to be "a catalyst and clearinghouse" for a much broader discussion of the necessary conditions for peace. Sommer ends, accordingly, with an invitation to take part. Through reading this book or participating in a study group, you have indeed joined the discussion Ferry and Sommer sought to start.

> *Patriotism today compels recognition that war itself now threatens our country.*

Peacework, the concise, earnest, and information-rich monthly journal published by the American Friends Service Committee's New England regional office, has in recent years won growing praise and been described as conveying "the authentic voice of the peace movement." In a special issue on "Movement-Building: Challenge and Opportunity" (1986), editor Pat Farren has assembled twenty-four pages of writing by thirty-five authors ranging from short responses to "What Keeps You Going?" and "How Can We Build a Better Movement?" to longer pieces on strategy, guidelines, and goals by Tom Wall, Joseph Gerson, Pam Solo, Andrea Ayvazian, and Muhammad Kenyatta.

For readers who have been active on one or a few issues but whose political outlook is relatively undeveloped, the most interesting parts of "Movement-Building" may be those on goals and strategy. For those who do not define themselves as activists, the most important parts may be those indicating the gravity of our common plight and challenging the reader to take responsibility for shaping the future. For those already working very hard, most valuable may be words on self-nurturance, and encouragement to spend time (in Kevin McVeigh's words) "enjoying the world we're trying to save."

Petra Kelly, a Member of Parliament in the Federal Republic of Germany, is probably the best-known spokesperson for "Green" politics.[26] Opposing missile deployments, challenging Soviet hosts on human rights, debating NATO intellectuals, sitting in at her country's consulate in South Africa, protesting in East Germany, holding hearings on civilian-based defense — she has shown herself a passionate, tireless tribune for the values of a new world. In "New Forms of Power" (1986), reprinted from *Breakthrough*, she outlines with characteristic conciseness and sweep the essentials of "The Green Feminist View," opposed to all patterns of domination. What would happen, she asks, if Green ideals became reality?

> Drastic reductions in military budgets; the first calculated steps out of our military alliances; the right to total conscientious objection; the beginnings of an authentic and honest human rights policy in every part of the world; stopping all weapons exports and civilian and military nuclear exports; developing forms of social and civilian-based defense; changing the production of arms to the production of socially useful and ecologically safe products; moving toward a just, peaceful and non-exploitative Europe of autonomous regions, including our neighbors across the Iron Curtain. It would mean the rise of new forms of power: power from the grass roots, from below.

The final voice presented here is that of Elvia Alvarado, a Honduran peasant leader. This passage, titled "Don't be Afraid, Gringo," is excerpted from her book[27] *Don't be Afraid, Gringo: A Honduran Woman Speaks from the Heart* (1987).

> It's hard to think of change taking place in Central America without there first being change in the United States. . . . So you Americans who really want to help the poor have to change your own government first. . . . You have to fight just like we're fighting — even harder. If you say, 'Oh, the United States is so big and powerful, there's nothing we can do to change it,' . . . you start to feel insignificant and your spirit dies. That's very dangerous. For as long as we keep our spirits high, we continue to struggle.
>
> We *campesinos* are used to planting seeds and waiting to see if the seeds bear fruit. We're used to working on harsh soil. And when our crops don't grow, we're used to planting again and again until they take hold. Like us, you must learn to persist.
>
> You have to begin educating people, telling them the truth about what's happening in the world. Because if the press in the United States is anything like it is in Honduras, the people aren't well informed. You have to teach them what's really happening, . . . what your government is doing. And once you've educated people, then get them organized.
>
> We're not asking for food or clothing or money. We want you with us in the struggle. We want you to educate your people. We want you to organize your people. We want you to denounce what your government is doing in Central America.
>
> From those of you who feel the pain of the poor, who feel the pain of the murdered, the disappeared, the tortured, we need more than sympathy. We need you to join the struggle. Don't be afraid, gringos. Keep your spirits high. And remember, we're right there with you!

Chapter 13
Where Do We Go from Here?

If to many people my thinking seems always to have a kind of surprising optimism, a
foolish optimism, my hunch is that it is because I keep trying to see people whole and
beginning — still growing — and then they seem less limited than they do to sociologists or
psychologists, politicians or journalists. But it doesn't much matter whether one has an
"optimistic" or "pessimistic" outlook, for the question still remains, Now what?

— Paul Goodman[1]

This book began with the issues of nuclear war as defined by top policy-makers and the mass
media: controversies about exotic technology and what decisions a handful of elite U.S. white
males should make about the quantity of weapons of mass destruction. We encountered major
redefinitions of those issues and moved to visions of how the whole world might function in a
condition of stable peace. We looked at trends toward peace and some of the social groups
worldwide whose actions make up or could aid those trends. Finally, we considered strategies that
aim to make our actions maximally effective and the varied voices of persons whose commitment
to work for change is part of the foundation for the future.

It may seem a long distance from the nightmare world of nuclear weapons, Star Wars fantasies, and
"low-intensity conflict" to the realities of our lives. Yet each of us is a human being on this earth
with a role in determining what its future will be.

Through reading this book, and perhaps also participating in a study group, you may have experienced something of how individuals and small groups of people can inform themselves and reflect
on possible ways to act to move toward a better future. In this chapter the focus is on how you
might sustain your sense that positive change is possible — how, if you choose to, you might
continue a process of learning, reflection, and action over the years ahead.

Future options

At the scheduled end of this particular learning experience, you the study group participant or
individual reader face a decision about the significance of what you have learned for the next part
of your life. For some people, what they hear about political and environmental dangers is just
"what's in the news" and feels disconnected to their personal reality. Like people in past doomed
civilizations, they are given warnings, but don't heed them.

Your reading of these words suggests you are someone aware that war is a serious problem, and
might possibly imagine you could do something to bring a peaceful world closer. Everything in
this chapter (to be quite frank) is meant to encourage you to become or remain active in work to
bring peace.

Readings: for study group use

A. (to be played during Session 15:) Audio cassette "The Freeze Revisited" (December 1986; interviews with Randall Forsberg and Randy Kehler; 29 minutes);

B. Brian Martin et al., "The Individual," pp. 98-111 from *Uprooting War* (1984; 14 pp.);

C. Sarah Conn et al., *Keeping Us Going: A Manual on Support Groups for Social Change Activists* (1986; 26 pp.);

D. Elise Boulding, "Epilogue," pp. 160-164 from *Building a Global Civic Culture* (1988; 5 pp.)

Because groups and individuals differ, rather than giving one kind of generalized advice we are suggesting several general and specific options among which you can choose, and processes to facilitate thoughtful choice.

(These pages address the situation of people doing a study group *ad hoc* on their own or under the auspices of a religious or social body or an adult education center. If you are a student using this book in a course, your situation is somewhat different. You will need to think whether what you have learned from the readings and class sessions is something to lay aside for now and leave to simmer in the back of your mind; or whether you are ready to consider summer or post-college planning to make work for peace a major part of your life, now or later, perhaps using some of the options that follow here.)

One general option: you don't have to do anything else. You can evaluate, declare the study group a success (or otherwise), and go your separate ways. (Limiting one's activity level is essential for preventing burn-out.) Some groups, reaching the end of this kind of study group, split up and the participants return to their previous activities, more knowledgeable about the world, and equipped with some new ideas about running meetings more efficiently and enjoyably. That's a worthwhile result.

You may take the most important or attractive or persuasive among the ideas encountered in *Building a Peace System*, figure out their implications for altering the work of the group or groups that you in the study group are already involved in, and aim to bring about appropriate changes.

Another general option is for an action group to evolve out of most or all of the study group's membership. In that case, at this "last" meeting of the study group, another meeting should be scheduled to inaugurate that action group.

Another variation is for one or more subgroups to form to do particular political projects together, or to find others outside the group to form support groups based on friendship or other affinity.

Another specific option: some groups using this participatory learning format have found it a profound, even transformative, experience. (One group continued to meet for over two years, choosing new readings — they didn't want to stop!) Some participants may feel like the individual who called one such study group "one of the most valuable educational experiences of my life." Whether or not you feel this strongly, you may decide that it's worthwhile political work for you to catalyze the organization of new study groups using *Building a Peace System*. You have access to a set of the materials, and you have experience being in a group. Whom do you want to help start learning these ideas? Friends, relatives, people in different peace or other activist groups, religious groups, students?

> **You could do something to bring a peaceful world closer.**

Remember that one option is to contact ExPro. We may have action ideas to suggest at the time when you finish your study group. We encourage you to contact us. Our address and phone number can be found in this book. Whatever the members of your group decide to do, we'd be grateful to hear from any of you about it.

Commentary on audiotape and readings

On the program "The Freeze Revisited" "two of the leaders of the national campaign for a nuclear weapons freeze discuss the movement's past, present, and future." Randall Forsberg originated the idea of a U.S.-Soviet nuclear freeze as a strategic focus for the U.S. peace movement. Randy Kehler was a primary organizer of the successful first local referendum on the freeze in 1980, which showed that the election of Reagan was not a mandate for an arms build-up. The following year he became national coordinator of the Freeze campaign.

This program gives perspective on the origins of the Freeze, its high and low points, and Forsberg's and Kehler's views of the current state of the movement and where it should next be headed. Forsberg presents an argument for two peace movement goals to be added to the goal of a U.S.-Soviet freeze: major cuts in NATO and Warsaw Pact forces, and a non-intervention "regime" (agreement about acceptable conduct) under which neither superpower would use military force to intervene in other countries' affairs. (These goals appeared as Steps Two and Three of her strategy article "A Step by Step Approach," a reading in Chapter 12.)

Building a Peace System

The program fits well at the concluding session of a study group on "building a peace system" because it reminds us that movements are begun, expanded, and changed not by anonymous "social forces" but by determined people. Movements are not created by the electoral system or the mass media, nor do they vanish when the media spotlight shifts elsewhere. Randy Kehler, who had been visiting and working with grassroots groups as a staff person of the Peace Development Fund's Exchange Project,[2] makes an assessment of the state of the peace movement (as of late 1986) worth quoting:

> The majority of Americans [still] think the Freeze would be a good idea. . . . I think what's happened with the Nuclear Weapons Freeze Campaign per se is that . . . the momentum has slowed, the excitement of it has worn off. Many people feel that we've come up against a fairly solid wall [of opposition maneuvers], some probably a direct result of our effort and our very success. There is a certain sense of "What do we do next? Where do we move?" There's a lot of head-scratching going on. There are many Freeze activists who are working on other issues now, on the Central America intervention issue most notably, but perhaps on South Africa, or the Middle East, or local issues in their own communities.

We encourage you to contact us.

> I think the positive thing that has to be kept in mind — and I see this from traveling all around the country and meeting with groups in every region of the country — is that there is in fact a grassroots disarmament / peace / freeze movement out there that did not exist five years ago — that is not smaller even than it was two or three years ago at the height of the Freeze; that is, if anything, larger. It can be said that it is not unified; that most groups are searching for focus; that they are trying to find meaningful work to do. But they are there, they are active in most cases, and they form the foundation of what I absolutely believe will be the next whole cycle of the disarmament movement, which will again be another upswing.

> If I look at the history of citizen movements, I don't see steady growth, steady momentum on the part of any movement, whether it's the movement for the abolition of slavery, or the women's movement, or the antiwar movement during the Vietnam War. Movements all go through cyclical changes, ups and downs, and I think there's no question that we've been in a down period at least since the '84 election. And what sustains my own hopes is seeing that the grassroots infrastructure — which in the end to me is where any movement derives its strength — is very much in place, and has the potential to come together again.

Kehler's viewpoint merits consideration. Compared to its media peak of 1982-83, the U.S. peace movement appears to have regressed; but a more perceptive assessment would recognize the learning — some of it hard lessons — and political development that have occurred in the movement since that time, as well as the other changes in the broader U.S. public and elsewhere. (Recall the Introductions to Parts One and Three.)

As you think about what you will be doing after the end of this study group, do so with awareness that you may have the opportunity to participate in a resurgence and expansion of the peace movement that will accomplish things beyond any previous period of history.

In his book *Uprooting War* Brian Martin asks: "What makes some individuals into social activists? What keeps other individuals non-active? How can individuals help themselves become more effective in acting against oppressive social institutions? What does it take to build and hold a commitment to helping achieve grassroots action against war and other social problems?"

Martin continues: "Rather than answering these questions just by myself, I have also asked a few friends ["who have been involved in social action five years or more"] to write about their own experiences." Each of the four statements is unique and down-to-earth. Recurring themes include: realistic appraisal of one's own character and needs; maintaining "mental calm" and avoiding "burn-out" by focusing one's efforts, and keeping up non-political activities or friendships; persistence, commitment, and common-sense practicality. Martin notes that individuals make choices within various constraints and suggests asking "what can be done to shape one's own social circumstances in order to provide a strong and lasting basis for both activism and personal needs?"

Social movement activity can be exhausting, frustrating, and disillusioning. It can also be exhilarating, fulfilling, and inspiring. Much has been learned in the last thirty years about how to do such work more effectively and enjoyably, and in a way that can be sustained over decades. Important parts of the knowledge gained through experience have been incorporated into a host of manuals.[3]

One of these is *Keeping Us Going: A Manual on Support Groups for Social Change Activists.* Prepared by members of Interhelp and Movement for a New Society, it is a complete "how-to" manual for support groups that can help peace activists meet needs for encouragement, problem-solving, personal attention, frank feedback, and celebration that are not adequately met in task-oriented groups.

Creating one or more support groups is an option that can enable study group participants who so desire to continue their connection with each other, without needing to think up a common project as an excuse to keep meeting. If the study group has been an important experience, this is understandable. Action projects involving others may grow out of support groups; but friendship and continuity are legitimate needs in themselves.

People may already be doing as much peace work as they want to be doing, yet desire a setting in which the needs for encouragement, etc. mentioned above can be met. A support group can provide a setting in which long-term issues can be addressed — such as how to change one's life to have greater opportunity to do effective peace work, or to enjoy more happiness while doing it. In a support group time can be allocated for explorations such as the "Whole Person Exercise" that are designed for reflection on goals and life planning.[4] Such explorations are important because strong groups and durable movements are best based on dedicated individuals who take time to think well about and nurture themselves and others.

The question with which Elise Boulding begins her "Epilogue" to *Building a Global Civic Culture* could also be asked about building a peace system. After a page of listing current examples of violence, folly, and injustice that make for danger and insecurity, she asks: "Is this the time to write a book about long, slow processes like the emergence of a world public interest . . . ?" She answers:

> If not now, when? Ever since I was young, people have been saying there is no time for long-range processes, that all energies must be bent to solving today's crises. Yet tomorrow has always brought another crisis. . . . [E]ither we have time or we do not. If we don't, that's that. If we do, then *taking time*, using it to ponder and act on the best possibilities for the human race, to develop our own capabilities to work for those possibilities, and finding our own role in the stream of history is the best we can do for our world.

> Taking time is the key. . . .

Strong groups and durable movements are best based on dedicated individuals who take time to nurture themselves and others.

Boulding speaks of "a way of living simultaneously on different time tracks" — learned when her five children were small — "which can keep us unrushed and centered, even in the midst of busyness." It involves awareness within the moment of the rhythm of the day, the week, and the season; and awareness of the longer, slower rhythms of life cycles, history, and "of creation itself. . . . Awareness of [that] larger rhythm cannot be taken for granted . . . . It has to be cultivated through reflection."

She concludes:

> The world civic culture, however fragmentary, is there ready to be named and worked with . . . . We can join the company of persons-in-becoming who are working to give it shape. . . . The choice is ours.

Afterword

At the beginning of this book "the peace system approach" was outlined. The approach involves conceiving war and peace as outcomes of complex systems rather than of one or two or a few policies or conditions. Peace may be considered a condition in which peace-making factors outweigh war-making ones. The peace system approach therefore indicates seeking to solve the problem of war by strengthening (or newly creating) the elements judged to be necessary for building a peace system.

After reading the preceding chapters, and perhaps also having read some of the suggested materials in a study group or on your own, you should have a better idea of what a peace system's elements would be. They would include improved mechanisms for global governance and reform, non-threatening national defense policies, and changes in economics and culture that would support peace with freedom by lessening inequalities and tensions and increasing peacemaking capabilities.

This book could have ended with an elaborate peace system model and a platform for action expressing the author's conclusions as to the best priorities for peace (and ecological and justice) activism. Detailed vision and strategy thinking is often valuable. But instead, because this book is above all a tool to inform *your* thinking, we choose here to pause to learn from your conclusions before elaborating our own.

ExPro's fundamental mission is to catalyze discussion and action for peace. Please send us your thoughts about the ideas in this book — or about ideas you consider better — and tell us how you act on them. Let us know if you would like to see a newsletter to make such communications publicly accessible.

Some final comments: the peace system approach is recognizably sociological (or, more broadly, social-scientific) in that it not only looks at government policies, but also beneath them, at the social phenomena from which they arise. In scholarly terms, this book might be considered to begin a project in participatory "action research" or "action science." Its hypothesis that a peace system could be built to end war can be fully tested only by historical experiment — by trying to create one. The knowledge sought is practical as well as theoretical.

This approach is also morally engaged. We do not only point to facts of global interdependence or international law, but advocate concern for the well-being of others anywhere on our planet and action based on a sense of individual responsibility for compliance — by ourselves and our societies — with the most enlightened of the emerging norms of "the global civic culture."

Although the peace system approach aims to be unusually comprehensive, it remains only one among contemporary frameworks for seeking peace. Among these perhaps the most widely discussed is "common security," first popularized in a book of that title by the Independent Commission on Disarmament and Security Issues (Palme Commission). The notion that in the nuclear

Building a Peace System

age countries have "common" security interests has seemed particularly timely as warming of U.S.-Soviet relations has raised the possibility of an end to the Cold War; and opportunities do now exist for demilitarization in Europe that could help to undercut the Cold War and its ideologies.

But the Cold War has had as much to do with enforcing capitalist or communist social relations within the superpowers' respective domains as with conflict between the two blocs. Third World militarization, poverty, debt, and unrest are not peripheral but as central as Europe to the ideology and practice of the Cold War. Consequently superpower detente in Europe must not be overrated. Global peace will require restructuring of economics, ecological practices, culture, and politics within the U.S. and other countries, and among all countries, in addition to arms treaties and military cutbacks.

Although common security work originally emphasized most the military standoff of NATO and the Warsaw Pact, its proponents in several countries are seeking to deepen the security agenda to include non-military factors like international environmental and economic challenges. With inclusion of calls for international cooperation and conflict resolution, the common security approach shows signs of converging with peace system thinking.

But although mobilizing people and their institutions to pressure governments for policy changes is always important, this activity must be supplemented by a simultaneous broader and longer-term strategy that aims to change the people and institutions themselves. Altering which information sources people rely on, introducing public financing of elections, challenging the racist, sexist, and nationalist premises of current policies, fostering different economic arrangements — such concerns may seem extraneous and counter-productive for the winning of any single peace movement policy objective.

Such efforts toward system transformation will, however, eventually be decisive for the fate of all peace movement goals. A sizable part of this book is therefore devoted to "Group Study Resources" — so that individuals can join to take steps toward more effective activism — and "Information Resources" through which people can sustain improved understanding and keep in touch with more distant efforts. Also offered in this book are extensive notes about the ideas mentioned in the preceding text. The notes to Chapter 7 on "Economic Development, Ecology, and Peace," for example, suggest how economic behaviors that can be changed right now could eventually help alter the structure of U.S. politics, the social character and political culture of our population, and the nature of the business decision-making that crucially affects our environment.

Long-term transformation efforts and influencing this year's public debate and government decisions are not inherently at odds; rather, they can complement each other. Those focusing on either would do well to learn from each other and seek to cooperate more closely. Such common efforts offer the best chance for success in building a peace system.

Notes

The Peace System Approach to Eliminating War

1. The familiar, handy phrase "arms race" is used here for convenience. But such use is not meant to endorse the theory the phrase incorporates as analytically adequate. That theory, often taken for granted, is quite debatable: the idea that U.S. and Soviet arms spending exhibit a competitive dynamic in which each side reacts to the arms spending of the other. Some have suggested instead that military spending may be impelled by domestic considerations, with reactions to foreign actions distinctly secondary in importance, perhaps providing only a handy rationale. Thus anticommunist writers often regard Soviet communism (or "totalitarianism") as inherently expansionist; Alan Wolfe makes a case for internal factors as decisive for the U.S. in *The Rise and Fall of the Soviet Threat: Domestic Sources of the Cold War Consensus* (Institute for Policy Studies, 1979; revised edition, South End Press, 1984).

German peace researcher Dieter Senghaas has presented significant evidence for regarding the superpowers' behavior as "autistic" rather than an action-reaction process; see the summary of his views in Juergen Dedring, *Recent Advances in Peace and Conflict Research* (Sage, 1976), pp. 79-83, and also p. 104, n. 20. For a brief overview and mention of more recent work in this vein, see Hanna Newcombe, "Survey of Peace Research" (*Peace Research Reviews* IX:6, 1984), pp. 23-26. Johan Galtung has written: "From the idea that [arms races] are not necessarily only reactions to external stimuli, the perceived threats from the outside, it does not follow that they are only reactions to internal stimuli, for instance capitalistic or bureaucratic expansionism. There is ample space for both [factors]" (*The True Worlds* [Free Press, 1980], p. 240, n. 29).

2. That neither the U.S.-Soviet military balance nor Soviet intentions are addressed in depth in this book does not imply dismissal of these issues' importance for influencing U.S. political attitudes. One survey has reportedly found that "individuals who were in favor of an armament buildup and who opposed a nuclear moratorium *did not materially differ*" from those holding the reverse opinions as to the consequences of nuclear war or their degree of anxiety about it. "They *did differ in their perception of the malevolence and motives of the Soviet Union*" (emphases in original). Seymour Feshbach, "Implications for Changing War-Related Attitudes," in Ralph K. White, ed., *Psychology and the Prevention of Nuclear War* (New York University Press, 1986), p. 528.

On Soviet motives, many works by George F. Kennan, Robert C. Tucker, Stephen F. Cohen, and other specialists on the U.S.S.R. offer a highly informed challenge to views of the Soviet Communist leadership as demonic or fanatically dedicated to world domination.

The military balance should presumably be a more objective matter than the interpretation of motives; and in proportion as the U.S.S.R. is weak or strong relative to the U.S., any Soviet malevolence would matter less or more. The case for enormous U.S. military spending is premised on arguments that we must stay ahead of (or catch up with) Soviet military power. How powerful are the Soviets?

Geopolitical differences greatly complicate comparisons. The U.S. is protected by oceans and is much larger than its two neighbors; the Soviets face China on the east as well as NATO on the west. Numerous factors create such asymmetries that, as the influential International Institute for Strategic Studies in London admitted in the 1987-88 edition of its publication, *The Military Balance*, "it is a misnomer to speak of a single, overall 'balance'" (*The Nation*, November 28, 1987, p. 616). Yet this has not forestalled decades of claims that the Soviets have, or are about to gain, military superiority.

In the 1960 presidential campaign John F. Kennedy charged that a dangerous "missile gap" favoring the Soviets loomed. In reality, according to Daniel Ellsberg (who held a high security clearance), "the United States had within range of Russia about 1000 tactical bombers and 2000 intercontinental bombers, 40 ICBMs [intercontinental ballistic missiles], 48 Polaris missiles, and another 100 intermediate range missiles based in

Europe. The Soviets had at that time some 190 intercontinental bombers and exactly *four* ICBMs . . . Officially, the precise figure cited [four ICBMs] . . . remains secret . . .: because public knowledge of the *scale* of the 'missile gap' hoax would undercut the recurrently-necessary tactic of whipping up public fears of imminent U.S. 'inferiority' to mobilize support for vastly expensive arms spending . . . ." Daniel Ellsberg, "Introduction: Call to Mutiny," in E. P. Thompson and Dan Smith, eds., *Protest and Survive* (Monthly Review, 1981), pp. vii-viii.

Major disparities in favor of the U.S. have continued to exist in more recent times as well. Michael T. Klare has demonstrated the "inherent limits on Soviet adventurism abroad" in "The Power Projection Gap: A Comparison of U.S. and Soviet Long-Range Intervention Capabilities," Appendix to *Beyond the "Vietnam Syndrome"* (Institute for Policy Studies, 1981), pp. 110-133. The U.S. surpasses the U.S.S.R. by margins ranging between 3 to 1 and 20 to 1 (p. 128) in factors like highly mobile manpower, transport and supply, and aircraft carriers and air support. Klare concludes: "Unlike the U.S., . . . the Soviet Union does not now possess a capacity for full-scale military intervention against a determined or well-equipped adversary located any distance from Soviet territory" (p. 133).

What this disparity means was summarized by the Boston Study Group (Randall Forsberg, Philip Morrison, Paul Walker, et al.) in their careful study of U.S. military forces in a global perspective: although the Soviets can, like the U.S., start a thermonuclear war of annihilation, when it comes to nonnuclear intervention capacity, "the United States stands alone: It is the world's only truly global power." *The Price of Defense* (Quadrangle / Times Books, 1979), p. 23.

All this may be difficult to believe, so accustomed are people in the U.S. to hearing that the Soviets rival us militarily and outspend us on defense ("by $300 billion" in the 1970s, said Ronald Reagan). Few in the U.S. know, however, that Soviet expenditures are reckoned by U.S. intelligence according to what it would cost the U.S. to do the equivalent; thus a pay raise for U.S. soldiers is counted as an increase in Soviet military spending! Noam Chomsky concisely summarizes other factors that render spending comparisons misleading in *Towards a New Cold War* (Pantheon, 1982), p. 193.

Independent-minded persons may want to examine for themselves detailed treatments of these matters. Perhaps the best place to begin is Tom Gervasi's *The Myth of Soviet Military Supremacy* (Harper & Row, 1986; $10.95), a recent comprehensive (545-page) critical examination of the U.S.-Soviet military balance.

A still more recent work that incorporates two contrasting viewpoints is Gervasi's *Soviet Military Power*—*"The Pentagon's Propaganda Document, Annotated and Corrected* (Vintage, 1988; large format paperback, 159 pp., $14.95), a detailed commentary on the Pentagon's annual *Soviet Military Power* that aims to expose "the hidden assumptions used to create incomplete and misleading comparisons of military power." Gervasi pulls no punches: "By every significant measure of comparison, the United States has always held, and continues to hold, a commanding lead in strategic power. Both the nuclear and conventional balances of power in Europe have always heavily favored NATO and continue to do so. The actual facts are not in dispute; the administration cannot really deny them. It can only avoid mentioning them, misrepresent them, or, as it does frequently in this book, simply lie." Gervasi's book is the most convenient way to compare what the U.S. government is saying side by side with an informed critique.

Who is so intent on increasing military spending, and why? Jerry W. Sanders's *Peddlers of Crisis: The Committee on the Present Danger and the Politics of Containment* (South End Press, 1983) is a thorough account of the mentality of some of the most powerful among those who wanted a massive increase in military spending after the Vietnam War.

In the wake of the Reagan-Gorbachev Intermediate Nuclear Forces (INF) agreement to eliminate some nuclear weapons, there have been calls for a conventional buildup to compensate for an alleged NATO disadvantage that is widely accepted as fact in the U.S. media. In contrast, Ken Silverstein's "Is the West Outgunned? Conventional Arms Myths in Europe," *The Nation* (June 11, 1988), pp. 822-826, buttresses Gervasi's assessment of the conventional balance in Europe.

Andrew Cockburn's *The Threat: Inside the Soviet Military Machine* (Vintage, 1983, 1984), drawing on interviews with Soviet defectors, gives a feel for the human reality of the Soviet military, afflicted by alcoholism, inefficiency, and poor equipment and training. Finally, the Center for Defense Information has published "Soviet Geopolitical Momentum: Myth or Menace?" (*Defense Monitor*, Vol. XV, No. 5, 1986), a very short, readable, and persuasive analysis of the balance of world power (available for $3.00 from CDI, 1500 Massachusetts Ave., N.W., Room 24, Washington, DC 20005).

These references may be helpful to those wishing to investigate these topics that fall outside this book's main focus.

3. See the end of this book for information about ExPro.

4. Mark Sommer, "Ten Strategies in Search of a Movement," *ExPro Paper* #6 (1987), p. 15.

5. For a typical statement of the view that deterrence has "kept the peace," see Alexander M. Haig's 6 April 1982 speech "Peace and Deterrence" (U.S. Department of State, Bureau of Public Affairs, Current Policy No. 383). That "living with nuclear weapons is our only hope" is the keynote proposition (p. 255) of the Harvard Nuclear Study Group's *Living with Nuclear Weapons* (Bantam, 1983).

6. Even so conservative a figure as historian and former diplomat George F. Kennan has written that "Elimination of nuclear weaponry . . . would not be enough [to safeguard human survival] . . . War itself, as a means of settling differences at least between the great industrial powers, will have to be in some way ruled out." We agree. More problematic, however, is Kennan's view that "It is the ingrained habits and assumptions of men, and above all of men in government, which alone can guarantee any enduring state of peaceful relations among nations." While enlightenment among officials is by all means to be encouraged, we do not look to them as the primary agents of peace. Our view is more structural, democratic, and (not least) feminist. Quotations from Kennan, *The Nuclear Delusion: Soviet-American Relations in the Atomic Age* (Pantheon, 1982), pp. xxviii, xxix.

7. Richard Healey, *Nuclear Times* (May-June 1987), p. 4. *Nuclear Times* has subsequently begun a regular section on "alternative security."

8. Of the books recommended in this volume, well over half were published in 1985, 1986, or 1987; the oldest of them dates back only as far as 1982. On the new projects and discussions, see Rob Leavitt, "Vision Quest," *Defense and Disarmament News* (August-September 1987), p. 7, and Chapter 12 of this book.

9. See Matthew Melko, *Fifty-Two Peaceful Societies* (Oakville, Ontario: Canadian Peace Research Institute Press, 1973) and (with Richard D. Weigel) *Peace in the Ancient World* (McFarland, 1981). The definition of peace used can be (and has been) criticized as too narrow, but this does not negate the value of these works.

10. Kenneth Boulding has done the most to popularize the phrase "stable peace"; see *Stable Peace* (University of Texas Press, 1978). The inclusion of war not being expected is derived from Karl W. Deutsch, by way of Carolyn Stephenson; see her *Alternative Methods for International Security* (University Press of America, 1982), p. 32.

11. Thucydides, *The Peloponnesian War* (Modern Library, 1951; Crawley translation), pp. 334, 331; cf. Rex Warner translation (Penguin Classics, 1954), pp. 404-5, 402.

12. Seyom Brown, *The Causes and Prevention of War* (St. Martin's Press, 1987), p. 76, quoting Kenneth Waltz, *Man, the State, and War* (Columbia University Press, 1959), p. 159. Although we cannot pursue the point here, it is important for anyone who theorizes to consider that some diagnoses (by a process perhaps analogous to the self-fulfilling prophecy) "do not so much define as *create* a pathological condition." (Paul Watzlawick, ed., *The Invented Reality* [W. W. Norton, 1984], p. 67.) To the extent — which should be carefully appraised, and not exaggerated — that the influential "realist" and "neo-realist" beliefs in the inevitability of the war system possibly do serve to perpetuate it as a reality, decisions to postulate that peace is possible may themselves constitute a real step toward peace.

13. Robert Jervis, "Cooperation under the Security Dilemma," in Robert J. Art and Kenneth N. Waltz, eds., *The Use of Force* (University Press of America; second edition, 1983), p. 36. Note that Jervis says "many," not "all." It is the view of many of the authors represented in this book that the existence of means of defense that do not threaten others indicates ways out of the "dilemma"; see Chapter 6.

14. Cf. "The Delicate Balance of Terror" by Albert Wohlstetter in *Foreign Affairs*, Vol. 37, No. 2 (January 1959).

15. Richard A. Falk and Samuel S. Kim, in their anthology *The War System* (Westview, 1979), defined that system as "an all-embracing structure of mutually interlocking organizational and behavioral variables, in which violence or force is accepted and legitimized as the ultimate arbiter of social conflicts at all levels of human society" (p. 2).

16. Robert Jervis, *The Illogic of American Nuclear Strategy* (Cornell University Press, 1984), p. 13.

17. See Seyom Brown, *op. cit.*, pp. 111-172 for a readable discussion of the limitations of some past efforts to end war — including some that ExPro members would appraise more positively than Brown does.

18. Leonard C. Lewin, ed., *Report from Iron Mountain on the Possibility and Desirability of Peace* (The Dial Press, 1967). Presented as a leaked secret government document, *Report from Iron Mountain* has been read mainly as satire. Its longest chapters are on "The Functions of War" and "Substitutes for the Functions of War." As W. H. Ferry has suggested, it still repays reading.

19. The notion of a "systems" approach is not without difficulties: "Nearly any integrative or interdisciplinary approach to anything is liable to be called a systems approach," Mark Davidson has observed in his *Uncommon Sense: The Life and Thought of Ludwig von Bertalanffy, Father of General Systems Theory* (J. P. Tarcher, 1983), p. 191. For a brief, accessible overview of "the systems movement," broadly conceived, and some applications of systems thinking in peace research, see pp. 191-210 and 163-168, respectively. Robert R. Holt stresses the importance of a systems approach in "Converting the War System to a Peace System" (1987; see Chapter 8); citing Einstein's call for "a new type of thinking," he offers 12 principles for systems thinking in "Can Psychology Meet Einstein's Challenge?" *Political Psychology* (June 1984), pp. 199-225. See also Joanna Macy's Foreword (pp. vii-ix) to George Lakey, *Powerful Peacemaking* (New Society Publishers, 1987; see Chapter 3); she regards a "systems view" as "the major cognitive revolution of our time."

Use of "systems" terminology about war and peace predates ExPro. Robert C. Johansen wrote of "the need for system change" and contrasted "the war system" with "a peace system" in *Toward a Dependable Peace: A Proposal for an Appropriate Security System* (Institute for World Order, 1978), pp. 13-18, esp. p. 16. The phrase "war system" gained increased currency with the publication of the 1979 Falk/Kim anthology cited in note 15. Falk and Kim also wrote of "the transition from the war system to a peace system" (p. 3) and "the conditions of peace and the design of a viable peace system" (p. 5), citing Falk's *A Study of Future Worlds* and Saul H. Mendlovitz, ed., *On the Creation of a Just World Order* (both published by The Free Press, 1975). Johan Galtung published an article (in German) on "the war system" in 1975; it appeared in English the following year in his *Essays in Peace Research*, Vol. II, pp. 94-123, and again in *The True Worlds* (1980), pp. 179-236.

Mark Sommer is primarily responsible for ExPro's adoption of the term "peace system." (Cf. *Beyond the Bomb*, pp. 88, 90-91.) Despite use of the same phrase, ExPro's approach is distinct from that of the "functionalism" of the late David Mitrany, author of *A Working Peace System* (1944). Commenting on Mitrany's work, Sommer demonstrates ExPro's characteristic concern for discerning what may be complementary in different approaches (see *Beyond the Bomb*, pp. 94-95).

These notes do not, of course, purport to be a thorough survey of the war system / peace system framework; roughly equivalent conceptions have been offered by others using different terms, including some authors represented in this book (e.g., Patricia Mische, Hanna Newcombe, and Carolyn Stephenson).

20. Cf. Falk and Kim, *op. cit.*, p. 2.

21. The idea of depicting a peace system by way of an analogy with Star Wars was suggested by Robert Borosage in an ExPro discussion, probably in January 1986. After writing this description, I found that Dietrich Fischer had described a peace system with four (slightly different) layers in his "Peace 2010" scenario that appears in Earl Foell and Richard Nenneman, eds., *How Peace Came to the World* (MIT Press, 1986), pp. 121-128; see comments in Chapter 9 of this book. See also Robert Irwin, "Creating a Peace System," in *Steps Toward a Peaceful World: The ExPro Papers*, #1 (1986), pp. 17-20.

22. "Cultural change" may sound mysterious. See Robert R. Holt, "Converting the War System to a Peace System" and Elise Boulding, "Two Cultures of Religion as Obstacles to Peace" (discussed in Chapter 8) for suggestions of needed cultural changes.

23. In 1988 ExPro undertook a program of research under the rubric of "The Peace System Project" that is designed to define the changes needed and what individuals and groups can do to bring them about.

24. There are deep-rooted reasons why we tend to believe that others have more than they deserve, while we have less. See the introduction to Part VI, "Ethnic Conflict," and the chapter on "Ethnocentrism and Hostility" in Roger Brown, *Social Psychology: The Second Edition* (The Free Press, 1986), pp. 533-585. Brown discusses the "minimal group" experiments of Henri Tajfel and his colleagues, which deserve to be better known.

25. Persons who put a high value on peace often seem to believe that a mutually acceptable solution is best in any situation; while those who believe that aggression or entrenched injustice cannot be compromised with often regard war and political violence as tragic necessities. Gene Sharp presents a challenging third position. He insists that in acute conflicts (e.g., against an invader, dictator, or South Africa's apartheid regime) a mutually acceptable solution will not be adequate to the demands of freedom and justice, and therefore the methods commonly included under the rubric of conflict resolution — mediation, negotiation, conciliation —

are inadequate: power is needed to force change.

Sharp argues that the required power need not be violent, but can (or could, with adequate refinement of the technique) be generated by the technique of nonviolent struggle. For Sharp's most explicit comments on these issues, see "Investigating New Options in Conflict and Defense," *Teachers College Record* (Columbia University), Vol. 84, No. 1 (1982), pp. 50-64; also in *Social Alternatives* (Brisbane, Australia), Vol. 3, No. 2 (March 1983), pp. 13-20; and in Douglas Sloan, ed., *Education for Peace and Disarmament* (Teachers College Press, 1983), pp. 50-64.

While Sharp's principal focus is on the further development of nonviolent struggle, it should not be overlooked that the methods of conflict resolution can presumably also be further refined and developed, so as potentially to handle successfully more acute problems than they ever have before.

26. In other words, a "well-established peace system," as defined here, would become possible only in the period after the most acute conflicts and severe forms of oppression, such as those cited by Sharp (see previous note), had been fought through and eliminated — preferably by means of nonviolent struggle.

27. The author of this book believes that at present, the task of creating conditions to permit every person to enjoy a decent life requires power struggles, extending sometimes to forcible revolutionary overthrow, to change oppressive situations. While struggle and a measure of coercion seem virtually unavoidable in resolving some conflicts at this stage in human history, the beginnings of major reductions in violence do seem possible now. Gene Sharp, author of *The Politics of Nonviolent Action* (Porter Sargent, 1973), has made a strong argument that war, social oppression, dictatorship, and genocide can be eliminated by development and application of nonviolent struggle. See Chapter Eleven, "The Societal Imperative" in his *Social Power and Political Freedom* (Porter Sargent, 1980), pp. 285-308. A sophisticated exploration of the possibilities of revolutionary change through the coercive force exerted by nonviolent struggle, outlining a five-stage process, is George Lakey's *Powerful Peacemaking: A Strategy for a Living Revolution* (New Society Publishers, 1987; earlier edition, 1973).

28. See Elise Boulding, *Building a Global Civic Culture* (Teachers College Press, 1988).

29. Civilian-based defense is defined by Gene Sharp as "a defense policy against foreign invasions and internal take-overs relying on prepared noncooperation and defiance by the trained civilian population and their institutions to deny the attacker's objectives and make lasting control impossible." Sharp, "'The Political Equivalent of War' — Civilian-based Defense," *Social Power and Political Freedom*, p. 196n. See Chapter 6 for more on this policy.

30. If a country's own (preferably non-provocative) military defense is counted as a fourth layer (probably functioning concurrently with the third layer of global and regional peacekeeping intervention), then a fall-back to civilian-based defense or improvised popular nonviolent resistance — or to improvised or paramilitary violent resistance, if these are what the society chooses — would be a fifth layer of national defense. The more layers the better, as far as security is concerned; it is only for clarity and ease of remembering that description in terms of a smaller number is preferable.

31. Efforts at "outright annihilation" are extremely rare, and likely to become rarer in a world where various steps toward a peace system are being taken by different parties. Yet for some time to come, no one will be able to be certain that no nuclear attacks will occur. In any case, contrary to widespread assumptions, it is possible to be skeptical, as is George Kennan, that nuclear "blackmail" or attacks would achieve major

political advantage. See Kennan, *The Nuclear Delusion*, p. 71; quoted in Sommer, *Beyond the Bomb*, pp. 81-82.

32. The importance of having some ultimate means of struggle if efforts to seek mutually acceptable solutions fail is emphasized by Sharp, who also examines the differing consequences of use of violent or nonviolent sanctions. See indexed references to "Ultimate sanction" in *Social Power and Political Freedom*.

33. "An integrated . . . trends" comes from Mark Sommer, "Ten Strategies in Search of a Movement," *ExPro Paper* #6 (1987), p. 4. "A wisely structured . . ." is from Sommer, "Constructing Peace as a Whole System," *Whole Earth Review* #51 (Summer 1986), pp. 15-16.

Part One: The Present Debate — and Beyond

How the Peace Movement Shaped the Present Debate

1. On the need for and importance of social movements, and for an original and useful analysis of the stages they typically go through, see William H. Moyer, "The Movement Action Plan," discussed in Chapter 12 (1986, revised 1987; available for $2.00 from Social Movement Empowerment Project, 721 Shrader St., San Francisco, CA 94117; 415-387-3361).

Social movements play a fundamental role in altering social perceptions of what is important. Often highly important matters — such as denial of democratic rights to blacks, the danger of nuclear annihilation, the disruption of the earth's ecology — are not "newsworthy" until a social movement makes them a public issue. This is true not only for long-standing or gradually worsening situations, but even for sudden events. Although the Three Mile Island accident in 1979 was "automatically" front-page news, the 1966 Fermi plant accident (described in John Fuller's *We Almost Lost Detroit*) was not. Why the difference? Three Mile Island followed three years of nonviolent direct action campaigns that had forced nuclear power onto the public agenda.

2. Allen Hunter and James O'Brien have written: "[T]he pacifist Left which existed after the collapse of the Marxist parties . . . found a focus for rebellion in its members' need to stand, alone if need be, against society's evils. From this absolute moralism and the nonviolent tactics of personal witness and mass civil disobedience, the New Left consciously and unconsciously adopted issues, tactics, and moral postures. In the late 1950s the Friends, the Fellowship of Reconciliation (FOR), and the Committee for Nonviolent Action (CNVA) opposed nuclear testing as well as the fearful anti-communism that justified such atomic insanity. Radical pacifists, working in CORE and other groups, also played an active role in civil rights activity in the early 1960s. This tradition of personal witness had a larger influence on the New Left than is generally recognized." "Reading About the New Left," *Radical America*, Vol. 6, No. 4 (July-August 1972), pp. 76-77.

For a sampling of the spirit of that tradition, see Albert Bigelow, "Why I am Sailing into the Pacific Bomb Test Area" and Juanita Nelson, "A Matter of Freedom," in Paul Goodman, ed., *Seeds of Liberation* (George Braziller, 1964). Lawrence S. Wittner, *Rebels Against War: The American Peace Movement, 1933-1983* (Temple University Press, 1984), provides a good overview, as does the pictorial history *The Power of the People: Active Nonviolence in the United States* by Robert Cooney and Helen Michalowski (1977; New Society Publishers). The latter two books contain extensive bibliographies.

On the civil rights movement, the best introduction is the video series "Eyes on the Prize," which conveys with unmatched vividness the courage and commitment required to make major changes in the direction of U.S. society. *Eyes on the Prize: America's Civil Rights Years* (Penguin, 1987), edited by Clayborne Carson et al., is an excellent reader and guide to the movement prepared in connection with the video series. Among a host of valuable works being published, two useful studies giving a sense of the day-to-day reality of movement activity are Aldon D. Morris, *The Origins of the Civil Rights Movement* (Free Press, 1984) and David J. Garrow, *Bearing the Cross: Martin Luther King, Jr., and the Southern Christian Leadership Conference* (William Morrow, 1986).

3. Douglas C. Waller, *Congress and the Nuclear Freeze* (University of Massachusetts Press, 1987), p. 27. Waller was a Congressional staffperson working on the Freeze.

4. See Lens's memoir *Unrepentant Radical: An American Activist's Account of Five Turbulent Decades* (Beacon Press, 1980), pp. 396-403, for details of this initiative.

5. The sketch in the preceding two paragraphs is drawn in part from Senator Edward M. Kennedy and Senator Mark O. Hatfield, *Freeze!* (Bantam, 1972). Cf. also Waller, *op. cit.*

6. It is sometimes possible to cite government action as playing a positive role in the growth of a social movement. In this case, Randall Forsberg's path to the Freeze was influenced by employment at the Stockholm International Peace Research Institute (SIPRI), funded by the Swedish government.

7. On the elite's shift, see Thomas Ferguson and Joel Rogers, *The Hidden Election* (Pantheon, 1981). On public opinion: "With the exception of the rise in support for increased military spending, which was rapidly reversed, there is little or nothing in the public-opinion data to support the claim that the American public moved to the right in the years preceding Reagan's 1980 victory. If American public opinion drifted anywhere over Reagan's first term, it was toward the left, not the right . . ." Ferguson and Rogers, *Right Turn: The Decline of the Democrats and the Future of American Politics* (Hill and Wang, 1986), p. 28. Ferguson and Rogers present a thought-provoking alternative explanation of Reagan's electoral victories in their opening chapter.

8. On the Freeze, see Waller, *op. cit.*, for a Congress-centered account. Pam Solo's *From Protest to Policy: Beyond the Freeze to Common Security* (Ballinger, 1988), is a major participant's analysis. Finally, see Joel Rogers and Joshua Cohen, *Rules of the Game* (South End, 1986), discussed in Chapter 11 of this book, for a concise analysis of the obstacles the American political system puts in the way of popular movements and majority rule.

9. Kehler was interviewed in "The Freeze Revisited" (Stanley Foundation, December 1986); see Chapter 13 for further quotation.

Chapter 1: Deterrence, Star Wars, and Peace

1. "Activists for the status quo": anonymous comment quoted in K. Magraw, "Arms Control: It's Academic?" in *Nuclear Times* (May 1985).

2. Smoke states that deterrence requires "some measure of violence, actual or threatened" (p. 16). Gene Sharp argues that deterrence can be achieved through a capacity for nonviolent struggle that can impose costs (political or economic) on an opponent. See Sharp's *Making Europe Unconquerable: The Potential of Civilian-Based Deterrence and Defense* (Ballinger, 1986), pp. 24-27, 67-84.

3. Robert Jervis, *The Illogic of American Nuclear Strategy* (Cornell University Press, 1984).

Chapter 2: Arms Control: Pro and Con

1. It should be recognized that "a better superpower relationship," while desirable to reduce the risk of the nuclear annihilation of humanity, is not an unmixed blessing. Although everyone has a common interest in survival, in other respects the common interests of the two superpower governments might conflict with the interests of people in other countries. See Chapters 9 and 10 for more on this.

2. The CBS News report is quoted from David M. Rubin, "Television Signs An INF Pact," p. 11 of *Deadline: A Bulletin from the Center for War, Peace, and the News Media*, insert in *Nuclear Times* (November-December 1987).

3. Petra K. Kelly, Annual Gandhi Lecture prepared for delivery October 3rd, 1988, p. 5. Available from Petra K. Kelly, MdB, Bundeshaus - HT 718, 5300 Bonn 1, Federal Republic of Germany. She quotes then Secretary of Defense Frank Carlucci as saying that it is "clearly in our interest to be able to retain the warheads on the missiles that are to be destroyed" (*International Herald Tribune*, 28 January 1988).

4. In April 1982 Secretary of State Alexander Haig asserted that a NATO declaration of "no first use" of nuclear weapons in Europe would require that the U.S. "reintroduce the draft, triple the size of its armed forces, and put its economy on a wartime footing." Haig, "Peace and Deterrence" (U.S. Department of State, Bureau of Public Affairs, Current Policy No. 383), p. 2.

5. Only in 1988 did the owls get so far as to publish a book with one chapter on "non-provocative and civilian-based defense." See Joseph S. Nye, Jr., Graham T. Allison, and Albert Carnesale, eds., *Fateful Visions: Avoiding Nuclear Catastrophe* (Ballinger, 1988). It would be a marvelous thing if tenured scholars with access to one of the world's greatest libraries could keep less than ten or twenty years behind the work in their field. Some people with fewer advantages did not wait until 1985 to "begin" — or rather, merely suggest beginning — a search for alternatives to nuclear deterrence.

But there may be a plausible explanation for the owls' belated call to "begin." Some readers may have observed discussions in which men repeat — or "clarify" — something a woman has said. Though repetitions or restatements can be useful, some men seem to feel that something has not really been said until a man has said it. Perhaps, in the eyes of these acolytes of nuclear deterrence and arms control, the search for alternatives has not *really* begun until *they* have started scrambling toward the front of the search party.

Chapter 3: Redefining the Issues: Aspects of the War System

1. This paragraph is primarily indebted to a speech by Daniel Ellsberg in the early 1980s that attempted to illuminate the nuclear danger by inquiring into when and how preparations for mass killing of civilians became accepted behavior. This speech included the reading of a memorable passage from physicist Freeman Dyson's memoir *Disturbing the Universe* (Harper & Row, 1979), in which Dyson described the step-by-step passage from his pre-war pacifist ideals to an active role in the engineering of mass killing (see pp. 30-31).

2. See Alva Myrdal, *The Game of Disarmament: How the United States and Russia Run the Arms Race* (1976; Pantheon, revised and updated, 1982). Even "conventional" (i.e., non-nuclear) war may become almost unavoidably "nuclear" in the sense of causing radioactive contamination if conducted in Western Europe or in any other countries with nuclear power plants. "The Bradford University School of Peace Studies [U.K.] has released a report showing that a conventional 'non-nuclear' war in Europe would 'spread radioactivity over wide areas and lead to vast tracts of land remaining uninhabitable for generations.' The fallout would come as conventional bombs ripped apart commercial nuclear power plants." Reported in *Greenletter* (Berkeley), Vol. 4, No. 3 (August 1988), p. 3.

3. Theodore Roszak, Introduction to E. F. Schumacher, *Small is Beautiful: Economics as if People Mattered* (Harper & Row, 1973), p. 4. Roszak wrote that Schumacher "belongs to that subterranean tradition of organic and decentralist economics whose major spokesmen include Prince Kropotkin, Gustav Landauer, Tolstoy, William Morris, Gandhi, Lewis Mumford, and, most recently, Alex Comfort, Paul Goodman, and Murray Bookchin." One might also mention Ralph Borsodi and Mildred Loomis. For a survey of social criticism and constructive thought in this tradition, see the closing chapters of Pyarelal, *Mahatma Gandhi: The Last Phase*, two volumes (Ahmedabad: Navajivan Press, 1956, 1958). Many books and pamphlets by and about Gandhi can be ordered from Greenleaf Books, RFD, Canton, Maine.

4. For information on PeaceNet, "the first global computer network for peace," linking people in the U.S. and over 70 other countries, contact PeaceNet (3228 Sacramento St., San Francisco, CA 94115; 415-923-0900).

5. The Rocky Mountain Institute's informative and entertaining newsletter lists in each issue dozens of high-quality technical and popular articles sold by RMI. Available on request from RMI, 1739 Snowmass Creek Road, Snowmass, CO 81654-9199; (303) 927-3128 or -3851.

6. The most readily available to U.S. readers of Galtung's many works is probably *The True Worlds: A Transnational Perspective* (Free Press, 1980), sold by mail by the World Policy Institute (777 U.N. Plaza, NY, NY 10017). See indexed references to "structural violence." The notes in that volume make frequent reference to Galtung's collected *Essays in Peace Research* (Copenhagen: Ejlers, 1975-1980; Atlantic Highlands, NJ: Humanities Press).

7. For discussion of the gender "subtexts" of such concepts as "citizen," "worker," and "consumer," see Nancy Fraser, "What's Critical about Critical Theory? The Case of Habermas and Gender," in Seyla Benhabib and Drucilla Cornell, eds., *Feminism as Critique: On the Politics of Gender* (University of Minnesota Press, 1987), pp. 31-56.

8. Alan Wolfe writes (with irony): "Since everyone in the United States aspires to the Aristotelian virtues of balance and moderation, a program of no more nuclear weapons combined with many more conventional weapons strikes many Americans as reasonable and sensible." He suggests that "the next step [in educating the U.S. public should be] to demonstrate some not especially known truths about conventional weapons: that they are as destructive as low-yield nuclear weapons; that they run the risk of actually lowering, rather than raising, the threshold against the use of nuclear weapons . . ." Alan Wolfe, "American Domestic Politics and the Alliance," in Mary Kaldor and Richard Falk, eds., *Dealignment: A New Foreign Policy Perspective* (Oxford and NY: Basil Blackwell for the United Nations University, 1987), p. 80. Cf. George F. Kennan, *The Nuclear Delusion*, p. xxviii.

9. James Peck, *The Chomsky Reader* (Pantheon, 1987), p. vii. Peck's introduction is a fine appreciation of Chomsky's unique role in American intellectual life. An inkling of the personal sacrifices made by Chomsky in sustaining an extraordinarily high level of writing and public speaking (and sometimes civil disobedience) for over twenty years can be gathered from the closing pages (54-55) of the interview that opens the volume.

Among Chomsky's more important collections of political writings are *American Power and the New Mandarins* (Vintage, 1969), *For Reasons of State* (Vintage, 1973), *Radical Priorities* (Montreal: Black Rose Books, 1981), and *Towards a New Cold War* (Pantheon, 1982). *The Fateful Triangle* (South End, 1983) focuses on the relations of the United States, Israel, and the Palestinians. See this book's annotated bibliography for Chomsky's most recent titles.

10. For a valuable analysis of the interaction of rational and irrational factors in the making of U.S. foreign policy, see Chomsky, "Vietnam and United States Global Strategy" in *For Reasons of State*, pp. 31-66, esp. pp. 53-66 (and accompanying notes); this discussion is reprinted in *The Chomsky Reader*, pp. 227-255 (esp. pp. 245-255). Cf. also *Turning the Tide* (published a dozen years later), pp. 55-58, 67. In the later book Chomsky terms the psychology of leaders and ideologues "rather boring" (p. 55).

The subject may, however, deserve careful attention, for two reasons. First, forming a moral interpretation of the behavior and mentality of government officials seems to be part of the process by which people who have previously accepted much of the official U.S. government view of the world begin to think more independently; this process may be facilitated by offering an interpretation that is both accurate and persuasive. And second, understanding the mentalities of policy-makers, journalists, etc. may be important for devising strategies for transforming the status quo.

Among useful basic sources on these matters are the works of Lloyd Etheredge and Robert Jervis. An excerpt from Etheredge's *Can Governments Learn?* (Pergamon, 1985) is discussed in Chapter 8 of this book. Jervis's *magnum opus* is *Perception and Misperception in International Politics* (Princeton, 1976); see also his other books. A brief introduction to his work is Jervis, "Hypotheses on Misperception," in Richard A. Falk and Samuel S. Kim, eds., *The War System* (Westview, 1979).

Friedrich Nietzsche touched on both elements in the complex blend of cognitive and moral factors in two remarks: "The most common lie is that with which one lies to oneself; lying to others is, relatively, an exception" and "Error . . . is not blindness, error is *cowardice*." Quoted from *The Antichrist*, section 55, in Walter Kaufmann, ed., *The Portable Nietzsche* (Viking, 1954), p. 640, and from the third section of the preface to *Ecce Homo* (in one volume with *The Genealogy of Morals*, Vintage, 1967), p. 218, respectively.

11. These are conducted by Macy and other members of Interhelp in many places. For addresses and phone numbers for 28 U.S. and ten international Interhelp members (as of November 1988), contact Interhelp, P.O. Box 8895, Madison, WI 53708-8895, U.S.A.; (608) 231-1219. Interhelp's quarterly journal *Awakening* may be

obtained from the same address. See also Macy's *Despair and Personal Power in the Nuclear Age* (New Society Publishers, 1983).

12. Peter Schwartz, quoted in "The World Information Economy: Stewart Brand interviews Peter Schwartz and Jay Ogilvy," *Whole Earth Review* No. 53 (Winter 1986), pp. 88-89.

13. This passage was drafted prior to the October 19, 1987 stock market crash, whose magnitude has been attributed in part to computer-programmed trading.

Part Two: Designing a Peace System
Why and How to Think About the Future

1. Kenneth E. Boulding, "The Prevention of World War III," *The Virginia Quarterly Review*, vol. 38, no. 1 (Winter 1962), pp. 1-12, reprinted in Richard A. Falk and Saul H. Mendlovitz, eds., *The Strategy of World Order*, Vol. 1: *Toward a Theory of War Prevention* (1966), pp. 3-13, quotation from p. 8.

2. Richard A. Falk, Samuel S. Kim, and Saul H. Mendlovitz, eds., *Toward a Just World Order* (Westview, 1982), p. 561.

3. Friedrich Engels, "Socialism: Utopian and Scientific." (Available in many editions. The quotation comes a half-dozen or ten pages into the text.) Martin Buber's *Paths in Utopia* (1949; Beacon, 1958) is indispensable reading on utopian socialism, anarchism, and the attitudes of Marx, Engels, and Lenin toward them. Marxian discouragement of utopian, or visionary, thinking has arguably had a very damaging effect on social change efforts, and not least on the history of countries where Marxists have come to power.

4. Robert Boguslaw, *The New Utopians: A Study of System Design and Social Change* (Prentice-Hall, 1965), pp. 9-12, 13.

5. Arthur Waskow, "Looking Forward: 1999," *Our Generation* (Montreal), Vol. V, No. 4 (1968).

6. Laurence H. Shoup and William Minter, *Imperial Brain Trust: The Council on Foreign Relations and United States Foreign Policy* (Monthly Review, 1977), p. 254.

7. Saul H. Mendlovitz and Thomas G. Weiss explain WOMP's choice of time span in "Towards Consensus: The Institute for World Order's Model World Orders Project," in Grenville Clark and Louis B. Sohn, *Introduction to World Peace Through World Law*, p. 80. (This 1973 booklet published by the World Without War Council reprinted the opening chapter of *World Peace Through World Law* and appended to it several other essays. The 1984 edition no longer contains the Mendlovitz/Weiss essay.) The Institute for World Order is now the World Policy Institute. The World Order Models Project continues at the WPI address, 777 U.N. Plaza, New York, NY 10017; (212) 490-0010.

8. The 200-year present is discussed in Elise Boulding, *Building a Global Civic Culture* (Teachers College Press, 1988), pp. 3-7, and in her "Learning to Learn" (1979), discussed in Chapter 7.

9. Any criticism that urges change implies that things could be different and thus sets up an implicit contrast between analysis and vision. Failure to articulate the vision in convincing form severely undercuts social criticism; for if there seems really to be no feasible alternative to the status quo (as is argued, for example — albeit unconvincingly — in *Living with Nuclear Weapons*), then criticism seems immature, pointless complaining. Further, without thinking through the nature of the desired alternative, one is less likely to recognize what is essential to the status quo, and more prone to focus on mere symptoms; thus, neglect of vision thinking tends to produce inadequate analysis.

Carmen Sirianni offers a well-balanced formulation: "Political strategy . . . cannot be derived from utopian theorizing alone, but must also base itself on analysis of the constraints and possibilities of existing social forces. An effective emancipatory politics cannot dispense with either of these dimensions. Utopia is essential to critical analysis and politics." Quoted from "Production and Power in a Classless Society: A Critical Analysis of the Utopian Dimensions of Marxist Theory," *Socialist Review*, No. 59 (September-October 1981), p. 74. In this book Part II is devoted more to "utopian theorizing," while Part III examines "existing social forces," emphasizing those that could contribute to creation of a peace system but not omitting to note those that constrain such efforts.

10. *Ecotopia: The Notebooks and Reports of William Weston* (Banyan Tree Books, 1975; Bantam, 1977) describes independent Ecotopia (Northern California, Oregon, and Washington) in 1999, as seen through the eyes of the first U.S. reporter allowed in since secession. The book became an underground bestseller. *Ecotopia Emerging* (Banyan Tree Books, 1981) recounts the growth of the movement for an ecologically-sound society, building to the dramatic events that make secession from the U.S. possible. Callenbach's Survivalist Party leaflets and party leader Vera Allwen's FDR-like "fireside chats" provide excellent models for "Green" propaganda in the 1980s and 1990s.

World War II seems inexhaustibly appealing to novelists; but to create a realistic novel of the world's struggle for peace, spanning the next few decades, would offer a new challenge that might prove irresistible to any novelist ambitious enough to be attracted by an epic theme and intellectually strong enough to handle the complexity of historical change proceses. Brian Stableford and David Langford's brilliant *The Third Millennium: A History of the World, AD 2000-3000* (Knopf, 1985) gives a hint of how fascinating such a novel could be.

11. The readings of Part II were of course not originally written to fit any scheme. The reader should therefore make allowances, there and throughout this book, for difficulties of fit and awkwardness of proportion. Also, some selections from a single book that might more logically both have been used in the same session have been discussed in separate chapters to avoid the possibly insuperable logistical hassle of two people sharing a book the same week. If your group believes a different arrangement of the readings will serve you better, by all means feel free to try it.

12. Editors' introduction, Paul C. Nystrom and William H. Starbuck, eds., *Handbook of Organizational Design* (Oxford University Press, 1981), p. xx.

13. The source of this quotation from Rene Dubos was unavailable at the time of writing.

Chapter 4: Envisioning and Designing a Future of Peace

1. In addition to *Peace Research Abstracts Journal*, Hanna and Alan Newcombe also publish six *Peace Research Reviews* each year; these are essays surveying or extending past peace research. See, for example, Hanna Newcombe's brisk, useful "Survey of Peace Research," *Peace Research Reviews*, Vol. IX, No. 6 (1984; 71 pp. of text, 25 pages of references; $4.00). They are excellent (and inexpensive) resources for the student, scholar, or activist. For a list of available publications, write Peace Research Institute—Dundas, 25 Dundana Ave., Dundas, Ontario, CANADA L9H 4E5.

2. Editors' introduction, Paul C. Nystrom and William H. Starbuck, eds., *Handbook of Organizational Design* (Oxford University Press, 1981), pp. xix-xx.

3. See "Recommended Periodicals" later in this book.

4. This quotation is taken from *Future Survey Annual 1983*, which contained a chart of fifty paths, rather than from the similar remarks introducing the more recent "Sixty Paths . . ."

5. For more on "alternative methods for international security," see Stephenson's essay reviewing the literature in her book of that title (University Press of America, 1982).

6. The term "threat system" is associated with Kenneth E. Boulding, who contrasts the use of threats with integrative and exchange systems in society. For a brief outline of these concepts, see Cynthia Earl Kerman, *Creative Tension: The Life and Thought of Kenneth Boulding* (University of Michigan Press, 1974), pp. 11-13.

7. See Fred Polak, *The Image of the Future* (1955; translated and abridged by Elise Boulding, Jossey-Bass/ Elsevier, 1972).

Chapter 5: World Governance

1. World federalist publications are full of such quotations. See, for example, Tom A. Hudgens, *Let's Abolish War* (1986) and Lawrence Abbott, "World Federalism: What? Why? How?" (no date; ca 1983). These are available from the Campaign for U.N. Reform and the World Federalist Association, respectively, both located at 418 Seventh St., S.E., Washington, DC 20003; 1-800-HATE-WAR.) Cf. also George Rathjens ("First Thoughts," *ExPro Paper #5*, p. 22): "Can our problem really be solved with anything short of true world government? (In the long term, I doubt it.)" The quotation later in the paragraph ("If we were to wait") is from Dietrich Fischer, *Preventing War in the Nuclear Age*, p. 5.

2. Truman quoted by Abbott, p. 16; Hudgens, p. 17; Benjamin B. Ferencz in collaboration with Ken Keyes, Jr., *PlanetHood* (Vision Books, 1988), pp. 41-42.

3. See Abbott, pp. 14-16, and Hudgens, p. 10. Ferencz and Keyes acknowledge "an unfortunate civil war between the southern and northern states" (p. 66) but suggest that without a federal union more bloodshed might have occurred among the states over the course of decades. Ronald J. Glossop makes a similar

argument at greater length in *Confronting War* (McFarland, 1987), p. 290. Ferencz and Keyes further indicate that secession from a world federation should be unacceptable and considered "synonymous with aggression" (pp. 105, 107).

4. Abbott, pp. 12-14.

5. Abbott, p. 14.

6. Ferencz and Keyes, p. 40; compare Abbott, p. 8.

7. Two paperback sources in which the Nuremberg Principles (and some related documents) can be consulted are Richard Falk, Gabriel Kolko, and Robert Jay Lifton, eds., *Crimes of War* (Vintage, 1971), pp. 88-108 and Arthur J. Laffin and Anne Montgomery, eds., *Swords into Plowshares: Nonviolent Direct Action for Disarmament* (Harper & Row, 1987; $8.95), pp. 207-208.

8. Quotation transcribed from report by John Hockenberry, "All Things Considered," National Public Radio, April 30, 1985.

9. The Ferencz collections of commentary and documents cited were published by Oceana Publications (Dobbs Ferry, NY) in 1975, 1980, and 1983, respectively; Oceana published Ferencz's *A Common Sense Guide to World Peace* in 1985.

10. Hudgens, p. 59.

11. Johan Galtung has presented a similar challenge to the thinking of disarmament advocates: "Disarmament does not seem to be the road to peace, but peace may be the road to disarmament." *The True Worlds* (Free Press, 1980), p. 202 (quoted in Fischer, *Preventing War in the Nuclear Age*, p. 111). For more of Galtung's viewpoint, see his *There Are Alternatives! Four Roads to Peace and Security* (1984), listed in this book's annotated bibliography.

12. The newsletter of Peace Brigades International is available from PBI, 4722 Baltimore Ave., Philadelphia, PA 19143. Witness for Peace can be reached at WFP, 198 Broadway, New York, NY 10038.

13. For a fascinating account of these negotiations, see William Wertenbaker, *The New Yorker* (August 1 and 8, 1983). Some of the "delegates expect [the International Seabed Authority established by the treaty] to be at least an experiment in world government, if not the prototype or embryo of one" (August 8, p. 56). Elliot Richardson, a prominent Republican and U.S. delegate to the negotiations, called them "the single most significant event in the development of international law and the peaceful cooperation among nations since the founding of the United Nations" (*New Directions*, Sept.-Oct. 1980, p. 2).

14. The flaws of Gross National Product have long been pointed out. More than twenty years ago Paul Goodman recalled John Kenneth Galbraith's still earlier example of "the man taking aspirin as the car radiator boils over in the traffic jam on the way to the overcrowded public beach: every part of this is good for the Gross National Product and will be subsumed under Recreation." *People or Personnel: Decentralizing and the Mixed System* (1965; Vintage pb. ed., 1968), p. 118.

More recently, Lester R. Brown has proposed adjusting production figures by an "ecological deflator" analogous to adjustment of GNP figures to factor out the misleading effects of price inflation. Brown states, for example, that "of the 52 million acres of cropland irrigated in the United States, 14 million are watered by pumping groundwater faster than it is recharged. . . . When the aquifers run dry . . . grain production will fall by an estimated 9 million tons." Considering also current use of "highly erodible cropland," Brown estimates that "taken together, grain output from unsustainable use of soil and water totals 51 million tons, one-sixth of the 300-million-ton U.S. grain harvest." *World Watch* (May-June 1988), p. 2. For a good discussion of the importance of indicators, see Johan Galtung, *The True Worlds*, Appendix, pp. 431ff, 460-461.

15. Michael Marien, *Societal Directions and Alternatives: A Critical Guide to the Literature* (Information for Policy Design, 1976), p. 10. Falk's *A Study of Future Worlds* is available from the World Policy Institute, 777 United Nations Plaza, N.Y., N.Y. 10017. See also other titles in their catalog.

Chapter 6: Alternative Security Policies

1. Kenneth N. Waltz, *Theory of International Politics* (Random House, 1979), p. 64. More explicitly, Waltz writes (p. 186): "John Herz coined the term 'security dilemma' to describe the condition in which states, unsure of one another's intentions, arm for the sake of security and in doing so set a vicious circle in motion. Having armed for the sake of security, states feel less secure and buy more arms because the means to anyone's security is a threat to someone else who in turn responds by arming." Waltz cites Herz, "Idealist internationalism and the security dilemma," *World Politics*, Vol. 2 (January 1950), p. 157. Whether or not "security" (as contrasted, say, with elite desires for prestige, power, and profit) is the primary motivation for arming, it is today the most commonly cited justification for it.

2. The qualification "significant," though imprecise, is necessary. People might cross a border with murderous intent armed with kitchen knives, but such an attack could easily be defeated and thus is not significant in the sense intended here.

3. John McPhee, *Place de la Concorde Suisse* (Farrar, Straus & Giroux, 1985; 149 pp.; $6.95).

4. For a list of Gene Sharp's publications, write the Program on Nonviolent Sanctions, Center for International Affairs, Harvard University, 1737 Cambridge St., Cambridge, MA 02138.

5. Sharp, "Making the Abolition of War a Realistic Goal," in Carolyn M. Stephenson, ed., *Alternative Methods for International Security* (University Press of America, 1982), p. 128.

6. Sharp, *Social Power and Political Freedom* (Porter Sargent, 1980), p. 196.

7. See Sharp's *Making Europe Unconquerable: The Potential of Civilian-Based Deterrence and Defense* (Ballinger, 1986), p. 163, note 6, for specifics.

8. Kennan's review of the first (1985) edition of *Making Europe Unconquerable* was reprinted in a new (1986) edition of the book.

9. Taylor, formerly an innovative designer of nuclear weapons, is the subject of another John McPhee book, *The Curve of Binding Energy* (Farrar, Straus & Giroux, 1974; 231 pp.).

10. The broadest coverage of this field is found in the international research newsletter *Non-Offensive Defence*, containing news of both political developments and new publications; it is published three to four times per year and is free on request from the Centre of Peace and Conflict Research at the University of Copenhagen, Vandkunsten 5, DK 1467 Copenhagen K., Denmark. Issue #9 appeared in May 1988 and was 57 pages long. Editor Bjorn Moller published a 123-page bibliography, also free on request, in 1987.

Defense & Disarmament Alternatives, published by the Institute for Defense and Disarmament Studies (2001 Beacon St., Brookline, MA 02146; 617-734-4216), has increased its emphasis on "alternative defense." The June 1988 issue was 12 pages long, November 1988's, four pages. A year's subscription (six issues) is sent free to Friends of the Institute ($25). (IDDS offers several publications, ranging from article to book length, on the subject.)

The Alternative Defense Project (c/o The Fund for Peace, 345 East 46th St., New York, NY 10017) has published Mark Sommer's "An Emerging Consensus: Common Security through Qualitative Disarmament" (1988; 16 pp.; $2.00), a pamphlet tracing the roots of current non-provocative defense thinking back to the 1930s.

11. See note 31 to "The Peace System Approach to Eliminating War."

12. The Pittsburgh Peace Institute offers an important model of local education on civilian-based defense and other peace-related topics. For a list of course offerings, write Pittsburgh Peace Institute, 1139 Wightman Street, Pittsburgh, PA 15217.

13. *Civilian-Based Defense: News & Opinion* is published bimonthly ($8/year in the U.S., $10 outside) by the Civilian-Based Defense Association, Box 31616, Omaha, NE 68131. It publishes surveys of developments, news of public discussion of CBD, and reviews of works in the field. See, for example, Brian Martin's review of Alex P. Schmid's *Social Defence and Soviet Military Power: An Inquiry into the Relevance of an Alternative Defence Concept* ('s-Gravenhage, Netherlands: Ministerie van Onderwijs en Wetenschappen, 1986; 469 pp.; 60 Dutch guilders). Schmid's book is an important critical assessment of CBD that finds it unsatisfactory as a substitute for, but possibly useful as a supplement to, military defense. Martin's review can be found in *Civilian-Based Defense: News & Opinion*, Vol. 4, No. 4 (May 1988). A review by Leonard Gambrell of Stephen Flanagan's chapter on "Nonprovocative and Civilian-Based Defenses" in Joseph Nye et al., eds., *Fateful Visions* (1988) appeared in the Fall 1988 (Vol. 5, No. 2) issue.

14. Sharp, *Gandhi as a Political Strategist, with Essays on Ethics and Politics* (Porter Sargent, 1979), p. 162.

15. The emphasis in this section on "alternative security policies" has been on defense against military attack. This subject will very likely — given the continuing decline in the utility of military power noted by observers of widely differing views — gradually become relatively less important in comparison with struggles using non-military forms of pressure, with economic measures looming largest.

One of the landmark volumes on CBD, *The Strategy of Civilian Defence* (Adam Roberts, ed.; Faber and Faber, 1967), began with a chapter on "Forms of Military Attack." A future book elaborating the peace system approach should include a typology of "Forms of Non-military Attack." Actions like Stalin's 1948 "salami tactics" vs. Czechoslovakia, U.S. destabilization of Chile's Allende regime through economic warfare and fomenting of a coup, C.I.A. and K.G.B. interference in foreign politics, the United States's post-1975 economic and diplomatic campaign against Vietnam, the causing of ecological damage to other countries — all deserve analysis. Adequate security policies will need to include ways to minimize or effectively resist and remedy such threats.

Chapter 7: Economic Development, Ecology, and Peace

1. Lester R. Brown, Worldwatch Institute, February 1988 letter advertising Lester R. Brown et al., *State of the World 1988* ($9.95 when prepaid; Worldwatch Institute, 1776 Massachusetts Ave., NW, Washington, DC 20036).

2. Brian Stableford and David Langford, *The Third Millennium: A History of the World: AD 2000-3000* (Knopf, 1985), chapter 9, "The Greenhouse Crisis," pp. 45-50. See this book's annotated bibliography for more about this extraordinary book.

3. Dianne Dumanoski, "Scientists Fear Fallout from Ozone Loss," *Boston Globe* (March 21, 1988), p. 3. More from this article: "The changes now occurring could cause 'big-time problems' in the near future. . . . 'This isn't 2050, this is us and our children,'" remarked scientist Irving Mintzer. "'We have enough information to know that we need to be concerned,'" said immunologist Margaret Kripke; "but, in the areas of greatest concern, she noted, 'we have the least information, specifically food crops, plant life, and marine organisms in the food chain. If we start messing around with the world's food supply, we're really in trouble.'" In addition, "research has shown that the skin plays an important role in the body's immune system and that ultraviolet radiation [increased through ozone layer thinning] can damage this immune function. . . . [Kripke] said such damage could inhibit the body's ability to fight off certain kinds of infectious diseases, with serious health consequences for the world."

Another scientist has found that "tiny plankton at the base of the Antarctic food chain are very sensitive to increased ultraviolet radiation, so the loss of ozone in that region could have a devastating effect on the marine food chain from plankton to fish, penguins, seals, and whales." That effect could in turn release carbon dioxide from the ocean, aggravating global warming. "'The apprehension one has is that too many of the things we are observing were unpredicted,'" observed a scientist. "The Antarctic ozone hole was something beyond the worst-case projections. . . . How many more [surprises] will we have?'" A colleague, noting that ozone losses "have been greater than the [computer] models have predicted [and] that future projections have been based on these models," remarked: "'So you have to ask the question. Are we underestimating the change in the future?'" F. Sherwood Rowland, a leading atmospheric scientist, warned: "'The potential consequences are severe. At this point, one cannot eliminate catastrophe as one of the possible conclusions.'"

4. Edward Goldsmith et al., *Blueprint for Survival* (1972; U.S. edition, Signet, 1974; 144 pp.), p. 3. Some important, readable early works calling attention to humanity's ecological crisis were: Barry Commoner, *The Closing Circle* (1971; 330 pp.); Dennis C. Pirages and Paul R. Ehrlich, *Ark II: Social Response to Environmental Imperatives* (1974; 344 pp.); Paul R. Ehrlich, Anne H. Ehrlich, and John P. Holdren, *Ecoscience: Population, Resources, Environment* (1977; 1051 pp.).

Although scientific knowledge has certainly advanced since the 1970s, general public understanding has lagged so far behind that these volumes can still be read with profit; the main ideas are not outdated. For more current information, see Lester Brown's annual *State of the World* volumes and Edward Goldsmith and

Nicholas Hildyard, eds., *The Earth Report: The Essential Guide to Global Ecological Issues* (Price Stern Sloan, 1988; 240 pp.). For an analysis of the ozone depletion problem and what to do about it, see Arjun Makhijani et al., *Saving Our Skins: Technical Potential and Policies for Elimination of Ozone-Depleting Chlorine Compounds* (Environmental Policy Institute, 218 D St., SE, Washington, DC 20003; September 1988).

5. On exponential growth and time lags in the perception of problems' seriousness, see Donella H. Meadows et al., *The Limits to Growth* (1972). For an analysis of seven global models, see Donella H. Meadows et al., *Groping in the Dark: The First Decade of Global Modeling* (Wiley, 1982). See also D.H. Meadows and J.M. Robinson, *The Electronic Oracle: Computer Models and Social Decisions* (Wiley, 1985), described in the annotated bibliography of this book.

6. See the ecologically-oriented ("Green") books by Bookchin, Callenbach, Capra & Spretnak, Hulsberg, Kelly, Sale, and Tokar included in the annotated bibliography.

7. Source cited in note 1 above. What any writer means by "economic progress," of course, nowadays requires scrutiny.

8. For a readable treatment of the "debt crisis," see Susan George, *A Fate Worse than Debt* (Grove Press, 1988). As an alternative to "debt slavery" — and also to cancelling or defaulting on the debt, which she opposes for several reasons (p. 235) — George offers a program of "creative reimbursement" that would require political backing in both North and South, greater unity among the debtors themselves, and less focus by them on international markets and more on their people's real needs (p. 236). Her program would combine forms of reimbursement tied to development progress and democratization in the debtor countries, and would include "reimbursement in kind" that could allow states "to pay off a part of their debt by *preserving their own national heritage*" — conserving species diversity, collecting traditional knowledge, and other activities that would serve to promote both development and pride (pp. 242-3). For additional elements and details, see pp. 229-254, "The 3-D Solution: Debt, Development, Democracy."

9. See Charles Perrow, *Normal Accidents* (Basic Books, 1984), chapter three, "Complexity, Coupling, and Catastrophe," especially pp. 89-100.

10. Paul and Percival Goodman's classic *Communitas: Means of Livelihood and Ways of Life* (Vintage, 1960) outlines three community models, one of them designed to provide guaranteed subsistence.

11. Journalist Alexander Cockburn has summarized the findings of Swedish social scientist Goran Therborn's *Why Some Peoples Are More Unemployed Than Others* (Verso, 1986):

"Mass unemployment is not ineluctable. Five countries in the advanced capitalist world have managed to keep unemployment low: Austria, Sweden, Norway, Japan and Switzerland. Those societies differ in political and economic texture, but they all share an institutionalized commitment to full employment. Austria, Sweden and Norway score high on unionization and social democratic political weight. Japan and Switzerland do not, but, Therborn suggests, they have a strong precapitalist component — quasi-feudal in the former, petit bourgeois in the latter — which contributes to a politico-economic perspective broader than the rate of return on invested capital. None of the five is a member of the E.E.C. [European Economic Community]; all are peripheral to the Atlantic alliance. Thus, national roads to full employment are possible. They require progressive control of the policies of the national bank; low real interest rates; direct government intervention in the economy; reflation geared to investment, both public and private; active labor-market policy measures; emphasis on productive over finance capital." *The Nation* (June 27, 1987), p. 877.

See also Robert Kuttner, *The Economic Illusion: False Choices between Prosperity and Social Justice* (Houghton Mifflin, 1984).

Leland Stauber presents an original proposal for decentralization of social power based on a detailed analysis of the Austrian experience in *A New Program for Democratic Socialism: Lessons from the Market-Planning Experience in Austria* (Four Willows Press, Box 322, Carbondale, IL 62903; 1987; 412 pp.; $35.00), reviewed in *In These Times* (March 23-29, 1988), p. 18. (Major portions of the book's final chapter can also be consulted in Leland Stauber, "A Proposal for a Democratic Market Economy," *Journal of Comparative Economics*, September 1977.)

While rejecting the huge wealth and power inequalities generated by capitalism, Stauber also acknowledges widely recognized drawbacks of socialized ownership: excessive concentrations of political and economic power, and reduced economic efficiency because of overly centralized planning and resistance to dismissing excess labor and closing inefficient plants.

Stauber offers a proposal that would, he argues, create "greater social equality while retaining all the essential advantages of a market economy" (p. 335). Its key element is that most corporations (excluding both small businesses and whatever giant organizations might be directly run by the national government) would function in a "market socialist" sector, "operated exactly as private firms, but with ownership vested in a system of local government investment funds" (p. 336). Private promoters would have "complete freedom of enterprise," but "for any venture requiring the corporate form," they would be required "to seek capital from the proposed capital market in publicly owned investment funds" (p. 338). Stauber's grounding in the largely successful but still problematic Austrian experience enables him to anticipate and address many potential problems.

Stauber also argues (pp. 354-359) that "the approach and concrete proposals advanced" in his book offer solutions to the problems the U.S.S.R., China, and other Communist societies are trying to solve. The proposals could be implemented gradually in both Communist and capitalist nations, and Stauber judges them politically feasible even in the U.S., suggesting conservative voters be asked: "Would you prefer to have the permanent stream of consumption income that now goes every year to the very wealthy go instead to your local government, either to reduce your present taxes or to allow more local public services without a tax increase?" (p. 362).

Stauber's proposal addresses major dilemmas of economic life and represents a carefully conceived synthesis of ideas drawn from the lessons of both market and socialist experience. Such mutual learning, he suggests, might even help to "moderate some of the East-West conflict itself" (p. 360). For a proposal somewhat resembling Stauber's, see David Morris, "Social Technology, Inc.," in *Defining Social Investment* ($3.00 from Co-op America; see address in note 19-C below).

12. See several of the chapters in Carmen Sirianni, ed., *Worker Participation and the Politics of Reform* (Temple University Press, 1987).

13. See Herman E. Daly "The Steady-State Economy: Toward a Political Economy of Biophysical Equilibrium and Moral Growth" in Daly, ed., *Toward a Steady-State Economy* (W.H. Freeman, 1973). See also Herman E. Daly, *Steady-State Economics* (Freeman, 1977).

14. George Lakey wrote (back in 1973) that "Third World peoples are demanding equality. If equality meant imitation, in this context, it would be like a poor youngster hoping someday to be like a grossly fat, corrupt rich person who is about to die of a heart attack." Lakey, *Powerful Peacemaking* (revised ed., 1987), p. 176.

15. Anne H. and Paul R. Ehrlich, *Earth* (London: Thames Methuen, 1987), p. 224.

16. For extensive discussion of some issues concerning scarcity, abundance, and equality, see Fred Hirsch, *Social Limits to Growth* (Harvard University Press, 1976), especially Part One on "social scarcity" and "the positional economy," and Michael Walzer, *Spheres of Justice: A Defense of Pluralism and Equality* (Basic Books, 1983).

17. Ordway, *Resources and the American Dream: Including a Theory of the Limit of Growth* (Ronald Press, 1953), p. 41. (This reference is derived from Michael Marien, *Societal Directions and Alternatives* [1976], p. 103. For more on Marien's book, see this book's annotated bibliography.)

18. On the practical level, *Taking Charge of Our Lives: Living Responsibly in the World,* Joan Bodner, ed., (American Friends Service Committee, San Francisco; Harper & Row, 1984) provides questions one can ask oneself to identify aspects of one's lifestyle one may desire to change, and includes a great deal of information on relevant books and social change organizations. To quote the book's back cover: *"Taking Charge of Our Lives* insists that real abundance is found in human creativity, in individual and shared self-reliance, in the richness of personal relationships, culture, and the human spirit — not in the unlimited acquisition of material goods in quantities far beyond what is economically or environmentally possible to share with the rest of the earth's people."

At the theoretical level, among dozens of authors who could be named, see those cited in Theodore Roszak's introduction to E.F. Schumacher, *Small is Beautiful* (Harper & Row, 1973), and Schumacher's classic "Buddhist Economics" in that volume. Mark A. Lutz and Kenneth Lux, *The Challenge of Humanistic Economics* (Benjamin/Cummings, 1979), was one early work seeking to explore the relation of "wants" and "needs"; see also their subsequent publications. For many concise reviews of relevant books, see current and back issues of Mark Satin's *New Options* newsletter (see "Recommended Periodicals" in this book). For recent creative economic thinking by economists and others, contact The Other Economic Summit (TOES/North America, c/o Susan Hunt, Economics Dept., University of Maine, Orono, ME 04469).

19. Some important elements for a democratic, peace-promoting, and ecologically sustainable transformation of the U.S. economy now exist. Here is a sketch to indicate how progress toward transformation might proceed, beginning from things you, the reader of this book, can do now. Following the sketch is information on how to take the actions suggested. These "phases" make a logical succession, not a temporal one. The more thoroughly the "earlier" ones are carried through, the more powerful the "later" ones are. But several elements from the "later" phases are in fact already under way.

Phase One: Concerned individuals, acting in their various roles, begin shifting resources to the more "socially responsible" sector of the economy. A) Credit card users switch to a card like the Working Assets Visa card, which contributes money to social change work with each use. B) Those with savings or invested money shift it to socially responsible uses. C) Consumers join Co-op America and increase the percentage of their money going to cooperatively-managed or worker-owned businesses. D) Consumers take steps — plenty of which involve no sacrifice in time or comfort, and can actually save money, like using more efficient lighting — to improve their lives' ecological effects. E) Consumers boycott General Electric and other socially irresponsible firms. F) Citizens push for their cities, towns, counties, and states to divest from and cease purchasing from firms making nuclear weapons or doing business with South Africa or other socially damaging activities.

Phase Two: G) Intellectuals study (and publicize their findings concerning) what forms of management, ownership, and social organization best contribute to socially responsible results — i.e., maximize employment, minimize pollution, maximize employee satisfaction, offer flexibility of working hours to accommodate family life and part-time work (so as to reflect an appropriately secondary place in life for jobs lower in intrinsic rewards). H) More stringent "screens" (beyond avoiding nuclear weapons and South Africa) for social investment are devised. I) Institutions offering technical assistance (on management, planning, market research) to firms that are democratically managed and/or worker-owned expand their expertise and scope of operations, helping such firms to increase their market share, expand to provide additional jobs, and enter new fields of operation. J) Foundations support conferences to increase cooperation and common strategizing on how different elements of the democratic and socially responsible sectors can support each other.

Phase Three: K) Growing federations of democratic and socially responsible firms, consumer groups, and secondary institutions (funds, banks, schools, technical consultants) set aside resources to enable them to increase their influence on government policies, domestic and foreign, that affect them. L) They seek also to increase the proportion of an individual's economic activity that can be conducted within the socially responsible sector, and the proportion of the population that has access to such opportunities. M) The invigorating effects of participation at the workplace and of reduced working hours enabling more time for reflection and enlightened civic action increase the influence of the majority public interest (in contradistinction to the interests of the wealthy whose campaign contributions and policy-making institutions normally outweigh and/ or decisively shape public opinion).

Phase Four: N) The growing democratic / socially responsible (D/SR) sector becomes a base for political action that shifts government resources to meeting human needs for shelter, better schooling, jobs, health care, etc., and increases the literacy, political awareness, and capacity for political action of a growing proportion of the population. The resulting political action overcomes the political dominance of corporations and establishes federal chartering of corporations and other strong legislation reducing the capacity of corporation managers and owners to damage human well-being. O) Individuals and organizations in the D/ SR sector implement ecologically sound policies themselves and push national and state governments to do the same. P) Those in the D/SR sector pressure national and global economic policy bodies (the U.S. Agency for International Development, the World Bank, and the International Monetary Fund) to pursue less damaging policies and encourage U.S. cooperation with multilateral programs for participatory "development" rather than programs designed to make poor countries complement the economic preferences of U.S. corporations. Through all the preceding changes and others initiated elsewhere, the world gradually becomes a better place.

The following list of actions you can take and activities you can support to transform the U.S. and global economy is very incomplete, thanks to the great growth of efforts in this area. This list is intended merely to enable you to choose and do a few things without delay. For much additional information, see Susan Meeker-Lowry's *Economics as If the Earth Really Mattered: A Catalyst Guide to Socially Conscious Investing* (New Society Publishers, 1988; $9.95), which is (at the time of this writing) the most comprehensive guide to socially responsible economic behavior, covering much more than investing in its 282 pages (including 38 pages of addresses for groups and periodicals and a five-page bibliography). ExPro does not endorse or guarantee anything about the groups mentioned below nor do we claim those named are superior to others not named; evaluate them carefully yourself.

A. Working Assets offers a Visa credit card that supports social change groups. "Since 1986, over 80,000 people have put a Working Assets VISA Card in their wallet. Together they have generated more than $140,000 for organizations such as Greenpeace, Amnesty International, Oxfam America . . ." (advertisement). For details, contact Working Assets, 230 California St., San Francisco, CA 94111 or call 1-800-533-FUND. Ask to see their prospectus and the newsletter *Money Matters*.

B. Concerning socially responsible investment, Working Assets (above) has a Money Fund. Another among many social investment funds is Calvert Social Investment Fund, 1700 Pennsylvania Ave., N.W., Washington, DC 20006; (800) 368-2745. The Fall 1988 issue of *Money Matters* states that the number of dollars committed to socially responsible investing, "including all divestment [from South Africa] and any money that has any social criteria attached to it," has grown from less than $100 billion in 1985 to over $400 billion — that's "billion" — by mid-year 1988.

C. For $15 per year one can join Co-op America and receive its catalog of excellent, reasonably priced products made by worker-managed and other socially responsible businesses — an excellent source of gift possibilities. Co-op America's quarterly newsletter, *Building Economic Alternatives*, sent free to members, is one of the best sources for up-to-date information, news, and good thinking about how to transform the economic relations that make up today's war-torn world. The newsletter also contains news of boycotts, the other side of socially responsible purchasing. The Winter 1988 *Building Economic Alternatives* on "Making the Links" is an excellent source on what is being and can be done to establish mutually beneficial economic relations between First and Third World people. Also very relevant is the issue on "Creating a Peacetime Economy" (Spring 1988). Back issues, $1. Contact Co-op America, 2100 M St. NW, Suite 310, Washington, DC 20063; 800-424-COOP or 202-872-5307.

D. To obtain a free catalog of products whose use can benefit our environment — ranging from water-saving toilets and efficient hot water heaters to many items suitable as attractive or entertaining gifts, contact Seventh Generation, 126 Intervale Road, Burlington, VT 05401; 802-862-2999. See also *Taking Charge of Our Lives* (in note 18 above); its bibliographies list other books and organizations that can help improve our lives — both ecologically and ethically.

E. On the General Electric boycott, see Chapter 11, note 16 and related text. For information comparing many major corporations on their relations with South Africa, treatment of labor, women, minorities, percentage of charitable giving, etc., see Steven Lydenberg et al., *Rating America's Corporate Conscience* (Addison Wesley, 1986).

F. See the work of Nuclear Free America and the *Bulletin of Municipal Foreign Policy*, both discussed in Chapter 11.

G. See the books and articles on Mondragon and Grameen Bank cited in notes below, and the references to the work of Jaroslav Vanek and others.

H. For examples of some current screening criteria, see the annual reports from Working Assets and Calvert.

I. One organization that offers technical assistance on worker buy-outs, democratic management, and other consultation and financing services for democratic businesses is the Industrial Cooperative Association, 58 Day Street, Somerville, MA 02144; (617) 629-2700. See also the periodicals *Changing Work: A Magazine about Liberating Worklife* ($14 for 4 issues; P.O. Box 261, New Town Branch, Newton, MA 02258; 617-736-3827) and *Workplace Democracy: The Magazine of Worker Participation and Ownership* ($18/year/4 issues; 111 Draper Hall, Amherst, MA 01003; 413-545-4875).

J. Paul Freundlich, Executive Director of Co-op America, has written: "Through Co-op America, we have already shown we can work together. The next steps are to shape our values and practice into an effective challenge to business as usual — part of a larger economic strategy combining justice with productivity." *Building Economic Alternatives* #14 (Summer 1988), p. 2.

K. In a recent survey, "nearly 90%" of the Calvert Social Investment Fund's shareholders "were supportive of the Fund becoming more outspoken in its efforts to curb defense outlays." (Quoted from Calvert's newsletter *Impact*, August 1988, p. 5.) A number of consumer groups already seek to influence public policies.

L. The availability of life and health insurance through Co-op America is a step in this direction, but still relatively few people are reached by socially responsible alternatives. Given the emergence in the last decade of the kind of organizations described in this note, however, there is now potential for an enormous expansion of the democratic / socially responsible sector. If enough people take steps of the kind suggested in this note, in the next ten years — or even the next five — an economic sector could be established that would strengthen support for better foreign and domestic policies. Ultimately, the building of such a base might prove indispensable for successfully countering the forces in the U.S. that make for war and ecological catastrophe.

M. On the relation of workplace participation to political participation and one's sense that one can be politically effective, see Carole Pateman, *Participation and Democratic Theory* (Cambridge University Press, 1970); Martin Meissner, "The Long Arm of the Job: A Study of Work and Leisure," *Industrial Relations*, Vol. 10, pp. 239-260. Concerning the effects of a measure of self-direction at the workplace on conformity and tolerance, see Melvin L. Kohn, *Class and Conformity* (University of Chicago Press, second ed., 1977) and Kohn and Carmi Schooler, *Work and Personality* (Ablex Publishing, 1983). The important but insufficiently known work of Kohn and his colleagues shows that "occupational self-direction" — of which having some control over what you do at work is a major component — is a factor ranking with higher education as a major promoter of tolerance and open-mindedness. Spreading these personality characteristics is highly important for creation of peace in a world of diverse cultures, and it is a lucky thing, though probably no coincidence, that the kind of workplaces that most foster it also appear to tend to be more economically productive.

N, O, P. This phase is at present more a vision of the future, but important efforts and some successes exist already. For example: ten states have developed adequate authority and regulations to mandate least-cost energy planning, according to Scott Ridley's *The State of the States '87.* (The Fund for Renewable Energy and the Environment [1001 Connecticut Ave., NW, Suite 719, Washington, DC 20036; 202-466-6880] publishes the *State of the States* annual ranking of state energy and environmental programs covering six areas including hazardous waste management, solid waste and recycling, and soil conservation. You can use it to pressure your state to adopt beneficial policies proven effective elsewhere.)

Some shortcomings of U.S. democracy are examined at the beginning of Chapter 11. Here, it can simply be noted that all the changes outlined above would make for a more democratic society: one in which people could better control the decisions that affect their lives. As Thomas Ferguson has written, "The prerequisites for effective democracy are not really automatic voter registration or even Sunday voting, though these would help. Rather, deeper institutional forces — flourishing unions, readily accessible third parties, inexpensive media, and a thriving network of cooperatives and community organizations — are the real basis of effective democracy." It is vital to consider "the resources available to individual voters to form and express an opinion." (Thomas Ferguson, "Party Realignment and American Industrial Structure," *Research in Political Economy*, 6.1-82, 1983; quoted in Noam Chomsky, *Turning the Tide* [South End, 1985], p. 222.)

Chomsky adds (p. 221): "Meaningful democracy presupposes the ability of ordinary people to pool their limited resources, to form and develop ideas and programs, put them on the political agenda, and act to support them. In the absence of organizational structures and resources that make this possible," democracy amounts to a choice among representatives of the wealthy who control effective candidacy through the financing of campaigns and ownership of the major media.

20. A reviewer of Amory Lovins's *Soft Energy Paths: Towards a Durable Peace* (1977) wrote that "the main reason for Lovins's importance is that he has managed to redefine the energy problem, and thereby to change the frame of reference of a large number of technical debates" (back cover, Harper paperback ed.).

The achievement of Lovins and his colleagues in the subsequent decade has been no less impressive. In 1977 the authors of a leading ecology textbook wrote that the chief camps contending over energy policy were those believing the main danger was having too little energy, too late and those believing the main danger was having too much, too soon. The groups favored "almost diametrically opposed" strategies: "The too-little-too-late group favors crash programs to develop and deploy all resources and technologies, with priority to whatever promises to be cheapest. The too-much-too-soon group wants to slow down, buy time by maximizing the efficiency of energy use, and use that time to select a mix of energy technologies that is as benign environmentally and socially as money and ingenuity can make it." (P. Ehrlich et al., *Ecoscience*, p. 498.)

Lovins and RMI have brilliantly transformed and transcended this debate by establishing that the cheapest source of "supply" *is* maximization of end-use efficiency. This being so, it has been possible for "soft path" advocates to seize the political advantage of calling for public utility commissions to use a "least-cost" criterion when they evaluate utility proposals for rate increases to pay for building nuclear or other generating plants. (See note 19, subnote N, above.) The utilities can be required to demonstrate that investing in new generation will be cheaper than the costs of reducing demand (in effect, "supplying" capacity) by investments in promoting greater efficiency (added insulation, more efficient motors and lighting, etc.) and offering users incentives that will reduce peak demand nearer average levels. In general, they cannot show generation to be cheaper, and the effects can already be counted in a number of states. Students of rhetoric will recognize that redefining "conservation" (which tends to evoke color photos of wilderness) and "efficiency" as "supply," and connecting the issue to a cultural axiom like "getting the most for your money," were crucial.

The effects of this conceptual breakthrough and RMI's ongoing empirical research are far-reaching and still continuing. (They can be followed in each issue of *RMI Newsletter*, free on request; address in "Recommended Periodicals" section of this book.) Note, for example, the May 1988 *RMI Newsletter* report on 150 state utility commissioners' visit to RMI headquarters.

The redefinition of "national security" seems a more difficult task than redefining the energy problem: instead of money and energy being wasted, it has been money and lives, and dispassionate analysis encounters still stronger emotions than over energy issues. Yet the approach undertaken in *Soft Energy Paths* (still worth reading) and by RMI — which has itself begun a Security Program — merits study for its extraordinarily adroit and successful use of conventional, even conservative, concepts to make the case for major policy changes.

21. Important and more recent elaborations of the 1948 Declaration are the "International Covenant on Economic, Social, and Cultural Rights" and the "International Covenant on Civil and Political Rights." The texts can be found in collections of U.N. documents.

22. For those in the industrialized countries Gran highly recommends Branko Horvat's *The Political Economy of Socialism* (M.E. Sharpe, 1982; $18.95), a work that does not advocate a state-dominated socialism, but rather a thoroughly democratic and decentralized system, with both its proposed workings and strategies for bringing it into existence in East and West, North and South specified in some detail.

23. See Chapter Eight, "The Participatory Economy as a Vehicle of Development," pp. 142-162 in Jaroslav Vanek, *The Participatory Economy: An Evolutionary Hypothesis and a Strategy for Development* (Cornell University Press, 1971).

24. See William Foote Whyte and Kathleen King Whyte, *Making Mondragon: The Growth and Dynamics of the Worker Cooperative Complex* (ILR Press [N.Y. State School of Industrial and Labor Relations, Cornell University, Ithaca, NY 14851], 1988; 336 pp.; $14.95), a thorough yet readable description and analysis of the origins and evolution of the Mondragon complex, plus reflections on its implications for the U.S. One focus of this important book is how Mondragon met the challenge of the worldwide recession of the 1980s, which hit Spain much harder than most countries. When workers are also responsible for the firm's survival, they can, to use Gilman's words, "make hard choices much more creatively and with more balance than [firms with

management and labor] locked into adversarial roles."

The Industrial Cooperative Association (see note 19, paragraph I, above) seeks to apply the lessons of Mondragon in its work. So also does Ohio's innovative and expanding Worker Owned Network (50 S. Court Street, Athens, Ohio 45701); write for WON's newsletter.

25. See Robert Oakeshott, "Mondragon: Spain's Oasis of Democracy" (1973), reprinted in Jaroslav Vanek, ed., *Self-Management* (Penguin, 1975), pp. 290-296.

26. The achievements of Mondragon began to become known in the U.S. around 1974. Another participatory development just now becoming known here, which may prove to be no less inspiring and influential, is the Grameen Bank of Bangladesh, an institution that loans money to the very poor and assists them in creating self-help structures that support them to start small businesses and improve their housing, diet, sanitation, morale, and general well-being. According to *Participation as Process: What We Can Learn from Grameen Bank, Bangladesh* (1986) by Andreas Fuglesang and Dale Chandler (see annotated bibliography), the Bank had by 1986 — just ten years after its founding as a small action research project —helped as many as one million people lift themselves above abject poverty. Concerning efforts now under way to apply this approach in Chicago and rural Arkansas, see the booklet *Defining Social Investment* (available for $3.00 from Co-op America), pp. 6-8.

Another economic innovation whose importance has so far been almost universally overlooked took place in Chile during the Allende years (1970-73) when the British cybernetic theorist and management expert Stafford Beer was invited to apply his ideas. Racing against efforts to crush the Allende regime, Beer and his Chilean colleagues designed and began implementing a system for electronically assembling economic data from "the whole social economy" on a daily, almost "real-time," basis and ingeniously processing it so as to make it comprehensible to an average worker, thus creating an unprecedentedly advanced system for national economic management and democratic socialism. Before the system was completed, the C.I.A.-sponsored "truckers' strike" threatened to topple the regime, but Beer's information-gathering system enabled the Allende government to deploy the trucks of those loyal to the regime so efficiently as to defeat the attack.

While of great importance as perhaps the first time in history that computer technology was used — successfully — to defend a popular regime against foreign subversion, Beer's work is of still wider significance for managing a complex world.

Green activists will be intrigued by Beer's argument that all complex organizations should be modeled on the most complex self-regulating system known — human neurophysiology. Decentralists and central planning advocates alike (as well as economists of all stripes) will want to explore how the real-time availability of an intelligible model of what is happening economically would affect decision-making by individual enterprises and government, and transform traditional debates.

Brain of the Firm (1972) outlined Beer's theory; the 1981 edition (published by John Wiley) added a gripping 150-page account of the Chile project. An interim report appeared at the end of Beer's *Platform for Change* (John Wiley, 1975). Alternative presentations of Beer's theory — enlivened by drawings and imaginary discussions of his views — are found in *Designing Freedom* (1974), *The Heart of Enterprise* (1980), and *Diagnosing the System: for Organizations* (1985), all published by Wiley.

27. See note 19, subnote M, above.

28. An international computer network was established in 1987 by the International Federation of Chemical, Energy and General Workers' Unions (ICEF), whose U.S. operational center is at the Industrial Union Depart-

ment of the AFL-CIO. Brecher and Costello note that its degree of availability to rank-and-file union groups still remains to be determined. For more information on domestic and international labor solidarity activity, Brecher and Costello recommend the periodical *Labor Notes* (7435 Michigan Ave., Detroit, MI 48210), the regular feature "Women and Global Corporations" in *Listen Real Loud: News of Women's Liberation Worldwide* (Nationwide Women's Program, AFSC, 1501 Cherry St., Philadelphia, PA 19102) and nine other sources. Brecher's articles on "Labor Today" appear bimonthly in *Zeta Magazine*; see "Recommended Periodicals" for subscription information. See also the workers' rights legislation mentioned in Chapter 11 following discussion of an essay by Paula Rayman.

Chapter 8: Psychology, Religion, Culture, and Peace

1. Damon Knight's "Rule Golden" is included in Joe Haldeman, ed., *Study War No More: A Selection of Alternatives* (St. Martin's Press, 1977), pp. 179-244.

2. This is not to imply that improved understanding and empathy are to be attained just by advocating them. Such progress has social preconditions, including an increase in the quantity and quality of the information that reaches the U.S. public through its news media. See this book's sections on periodicals and other media for some discussion and practical suggestions.

3. See, for example, Gordon Adams, *The Politics of Defense Contracting: The Iron Triangle* (Transaction Books, 1982), and Seymour Melman, *The Permanent War Economy* (1974; revised edition, Touchstone, 1985).

4. For research on misperception, see Robert Jervis, "Hypotheses on Misperception," in Richard Falk and Samuel S. Kim, *The War System* (Westview, 1980), and chapters and references in Ralph K. White, ed., *Psychology and the Prevention of Nuclear War* (New York University Press, 1986).

5. See Sharp's article cited in note 25 to "The Peace System Approach to Eliminating War."

6. See, for example, Joan V. Bondurant, *Conquest of Violence: The Gandhian Philosophy of Conflict* (1958; Princeton University Press, 1988), and Gene Sharp, "Types of Principled Nonviolence," in *Gandhi as a Political Strategist, with Essays on Ethics and Politics* (Porter Sargent, 1979).

7. Quoted by Bello, p. 74, from Cynthia Adcock, "Fear of 'Other': The Common Root of Sexism and Militarism," in Pam McAllister, ed., *Reweaving the Web of Life: Feminism and Nonviolence* (New Society Publishers, 1982), p. 210.

8. Consider Kull, "Nuclear Nonsense," discussed in this chapter; his *Minds at War: Nuclear Reality and the Inner Conflicts of Defense Policymakers* (Basic Books, 1988); several books authored or co-authored by Robert Jervis; and Lloyd S. Etheredge's books *A World of Men: The Private Sources of American Foreign Policy* (MIT Press, 1978) and *Can Governments Learn? American Foreign Policy and Central American Revolutions* (Pergamon, 1985). See also Carol Cohn, "Sex and Death in the Rational World of Defense Intellectuals," *Signs*, Vol. 12, No. 4 (Summer 1987), for a longer essay examining the same evidence as her article discussed in this chapter but from a more explicitly feminist standpoint. Its notes contain references to the growing literature critiquing the dominant (masculine) version of "rationality" and discussing the relation of conventional masculinity to the arms race.

9. See, for example, Sara Ruddick, "Maternal Thinking," in Joyce Trebilcot, *Mothering: Essays in Feminist Theory* (Rowman & Allanheld, 1984); Cynthia Enloe, "Feminists Thinking About War, Militarism, and Peace," in Beth B. Hess and Myra Marx Ferree, eds., *Analyzing Gender: A Handbook of Social Science Research* (Sage, 1988); Cynthia Enloe, *Making Feminist Sense of International Politics* (forthcoming); Betty Reardon, *Sexism and the War System* (Teachers College Press, 1985). Jean Bethke Elshtain's *Women and War* (Basic Books, 1987) contains a lengthy bibliography.

10. See anthropologist Peggy Reeves Sanday's learned yet readable *Female Power and Male Dominance: On the Origins of Sexual Inequality* (Cambridge University Press, 1981). Sanday offers a sophisticated discussion of symbolic representations of female and male roles and their complex relation to material conditions. She finds that "Generally, male dominance evolves as resources diminish and as group survival depends increasingly on the aggressive acts of men. . . . If there is a basic difference between sexes, other than the differences associated with human reproductivity, it is that women as a group have not willingly faced death in violent conflict" (pp. 210-211).

11. Boulding cites Anselm Strauss's book *Negotiations: Varieties, Contexts, Processes and Social Order* (Jossey-Bass, 1978).

12. Evan Luard, *Types of International Society* (Free Press, 1976), p. 380.

13. Elise Boulding, "Global Altruism and Everyday Behavior," in T. F. Lentz, ed., *Humatriotism: Human Interest in Peace and Survival* (The Futures Press, 1976), p. 62.

14. See chapters 3 and 7 in Elise Boulding, *Building a Global Civic Culture* (Teachers College Press, 1988), pp. 35-55 and 118-139.

15. Etheredge, p. 80. The campaign of economic sabotage tallied neatly with the perennial theme of U.S. propaganda — true in important respects, of course — that Communist economies function inefficiently.

16. Etheredge, p. 85.

17. Perhaps the name "MONGOOSE" will become more familiar, though not the historical facts. Late in 1987 William F. Buckley, Jr., published *MONGOOSE, R.I.P.*, a thriller novel in which Fidel Castro plots to kill John F. Kennedy in Dallas in 1963 using a secretly retained Soviet nuclear missile (and thus causing hundreds of thousands of other deaths) in revenge for JFK's MONGOOSE attempts on his own life. The plot is foiled at the last minute. Inventing imaginary criminal plans by Castro worse than the actual historical crimes by the U.S. against Cuba doubtless restores to a dogmatically right-wing mind a consoling image of the world as it ought to be.

18. See *Living with Nuclear Weapons*, pp. 16-17. Albert Carnesale, Paul Doty, Stanley Hoffmann, Samuel P. Huntington, Joseph S. Nye, Jr., and Scott Sagan write of the need to discourage "future Soviet aggressive behavior" but say literally not one word about the U.S.'s preceding unsuccessful invasion and subsequent year-long campaign of killing and sabotage. Yet most of Etheredge's principal sources were published from three to seven years prior to the writing of the Harvard book, and the significance and pertinence of the events described are unmistakable. How is such a striking omission to be justified, or even explained? It recalls George Orwell's observation that "The nationalist not only does not disapprove of atrocities committed by his own side, but he has a remarkable capacity for not even hearing about them." ("Notes on National-

ism," 1945; quoted in Noam Chomsky and Edward S. Herman, *The Washington Connection and Third World Fascism*, South End, 1979, p. vii.)

19. Etheredge, pp. 198, 87.

Part Three: Making Peace a Reality
Prospects for Building a Peace System

1. Richard Falk, Samuel S. Kim, and Saul H. Mendlovitz, "Introduction" to Section 9, "Orientations to Transition," in *idem*, eds., *Toward a Just World Order* (Westview, 1982), pp. 559, 560. Cf. Mark Sommer's similar point: "We will need somehow to harness events and trends already present in the culture in order to gain sufficient momentum for a transformation." *Beyond the Bomb*, p. 139.

The "faith in rationality" Falk et al. criticize might be attributed to world federalists who believe that showing people the alleged advantages of world government and the existence of careful plans for it can mobilize adequate public support to bring about such a government. On a similar faith in appeals to reason by distinguished individuals, see Otto Nathan and Heinz Norden, eds., *Einstein on Peace* (1960; Avenel, 1981), p. xii.

Marx and Engels rightly conceived their approach as an advance over what they termed "utopian socialism," in that "scientific socialism" gave serious attention to existing social forces that were believed to be leading toward the future deemed desirable. But the Marxian approach contained its own severe flaws. First, the lack of an elaborate delineation by Marx and Engels of the socialist future weakened (though it did not wholly destroy) the ability of the Soviet peoples and others to criticize the injustices of the U.S.S.R. and later self-described Marxist states as falling short of clear-cut standards of socialist democracy.

Second, Marx and Engels adopted from Hegel the false conception that the desired future was inherent in the logic of history, and was coming "with the inevitability of a law of nature" (see Marx, *Capital*, chapter 32). In the year 2089 it may be possible to say (though it will still risk misleading) that human reason and the natural desire for survival made the achievement of peace a logical development. But before the fact, such statements risk fostering — or at least "[failing] to correct" — a kind of "paralyzing and debilitating optimism" that (in the view of historian Gabriel Kolko) was a disastrous influence of Marxism on the socialist movement. See Kolko, "The Decline of American Radicalism in the Twentieth Century," in James Weinstein and David W. Eakins, eds., *For a New America* (Vintage, 1970), pp. 198-201.

Intellectually avid readers will also want to know of important recent work in the natural sciences and social theory and practice that may reshape in a helpful way dominant assumptions and attitudes about knowledge, necessity, and the possibilities for changing society for the better.

Concerning the kind of "necessitarian" thinking criticized above in Marx, see Roberto Mangabeira Unger's stimulating *False Necessity: Anti-Necessitarian Social Theory in the Service of Radical Democracy* (Cambridge University Press, 1987). Unger writes (p. 230) that "what at first seem to be governmental, economic, and legal arrangements strongly determined by a combination of inexorable technical requirements and irresistible social influences turn out, on close inspection, to have been a series of complicated and precarious settlements, the outcomes of many loosely connected lines of invention and habit, compromise and coercion, insight and illusion." Compare the closing pages (272-278) of Charles Perrow's *Complex Organizations* (3rd ed., Random House, 1986): "We should not assume a 'historical necessity' . . ." (p. 275). See also Warren Ziegler, *Envisioning a World Without Weapons,* cited in this book's section on doing an imaging workshop: "Keep in mind that no story *has* to happen. Avoid the language of necessity" (p. 50; cf. p. 51). For additional references and discussion, send a self-addressed, stamped envelope to ExPro requesting Robert A. Irwin, "Marx's 1859 Preface and Necessitarianism" (unpublished manuscript, 1985; 11 pp.).

James Gleick's highly readable book *Chaos: Making a New Science* (Viking, 1987) describes new mathematics and experimental findings that indicate how highly complex systems (like weather or human society) are unpredictable and why huge changes can result from tiny causes (see his discussion of "what is only half-jokingly known as the Butterfly Effect — the notion that a butterfly stirring the air today in Peking can transform storm systems next month in New York"). Kenneth Boulding has written that "In the light of evolutionary history, the universe looks much less like a clock wound up in the beginning and much more like a play, a play moreover in which the authors are part of the action and the script changes unpredictably all the time. . . . When even quite improbable events happen, the history of the universe thenceforth is different." From "Foreword" to Erich Jantsch, ed., *The Evolutionary Vision: Toward a Unifying Paradigm of Physical, Biological, and Sociocultural Evolution* (Westview, 1981), pp. xv-xvi.

For a critique of passive conceptions of knowledge, an argument that "one of the best ways to understand the world is to try to change it" (p. xii), an emphasis on "pragmatic explanation" and "practical knowledge," and much more, see Chris Argyris, Robert Putnam, and Diana McLain Smith, *Action Science: Concepts, Methods, and Skills for Research and Intervention* (Jossey-Bass, 1985).

The present writer's conclusions can be simply put: we should neither regard present circumstances as unchangeable, nor assume either better or worse futures to be inevitable. We should recognize that the choices each of us makes will certainly have some effect — possibly a large effect — on the future. The challenge is to make those choices with courage and with maximum intelligence and awareness of how we can better the conditions of human and other life worldwide. Doing this is no simple matter. That is why systems thinking — see Holt's second article cited in note 19 to "The Peace System Approach" — is so important to learn and apply thoroughly. (See also Kenneth Boulding's comments on "perverse dynamics" in "Twelve Friendly Quarrels with Johan Galtung," *Journal of Peace Research,* XIV:1 [1977], pp. 75-86.)

2. "A typical, ever-recurring formulation [in early thinking on mass noncooperation] was, 'If everyone does this and this, then . . .' To the question of how such a decision should come to pass, little attention was devoted. In place of technical details stood pictures and parables; in place of the names of groups and organizations capable of acting, stood abstract concepts." Theodor Ebert, *Gewaltfreier Aufstand* [Nonviolent Uprising] (original ed., 1968; Waldkirch, West Germany: Waldkircher Verlagsgesellschaft, abridged and revised ed., 1970), p. 84. Similar "if everyone" thinking is still often encountered today.

3. "As Kenneth Boulding once pointed out, agreement is a scarce resource — whenever we can do without it, this is preferable." Dietrich Fischer, *Preventing War in the Nuclear Age* (Rowman & Allanheld, 1984), p. 8. Note that the word "preconceived" in the text distinguishes its point from achievements like the Law of the Sea Treaty. The Law of the Sea negotiations were a protracted process of seeking agreement; they illustrate both that agreement is difficult, and that it can be reached.

4. John Gall, *Systemantics: How Systems Really Work and How They Fail* (second ed., 1986; General Systematics Press, 3200 West Liberty, Ann Arbor, MI 48103; 319 pp.; $14.95), quoted in J. Baldwin, ed., *The Essential Whole Earth Catalog: Access to Tools and Ideas* (Doubleday, 1986), p. 24.

5. Although building a peace system is a gradual process, viewed from a global perspective, it can include relatively rapid changes in particular countries.

6. Egon Bittner, *The Functions of the Police in Modern Society* (Oelgeschlager, Gunn & Hain, 1980; reprint of 1970 edition), pp. 17, 20. Bittner is no sentimental idealist. He writes: "Though these developments reflect the growth of humane sentiments, they derive more basically from a shift of values in which the virtues associated with material progress and assiduous enterprise gained ascendancy over the virtues of masculine prowess and combative chivalry" (p. 17). The real progress toward peace, Bittner believes, has derived from "neither religious faith nor humanistic concern," but from "the lackluster ethic of utilitarianism" and the "realization that [violence] is foolish. Forceful attack and the defense it provokes have an unfavorable input/ output ratio; they are a waste of energy" (p. 20).

This utilitarian logic is explicit in such slogans as "Being dead is bad for business." See the article with that title in Don Carlson and Craig Comstock, eds., *Securing Our Planet* (Jeremy P. Tarcher / St. Martin's Press, 1986), pp. 144-159.

The declining legitimacy of violence even among revolutionaries is discussed in Susanne Gowan et al., *Moving Toward a New Society* (New Society Publishers, 1976), pp. 238-240.

7. International law professor Francis Anthony Boyle presents trial materials arguing the illegality of nuclear weapons under international law in his *Defending Civil Resistance Under International Law* (1987; 1988). See this book's annotated bibliography for how to obtain this book in paperback.

8. An August 1987 *Atlantic Monthly* cover article was entitled "The (Relative) Decline of America"; it was excerpted from the subsequently widely discussed book by Paul M. Kennedy, *The Rise and Fall of the Great Powers* (Random House, 1988).

9. Reluctance of NATO countries to accept missile deployments in Western Europe, New Zealand's refusal to accept (and Denmark's resistance to) visits by nuclear-armed warships, and several NATO countries' noncooperation with the United States's bombing of Libya are examples.

10. Interview with Lester Brown, *Utne Reader*, #23 (Sept./Oct. 1987), p. 91.

11. See Richard Rosecrance, *The Rise of the Trading State: Commerce and Conquest in the Modern World* (Basic Books, 1986). Alexander George describes the book (on its back cover) as one "that identifies trends which offer opportunities for constructing a more peaceful international system." Creditably, Rosecrance also devotes a chapter to "Prospects for Atavism" — a resurgence of international violence. Also pertinent is an August 11, 1988 *Wall Street Journal* headline that read: "Strategic Shift: U.S. Redefines Its Views on Security To Put More Emphasis on Global Economic Factors" (pp. 1, 16). That the bipartisan shift described might be motivated largely by recognition that economic power is required to finance military power does not annul the short-run significance of the shift.

12. On the ecological effects of growth, recall works cited in Chapter 7's notes. Concerning tensions with Japan, see Chapter 10 below. On the drawbacks of competition more generally, see Alfie Kohn, *No Contest: The Case Against Competition* (Houghton Mifflin, 1986).

13. See Robert A. Irwin, "Nonviolent Struggle as Social Technology: Evolution in the 'Mode of Conflict'" (unpublished manuscript, 1986; available for a self-addressed stamped envelope from ExPro), for a brief

review of the development of nonviolent struggle in the twentieth century. The effects of a given use of nonviolent struggle are not invariably positive, as these examples are meant to show.

14. Elise Boulding, *Building a Global Civic Culture* (Teachers College Press, 1988), pp. 35-36. The language of this whole paragraph on INGOs is drawn from Boulding.

15. Cf. Robin Morgan, *Sisterhood is Global* (Anchor, 1984) and Jessie Bernard, *The Female World from a Global Perspective* (Indiana University Press, 1987).

16. On Greenham Common, see Alice Cook and Gwyn Kirk, *Greenham Women Everywhere* (South End Press, 1983) and Barbara Harford and Sarah Hopkins, eds., *Greenham Common: Women at the Wire* (London: The Women's Press, 1984). For the Seneca Falls encampment, see Mima Cataldo et al., *The Women's Encampment for a Future of Peace and Justice: Images and Writings* (Temple University Press, 1987). See also Puget Sound Peace Camp, *We Are Ordinary Women* (Seattle: The Seal Press, 1985). The poster "Patchwork Power" ($6.75 from Syracuse Cultural Workers, Box 6367, Syracuse, NY 13217; 315-474-1132) lists 41 women's peace encampments in 12 countries.

17. The Great Peace Journey "began as an initiative of a local branch of the Swedish section of the Women's International League for Peace and Freedom and resulted in the creation of a series of local teams of women and men who visited the heads of government of small and medium-sized governments in Europe in 1985 to pose five [peace-oriented] questions: . . . on the willingness to shift to a purely defensive military, to eliminate production of mass-destruction weapons, to eliminate their [arms] trade, to share Earth's resources more equitably, and to utilize UN machinery for the peaceful settlement of disputes." Additional steps have been carried out or planned, including a "people's summit to discuss the government responses and decide on further strategies." Elise Boulding, *Building a Global Civic Culture*, p. 46.

18. See George Lakey, "The Identity Functions of the War System," *Powerful Peacemaking* (New Society Publishers, 1987), pp. 13-21.

19. Why the mass media rarely question the legitimacy of U.S. aggression is illuminated by Edward S. Herman and Noam Chomsky, *Manufacturing Consent: The Political Economy of the Mass Media* (Pantheon, 1988).

20. In 1987 seven state governors "publicly stated that if asked to send their [National Guard] troops to Central America they would refuse." Paul Little, "Blazing a Road to Nowhere," *In These Times* (January 13-29, 1988), p. 12.

21. For an overview, see Mark Sommer and Gordon Feller, "'Independent Initiatives': Better than Arms Control?" in *New Options* #32 (October 27, 1986).

22. See Yankelovich and Doble article cited in Chapter 2.

23. Falk et al., *op. cit.* in note 1 above, p. 562, summarizing Kothari's position.

24. Kothari, "Towards a Just World," reprinted in Falk et al., *op. cit.* in note 1 above; quotation from p. 601.

25. Shallow or misplaced optimism is a mixed blessing at best. Consider Kolko, as cited in note 1 above, and

see Michael Marien's articles and Mark Satin's review of Harman's *Global Mind Change*, both in Chapter 12. It is not certain that efforts to create peace will be successful. But the potential is definitely there.

Randy Kehler has written that "I am often asked whether I am optimistic about stopping and reversing the nuclear arms race. The answer is no, I am not optimistic. But I *am* hopeful. That is to say, I am not convinced that we *will* stop the nuclear arms race. . . . But I am absolutely convinced that it is *possible* for us to stop it. For me, this is a matter of faith. And because I have faith that the possibility exists, I believe that we must keep trying. In short, I know that for myself I must cultivate not only faith but fortitude." "The Freeze: Three Years After," *Fellowship* (July-August 1984), quoted in Gordon C. Bennett, *The New Abolitionists: The Story of Nuclear Free Zones* (Brethren Press, 1987), pp. 229-230.

In the words of Elise Boulding: "What lies ahead we do not know. Humility is appropriate." She concludes an article by quoting an interviewee: "'The world *may* make it.'" Elise Boulding, "Evolutionary Visions, Sociology and the Human Life Span," in Erich Jantsch, ed., *The Evolutionary Vision* (Westview, 1981), p. 192.

Chapter 9: The Superpowers

1. H. D. S. Greenway, "Superpowers at the Summit," *Boston Sunday Globe* (December 6, 1987), p. 1.

2. Several of Chomsky's references to U.S. subversion — the cases following the dash, from Greece to El Salvador — are likely unfamiliar to many U.S. readers. Chomsky lists them chronologically; relevant information can be found in several of his books. See *The Political Economy of Human Rights, Vol. I: The Washington Connection and Third World Fascism* (1979; co-authored with Edward S. Herman); *Towards a New Cold War* (1982); *Turning the Tide* (1985); *The Chomsky Reader* (1987). The first and third are published by South End Press, the other two by Pantheon.

3. Joseph Gerson, "Introduction," *The Deadly Connection*, p. 5.

4. Maxwell Taylor, "Foreword" to Amos A. Jordan and Willam J. Taylor, Jr., *American National Security* (Johns Hopkins University Press, 1981), pp. vii-viii. The book in which this definition occurs, while not an official government document, carries praise from a bipartisan array of former cabinet-level officials such as James Schlesinger, Alexander Haig, and Carter administration CIA director Stansfield Turner.

5. In Chapter Two, "The Pentagon-CIA Archipelago," of *The Political Economy of Human Rights, Vol. I*, Noam Chomsky and Edward S. Herman present evidence from ten countries that U.S. aid correlates positively with a "favorable investment climate" (measured by easing of tax laws and repression of labor) and the violation of human rights (measured by torture, death squads, and political prisoners).

6. The views quoted are those of a Cuban official, summarized in *Toward Freedom* (Dec. 1987 / Jan. 1988), p. 72.

7. Kurt Waldheim, "Foreword," in Earl Foell and Richard Nenneman, eds., *How Peace Came to the World* (MIT Press, 1986), p. viii.

8. Lincoln P. Bloomfield, *ibid.*, p. 236.

9. Foell and Nenneman, *ibid.*, p. 5.

10. "All of the presidential candidates except Jackson favor some sort of buildup in conventional weapons," reported Michael T. Klare during the 1988 campaign. The rationale was the widespread but false contention that the Soviets have superiority in conventional weaponry (see note 2 to this book's essay on "The Peace System Approach" for references refuting the contention). See Klare, "Arms and the Candidates: The U.S. and the World After Reagan," *The Nation* (March 12, 1988), pp. 325, 340-345.

Chapter 10: Beyond the Superpowers: Other Actors

1. One of the most important areas neglected herein is Eastern Europe. Good coverage of the issues faced by movements for peace and freedom in Eastern Europe can be found in the journal *Across Frontiers* (quarterly; $10; Box 2382, Berkeley, CA 94702) and in *Peace and Democracy News*, the semi-annual bulletin ($5/year) of the Campaign for Peace and Democracy/East and West (P.O. Box 1640, Cathedral Station, New York, NY 10025; 212-724-1157).

2. See Singham and Hune, *Non-alignment in an Age of Alignments*, pp. 33, 43-47.

3. For more on the Palauans' struggle to retain their constitution against U.S. pressure, and for a survey of the "new regional spirit supporting a nuclear-free and independent Pacific," see Glen Alcalay, "South Pacific Regionalism: Connecting the Dots on the Map," *The Nation* (August 1-8, 1987), pp. 84-87.

4. Yoshi Tsurumi, "The Challenges of the Pacific Age," *World Policy Journal*, II:1 (Fall 1984), p. 63. Tsurumi is Professor of International Business at Baruch College of the City University of New York.

5. For further information see Zarsky et al., *American Lake: The Nuclear Peril in the Pacific*, (Viking-Penguin, 1987).

6. The symposium was held at Harvard University. See *Harvard Magazine* (Jan.-Feb. 1987), p. 48. The research cited is in Thomas K. McCraw, ed., *America Versus Japan: A Comparative Analysis* (Harvard Business School Press, 1986).

7. Johan Galtung finds the Japanese civilization, along with the occidental (European-North American) civilization in its "expansion mode," to have an aggressive character. See "Peace and the World as Inter-civilizational Interaction," in Raimo Vayrynen et al., eds., *The Quest for Peace* (Sage, 1987), pp. 330-345, esp. 339-344.

8. "For every American student living in Japan, no fewer than fifteen Japanese are studying at American colleges and universities. Considering the disparity in the two countries' populations, this amounts to a 30-fold effort by the Japanese to understand the United States, compared with the American effort to understand Japan." Thomas K. McCraw, *op. cit.*, p. 382.

9. Although Japan has one of the world's strongest peace movements, it surely reflects neglect by U.S. activists as well as inadequate research that it proved impossible to find a good recent article on that movement to recommend in this book.

10. Quotations from Charles Derber, "Peace Politics: New Perspectives from Europe," *The ExPro Papers* #1 (1986). The Alternative Defence Commission has produced another book, *The Politics of Alternative Defence: A Role for a Non-nuclear Britain* (London: Paladin Grafton Books, 1987). In the U.S. it can be ordered for $11.00 from the Institute for Defense and Disarmament Studies, 2001 Beacon St., Brookline, MA 02146.

11. A. W. Singham and Shirley Hune, "From Third World Non-alignment to European Dealignment to Global Realignment," in Kaldor and Falk, eds., *Dealignment*, pp. 202-203. On differences of outlook and instances of cooperation between Europe's neutral countries and the non-aligned countries, see Raimo Vayrynen, "Neutrality, Dealignment and Political Order in Europe," esp. pp. 165, 168, in Kaldor and Falk.

12. What became controversially known in the U.S. as an "assassination handbook" was prepared by the CIA "to teach the conventionally minded *contra* forces the more sophisticated techniques of low-intensity conflict and encourage greater discrimination in the choice of targets" (Miles, p. 34). This book can be purchased in the U.S. (*Psychological Operations in Guerrilla Warfare*, Vintage, 1985; with essays by Joanne Omang and Aryeh Neier). "Psychological operations" means avoiding indiscriminate violence against civilians in favor of (in Miles's words) "targeted torture and assassination of teachers, health workers, agricultural technicians and their collaborators in the community," carried out as a "logical and systematic policy."

13. Quoted in Noam Chomsky, *On Power and Ideology* (South End Press, 1987), p. 108, from *International Security* (Summer 1981).

Chapter 11: Making Changes: Analyses and Approaches

1. Galtung, "Self-Reliance: An Overriding Strategy for Transition" in Falk, Kim, Mendlovitz, eds., *Toward a Just World Order* (Westview, 1982), p. 602; originally in Galtung, *The True Worlds: A Transnational Perspective* (Free Press, 1980), p. 393.

2. The term "peace movement" is sometimes used in the U.S. in a way that limits its meaning to middle and upper class white people worried about nuclear holocaust. Since the term has very different meanings to different people, let us clarify its meaning for the U.S. by distinguishing five important groupings, in approximate order of increasing size. A first grouping includes politically active pacifists, such as members of pacifist organizations (secularly or religiously oriented) and politically active members of "the historic peace churches" (Brethren, Mennonites, Quakers).

Second are people who actively oppose U.S. military interventions, U.S. overt and covert efforts to dominate Central America, the Middle East, and other regions, and U.S. support for repressive governments such as South Africa's. Though such persons vary in their political outlooks and may be less numerous than pacifists if defined by organizational membership, they can from time to time mobilize far more people around particular oppositions (consider the anti-Vietnam War movement) than the number of those who adhere to forms of pacifism. On particular issues at times — e.g., opposition to aiding the Nicaraguan *contras* — they represent majority public opinion. Members of the Committee in Solidarity with the People of El Salvador (CISPES) and TransAfrica exemplify this grouping.

Third are persons worried about nuclear war: those making up such organizations as the Freeze, SANE (these first two merged in 1987), Physicians for Social Responsibility (and similarly named groups of educators and other occupational groups), Women's Action for Nuclear Disarmament, Peace Links, and many others. Some arms control groups fit in this category.

A fourth grouping would be those who think U.S. military spending is too high and want to shift our society's resources to domestic needs. The size of this group varies, but polls indicate it includes millions. Politicians echoing these sentiments are usually identified as liberals and are often Democrats; but the two major parties take positions that differ only by a few percentage points in the rate of growth of military spending they favor. Neither stands for a lowered military budget and a major shift to meeting domestic needs. The Congressional Black Caucus and the Populist Caucus in Congress sometimes articulate the popular desire for a shift in national spending priorities — as do, to a lesser degree, some of the periodic conferences of governors and mayors. There are hundreds, probably thousands, of local, state, and national citizen groups who favor such a shift, varying from some who make it a priority for their programmatic work to others who regard it as an implicit means or corollary to their goals.

The fifth, and probably largest, grouping are the supporters of the Freeze, no-first-use of nuclear weapons, and related policies and judgments. As the Public Agenda Foundation research reported by Daniel Yankelovich and John Doble in 1984 indicates, as many as 96 per cent of the public have adopted some opinions promoted by the groups worried about nuclear war. Poll results, of course, depend a great deal on exactly how questions are posed, and contradictions are not difficult to elicit about questions remote from people's daily lives (e.g., "Should the U.S. have a policy of no-first-use of nuclear weapons?") Nevertheless, Yankelovich and Doble found that "the public feels it is time to change course and, in doing so, to take some initiatives in the cause of peace" (*Foreign Affairs*, Fall 1984).

Many people fit into more than one of these five categories, and many have concerns or take actions (some of which might seem contradictory to an observer) without articulating a position that puts them neatly into a category.

This discussion describes the U.S. situation; in addition to the role of other countries' peace movements as forces for building a peace system, it is also reasonable (as suggested in the Introduction to Part III) to regard governments active in the Non-Aligned Movement, and at times, other governments, nongovernmental organizations, and regional or global inter-governmental institutions as forces for peace.

3. G. William Domhoff, *Who Rules America Now?* (Prentice-Hall, 1983), p. 117. See pp. 117-118 regarding further literature on the effect of political systems on parties and political representation systems. In the same chapter ("The Power Elite and Government") Domhoff presents evidence that there is a "power elite" based in the social upper class of the wealthiest people that successfully "operates within — not outside — the democratic process, including the two-party system" (p. 119). See also G. William Domhoff, *The Powers That Be: Processes of Ruling Class Domination in America* (Vintage, 1979).

4. Joshua Cohen and Joel Rogers, *Rules of the Game* (South End, 1986), pp. 20-21.

5. Cohen and Rogers, *ibid.*, p. 23.

6. "One analyst": Thomas Byrne Edsall, *The New Politics of Inequality* (Norton, 1984), p. 201, quoted in Noam Chomsky, *Turning the Tide*, p. 243. 1984 Times/CBS poll: quoted in Chomsky, *ibid.*, p. 244, from *New York Times*, November 19, 1985.

7. Cohen and Rogers, *ibid.*, p. 40. These statements run counter to an almost universal impression. But for a discussion of recent trends in public opinion, Cohen and Rogers recommend Thomas Ferguson and Joel

Rogers, *Right Turn: The Decline of the Democrats and the Future of American Politics* (Hill & Wang, 1986), chapter one.

8. See Joseph Schumpeter's definition of democracy and the contrasting "classical" view, both discussed in Carole Pateman, *Participation and Democratic Theory* (Cambridge, 1970), pp. 1-44. In the classical view (of Rousseau and J.S. Mill — and one could add the name of Thomas Jefferson), democracy was not just periodic elections, but ongoing self-government that educated its participants — thereby enabling them to become more enlightened citizens — through the participatory process itself.

9. See Daniel Cantor and Juliet Schor, *Tunnel Vision: Labor, the World Economy, and Central America* (South End, 1987).

10. Conversion expert Seymour Melman's most recent book is *The Demilitarized Society: Disarmament and Conversion* (Montreal: Harvest House, 1988).

11. Matt Witt, "Linking Human Rights with International Trade," *In These Times* (Oct. 26-Nov. 1, 1988), p. 8.

12. For a more detailed treatment of racism in the U.S. that will be eye-opening for most white (and many non-white) readers, see Paul Jacobs and Saul Landau (with Eve Pell), *To Serve the Devil: A Documentary Analysis of America's Racial History and Why It Has Been Kept Hidden* (Vintage, 1971; 2 volumes). These fascinating volumes treat not only white-black relations but the experience of native Americans, Chicanos, Puerto Ricans, and Asian-Americans as well.

13. A fine, comprehensive anthology based on testimony at the 1982 Ad Hoc Hearings on the Full Implications of the Military Budget conducted by Dellums is Ronald V. Dellums, *Defense Sense: The Search for a Rational Military Policy* (Ballinger, 1983; 342 pp.). The last chapter summarizes Dellums's alternative budget approach, based on international cooperation, rejection of "the attempted domination of the world through overt or covert intervention," and a "doctrine of nuclear arms 'sufficiency' rather than 'superiority'" (p. 285). The following news item, reported by Alexander Cockburn in his column in the socialist weekly *In These Times* (May 24-June 6, 1989), gives a clue as to why neither the fact of the Black Caucus's political leadership nor the substance of its proposals are known to much of the U.S. population: "On April 18 the Congressional Black Caucus released its comprehensive Alternative Budget for the fiscal year of 1990 to challenge the nation's crisis in housing, drugs, education, health, and employment stability. Rep. Ronald Dellums (D-CA), the chairman of the Black Caucus, presented the CBC budget as 'the People's Alternative.' The press conference to launch this budget was ignored by almost all mainstream corporate media, including the *Washington Post* and the *New York Times*." We are fortunate that the corporate media protect us from getting all riled up over the notion that our society could solve its problems, when we have the more important responsibilities of watching TV commercials and using our credit cards to attend to.

14. *Bulletin of Municipal Foreign Policy* (Autumn 1987), p. 3; Winter 1987-88 issue, p. 15. *The Bulletin* can be obtained for $35/year from the Center for Innovative Diplomacy, 17931-F Sky Park Circle, Suite F, Irvine, CA 92714; 714-250-1296. CID seeks to "democratize foreign policy making throughout the world." The Winter 1986-87 *CID Report* summarizes CID's origins and purposes and its array of impressive projects focused on local elected officials, municipal foreign policy, citizen diplomacy, and alternative security. Two of CID's co-founders also helped start PeaceNet, the computer network and communications system for peace activists (contact 3228 Sacramento St., San Francisco, CA 94115; 415-923-0900). CID offers attractive publications

designed to help local elected officials and ordinary citizens work for peace.

15. Contact Nuclear Free America, 325 East 25th Street, Baltimore, MD 21218 (301-235-3575), for nuclear-free zone organizing and boycott information.

16. Figures from *Nuclear Times* (November-December 1987), p. 9. For up-to-date information on the GE campaign, contact INFACT, 256 Hanover Street, Boston, MA 02113 (617-742-4583).

17. Paul Goodman, "A. J. Muste and People in Power," published in *Liberation* (November 1967), was reprinted in the 1968 Vintage paperback combining *People or Personnel* and *Like a Conquered Province*. In the passage quoted in this book, the sentence containing the words from "was both rational" to "yet mediating" actually appears later in the essay.

A. J. Muste (pronounced MUS-tee; 1882-1967), a minister, labor leader, pacifist, and chairman of the first broad coalition against the Vietnam War, was a pioneer of "revolutionary nonviolence." For an excellent biography, see Nat Hentoff, *Peace Agitator: The Story of A. J. Muste* (1963), now available in paperback for $6.50 from the A. J. Muste Memorial Institute, 339 Lafayette St., New York, NY 10012; 212-533-4335.

18. Paul Goodman, "The Duty of Professionals," reprinted in *Drawing the Line* (Free Life, 1977), p. 170n. (This collection should not be confused with Goodman's 1962 book of the same title.) See also "Quantity and Quality in Nonviolent Action," in Gene Sharp's *The Politics of Nonviolent Action* (Porter Sargent, 1973), pp. 475-479, for a discussion based in part on George Lakey's work.

19. "Nuclear Armaments: An Interview with Daniel Ellsberg" (1979), published by Conservation Press (Box 201, 2526 Shattuck Ave., Berkeley, CA 94704).

Chapter 12: Considering Strategies

1. See this book's section on periodicals for suggestions on how to learn about (and participate in!) ongoing discussions in the movements for peace, social change, and ecological survival. Among valuable publications too recent to be integrated into Chapter 12 are: Tom Atlee et al., eds., *Moving Toward Peace: A Study of Peace Movement Strategies and Tactics* (1989), a 42-page collection of articles available for $2.50 (postpaid; less in bulk) from San Francisco Study Group for Peace and Disarmament, 2735 Franklin St., San Francisco, CA 94123 (the group has announced a new written forum for dialog, supplementing its journal *Thinkpeace* — inquire for details); *Annual Review of Peace Activism* (1989), a new publication sponsored by the Winston Foundation for World Peace, available for $9.00 from P.O. Box 351, Kenmore Station, Boston, MA 02215 (or from 1-800-827-8900); "Towards a New Millennium of Peace: Abolish Nuclear Weapons by the Year 2000 and Establish Common Security" (1988), a 6-page statement by the Disarmament 2000 / Common Security Working Group (copies available from WILPF, 1213 Race St., Philadelphia, PA 19107).

2. See *Nuclear Times* (March/April 1988), pp. 33-34 for a report on Forsberg's November 1987 speech to the first National Congress of SANE/Freeze, now the largest U.S. peace organization. "Forsberg was talking about . . . something called alternative defense policy, an unwieldy term for a set of midterm policies on nuclear and conventional forces that the peace movement is beginning to promote. The Freeze, the comprehensive test

ban, and the INF Treaty have always been proposed as mere first steps, with further steps to be announced. But in the absence of carefully spelled-out additional proposals, the media, Congress, and the establishment have conveniently presumed that first steps are all the movement wants." Forsberg's Institute for Defense and Disarmament Studies has initiated an Alternative Defense Network.

3. The "functional" image of a peace system conceives it as having several "layers" that work to prevent military aggression (and other actions destructive of human well-being) from occurring or succeeding. See "The Peace System Approach to Eliminating War."

4. This description comes from *Toward a Just World Order* (1982), but of course WOMP's evolution did not stop in 1982. Falk describes the evolution of his own outlook in Chapter One, "The World Order Approach," of his *The Promise of World Order* (Temple University Press, 1987), pp. 14-24; see especially pp. 21-24. As of 1988, WOMP's work included assisting the activities of the Committee for a Just World Peace (led by Saul Mendlovitz and Yoshikazu Sakamoto), carrying out the work of the Grass-roots Activism: Global Implications Project (GRAGI), "supporting through research, writing, and public dialogue efforts to mobilize a global social movement for a just world peace," and co-publishing (with India's Centre for the Study of Developing Societies) the bimonthly journal *Alternatives: Social Transformation and Humane Governance* ($18/year). For more information contact the World Order Models Project, 777 United Nations Plaza, New York, NY 10017; (212) 490-0010.

5. ExPro's work as of June 1989 included encouragement of peace system study groups; a Peace System Project supporting research on the conditions of peace; and co-sponsorship of the Soviet-American Initiative for a Citizens Ecological Treaty (Patricia Mische, Global Education Associates, U.S. coordinator).

6. Concerning the World Policy Institute's Security Project, see William Greider, "The Economics of Security," pp. 165-171 in Don Carlson and Craig Comstock, eds., *Securing Our Planet* (Tarcher, 1986). The Security Project has produced the book *Post-Reagan America* (WPI, 1987; 174 pp.). For further information, contact World Policy Institute, 777 United Nations Plaza, New York, NY 10017; (212) 490-0010. (Yes, same address as WOMP.)

7. The Exchange Project offers training to increase the organizational effectiveness of grassroots peace groups. It publishes a newsletter and produces written and video resources. For more information, contact The Exchange Project, Peace Development Fund, 44 North Prospect St., P.O. Box 270, Amherst, MA 01004; (413) 256-8306.

8. Although Gandhi's recently deceased colleague Khan Abdul Ghaffar Khan (1890-1988) did not win the 1985 Nobel Peace Prize, most if not all of the events described as prior to 1985 are factual. The story of Mrs. Degranfenried has also been memorialized by singer/songwriter Fred Small. Concerning Witness for Peace and Peace Brigades International, see the addresses in Chapter 5, note 12. These groups need money as well as qualified volunteers.

9. Bello, p. 115 (ellipses in original). Lest we "overestimate the positive character" of apparent trends toward "stable peace," however, Bello suggests that we be aware that "a long period of peace may merely mask the accumulation of tensions which then erupt, not in a series of limited wars, but in one massive cataclysm. Also, maintaining peace at the center — the Soviet-U.S. relationship — may involve a displacement of conflict to the periphery, to the Third World. The post-1945 history of the Third World appears to support this thesis" (p. 109).

10. For example, Smoke and Harman write that "old-fashioned 'gunboat diplomacy,' in which powerful, technically advanced nations intervened militarily in the affairs of weak Third World nations, can no longer be undertaken without immense outcry and is now rarely attempted" (p. 63). The "fashion" may vary — sometimes bombers replace gunboats, or covert replaces overt action — but the histories of Grenada, Libya, Central America, southern Africa, and Afghanistan (to take examples, including protracted ones, only from the last ten years) indicate that such attacks are more than a rarity. The resurgence of military interventionism under Reagan has been widely noted.

Smoke and Harman also state (p. 98) that "Actual social change comes from people's beliefs and images. There is no place else it can come from." This is only true if everything is defined as involving beliefs and images, even the most mindless or unwilling behavior. The young man or woman skeptical about war but who enlists in the armed forces for lack of civilian job opportunities is far more likely to function as a reliable component perpetuating the war machine than to transform that machine from within. The beliefs we express and act on are greatly influenced by the social situations we find ourselves in. Beliefs about how to preserve one's own life and avoid dishonorable discharge become more salient than generalized beliefs about war (which may shift over time toward "war preparedness is an evil, but a necessary one — because of the other side"). Behavior (possibly strongly influenced by unintentionally created circumstances) is mutually dependent with beliefs, and both contribute to social change and stability.

11. If the wealthiest 2% of the U.S. population hold most key cabinet posts and Congressional committee chairmanships, determine through financing of campaigns which political candidates are "serious" ones, own the mass media, control and manage the major foundations that fund social research, govern (as trustees) most major universities, coopt top media personnel and intellectuals into organizations whose agenda is set by the wealthy, and produce a steady stream of "educational" materials designed to steer the more attentive parts of the public into seeing things their way, — then the beliefs of that minority may play a much greater role in determining policy than the beliefs of (say) the least wealthy 70%.

For some references (out of dozens that might be given) to substantiate the preceding sketch as applicable to the U.S., see Gabriel Kolko, *The Roots of American Foreign Policy* (Beacon, 1969); Laurence H. Shoup and William Minter's *Imperial Brain Trust: The Council on Foreign Relations and United States Foreign Policy* (Monthly Review, 1977), which sheds light (pp. 31, 69-75) not only on the CFR but also on the role of such groups as the Foreign Policy Association, closely interlocked with the CFR and one of the bodies serving as "channel-ways of expression" (p. 71) for the upper-class-dominated outlook promoted by the CFR; Susanne Gowan et al., *Moving Toward a New Society* (New Society Publishers, 1976), p. 160, n. 30; G. William Domhoff, *The Higher Circles* (Vintage, 1970) and *Who Rules America Now?* (Prentice-Hall, 1983).

For anyone whose mind formed the phrase "conspiracy theory" while reading the preceding two paragraphs, the final two chapters of Domhoff's *The Higher Circles* are indispensable reading. In "Dan Smoot, Phyllis Schlafly, Reverend McBirnie, and Me" and "Where a Pluralist Goes Wrong," Domhoff spells out with painstaking care (and good humor) exactly where he agrees with and differs from the ultra-conservative "conspiracy" notion believed by many poorer Americans and the liberal "pluralist" viewpoint dominant among academics and many middle-class people.

12. As Tom Greening (editor of the *Journal of Humanistic Psychology*, in which the essays in *Politics and Innocence* first appeared) reports in his introduction, the publication of Marien's reply to *Aquarian Conspiracy* author Marilyn Ferguson's response to his article led to her resignation from the journal's editorial board.

13. But be sure to give full publication details so that people who want to read the guidelines in context can obtain the whole book. ExPro is grateful to editor Tom Greening and Saybrook Publishers, who kindly gave

permission for reproduction of excerpts from *Politics and Innocence* for study group use, one copy per group.

14. Marien and Satin insist that we distinguish envisioning a desired future from wishful thinking that obscures what must be done to make that future a reality. One widely-circulated, well-intentioned example of erroneous wishful thinking was Ken Keyes, Jr.'s *The Hundredth Monkey* (Vision Books, 1981), an anti-nuclear tract whose title was based on a "New Age" pseudo-scientific myth. Keyes repeated the story that when a certain number of monkeys on a Japanese island learned to wash sweet potatoes, suddenly all the monkeys on nearby islands became likewise enlightened. "There is a point at which if only one more person tunes-in [sic] to a new awareness, a field is strengthened so that this awareness is picked up by almost everyone!" (1985 ed., p. 17). Awareness of the danger and folly of nuclear weapons, Keyes suggested, would, if spread far enough, suddenly emerge in everyone, leaders and all. "In [this phenomenon] may lie our only hope of a future for our species" (p. 10).

It's a good thing this isn't our only hope. The monkey story has been shown — in *Whole Earth Review* #52 (Fall 1986) — to lack a solid factual basis. That issue of *Whole Earth Review* (recently issued in book form as Ted Schultz, ed., *The Fringes of Reason*; 1989; 223 pp.; $15.00) contains a whole section on the Hundredth Monkey myth, including an examination of the scientific articles that were misrepresented as supporting it, a reply by the myth's initial launcher, and an essay on the inclination of people to spread such ideas.

15. To arrange a workshop or obtain other information about the Movement Action Plan, contact William H. Moyer, Social Movement Empowerment Project, 721 Shrader Street, San Francisco, CA 94117; 415-387-3361. Andrea Ayvazian calls Moyer's MAP "an invaluable guide for social change activists . . . the single most useful tool I have uncovered yet." Single copies are $2.00; lower rates are available for bulk orders (five or more).

16. On nonviolent struggle, see Gene Sharp, *The Politics of Nonviolent Action* (Porter Sargent, 1973). "Nonviolent action" is defined by Sharp (pp. 64-67) in contrast not only with political violence but also with "peaceful institutional procedures backed by threat or use of sanctions" (p. 65). His usage is followed in this book, except that the term "nonviolent struggle" is generally preferred because "struggle" conveys the essential idea that action in a conflict situation is meant (as is made clear by Sharp, pp. 64-65, 66). Some people think of "civil disobedience" as roughly synonymous with nonviolent struggle. Sharp, the most influential conceptual analyst in the field, defines civil disobedience ("deliberate, open and peaceful violation of particular laws, decrees [etc.] . . . which are believed to be illegitimate"; see pp. 315-316) as only one of 198 methods of nonviolent action.

17. Gene Sharp pioneered awareness of nonviolent struggle in the American Revolution with many references (see index) in *The Politics of Nonviolent Action*. An important volume entirely focused on that subject has subsequently been published: *Resistance, Politics, and the American Struggle for Independence, 1765-1775* (Lynne Rienner Publishers, 1986), edited by Walter H. Conser, Jr., Ronald M. McCarthy, David J. Toscano, and Gene Sharp. This 592-page book contains fourteen chapters by British and American scholars that explore the Stamp Act resistance, the resistance to the Townshend Acts, and the Continental Association of October 1774 (which Sharp has described as probably the most sophisticated program of phased nonviolent resistance before Gandhi). This decade of resistance was highly significant for developing the capacity for self-government that enabled the colonies to undertake to win independence from British rule. Today, the spread of awareness of the role of nonviolent struggle in the origins of the United States might aid the progress of movements for peace and alternative defense policies.

18. On the necessity defense, see the defense's closing argument, the judge's instructions, and related material in *Por Amor Al Pueblo*, pp. 138-173. For extensive information on necessity, Nuremberg, international law, and other legal defense strategies, and much interesting related material on "peace law," contact the Meiklejohn Civil Liberties Institute, Box 673, Berkeley, CA 94701. Newsletter and order form free on request. *A Peace Law Docket* of over 369 cases is available for $20.00 plus $5.00 postage and handling. See also F. A. Boyle's important *Defending Civil Resistance Under International Law*, listed in this book's annotated bibliography.

19. Randy Kehler, *Nuclear Times* (Jan.-Feb. 1988), p. 5.

20. "In good hands" was the remarkable expression used by one of the jurors who acquitted former President Carter's daughter Amy Carter, Abbie Hoffman, and others in a 1986 trial in Western Massachusetts.

21. To get in touch with this network, contact National War Tax Resistance Coordinating Committee (NWTRCC), P.O. Box 85810, Seattle, WA 98145; (206) 522-4377. One of the stronger regional groups is New England War Tax Resistance, Box 174, MIT Branch P.O., Cambridge, MA 02139; (617) 731-6139.

22. A brochure explaining how the fund works is available from War Tax Resisters Penalty Fund, P.O. Box 25, N. Manchester, IN 46962.

23. At the October 1987 convention of the National Rainbow Coalition, Jackson "outlined a new foreign policy plan he called 'the Jackson Doctrine.'" The first of its three principles was "to strengthen and support the rule of international law." Salim Muwakkil, "Pot of gold at end of Jackson's Rainbow?" *In These Times* (October 21-27, 1987), p. 7. Jackson reiterated this stance in a July-August 1988 *Mother Jones* article.

Michael Dukakis, too, spoke of respecting international law in his campaign for the Democratic nomination. Regrettably, he also expressed positions contrary to international law, such as indicating invading Nicaragua would be justified if it introduced "Soviet offensive weapons." The United States, of course, reserves the right to put offensive weapons anywhere. For a case study that notes the assumption, prevalent among the dominant U.S. politicians and media, that the U.S. has special rights no other nation on earth has, see Stephen R. Shalom, "The Cuban Missile Crisis," *Zeta Magazine* (June 1988), pp. 69-80.

24. Co-editors Felice and Jack Cohen-Joppa wrote in *The Nuclear Resister* #44 (February 2, 1987) that "Civil disobedience opposing nuclear weapons has become so widely recognized as justified under International Law that many resisters have begun to refer to their actions not as civil disobedience but as 'Nuremberg actions.' There are now several instances on record where judges are willing to entertain this legal argument and even let juries judge the matter themselves — a significant milestone compared to the judicial intransigence apparent only a few years ago." They go on to ask: "When will the leading national groups working in the 'legal' arena for nuclear disarmament begin to follow these committed activists and integrate civil disobedience into their strategy for the social change our very survival depends on?"

25. W. E. B. DuBois, *The Suppression of the African Slave-Trade to the United States of America, 1638-1870* (1896; Dover, 1970), p. 199.

26. *Fighting for Hope* (South End, 1984) is the first of Petra Kelly's books to become available in English. For an introduction to the West German Greens, see the books and articles cited in Brian Tokar's *The Green Alternative* (1987; see this book's bibliography), pp. 151, 157-8. In addition, see Werner Hülsberg, *The*

German Greens: A Social and Political Profile (Verso, 1988). The West German Greens can be contacted at: Die Grünen, Bundesgeschäftsstelle, Colmanstr. 36, 5300 Bonn, West Germany. Some publications are available in English. The 8-page German-language weekly *Die Grünen* (The Greens) is available for 6 marks per month from Postfach 20 24 22, 8000 München 2, West Germany. To contact the nearest U.S. Green group, write Committees of Correspondence, P.O. Box 30208, Kansas City, Missouri 64112.

27. *Don't Be Afraid, Gringo* was published in 1987 by Food First Books, 145 Ninth Street, San Francisco, CA 94103, and in 1989 by Harper & Row. Thanks are due to the journal *Toward Freedom: Report on Non-alignment and the Developing Countries*, in whose October 1987 issue this excerpt (here further abridged) was included.

Chapter 13: Where Do We Go From Here?

1. Paul Goodman, preface to *Utopian Essays and Practical Proposals* (Vintage, 1962), p. xiv.

2. Concerning the Exchange Project, see Chapter 12, note 7.

3. One of the most comprehensive and widely used of these is Virginia Coover et al., *Resource Manual for a Living Revolution*, available from New Society Publishers. NSP emphasizes books that are skill-oriented, including training manuals and other books on democratic decision-making, group dynamics, nonviolent action strategies and tactics, childrearing, and worker self-management. For a catalog, contact NSP, 4527 Springfield Avenue, Philadelphia, PA 19143; (215) 382-6543.

4. Instructions for the "Whole Person Exercise" and many other tools and exercises for personal and group decision-making, education, conflict resolution, affirmation, and fun are contained in *Resource Manual for a Living Revolution*. Information on residential workshops designed to help women discover or deepen their identities as spiritually grounded social change agents is available from Sandra Boston deSylvia, 15 Abbott St., Greenfield, MA 01301; 413-774-5952. In addition to workshops and other group activities, a very convenient and (after the initial outlay) inexpensive way to relax, improve one's sense of well-being, and strengthen one's ability to cope with the stresses of everyday life and social change work, is to use audio tapes. One need not accept unproven theories about "self-programming" to benefit from a relaxing half-hour listening to a tape. Of the many on the market, the following have won praise and can be vouched for by the present writer. Effective Learning Systems (5221 Edina Ind. Blvd., Edina, MN 55435; 612-893-1680) sells several dozen 30-minute tapes offering gentle, positive suggestions on topics ranging from "Deep Relaxation" to "Overcoming Worry" and "Taking Charge of Your Life." "Self-Image II" and the 10-minute "Alpha Break" tape are especially recommended. $9.98 per tape plus $3.00 shipping. The Changeworks (P.O. Box 4000-D, Berkeley, CA 94704; 415-540-5707) offers a half-dozen tapes based on Ericksonian hypnosis and featuring remarkable special effects (stereo headphones recommended) within extended metaphors. "Great care has been taken to make the tapes not only effective but *interesting* enough to listen to often." With plays on words and multiple voices, one can enjoy new aspects of the tapes with repeated listening. Twenty to forty minutes long; $12.95 per tape plus $1.85 postage/handling for first tape, 75 cents each additional. The beautiful and inspiring "Natural Self-Confidence" tape is particularly recommended. Catalogs free on request.

Group Study Resources

Introduction
A: How to Organize a Peace System Study Group
B: Principles for Democratic Social Change
      Study Groups
C: How to Do a 15-Session Study Group
D: How to Do a 7-Session Study Group
E: How to Base a College Course on This Book
F: How to Order the Materials
G: How to Do an "Imaging a World Without War"
      Workshop
H: Evaluating Your Study Group Experience

Group Study Resources:
Introduction

This book is designed so that you can use it in several ways. While you can read it straight through as an individual, you can also gain added benefits by forming a group or arranging a course in which you and others can divide the cost of acquiring the readings and tapes mentioned in it, and can develop deeper insights through the process of discussing what you are learning with each other. The improved and larger-scale learning that group study can make possible may well be essential if human beings are to solve the problems of war, poverty, oppression, and ecology that we face. Discussion of the nature of these problems, and of the proposed solutions to them that we may choose to implement, is essential for effective democracy.

This part of the book contains several different sections to help you do a study group or course successfully:

> A. How to organize a peace system study group
> B. Principles for democratic social change study groups
> C. How to do a 15-session study group
> D. How to do a 7-session study group
> E. How to base a college course on this book
> F. How to order the materials
> G. How to do an "Imaging a world without war" workshop
> H. Evaluating your study group experience

Section A explains the basics of how to organize a peace system study group, including recommended agendas. Section B explains why the processes recommended in Section A have been chosen, and clarifies the underlying principles. Fifteen or seven-session study groups or courses sponsored by a college, church, union, or other institution are all possibilities; how to use this book for those options is explained in Sections C, D, and E. Section F tells what the materials needed for the 7- or 15-session versions are, what they cost, and how to order them.

The 15-session study group is intended to consist of an introductory session for getting organized, acquainted, and familiar with the format to be used, thirteen sessions in which readings are discussed (corresponding to the thirteen chapters in this book), and a workshop on envisioning a world without war to be done part way through (ideally, as the fifth session). Section G explains how you can either get an outside resource person to conduct such a workshop or do it on your own.

Finally, Section H includes a form you and other members of your group can use to report back to ExPro on your experience, including suggestions on how this book might be improved in future editions. Your ideas might benefit many others. We hope to hear from you!

A: How to Organize
a Peace System Study Group

Getting Started

Groups from 7 to 12 in number usually work best, though smaller and larger groups can also succeed. The group can meet however frequently it wishes; once a week gives a good balance between enough time to do reading between sessions yet not so much as to lose the continuity of the discussions. Prior to the first meeting the group acquires a set of books and articles to share, plus a copy of *Building a Peace System* for each individual; five members report each session on articles or books read in the sequence recommended in this book. (Each member reports on different readings averaging about 50 pages in length.) The group discusses the readings and how to apply what is being learned to bringing about peace. A session normally lasts three hours. Various "tools" and exercises are used by the group, as it chooses, to facilitate learning and empowerment. A "convenor" starts the study group by finding participants, acquiring reading materials, and getting the first session off to a good start.

The following information is written with a 15-session study group in mind. A 7-session study group may better suit some groups' circumstances; if so, you should consult this book's section on how to do a 7-session version of the kind of group described in the following pages.

Finding participants. Maybe you already belong to a group of people concerned about the arms race, who wish to work more effectively. Ask others if they want to help organize a study group on peace. If you do not know anyone who might be interested, post fliers advertising the idea and/or contact organizations you've heard of to ask if they know of interested people in your area.

Acquiring the materials. As soon as you're sure there is enough interest to have a group, order materials right away so you'll have them when you need them. Refer to "How to Order the Materials" for details. If you can find (through ExPro or through other connections) a group that has already done a peace system study group, you may be able to borrow, rent, or buy a full set of materials from them. If you are buying, materials for a 7-session study group, including copies of this book for ten participants, cost about $260; for a 15-session study group, about $380. Divided among eight to twelve persons, this cost comes to between $2.20 and $4.70 per person per session — with the group owning all the materials at the end. Costs can be shared among members of the group or underwritten by a sponsoring organization. The materials should be organized when they arrive in such a way that those needed can reliably be brought to each session.

Arranging an "Imaging a World Without War" workshop. At the beginning of Part Two is a logical point at which to do a workshop on "Imaging a World Without War." If you want to arrange for an experienced facilitator to lead the group through such a workshop (as is recommended), it will be necessary to plan ahead; but if such an arrangement is not feasible for your group, you can do such a workshop on your own. See Section G below for further information.

Getting the first sessions off to a good start. Once the study group is under way, the members will (if they follow the recommended format) evaluate how it is going at the end of each session and make any changes they desire in how the group functions. To help the group get to the point of being self-managed is the responsibility of the convenor(s) — the person or persons starting the study group. The convenors should read this whole section on "How to Organize a Peace System Study Group" carefully so they understand the recommended format and can explain it at the first meeting.

The format and processes have been carefully conceived and tested, but are not meant to be followed rigidly. Since a mechanism for change is built in via the evaluation part of each session, it is possible to start with this model and then to experiment with changes, even drastic ones. Use the model presented here critically, adjusting it when necessary to meet your own group's needs. Discuss the format explicitly at the beginning so that all group members can start with a common understanding. Each member of the group should read "Principles for Democratic Social Change Study Groups" before the first meeting, if at all possible, or by the second meeting, at the latest.

To cover a large amount of material in a relatively short time, the following format is recommended. In each session, five members of the group give concise (5-7 minute) reports, each on a different reading (or group of readings) recommended in this book. The readings for each report are usually 30-70 pages long. Every member of the group should read this book's commentary on the readings. Toward the end of each session, five other members should volunteer to do the reports for the next session. (You can also plan two sessions ahead to allow more time to get reading done.) In this way a participant need read only an average of about 50 pages every other week (if the group meets weekly), in addition to reading the commentary in this volume. (In an academic setting, however, it may be possible for participants to read a much higher percentage of the total materials.)

The reports, together with eight to ten minutes of clarifying questions and discussion following each one, make up a little less than half of each session. Another portion of time goes to opening and closing activities that help the group generate and maintain a sense of community and conscientious participation and help it plan and evaluate. Further discussion or the use of planned exercises occupy the remaining time in a typical session.

The format and approach recommended have three features: 1) a format that encourages and equalizes participation by group members; 2) an efficient process for covering a lot of reading material; and 3) the use of exercises that help people relate what they are learning to their lives and apply it in effective social change work. The following pages explain the roles and processes that are designed to create these features.

Roles

The role of the convenor has already been indicated. Other process-related roles to be taken on in turn by the different members of the group are:

Facilitator. The facilitator's task is to "chair" the session, enabling or "facilitating" the smooth working of the group and helping it accomplish what it wants. The facilitator should:

Write a proposed agenda for the session beforehand on a large sheet of paper.

Get the session started on time and suggest when it is appropriate to move on, keeping reports, discussion, and other agenda items within the time limits that the group has agreed to. (The facilitator should not mistake those limits for an external authority, but rather should remind the group, if and when it has strayed from its agenda, to think whether it wants to return to that agenda or change it.)

Be sensitive to the feelings of the group; expressions of emotion, types of questions being asked, and general mood may indicate that some variation in process is called for.

Try to get unspoken but important frustrations, needs, fears, expectations, etc. out in the open so they can be dealt with directly. (Hidden concerns are often a source of frustration and failure in groups.)

Help everyone share in the discussion. Be sensitive to shyer people being cut off or intimidated by those more extroverted. It's often good to ask part way through a meeting if people who haven't spoken much have anything they want to say.

When people seem not to be understanding each other's ideas, encourage them to paraphrase in their own words what they think the other person is saying and ask the person if that's accurate.

Assistant facilitator. The assistant facilitator should be in touch with the facilitator a few days before the session in case there is anything tricky about the session's agenda or logistics (e.g., is a tape player needed?). During the meeting the assistant facilitator may serve as recorder or time-keeper (see below), and should stay aware of how the session is going and make suggestions as appropriate. Paying special attention to the group's process is practice for the following session, when this person becomes the facilitator.

Recorder. The recorder can, if the group wishes, write on flip-chart paper important ideas that come out of the reports or discussion (helping the group keep track of them throughout the session), and should record the evaluation comments at the end of the session.

Timekeeper. The timekeeper reminds people (gently) of the time. People giving reports may request two-minute warnings so they can be sure to cover all the essentials. When a planned allotment of time is used up, don't say "Stop! Time's up!" Say (for example): "That's been ten minutes of discussion." If the group wants to spend an hour discussing a report, great! That's its privilege. It's the facilitator's job to point out when such choices will require shortening something else (or adding another session to the study group's length). Aim to end on time.

These are the formal roles we recommend. Rotating roles is valuable for the group. The roles of facilitator and assistant facilitator should be filled by as many members of the group as possible so that the experience and the responsibility can be shared. Recording and timekeeping can be done by the assistant facilitator or can be separate roles taken on by volunteers at each session.

All this may sound complicated, but experience suggests it soon becomes familiar and makes for maximum learning and a smooth-running study group.

Processes

Included with the materials sold by ExPro to study groups is a reprint from *Organizing Macro-Analysis Seminars*, a booklet that discusses many variations of process a group can try, and solutions to common problems of study groups.[1] The convenor should read that reprint before the group's first meeting, and other participants are encouraged to read it before playing the facilitator role. A 15-session study group will have more time to experiment than a 7-session one, but both can do so successfully.

"Excitement sharing." This is a good way to start each meeting on an "up" note. Sometimes it can be used to draw the group together if people are still milling around and saying hello. The facilitator can call people together and when most are seated ask, "What is something good that has happened in your life since we last met?" Each person then has the opportunity to share an event, accomplishment, insight, experience, etc. that was exciting or a "plus" during the week. Input should be brief, comments limited.

Some advantages of excitement sharing are: it starts the meeting on a positive note, it develops a more personal tone among the participants, and it is enjoyable (and thus may encourage people to arrive on time). Caution: one danger is that excitement-sharing could go on for hours, therefore don't go beyond an agreed-upon time (say, ten minutes).

Agenda review. Near the beginning of every session, the facilitator should present the proposed agenda for the meeting. The agenda can then be reviewed and changed if necessary to accommodate new ideas or different priorities. The agenda should be written on a big sheet of paper in plain view so everyone can see throughout the session what they've decided to do.

Personal introductions. Even groups in which members know each other are encouraged to spend some time on this at the first meeting. Groups can choose (don't try to do all these at the first meeting!) from the following list of things to be shared by participants, or do others, as you wish.

1. Name
2. Where you're from
3. How you heard about the peace system study group
4. Why you're interested in it
5. What effect you believe your economic/social/cultural background has had on your political viewpoint (a brief comment, not an autobiography!)
6. One thing you have done well in work for peace (if you have been active in some way), and one thing you would like to be able to do better
7. One thing you would like to be doing to work for peace; what is preventing you from doing that; and what you can do about the obstacle

Where size permits, it may be possible, and is probably preferable, for the whole group to listen to each person address several of these. Another option is for people to pair off (preferably with someone they know less well or not at all) and take five minutes each to listen to the other, then have everyone introduce his/her partner to the whole group. The facilitator for the meeting should propose one of these options or a substitute process.

It is not a good idea to ask people simply to tell what social change work they have done, since often a few people talk at length about their experience while others feel inadequate because they have had less experience. No matter what introductory process is used, each person's comments should be fairly brief and each person should have approximately equal time to share with the group. This basic principle is important to keep in mind throughout the study group.

Evaluation. It is important to have an evaluation near the end of every session. It enables positive and exciting things to be mentioned and affirmed. ("This is a nice place to meet"; "I'm glad we keep consistently starting and ending on time"; "Jane, I thought your report was really interesting and also very well prepared"; "You did a good job of facilitating"; "Ted, thanks for continuing to bring the next set of readings each time.") Also, equally importantly, it allows participants to identify things they didn't particularly like and to make suggestions for change. ("I would like it if we could meet in a room with better lighting"; "How about if we try hearing all the reports first before we have any discussion?")

A good format for evaluation is to ask first "What was good about the meeting?" Evaluation can cover the readings, process, and logistics (meeting place, etc.). Next, ask "What wasn't so good?"

Finally, "Any suggestions for improvements for next time?" Lengthy discussion should be avoided; contradictory comments need not always be reconciled. Just record them on flip chart paper for the use of the next session's facilitator. When several people would like to try a change, often it's better to agree to try it once rather than debate endlessly whether it would be an improvement. Planning details can usually be left to the next facilitator and assistant facilitator.

Giving reports. Five minutes is little time for a rambling report, but a well-organized one can say a great deal. (Think of the impact of a one-minute television commercial.) Rather than only summarizing as much of the readings as you can, it is good also to emphasize the two or three points you consider most important. (Sometimes it may be helpful to the group for you to prepare ahead of time a diagram listing key points that people can look at as you talk.)

Read critically. Are the key assertions made adequately supported? Do there seem to be unstated assumptions you disagree with? As you read, think about what problems are being identified, what solutions are being suggested, and what the implications are. In the last minute of your report, discuss those implications. Should peace groups you're familiar with be doing something different in the light of what you've read? If you were unable to cover everything you wanted to in the report time, perhaps some points can be added during the discussion. Be as concise as you can.

Reports and discussion. Much of each session is essentially a long discussion enriched by new information via reports every ten or fifteen minutes. Having time limits and prepared reports interspersed through the discussion helps people to focus and keep from getting sidetracked too much, and it adds a sense of progress and accomplishment to the meeting. The five minutes for reports and ten minutes for discussion are suggested times; each group will want to work out for itself the rhythm it prefers. Whatever is chosen, people should be disciplined in keeping to it.

Relating what's been learned to social change possibilities. The main purpose of a peace system study group is to encourage thinking that can be used to make work for peace more effective. Consequently, to maximize the potential benefit, it's a good idea to devote portions of group time to think about how to apply what's been learned. Many processes have been developed to help people create better social change activities and overcome barriers they may encounter. See pp. 23-24 of the Macro-Analysis reprint cited above for several methods that can be used. Consider allocating some time every two or three meetings to this, in addition to the attention it is given in the last minute of reports and (probably) in discussion times.

Agendas

Recommended agenda for Session 1: Getting Started

Explanations for terms used in this suggested agenda can be found in the preceding pages. This agenda assumes that the group's convenors have ordered and received the needed materials (including a copy of *Building a Peace System* for each member). The convenor(s) should bring large sheets of paper (flip charts or discarded computer printouts), crayons or markers to write with, an easel or masking tape, etc., and prepare a "Proposed Agenda" like the one below big enough for everyone to read. The convenor(s) can facilitate the session, or possibly invite a member of the group who has already read this section of *Building a Peace System* to share the job.

Agenda item	Minutes
1. Welcome by convenors	5
2. Agenda review	5
3. Personal introductions (* varies with group size and prior acquaintance)	* 30-60
4. Introduction to the democratic study group format	15
5. Break (here or whenever seems best)	15
6. Discuss expectations and wishes for study group	15-25
7. Initial business (money, time, place, etc.)	30
(If time: answer questions presented below)	(15-25)
8. Brainstorm questions about peace and what you hope to learn in the study group	10-30
9. Decide who'll prepare the first reports on readings and hand out the reading materials; choose assistant facilitator for next meeting	5-10
10. Evaluation	5-10
Total	**160-180**

If less time than indicated above is needed for the first seven items, the group may choose, before doing item #8, for everyone to respond briefly to the following questions:

"Do you think that it is possible to achieve permanent worldwide peace in the sense of wars neither occurring nor being prepared for? If you answer no, why not? Do you think that human-kind will destroy itself through war, or that things will continue indefinitely about as they are now (with a few dozen wars happening)? How will war affect your life?

"If you answer yes, do you think that peace can be achieved in your lifetime? How long do you think it will take to achieve it? What events do you imagine would lead to peace? Do you think you will play a role in bringing about peace? How would peace affect your life?"

There is no need to discuss the answers given; they will help group members to know their own and each other's minds better as the study group begins.

If you are reading this book on your own, we suggest you pause to formulate your answers to these questions. You might find it valuable to write the answers down, and then ask yourself the questions again when you have finished reading the whole volume.

Recommended agenda for Session 2: Deterrence, Star Wars, and Peace

Agenda item	Minutes
1. Excitement sharing	10
2. Agenda review	5
3. Choose recorder and timekeeper	2
4. Any remaining business, discussion of format, etc.	10-20
5. Discuss (if desired) "The Peace System Approach to Eliminating War" and "How the Peace Movement Shaped the Current Debate"	10-20
6. 1st report (5-7 min.) and clarifying questions and discussion (8-10 min.)	15
7. 2nd and 3rd reports (same format as 1st)	30
8. Break	10
9. 4th and 5th reports (same format as before)	30
10. General discussion	30-40
11. Decide next assistant facilitator and who'll report on next session's readings	5
12. Evaluation	10
Total	**180**

The second session follows a format more typical of the whole study group than the first, but still allows some time for "getting started" business. Between the first and second sessions all participants should complete reading the portions of this book indicated for the first two sessions on page 231 (for the 15-session version) or pages 237-238 (for the 7-session version).

In later meetings the time spent in the first two sessions on business and becoming familiar with the format of the sessions and each other will be available for exercises, as indicated in the following agenda. These exercises can be very important. (See the discussion and examples given following the agendas.)

Recommended agenda for Session 3 and later sessions

Agenda item	Minutes
1. Excitement sharing	10
2. Agenda review	5
3. Choose recorder and timekeeper	2
4. 1st report (5-7 min.) and clarifying questions and discussion (8-10 min.)	15
7. 2nd and 3rd reports (same format as 1st)	30
8. Break	10
9. 4th and 5th reports (same format as before)	30
10. General discussion	30-40
11. Exercise (see examples below)	25
12. Decide next assistant facilitator and who'll report on next session's readings	5
13. Evaluation	10
Total	**180**

Recommended agenda for final session

Agenda item	Minutes
1. Gathering; excitement sharing	10
2. Agenda review	5
3. Play Forsberg/Kehler audio cassette	30
4. Discussion: the current situation and prospects of the U.S. peace movement	15
5. Report on Brian Martin, "The Individual," from *Uprooting War*, plus 5 min. discussion	10
6. Report on Sarah Conn et al., *Keeping Us Going*, plus 5 min. discussion	10
7. Report on Elise Boulding, "Epilogue" to *Building a Global Civic Culture*, plus 5 min. discussion	10
8. Time in pairs to propose options for the group	10
9. Reporting ideas back to whole group	15
10. Break	15
11. Small group discussion and/or determining any next steps; or further whole-group discussion	25
12. Group housekeeping (where do readings go, etc.)	5
13. Evaluation of whole study group experience	15
14. Closing (song, ritual, silence)	5
Total	**180**

Exercises and Tools

The skillful use of activities we term "exercises" or "tools" can lift a study group from being mere acquisition of knowledge to being a life-changing experience. Some seemingly simple ideas and procedures can be useful for years afterwards as powerful tools for analyzing situations, solving problems for individuals or organizations, and making decisions about political strategy or the direction of one's own life.

There is a large repertoire of exercises and tools from which to choose. Rather than squeeze an inadequate selection from them into this volume, we refer you instead to two sources. The first is the reprint from *Organizing Macro-Analysis Seminars* mentioned earlier; a copy is included along with the other reading materials provided by ExPro to study groups. (You are free to reproduce it on a nonprofit basis.) It contains such exercises and tools as Web Chart, Brainstorming Reasons Why It's All Hopeless, and Problem-Solving.

A second excellent (and much more comprehensive) source is the book *Resource Manual for a Living Revolution* by Virginia Coover et al., which contains several dozen exercises and tools ranging from Force Field Analysis to Risk List and the Whole Person Exercise.[2] Several other books are also useful sources.[3]

Some of the exercises and tools aid analytic thinking; others aim to increase awareness of our own selves and what has shaped us; others help in making personal and political decisions. (Some arguably involve all three.) That they are not contained within this book may seem an invitation to neglect them. Such neglect would be a great mistake.

Why? Because the dangers posed by modern war have developed in part through the existence of a gulf between abstract theorizing and war planning, on the one hand, and, on the other, a personal, emotional, and moral realization of the human meaning of mass murder and preparation to commit it. People who want to move from endless war to peace should try to learn in a way that integrates the intellectual, moral, and emotional. To create a world of stable peace, men as well as women need to grow in awareness of the emotional, nurturance, and personal growth needs of groups and individuals, and to take responsibility for addressing them.

Therefore, all participants in peace system study groups are strongly encouraged to read through the macro-analysis reprint (especially pp. 19-21 and 97-101) and to select exercises appropriate to your group, adapting them to the peace system themes of this book. It is also hoped that some members of the group will get hold of the *Resource Manual* (available by mail, and found in many bookstores and libraries) to draw exercises from it as well and use them wherever they seem most suitable in the group's sessions.

Exercises for Sessions 3 and 4 (of a 15-session study group) are suggested here to help the group get accustomed to including exercises in its meetings, but subsequent ones should be chosen from the *Organizing Macro-Analysis Seminars* reprint or other sources by the facilitators of the later sessions, assuming the group's willingness.

Recommended exercise for Session 3. (The group can choose to do this exercise either before or after the "general discussion" time.) What event (whether well-known or obscure) can you recall that best represents for you wise and effective action in the cause of peace? Is there an event you have been involved in that you recall with pride as representing such action, or a peace-related ideal — that perhaps gave you a feeling of "this is the way it should be"? (Format: 2-5 minutes thinking, 2 minutes each to share back. Total: 25 minutes.)

Recommended exercise for Session 4. Choose one of the problems identified in the reports for Session 4. If the members of your study group decided to drop other activities and become an action group focusing your efforts on that problem, what could you do toward solving it? Aim for mind-stretching imaginativeness as well as practicality. "Brainstorm" — generate many action ideas quickly without criticizing them. Write the ideas as they come on a flip chart. Then evaluate the ideas: which would be best to do? Precision and consensus are not essential. Consider both your group's own immediate resources and those it could connect with or mobilize. (Format: 3-5 minutes to choose problem; 10 minutes for brainstorming action ideas; 10 minutes for discussion. Total: 25 minutes.)

Make your own choices for the later sessions. It's your study group. Good luck!

Notes

1. *Organizing Macro-Analysis Seminars: A Manual* (Philadelphia Macro-Analysis Collective, 1975; out of print).

2. *Resource Manual for a Living Revolution* is available for $12.95 (plus $1.50 postage/handling) from New Society Publishers, P.O. Box 582, Santa Cruz, CA 95061-0582.

3. See those listed in the notes to "How to Do an 'Imaging a World Without War' Workshop."

B: Principles for Democratic Social Change Study Groups

The participatory format and processes used in this book originated in the "macro-analysis seminar" movement. That movement began in the early 1970s among veterans of the civil rights, anti-poverty, and antiwar movements. Many of those activists had believed that the U.S. was a prosperous and democratic society whose remaining problems — pockets of poverty, racial inequality — could and would be solved by citizen initiatives to prompt government action. Instead, they found a stubborn power structure responsive only to extraordinary efforts and sacrifice (as in the civil rights movement) and more interested in waging war in Southeast Asia than in ending poverty or redressing inequality at home. As the 1960s drew to a close, with war, racism, and poverty persisting, a host of new problems entered public awareness, beginning with the emergence of the women's liberation, gay liberation, and ecology movements.[1]

Parallels and interconnections among such problems and the conditions that perpetuated them led many activists to decide that they were up against a "system." While a few felt confident they could define that system, many found old categories and prescriptions inadequate and felt the need to increase their understanding of what was wrong, how things might be different, and how change could be brought about.

Traditional education, compartmentalized into disciplines, slow to recognize new realities, and complacent toward injustice, was not the answer. Yet independent study groups faced difficulties, too: Where to begin? How to make the costs in time and materials manageable? How to insure that the learning process fostered rather than undermined activism, and remedied rather than accentuated the inequalities of expertise and educational background participants brought to the group?

Macro-analysis seminars were devised with these concerns in mind. (The term "macro-analysis" was coined to indicate the importance of getting the "big picture" — "macro" is Greek for "big" — of how different problems were related, but soon "macro seminar," "macro format," and "macro process" referred equally much to the unique combination of learning and empowerment processes used.)

The pioneering participants realized that much more material could be covered if participants reported on different readings rather than everyone reading the same thing. Ideas as to useful subject matter, and growing expertise, could be shared if study group participants published a recommended outline of topics and readings that could be revised over time as other groups used it and found newer or better materials. Practices from group dynamics, the women's movement, and other sources could equalize participation and maximize the social change impact of the learning process.

The first edition of *Organizing Macro-Analysis Seminars: A Manual* was published in 1972 (in mimeograph) by the Philadelphia Macro-Analysis Collective. It contained extensive group process suggestions and an outline of 24 (or, optionally, 12) weeks of readings grouped in five parts:

223

ecological problems, U.S. relations with the Third World, U.S. domestic problems, visions of a better society, and strategies for getting from here to there. From 1972 through the early 1980s some 500 macro-analysis seminars were conducted in the U.S., Canada, and other countries, and several revised editions of the reading list were prepared. Most seminars were organized by social change activists, many through religious groups, and many also in over a dozen colleges and universities which conducted macro seminars for course credit at the initiative of faculty or students.

The "macro" format and processes were used in other "macro manuals" with readings adapted to other countries, or focused on subjects such as Peace Conversion, Urban Transportation, Political Theory and Strategy, Multinational Corporations, and Central America.

Portions of the 1975 "macro manual," reproduced verbatim or slightly revised, make up part of the "How to Organize a Peace System Study Group" section of this book. The name "macro-analysis seminar," never very clear to newcomers, has been dropped in favor of the wordy but less opaque "democratic social change study group"; but all the essentials of the participatory, activism-oriented approach have been retained.

The text that follows, originally entitled "Underlying Principles of Macro-Analysis" (1975), was, if memory serves, mostly written by the late Jim Nunes-Schrag, a lively and dedicated grassroots educator who is sorely missed. It has been abridged and slightly revised to improve its clarity and relevance for peace system study groups. The "we" in the text, referring to the Philadelphia Macro-Analysis Collective, no longer exist as such. But, as in 1975, it seems important — precisely because participants are strongly encouraged to adapt the format and processes to their own needs — to spell out the principles that have made for successful democratic study groups.

• • •

This text makes explicit the principles, values, and assumptions we have found valuable for democratic social change study groups. In addition to making the principles clear, it should help study group organizers and participants make changes if they want to (a) agree that a certain principle is good and innovate in how to apply it; (b) lay aside a principle and develop an alternative one, and practical ways of implementing it; (c) incorporate new principles and ways of implementing them. Any of these may work out well as long as the innovators are conscious of what they are doing. It is important to be really familiar with the format and the various processes and the part they play in implementing the guiding principles before trying to change them.

This is not to discourage creativity — only to caution that inadequately thought-out changes may disorient a study group or damage its morale. Experience and thoughtful experimentation, on the other hand, can yield valuable lessons. For example, a major lesson of past study groups is the importance of encouraging a positive, hopeful, mutually affirming and trusting attitude among participants. Why? Because a major goal of the groups is helping people become more effective social change agents, and we have found that the attitudes and spirit we create in our work together play a large part in sustaining our capacity to continue learning and working.

A. Group Process

1. *The maintenance of participatory democracy in all the activities of the study group is vital.* This is so for many reasons, two very important ones being that (a) participatory democracy is a crucial part of our vision of a better society, and we will best achieve that by practicing it now at every possible opportunity; and (b) the evidence of many democratic study groups, especially when contrasted with standard high school and college learning situations, is that people learn faster and more effectively, and are more likely to move on to social change applications of their learning, when they are in charge of the learning situation.

Participatory democracy is maintained primarily through procedures that encourage: a) equal participation in the group, and b) equal sharing within it of the power and information necessary for decision-making. Equal participation is aided by: everyone's possession of, and familiarity with, the texts explaining the format and processes;[2] regular rotation of the role of facilitator; and an agenda which is on a large sheet of paper in view of everyone and which is reviewed each meeting and is open to changes suggested by any participant. Procedures encouraging equal participation include: several occasions on which the person speaking is not to be interrupted, including report giving, brainstorming, and "think and listen"; and the availability of exercises to raise the consciousness of people who tend to speak too frequently (e.g., giving up one of a small number of allotted matches each time one speaks, and not being permitted to speak when one's matches are gone); the reports format in which each person has the opportunity to contribute information; and agenda items like excitement sharing which include everyone.

2. *Participants need to get to know one another more deeply than just in the limited role of co-learners.* If group members come to trust and appreciate each other more and more as the study group goes on, the collective learning will be a more enjoyable experience; the group will come to mean more to each participant; more effective learning will occur, because people will feel trustful enough of the group to share ideas they aren't really sure about; participants will be more likely to develop meaningful and implementable social action plans; and the quality of meetings will improve because everyone will genuinely care about giving good reports, being an alert facilitator, timekeeper, etc.

Procedures which encourage this deepening level of trust include the values clarification exercises[3] and other structured sharing in the introductory sessions of the study group; excitement sharing, and occasional extended excitement sharing; potluck meals together, etc.

3. *All of us can develop a kind of learning/teaching experience that is empowering* to us because we will grow in our reliance on and respect for our ability both to think clearly and to successfully tackle problems, rather than concluding that only the "experts" know enough to act on these issues. This principle breaks down into two more specific ones:

(3A) *Each group knows best what its own unique needs are.* A variety of options are available for dealing with a specific topic, situation, need, etc. Each group should assess its own needs, and then determine how best to meet them in the context of the overall structure.

(3B) *Each group needs to keep doing the things that will build a solid, authentic sense of achievement, and the things that will help it recognize and appreciate what it is achieving.* Factors important in producing this sense of achievement include:

(a) Careful adherence to suggested time limits. If each report is finished on time, there will be time in the session to relate new information to social change, and the session will finish on time. These achievements in turn lead to finishing topics as expected, creating an ongoing sense of momentum and achievement. If reports are repeatedly too long, sessions will run overtime, the group may get behind schedule, etc., and a sense of failure can easily set in.

(b) Sensitivity in judging how much time is worth allotting to completely open-ended discussion. Participants in many groups have found it frustrating and unproductive to discuss at length points for which documenting information is not at hand. Similarly, it can be very unsatisfying to get off on tangents and not end up where you wanted to be.

(c) Being careful to allow significant amounts of time for relating what's learned to what can be done with it. This may seem unimportant if action ideas generated aren't acted on immediately, but is in fact valuable for two reasons. First, participants will usually take these ideas back into their own lives, and into other groups they're involved in, e.g., ecology, peace, social justice. Second, generating ideas for social change activities (and reviewing them periodically) reminds the group of all the things that could be done. This is an important counter-balance to the disturbing and discouraging nature of some of the information the reports bring to light. Reviewing the action ideas generated over the course of the study group also reminds the group how much it has accomplished.

(d) Sensitivity in making efficient use of overall session time, but not overburdening the group. Work toward finding your group's balance between the amount of information input and discussion that feels positive and exciting, and the amount that feels too intense and overwhelming.

4. *Doing enjoyable, energizing things to help keep the group's morale and energy level high is very important.* Precisely because social change study groups have a very serious purpose, we need

energy from many sources. One is the attainment and appreciation of solid achievement described above. Others (in addition to excitement sharing) are singing, stretches, and active games that can be inserted at low-energy points in a session.[4] These raise our energy level for more creative work, release tension, and help us to start implementing now a vision of a society in which people enjoy each other through both work and play.

5. *Regular carrying out of effective evaluations.* This principle is placed at the end of the group process section because in some ways it encompasses all the previous principles. An evaluation that is both frank and honest, and at the same time sensitive and supportive of participants, is a crucial mechanism for sharing everyone's assessment of how well things are going in terms of the principles outlined above, and for making use of the collective wisdom of the group in making improvements for the future. It is the major opportunity to implement the process of molding the study group structure to meet the group's particular needs; and to strengthen group morale and increase energy by reflecting on things that went well.

B. Topics and Readings

6. *Maintenance of the overall framework of the topics studied.* This is important because the study of a set of topics which have been arranged to create an intellectual framework helps people build a sense of things falling into place which the study of a random series of topics usually doesn't produce. This excitement helps maintain a high level of enthusiasm about the study group. A group that feels a need to change the order of, add, or delete topics should try to gauge the probable effect of the change on the coherence of the learning experience.

7. *Any new topics added are relevant to action.* Action for social change is, of course, the major purpose of social change study groups. Any new topics about which members of the group may be curious should be assessed according to how their study might strengthen efforts for social change.

8. *An emphasis on readings, both those prescribed in this book and any new ones added by groups, that go to the roots of problems.* "Going to the roots of a problem" means raising questions about what is really necessary to solve the problem, and not stopping short of that because of vested interests which would be threatened if a true resolution of the problem were approached. Many of the readings prescribed in this book advocate fundamental change in political and economic policies. This emphasis has been chosen for two reasons. First, these viewpoints favoring fundamental change are ones which are rarely familiar or accurately known, whereas we are all constantly immersed, via the mass media (including the prestigious newspapers and magazines), in various shorter-range reform arguments as well as arguments denying that the things we study are problems at all. Second, often the case for fundamental change is a sound one, with which peace activists should therefore become familiar. Participants may also choose, however, to include addi-

tional readings defending the status quo or advocating minimal reforms so that the different perspectives can be examined side by side.

9. Any *new readings* a group may introduce *should include one or more of the following: new knowledge;* proposed *values* or guidelines with which to approach the subject; insights into *links between ostensibly different topics;* proposals for *solutions;* and ideas about *strategy* for making the solutions happen.

C. Action

10. *A small group of people, such as the participants in a peace system study group, can undertake meaningful and successful political action toward solving the problems they are studying.* The sit-in movement, started in 1960 by four black college students determined to end lunch-counter segregation, is one dramatic example, but innumerable others could be given.[5]

11. *The success of a social change study group should be evaluated primarily on the basis of its influence on our actions for social change.* As suggested earlier, this can take several forms besides that of the study group members' deciding to do an action project together. These can include the introduction of new ideas to other social change groups, the spreading of more effective and enjoyable ways of conducting meetings, and organizing new study groups, among other possibilities.

12. *We are all victims of the problems we are studying,* not just altruistic reformers working on someone else's problems. This should be kept in mind as we consider how to confront various aspects of the world's problems and work toward solutions. Reflection and discussion should show that these problems affect us personally and are not just abstract subjects. The better we understand that, and look upon our social change efforts as steps toward improving the quality of our own lives, the more strength we will have to draw on in the struggle.

Notes

1. For an active participant's discussion of this period, see Dave Dellinger, *More Power Than We Know: The People's Movement Toward Democracy* (Anchor Press / Doubleday, 1975), passim, but especially "Preparing the Future: Fragmenting and Deepening," pp. 15-22.

2. For peace system study groups, these texts appear in three places: a) the section of this book you are now reading; b) the section "How to Organize a Peace System Study Group" elsewhere in this book; and c) the reprinted pages from *Organizing Macro-Analysis Seminars: A Manual* that are supplied along with the other readings purchased from ExPro. Decide for yourselves if you want to make copies of the last item for everyone in your group. It's worth doing if people will in fact read it.

3. See *Organizing Macro-Analysis Seminars*, pp. 19-20.

4. See Virginia Coover et al., *Resource Manual for a Living Revolution*, pp. 78-79, 112. A songbook full of old and new favorites is *Rise Up Singing*, edited by Peter Blood-Patterson, published by *Sing Out!* magazine and distributed by New Society Publishers (P.O. Box 582, Santa Cruz, CA 95061-0582) for $12.95 (paperback) or $14.95 (spiral binding) plus $1.50 postage for first book, 50 cents each additional.

5. Richard K. Taylor's *Blockade* (Orbis Books, 1977) is a dramatic account, complete with photographs, of a nonviolent direct action campaign that succeeded in stopping U.S. arms shipments to a dictatorship engaged in mass killing. See pp. 4-8 for how the campaign originated in a macro-analysis study group.

C. How to Do a
15-session Study Group

Below are recommended instructions for participants and facilitators to keep in mind for each session. They should be read and followed before each session begins. Most sessions follow one basic format; sessions 1, 2, 5, 8, and 15, have different formats.

Session 1: Getting Started

Convenor. If people interested in being in the study group have been able to acquire and read the sections "How to Organize a Peace System Study Group" and "Principles for Democratic Social Change Study Groups" before the first meeting, that will help the participants establish clear common expectations about the goals and operation of the group.

Consult "How to Organize a Peace System Study Group," especially "Recommended agenda for Session 1" in the "Agendas" subsection. (When preparing the agenda be sure to include time for five participants to divide up the reading assignments listed in Chapter 1; the readings are to be reported on in Session 2.)

Session 2: Deterrence, Star Wars, and Peace

Participants. All participants should read "The Peace System Approach to Eliminating War," "How the Peace Movement Shaped the Current Debate," and Chapter 1, "Deterrence, Star Wars, and Peace."

Facilitators. Consult "How to Organize a Peace System Study Group", especially "Recommended agenda for Session 2" in the "Agendas" subsection. Prepare the agenda. Be sure to include time for five participants to divide up the reading assignments listed in Chapter 2; the readings are to be reported on in Session 3.

Session 3: Arms Control: Pro and Con

Participants. All participants should read Chapter 2, "Arms Control: Pro and Con."

Facilitators. Consult "How to Organize a Peace System Study Group," particularly the "Agendas" and "Exercises and Tools" subsections. Note that there is a recommended agenda and exercise for this session. (When preparing the agenda be sure to include time for five participants to divide up the reading assignments listed in Chapter 3; the readings are to be reported on in Session 4.)

Session 4: Redefining the Issues: Aspects of the War System

Participants. All participants should read Chapter 3, "Redefining the Issues: Aspects of the War System."

Facilitators. Consult "How to Organize a Peace System Study Group," particularly the "Agendas" and "Exercises and Tools" subsections. Note that there is a specific recommended agenda and exercise for this session. (When preparing the agenda be sure to include time for five participants to divide up the reading assignments listed in Chapter 4; the readings are to be reported on in Session 6.)

Session 5: Imaging Workshop

See Section G, "How to Do an 'Imaging a World Without War' Workshop."

Session 6: Envisioning and Designing a Future of Peace

Participants. All participants should read "Why and How to Think About the Future" and Chapter 4, "Envisioning and Designing a Future of Peace."

Facilitators. Consult "How to Organize a Peace System Study Group," particularly the "Agendas" and "Exercises and Tools" subsections. Choose or invent an exercise for the group to do during the session. When preparing the agenda be sure to include time for five participants to divide up the reading assignments listed in Chapter 5; the readings are to be reported on in Session 7.

Session 7: World Governance

Participants. All participants should read Chapter 5, "World Governance."

Facilitators. Consult "How to Organize a Peace System Study Group," particularly the "Agendas" and "Exercises and Tools" subsections. Choose or invent an exercise for the group to do during the session. When preparing the agenda be sure to include time for five participants to divide up the reading assignments listed in Chapter 6; the readings are to be reported on in Session 8.

Session 8: Alternative Security Policies

Participants. All participants should read Chapter 6, "Alternative Security Policies."

Facilitators. Consult "How to Organize a Peace System Study Group," particularly the "Agendas" subsection. When preparing the agenda be sure to include time for five participants to divide up the reading assignments listed in Chapter 7; the readings are to be reported on in Session 9. Please note: there is a 29-minute audio cassette to be played during this session. Unless you wish to lengthen the meeting time for this session, it is suggested you make room for the cassette by omitting the time normally allotted to an exercise.

Session 9: Economic Development, Ecology, and Peace

Participants. All participants should read Chapter 7, "Economic Development, Ecology, and Peace."

Facilitators. Consult "How to Organize a Peace System Study Group," particularly the "Agendas" and "Exercises and Tools" subsections. Choose or invent an exercise for the group to do during the session. When preparing the agenda be sure to include time for five participants to divide up the reading assignments listed in Chapter 8; the readings are to be reported on in Session 10.

Session 10: Psychology, Religion, Culture, and Peace

Participants. All participants should read Chapter 8, "Psychology, Religion, Culture, and Peace."

Facilitators. Consult "How to Organize a Peace System Study Group," particularly the "Agendas" and "Exercises and Tools" subsections. Choose or invent an exercise for the group to do during the session. When preparing the agenda be sure to include time for five participants to divide up the reading assignments listed in Chapter 9; the readings are to be reported on in Session 11.

Session 11: The Superpowers

Participants. All participants should read "Prospects for Building a Peace System" and Chapter 9, "The Superpowers."

Facilitators. Consult "How to Organize a Peace System Study Group," particularly the "Agendas" and "Exercises and Tools" subsections. Choose or invent an exercise for the group to do during the session. When preparing the agenda be sure to include time for five participants to divide up the reading assignments listed in Chapter 10; the readings are to be reported on in Session 12.

Session 12: Beyond the Superpowers: Other Actors

Participants. All participants should read Chapter 10, "Beyond the Superpowers: Other Actors."

Facilitators. Consult "How to Organize a Peace System Study Group" section, particularly the "Agendas" and "Exercises and Tools" subsections. Choose or invent an exercise for the group to do during the session. When preparing the agenda be sure to include time for five participants to divide up the reading assignments listed in Chapter 11; the readings are to be reported on in Session 13.

Session 13: Making Changes: Analyses and Approaches

Participants. All participants should read Chapter 11, "Making Changes: Analyses and Approaches."

Facilitators. Consult "How to Organize a Peace System Study Group," particularly the "Agendas" and "Exercises and Tools" subsections. Choose or invent an exercise for the group to do during the session. When preparing the agenda be sure to include time for five participants to divide up the reading assignments listed in Chapter 12; the readings are to be reported on in Session 14.

Please pass on to the people reporting on Chapter 12 the following tip: Chapter 12 readings include more separate items than has been the case in previous sessions, making it difficult to summarize them all adequately in the time allotted to reports. Don't feel obliged to say something about every item. Remember that every member of the group is expected to read Chapter 12's commentary and thus will get some sense of the readings. (Many are summarized at greater length in this chapter than in previous ones.) Read all the items in your set and report on whatever seems most important to you (but be prepared to answer questions from your group members about any item that you don't mention).

Session 14: Considering Strategies

Participants. All participants should read Chapter 12, "Considering Strategies."

Facilitators. Consult "How to Organize a Peace System Study Group," particularly the "Agendas" and "Exercises and Tools" subsections. Choose or invent an exercise for the group to do during the session. When preparing the agenda be sure to include time for five participants to divide up the reading assignments listed in Chapter 13; the readings are to be reported on in Session 15.

A process and planning note: At the end of Session 14, think ahead to the next one — the last scheduled meeting. Choose two or three persons who have a good sense of the group and can think about which (if any) of the options for possible future group activity outlined in Session 15 might be most suited to the group. Between this session and Session 15 any of you in the group who wish to can give those persons your suggestions for how best to use that session.

Session 15: Where Do We Go from Here?

Participants. All participants should read Chapter 13, "Where Do We Go from Here?"

Facilitators. Consult "How to Organize a Peace System Study Group," particularly the "Agendas" subsection which has a specific recommended agenda for this final session.

D: How to Do a
7-session Study Group

If you want to do a peace system study group but prefer one shorter than fifteen sessions, here's a design for one that only takes seven sessions. (Of course, you can custom design a study group of any length using this book as a resource, but that will be up to you.) The trick, of course, is doing fewer readings. To do the seven-session version, you will need only the asterisked items listed in "How to Order the Materials," and need only do the readings indicated below.

As you can see elsewhere in this book, at the beginning of each chapter is a list of readings grouped in reports (A, B, C, D, E). Roughly half of those have been selected and regrouped somewhat differently here. To minimize confusion, Roman numerals are used to designate sessions in this 7-session version. (The readings are in most cases still read in the same sequence. Except for the Scialabba article from Chapter 3 that is read in Session V here, and the part of Bello from Chapter 4 read in Session II here, the readings for each session listed below come from the chapters in this book that are being read for that session.)

The number of pages is given after each report. The reports are sometimes longer than those in the 15-session version. If you think you might have trouble doing the reading for a given report, say so when you're taking on the assignment, and you and the group can decide together what to do. Remember that it's your study group. Your responsibility is not to what's written in this book but to yourself and the other participants. Keep in mind that more pages are not necessarily harder to report on than fewer; our experience has been that 80 pages from one coherent reading can be easier to report on well than 40 pages from three quite different items. The readings have (with several unavoidable exceptions) been grouped to help give reports a unity of theme.

For recommended agendas, see "Agendas" subsection in "How to Organize a Peace System Study Group."

Session I: Getting Started; Questions about Peace

Everyone read the beginning parts of this book, from "How to Use This Book" through "The Peace System Approach to Eliminating War" and "How the Peace Movement Shaped the Present Debate" (the introduction to Part One); and read "How to Organize a Peace System Study Group" and "Principles for Democratic Social Change Study Groups." (This and the reading to be done by everyone in Session V are the two largest amounts of reading from *Building a Peace System* that you'll have to do for any session.)

Session II: Star Wars; Arms Control; Redefining the Issues

Everyone read Chapters 1 through 3. The facilitators for this session (and, in turn, each successive facilitator) should also read the reprint from *Organizing Macro-Analysis Seminars* mentioned in "How to Organize a Peace System Study Group."

A. Patricia Mische, pp. v-viii, 1-53, and "Why Arms Control is Needed," "Compliance: Won't the Russians Cheat?" and "Doing It Better: Planning for Success," pp. 58-81, in *Star Wars and the State of Our Souls: Deciding the Future of Planet Earth* (1985). Total = 80 pp.

B. Richard Smoke, "What is Peace?" "Nine Paths to Peace," "Traditional Paths to Coping with Conflict," and "Traditional Paths to Preventing Conflict," pp. 1-30 in *Paths to Peace: Exploring the Feasibility of Sustainable Peace* (1987);
Daniel Yankelovich & John Doble, "The Public Mood: Nuclear Weapons and the USSR," from *Foreign Affairs* (Fall 1984; 15 pp.);
"An Interview with Michael Howard: Peace Movements and the Meaning of Peace," from *Peace and Security* (1987; 2 pp.).
Total = 45 pp.

C. George Rathjens and Jack Ruina, "The Real Issue in the Geneva Talks"; George Rathjens, "Reducing the Risk of Nuclear War: SDI and Alternatives";
Kirkpatrick Sale, "August is the Sanest Month"; Mark Sommer, "The Real Enemy is War Itself"; W. H. Ferry, "The Choice: Nonviolence";
Dietrich Fischer, "An Active Peace Policy"; all from *The ExPro Papers #1, Steps toward a Peaceful World* (1986; 24 pp.; it is suggested these be read in this order, not their order in the booklet.);
George Rathjens, "First Thoughts on Problems Facing ExPro," *The ExPro Papers* #5 (1986; 23 pp.);
William A. Schwartz and Charles Derber, "Arms Control: Misplaced Focus," from *Bulletin of the Atomic Scientists* (March 1986; 6 pp.).
Total = 45 pp.

D. Kirkpatrick Sale, "Centrifugal Force: Making the World Safe from Mass Society," *The ExPro Papers* #2 (1986; 10 pp.);
Hal Harvey, "The Best Defense is Dealing With the Roots of Conflict," *New Options* newsletter (April 30, 1987; 2 pp.);
Gernot Kohler, "Global Apartheid," *World Order Models Project Working Paper* #7 (1978; 13 pp.);
Ethel Jensen, "How Feminists View Peace and Conflict," from "Feminism and Peace" (1982), pp. 11-19;

Gerald Mische, "A Tale of Two Tables: The Link Between Economic and Military Security" from *Breakthrough* (1985; 5 pp.).
Total = 39 pp.

E. Walden Bello, "Religion and the Vision of Peace" and "Envisioning Peace in Three Intellectual-Ethical Traditions," pp. v-vi, 1-62 in *Visions of a Warless World* (1986). Total = 59 pp.

Session III: Envisioning Peace; World Governance

Everyone read "Why and How to Think About the Future" (the introduction to Part II), Chapters 4 and 5, and "How to Do an 'Imaging a World without War' Workshop."

A. Kermit Johnson, "What is Peace? Judeo-Christian Insights," *The ExPro Papers* #4 (1987; 9 pp.);
Elise Boulding, "Image Before Action," from *Peace and Freedom* (June 1987) (1 p.);
Elise Boulding, "The Social Imagination and the Crisis of Human Futures: A North American Perspective," from *Forum for Correspondence and Contact*, 13:2 (February 1983), pp. 43-44, 49-56 (small print, equivalent to approx. 18 pp.);
Michael Marien, "Sixty Paths to U.S. and Global Security" from *Future Survey Annual 1984* (2 pp.).
Total = 29 pp.

B. Kenneth Boulding, "Research for Peace" (1978), pp. 158-169 in Stephenson, ed., *Alternative Methods for International Security* (1982);
Carolyn Stephenson, "A Research Agenda on the Conditions of Peace," *The ExPro Papers* #7 (1987; 22 pp.);
Patricia Mische, "Re-Visioning National Security: Toward a Viable World Security System" (1981), pp. 71-84 in Stephenson, *Alternative Methods for International Security*.
Total = 48 pp.

C. Dietrich Fischer, "Introduction," pp. 1-10 in *Preventing War in the Nuclear Age* (1984);
Kenneth Boulding, "Foreword,"; and
Mark Sommer, "Alternative Futurism: Toward More Practical Utopias," "Alternative Security," "World Order," "Peace Research," "Negotiation," and "Game Theory," pp. iii-vi, x-xiii, 111-135, 27-47, 87-95, 101-109 in *Beyond the Bomb* (1986);
Richard Smoke, "The Path of Alternative Conflict Resolution," pp. 55-62 in *Paths to Peace* (1987).
Total = 74 pp.

D. Benjamin Ferencz with Ken Keyes, Jr., *PlanetHood* (1988), pp. 25-110. Total = 77 [small] pp.

E. Ronald J. Glossop, "Institutional Aspects of the Contemporary Situation" and "Legal Aspects of the Contemporary Situation," pp. 178-203, 204-216 from *Confronting War* (1987; 39 pp.); Richard Falk, *Future Worlds* (1976), pp. 3-60 (58 pp., including twelve diagrams). Total = 97 [mostly small] pp.

Session IV: Alternative Security; Economics; Religion, Culture & Psychology

Everyone read Chapters 6 through 8.

A. Dietrich Fischer, "The Dual Meaning of 'Strength,'" "Defensive vs. Offensive Arms," "Does Balance of Power Promote Security?" "Transarmament Before Disarmament," "Nonmilitary Defense," "Entangling Alliances," "General Defense," and "Conflict Resolution," pp. 29-53, 61-62, 102-141, 154-163, 171-186 in *Preventing War in the Nuclear Age* (1984). Total = 90 pp.

B. Audio cassette: "A Modern Alternative to War" (Common Ground interview with Gene Sharp, June 1983; 29 minutes);
Gene Sharp, "National Security Through Civilian-Based Defense," "Ten Points about Civilian-Based Defense," "Questions about the Applicability of CBD," "Steps in Consideration of CBD," and "Key Definitions," in *National Security Through Civilian-Based Defense* (1985), pp. 9-10, 13-52;
Theodore B. Taylor, review of Sharp, *Making Europe Unconquerable: The Potential of Civilian-based Deterrence and Defense* (1985, 1986), from *Bulletin of the Atomic Scientists* (January-February 1987; 1 p.);
Gene Sharp, postscripts to "Gandhi's Defense Policy" and "Gandhi as a National Defense Strategist" from *Gandhi as a Political Strategist* (1979), pp. 161-164, 191-195. Total = 50 pp.

C. Mark Sommer, "Alternative Defense" and "Nonviolence," pp. 3-25, 67-85 in *Beyond the Bomb* (1985; 40 pp.);
Richard Smoke, "Alternative Paths to Coping with Conflict" (alternative defense, civilian-based defense), pp. 39-54 in *Paths to Peace* (1987);
Liane Norman, "Defending America Without War: A Guide for Thought and Discussion" (1987), 4 pp.;
Robert Irwin, "Coercion, Force, and Nonviolent Sanctions: Their Place in a Peace System" *The ExPro Papers* #3 (1986; 17 pp.). Total = 76 pp.

D. Robert Gilman, "Mondragon: The Remarkable Achievement," from *In Context* (Spring 1983; 3 pp.);

Guy Gran, "Mondragon," from *Learning from Development Success* (1983; 3 pp.);
Women's International League for Peace and Freedom, *The Women's Budget* (2nd ed., 1987;
    40 pp.);
Elise Boulding, "Two Cultures of Religion as Obstacles to Peace," from *Zygon* (December 1986;
    17 pp.).
Total = 63 pp.

E.   Walden Bello, "Understanding War: The Psychological Perspective" and "Understanding War:
         The Feminist Perspective," pp. 63-71, 73-79 in *Visions of a Warless World* (1986);
     Robert R. Holt, "Converting the War System to a Peace System: Some Contributions from
         Psychology and Other Social Sciences" (1987; 63 double-spaced pages, = approx. 40 pp.);
     Paul Wachtel, "Economic Growth — or Human Growth?" and Herman Daly, "Economic
         Growth — or Moral Growth?" from *New Options* (November 30, 1987; 3 pp.).
     Total = 58 pp.

Session V: Changes and Change Efforts in Today's World

Everyone read "Prospects for Building a Peace System" (the introduction to Part III) and Chapters 9
through 11.

A.   Mark Sommer, "The Gorbachev Experiment," in *The ExPro Papers* #1 (1986; 3 pp.);
     Robert Irwin, "Redefining the 'National Interest'" (1982; 6 pp.); and "Changing U.S. Foreign and
         Defense Policy" (1982; 15 pp.);
     George Perkovitch, "New Soviet Thinking" from *Nuclear Times* (May/June 1987; 3 pp.);
     Joergen Dragsdahl, "Are the Soviets Really Serious?" from *Nuclear Times* (May/June 1988;
         3 pp.);
     Robert C. Tucker, "Keeping Peace Between the Superpowers: Toward a Cooperative Regime
         of War Prevention" (1985; 7 pp.);
     Dietrich Fischer, "Peace 2010" scenario, pp. 121-128 from Earl Foell and Richard Nenneman,
         eds., *How Peace Came to the World* (1986; 7 pp.).
     Total = 44 pp.

B.   A. W. Singham and Shirley Hune, "Introduction," "Principles of Non-alignment," "Structure and
         Organization," and "Non-alignment: Retrospects and Prospects Within a Global Context,"
         pp. 1-56 (especially 1-3, 13-35, 42-47) and 364-376 from *Non-alignment in an Age of Align-
         ments* (1986) (= 39-65 pp.);
     Walden Bello, "Third World Visions of a Warless World," pp. 81-93 in *Visions of a
         Warless World* (1986);
     Elise Boulding, "The Rise of INGOs: New Leadership for a Planet in Transition," from *Break-
         through* (Fall '87 / Spring '88), pp. 14-17.
     Total = 56 pp.

C. John W. Dower, "America's Japan: The End of Innocence," from *The Nation* (September 12, 1987; 3 pp.);

David Freedman, "Low-Intensity Warfare," *The Nonviolent Activist* (October-November 1988), pp. 11-13;

Noam Chomsky, "Is Peace at Hand?" from *Zeta Magazine* (January 1988), pp. 6-14;

Carole Collins, "Voices from Apartheid's Other War" (American Friends Service Committee, 1987; 14 pp.);

George Scialabba, "Watergate and Contragate: The Essential Continuity," from *The Activist Review* (1987; 2 pp.).

Total = 31 pp.

D. Joshua Cohen and Joel Rogers, *Rules of the Game: American Politics and the Central America Movement* (1986), pp. 1-43;

Rick Jahnkow, "Electoral Politics: Progress or Pitfall?" from *The Nonviolent Activist* (March 1987); 2 pp.;

Jobs with Peace Campaign, "A National Budget for Jobs with Peace" and "Jobs with Peace: A Healthy Economy in a Peaceful World" (1987; approx. 6 pp.);

Jeb Brugmann and Michael Shuman, "Thinking Globally, Acting Locally" in *Nuclear Times* (May-June 1987; 3 pp.);

"New Partnership Forged in Nevada Desert," *Bulletin of Municipal Foreign Policy*, II:1 (Winter 1987-88; 2 pp.).

Total = 56 pp.

E. Liane Norman, "The 'Politics of Love' in the Cause of Peace" from *The Center Magazine* (March/April 1984; 11 pp.);

"The Nonviolent Alternative: An Interview with Liane Norman" from *The Center Magazine* (January/February 1987; 6 pp.);

Paul Goodman, "A. J. Muste and People in Power" from *Liberation* (November 1967; 5 pp.);

Daniel Ellsberg, affidavit prepared for *U.S. v. David Biviano et al.* (October 11, 1986; 11 pp.);

John Swomley, "Stopping Nuclear War with Little Boats" from *The Christian Century* (September 24, 1986; 2 pp.).

Total = 35 pp.

Session VI: Considering Strategies

Everyone read the introduction to Chapter 12. You may want to add or substitute any recent publications that members of the group think represent developments in peace movement thinking and action that would be important to discuss.

A. Rob Leavitt, "Vision Quest," *Defense and Disarmament News* (August-September 1987; 1 p.);

Committee on Common Security, "Common Security and Our Common Future: A Call to Action" (1989; 3 pp.);

Michael Klare, "Road Map for the Peace Movement: Getting from Here to There," from *The Nation* (June 29, 1985; 4 pp.);

Mark Satin, "Visioning Our Way Out of Here," from *New Options* (November 30, 1987; 2 pp.);

Andrea Ayvazian and Michael Klare, "Decision Time for the American Peace Movement," from *Fellowship* (September 1986; 3 pp.);

Patricia Mische, "The Soul of the Universe," pp. 113-130 in *Star Wars and the State of Our Souls* (1985);

Michael Nagler, "Peace 2010" scenario, from Earl Foell and Richard Nenneman, eds., *How Peace Came to the World* (1986), pp. 151-159.

Total = 39 pp.

B. Walden Bello, "Toward a Warless World," pp. 107-115 in *Visions of a Warless World* (1986);

Richard Smoke (with Willis Harman), sections on "the delegitimation of war" and "changing atitudes," plus "Recapitulation," "Some Elements of an Image," "The Plausibility of Transformative Change," "The Shape of the Next Age," "Reassessing the Possibility of Peace," and "Conclusion," pp. 62-71, 78-80, 87-99 in *Paths to Peace* (1987);

Tom Greening, "Introduction" (1986; 2 pp.);

Michael Marien, "The Transformation as Sandbox Syndrome" (1983; 8 pp.);

Marilyn Ferguson, "Transformation as Rough Draft" (1983; 2 pp.); and

Michael Marien, "Further Thoughts on the Two Paths to Transformation: A Reply to Ferguson" (1983; 8 pp.); all from Tom Greening, ed., *Politics and Innocence: A Humanistic Debate* (1986), pp. 43-45, 52-59, 59-61, 61-69;

Mark Satin, "Harman: Best and Worst of the New Age" (review of Willis Harman, *Global Mind Change*), from *New Options* (December 28, 1987; 1 p.).

Total = 53 pp.

C. William H. Moyer, "The Movement Action Plan: A Strategic Framework Describing the Eight Stages of Successful Social Movements" (second ed., 1987; 16 tabloid-size pp.).

D. Robert Irwin, "Nonviolent Struggle and Democracy in American History," from *Freeze Focus* (September 1984; 2 pp.);

David Dellinger, "Introduction" to *Por Amor al Pueblo: Not Guilty! The Trial of the Winooski 44* (1986; 5 pp.);

National War Tax Resistance Coordinating Committee, brochures on war tax resistance;

Eileen Sauvageau, Karl Meyer, speeches; Nancy Brigham, interview by Lynne Weiss in *Life and Taxes* #3 (1988; 8 pp.);

World Federalist Association, "Will Uncle Sam Remain an International Outlaw?" (1987; brochure);

Robert Irwin, "Nonviolent Direct Law Enforcement" (1989; 11 pp.).
Total = 30 pp.

E. Randall Kehler, "Thoughts on War and Patriotism," in *The ExPro Papers* #1 (1986; 5 pp.);
Mark Sommer, "Ten Strategies in Search of a Movement," *ExPro Paper* #6 (1987; 15 pp.);
"Peace is Life Work of Scarsdale Man [W. H. Ferry]" (*New York Times*, February 1, 1987; 1 p.);
Petra Kelly, "New Forms of Power: The Green Feminist View," from *Breakthrough* (Summer 1986; 1 p.);
Thirty-five authors (Pat Farren, ed.), "Movement-Building: Challenge and Opportunity," *Peacework* special issue (1986; 24 pp.);
Elvia Alvarado, "Don't Be Afraid, Gringo," from *Don't Be Afraid, Gringo: A Honduran Woman Speaks from the Heart* (1987), excerpted from *Toward Freedom: Report on Non-alignment and the Developing Countries* (October 1987; 1 p.).
Total = 47 pp.

Session VII: Where Do We Go From Here?

Everyone read Chapter 13 and think about the meaning and implications of what has been learned during the study group. See recommended agenda in "How to Organize a Peace System Study Group."

A. (to be played during Session VII:) Audio cassette "The Freeze Revisited" (December 1986; interviews with Randall Forsberg and Randy Kehler; 29 minutes);

B. Brian Martin et al., "The Individual," pp. 98-111 from *Uprooting War* (1984; 14 pp.);

C. Sarah Conn et al., *Keeping Us Going: A Manual on Support Groups for Social Change Activists* (1986; 26 pp.);

D. Elise Boulding, "Epilogue," pp. 160-164 from *Building a Global Civic Culture* (1988; 5 pp.).

E: How to Base a
College Course on This Book

This book outlines a 15-session course of study, 12 sessions of which include (very roughly) about 250 pages each of readings from articles and books, to which should be added the reading of this book itself. The simplest way (though not necessarily the best) to adapt this package to teaching a college course would be to subtract (or add) some sessions to fit the length of your semester, and drop some books and articles to reduce the cost of materials and the amount of reading you require of your students (if 250 pages seems excessive).

You will know best how to use this book in your situation. Here, nevertheless, are some ideas to consider about using it in a college setting. We're writing as if you're a teacher; however, if you're a student, be aware that you could take the initiative to persuade a faculty member to offer a course based on this book, or if that proves impractical, you could arrange an independent study group. During the past two decades many colleges and universities — such places as Stanford, Colgate, the University of Michigan, and Wesleyan — have conducted courses using this participatory format, so it's quite possible.

Here are the options we suggest:

1) You can limit the class size to a dozen students, obtaining the needed materials in advance and conducting the course using the participatory processes of this book, deviating from the plan of readings only if necessary to match the number of sessions to the length of the semester. You could use the 7-session model and add other readings, or use the 15-session model and drop some sessions.

1A) A variation on 1) is to have several groups meet (each with its own set of materials), making the course available to larger numbers of students.

2) You can use this book as a supplementary textbook in an already established course to provide an overview of a range of issues and readings, some of which you will also assign. You might, for example, develop a course in which each student buys and reads *Building a Peace System* and also *Preventing War in the Nuclear Age, Beyond the Bomb, National Security Through Civilian-based Defense, Design for a Better World,* and *Building a Global Civic Culture,* along with other books not included herein.

This plan has the disadvantage that students do not encounter as wide a range of subject matter, but the advantage that they can read books in their entirety, including ones like Hanna Newcombe's *Design for a Better World,* whose cumulative nature made its later parts less suitable to being divided into multiple reports, and ones like Elise Boulding's *Building a Global Civic Culture,* reluctantly omitted on grounds of expense, but not unreasonable to ask a student to buy (and maybe in paperback by the time you are teaching). You may wish to substitute some of the recent books cited in the annotated bibliography for those prescribed for purchase in this volume.

3) You can use this book as a source of ideas and readings for designing a new course, selecting some of its recommended readings to assign.

If you choose 1) or 2), you will probably want each member of the class to buy a copy of *Building a Peace System.* It provides: a) an overview of the peace system approach; b) introductions and critical commentary on a large number of readings; c) a wealth of references to additional literature and information sources; and d) an annotated bibliography. Each of these should be useful in a wide variety of kinds of courses.

The readings reprinted by ExPro can be purchased and responsibility for reading them divided among students, or you may seek permission to reproduce copies for each student. If you wish to do the latter, be sure to request the appropriate permissions from the original sources indicated on the single copies ExPro supplies.

The format of a democratic social change study group is an interesting change from typical college classes. Modifying the teacher-student dichotomy may be accomplished through conscientious use of the suggested format, but the notion of combining learning with an action orientation can also pose a challenge in a college setting. Students often have a problem thinking in terms of action because of their relatively short-term commitment to the class and often, also, to the community in which they are living. Given the urgency of humankind's situation, however, it is a challenge worth tackling.

Many classes using this democratic format have been initiated by students through provisions their schools have made for "experimental" courses. Such courses can sometimes be "institutionalized" to continue year after year as student-designed courses under the oversight of an ongoing student committee.* (This has been done for years with a "Nonviolence and Social Change" course at Williams College.) Other courses have been done with the professor as convenor and with required papers. When study groups are done for credit, some participants have found that the grading process, in which a teacher evaluates a student, conflicts with the democratic process in which all participants act as equals. A non-graded or pass/fail system might be preferable, but if grades are required, a substantial element of self-evaluation can be useful to include.

In some schools participants have used the participatory format while incorporating new readings. Others have taken the readings and incorporated them into the normal classroom situation. Some groups have included sessions in which they explore how the participants' differing class and social backgrounds affect the way they think about the issues studied, thus clarifying the nature of

---

* For help setting up student-run courses, see Center for Common Security in "Some Peace Organizations" (later in this book).

differences of opinion that emerge. Other groups include a combination of professors, students, and townspeople, providing a broader range of perspectives.

On some campuses the legitimacy of a course dealing with peace may be challenged as "too political" or "biased." Advocates of such a course should respectfully point out that judgments about what ideas and viewpoints merit attention are implicit in every course on campus. Courses that include only familiar ideas supporting the status quo are just as "political" as a course exploring ideas that challenge it — they are just not as obviously so.

In that respect, unconventional courses may better serve the cause of education. As John Stuart Mill argued, viewpoints contrary to prevailing thought can, even if wholly mistaken, make a valuable contribution to clarifying the rationales for generally accepted ideas (in this case, ideas of the virtues of nuclear deterrence and arms control or the permanent necessity of war preparations). And if the new views are not wholly mistaken, they contribute even more.

Colleges interested in intellectual vigor may find it worthwhile to respond to the call of President Jean Mayer of Tufts University and other distinguished educators (the 1988 "Talloires Declaration") for greater attention to peace within institutions of higher learning.

Making peace the focal point of a course is likely to help remedy a neglect often present in college courses in history, political science, law, international relations, and diplomacy. But proponents of peace studies should be aware that teachers of courses in these fields may also welcome inclusion of scholarly explorations of peace into their courses. Share this book with them, and be alert to new opportunities for collaboration.

F: How to Order the Materials

We have eased the task of obtaining the books, cassettes, and reprints needed to conduct the study group in several ways. ExPro has reprinted a large number of items that otherwise would have been difficult or impossible to obtain. We have arranged for the bookstore Food for Thought to supply by mail all the books needed in one promptly available package so you need not deal with many publishers and be delayed while waiting for all of them to respond. ExPro has also ordered booklets, magazines, cassettes, etc. from more than a dozen sources to save you writing to each one separately. But you should still allow yourself ample time — several weeks, to be on the safe side — to order materials and receive them by the time your study group is to start.

Paying for the study group. Although the cost per person of doing either the 7-session or 15-session version of the study group is quite low compared, say, to taking a university course, the total outlay of money must be made all at once a few weeks in advance in order to have all the materials available by the first meeting. That cost may be more than an individual study group convenor can afford to advance on behalf of the group for those weeks. Sometimes a sponsoring group will pay this cost, or the group may be able to rent or obtain free a set of materials that has been used by another group; if not, the initial cost can be made manageable if several persons who plan to be in the group put up the money in advance. Later, by the first or second meeting of the group, payments by the other study group members can reimburse them, equalizing the cost for everyone. (Some groups may also choose to subsidize some members' costs to enable persons with less money to participate in the study group.)

Asterisks and numbers. If you are doing the 7-session rather than the 15-session version of the study group, you only need the items listed below with asterisks (*) by their names; adjust your payments accordingly. Numbers to the left of the items indicate which chapters of this book they are discussed in. When the materials arrive, sort them according to the first session each is used in.

How to Order the Books

The titles listed below are all supplied by Food for Thought Books, 67 N. Pleasant St., Amherst, MA 01002; (413) 253-5432. Orders must be prepaid by check, and are shipped within one week of receipt via UPS. (Give a street address; UPS cannot deliver to a post office box.)

Since prices are subject to change, don't be surprised if an invoice for a few additional dollars accompanies the package of books. (If so, please pay it promptly.) If you want to confirm the amount in advance, write or phone the bookstore. (If phoning, explain "I have a question about the books for the ExPro study groups.")

If members of your group already own some of the books, you may wish to photocopy the list that follows, cross out the titles you don't need, and subtract their prices from the check you send. Keep in mind, though, that your group may wish to sell or rent the set to another group when you are finished with it, in which case it would be better to have a complete set.

Building a Peace System

Discussed in Chapter	Books to be ordered from Food for Thought	Cost
11	Michael Albert & Dave Dellinger, *Beyond Survival*	8.00
2	Graham Allison et al., *Hawks Doves & Owls*	6.95
* 4, 8, 10, 12	Walden Bello, *Visions of a Warless World*	5.00
1, 2, 9, 10, 12	Don Carlson/Craig Comstock, *Securing Our Planet*	11.95
1, 2, 9	Albert Carnesale et al., *Living with Nuclear Weapons*	(see note below)
3, 9	Noam Chomsky, *Turning the Tide*	10.00
* 11	Joshua Cohen & Joel Rogers, *Rules of the Game*	4.75
* 5	Benjamin Ferencz, *PlanetHood*	2.50
* 4, 5, 6, 7	Dietrich Fischer, *Preventing War in the Nuclear Age*	12.50
3	Joseph Gerson, *The Deadly Connection*	10.95
3, 6	George Lakey, *Powerful Peacemaking*	9.95
* 1, 2, 12	Patricia Mische, *Star Wars and the State of Our Souls*	4.95
4, 5	Hanna Newcombe, *Design for a Better World*	17.50
* 1, 2, 4, 5, 6, 7, 8, 12	Richard Smoke, *Paths to Peace*	11.95
* 6	Gene Sharp, *National Security through Civilian-based Defense*	4.95
* 4, 5, 6, 8, 9	Mark Sommer, *Beyond the Bomb*	7.95
* 4, 5	Carolyn Stephenson, *Alternative Methods for International Security*	11.00
	handling and shipping	4.00
	BOOKS for 7-session study group	$69.55
	BOOKS for 15-session study group	$144.85

Make your check payable to Food for Thought Books and send it to 67 N. Pleasant St., Amherst, MA 01002. If you do not receive the books within two weeks, phone Food for Thought at (413) 253-5432.

Note: The $4.50 Bantam edition of the Harvard Nuclear Study Group's *Living with Nuclear Weapons* has gone out of print. Rather than spend $15.00 to buy the Harvard University Press edition, it is suggested you borrow this book from a library.

How to Order the Other Materials

Obtain these directly from ExPro, 1601 Connecticut Ave., NW, 5th floor, Washington, DC 20009; 202-232-5477.

1. **Building a Peace System.** Every member of the group should have a copy of this book. Single copies are $14.95. If you find the ideas in this book worth spreading around, we encourage you to order additional copies and sell them at conferences, rallies, workshops, and meetings (or, if your group has a newsletter or does mailings, by mail). The discounts offered enable your group to raise funds by doing this. All price and discount information is subject to change. Bookstores, please inquire as to terms.

1-9 copies	retail	$14.95 each
10-29 copies	20% discount	$11.95 each
30 or more copies	40% discount	$8.97 each

2. **ExPro Papers**. #1 costs $2.50; others are $1.50 each.

* 1, 2, 9, 12   The ExPro Papers #1: Steps toward a Peaceful World
* 3   ExPro Paper #2 Kirkpatrick Sale, Centrifugal Force
* 6   ExPro Paper #3 Robert Irwin, Coercion, Force and Nonviolent Sanctions
* 4   ExPro Paper #4 Kermit Johnson, What is Peace? Judeo-Christian Insights
* 2   ExPro Paper #5 George Rathjens, First Thoughts on Problems Facing ExPro
* 12   ExPro Paper #6 Mark Sommer, Ten Strategies in Search of a Movement
* 4   ExPro Paper #7 Carolyn Stephenson, A Research Agenda . . .
   9   ExPro Paper #8 Robert Johansen, Toward National Security Without Nuclear Deterrence

Subtotal for 7-session group: 11.50

Subtotal for 15-session group: 13.00

3. Other ExPro items:

* all	*Organizing Macro-Analysis Seminars* reprint	1.35
1	Gray & Payne, Victory is Possible	.35
* 1	Interview with Michael Howard, Peace and Security	.10
2	Alperovitz, Naked NATO: America's Europe Problem	.15
* 2	Yankelovich & Doble, The Public Mood	.70
* 2	Schwartz & Derber, Arms Control: Misplaced Focus	.30
2	Johansen, The Future of Arms Control	3.00
* 3	Harvey, The Best Defense is Dealing with the Roots...	.10
* 3	Kohler, Global Apartheid	2.00
* 3, 8	Jensen, Feminism and Peace	1.50
* 3	Scialabba, Watergate and Contragate	.10
* 3	G. Mische, A Tale of Two Tables ...	.25
3	Deudney, Whole Earth Security	2.00
* 4	E. Boulding, Image Before Action	.05
* 4	E. Boulding, The Social Imagination and the Crisis...	.70
* 4	Marien, Sixty Paths to U.S. and Global Security	.10
5	Reves, Why Waste Time Discussing Disarmament?	.20
5	World Fed. Assn., We the People; Getting from Here to There	.25
* 5	Glossop, Institutional Aspects ...; Legal Aspects ...	2.25
5	Johansen and Mendlovitz, The Role of Enforcement ...	.80
5	Satin, Reforming the U.N.	.15
* 5	Richard Falk, Future Worlds	3.00
* 6	Sharp, A Modern Alternative to War — cassette	4.00
* 6	Taylor, review of Sharp, *Making Europe Unconquerable*	.10
* 6	Liane Norman, Defending America Without War	.50
6	Irwin, Civilian-Based Defense	.55
* 6	Sharp, postscripts to chapters 8 & 9 in *Gandhi as a Political Strategist*	.50
6	B. Martin, Social Defence: Grassroots or Elite	.50
6	H. Newcombe, Collective Security, Common Security...	.60
7	Carothers, Small Wonders	.40
7	Rocky Mountain Institute, America's Stake in Soviet...	.20

7	Universal Declaration of Human Rights	free
7	UN Environment Program, World Charter for Nature	free
7	Alperovitz & Faux, excerpts from *Rebuilding America*	1.75
7	Gran, excerpts from *Development by People*	1.30
* 7	Gilman, Mondragon: The Remarkable Achievement	.15
* 7	Gran, Mondragon, *Learning from Development Success*	.25
7	Brecher & Costello, Labor Internationalism	.45
7	Leghorn, Economic Roots of the Violent Male Culture	.30
* 7	WILPF, *The Women's Budget*	2.50
7	E. Boulding, Learning to Learn: North Responds ...	.70
7	Makhijani & Browne, Restructuring the International Monetary System	3.00
8	Kull, Nuclear Nonsense	.60
8	Richards, Moving Heaven and Earth Together	.30
* 8	E. Boulding, Two Cultures of Religion as Obstacles	.90
8	Cohn, Slick'ems, Glick'ems, Christmas Trees, and ...	.40
8	P. Mische, Women/World Order; Women/Power	2.00
* 8	Holt, Converting the War System to a Peace System	3.55
* 8	Wachtel, Daly, Economic Growth Is Not the Answer	.15
8	E. Boulding, Learning Peace	.50
8	Etheredge, excerpts from *Can Governments Learn?*	1.45
9	Gorbachev, 12/88 United Nations speech	1.20
* 9	Irwin, Redefining the National Interest	.35
* 9	Irwin, Changing U.S. Foreign and Defense Policy	.45
9	Tucker, Where is the Soviet Union Headed?	2.00
9	Johansen, The Reagan Administration and the U.N.	3.00
* 9	*Nuclear Times* May-June 1987	3.00
* 9	Perkovitch, in *Nuclear Times* May-June 1987	
* 9	Dragsdahl, Are the Soviets Really Serious?	.15
* 9	Tucker, Keeping Peace Between the Superpowers	.40
* 9	Fischer, Peace 2010 scenario	.40
9	Klare, Policing 3rd World: Blueprint for Intervention	.20
* 10	Singham & Hune, excerpts from *Non-alignment in an Age of Alignments*	2.05
10	Parliamentarians Global Action; Ending the Deadlock	.30

* 10	E. Boulding, The Rise of INGOs: New Leadership ...	.25
10	Zarsky et al., in *Nuclear Times* May-June 1987	
10	Carothers, Loose Cannons: The Nuclear Navies and ...	.30
10	Bennett, excerpt from *The New Abolitionists*	.50
* 10	Dower, America's Japan: The End of Innocence	.20
10	van Wolferen, The Japan Problem	.80
10	Thompson, Beyond INF: The Peace Movement's Next Task	.15
10	Kaldor & Falk, excerpt from *Dealignment: A New Foreign Policy Perspective*	.75
10	Miles, The Real War	2.20
* 10	Freedman, Low-Intensity Warfare	.15
* 10	Chomsky, Is Peace at Hand?	.60
* 10	Collins, Voices from Apartheid's Other War	3.00
* 11	Jahnkow, Electoral Politics: Progress or Pitfall?	.10
* 11	A National Budget for Jobs With Peace	1.00
* 11	Jobs With Peace: Healthy Economy in Peaceful World	1.00
11	Dellums, Dellums Defense Alternative	.30
11	Deudney, Forging Missiles into Spaceships	3.00
11	Deudney, Darnovsky exchange	.20
* 11	Brugmann, in *Nuclear Times* May-June 1987	
* 11	New Partnership Forged in Nevada Desert	.10
11	A. & H. Newcombe, Mundialization ...	1.00
11	*The New Abolitionist*, boycott info	3.00
* 11	Norman, The Politics of Love in the Cause of Peace	.55
* 11	Norman, The Nonviolent Alternative: An Interview ...	.30
* 11	Goodman, A. J. Muste and People in Power	.30
* 11	Ellsberg, affidavit prepared for U.S. v. D. Biviano	.55
* 11	Swomley, Stopping Nuclear War with Little Boats	.10
12	Sommer, Constructing Peace as a Whole System	.40
12	Falk, Kim, Mendlovitz, from *Toward a Just World Order*	.70
* 12	Leavitt, Vision Quest	.05
12	*Nuclear Times* November-December 1987	3.00
12	Birchard & Leavitt, in *Nuclear Times* Nov.-Dec. 1987	
12	Auster, in *Nuclear Times* Nov.-Dec. 1987	

* 12	Committee on Common Security, "Common Security"	.15
* 12	Klare, Road Map for the Peace Movement	.20
* 12	Satin, Visioning Our Way Out of Here	.10
* 12	Ayvazian & Klare, Decision Time for American Peace Movement	.15
* 12	Nagler, Peace 2010 scenario	.30
* 12	Marien, Ferguson, Sandbox / Transformation	.70
* 12	Satin, Harman: Best and Worst of the New Age	.05
* 12	Moyer, The Movement Action Plan	1.00
* 12	Irwin, Nonviolent Struggle & Democracy	.10
* 12	Dellinger, introduction to *Por Amor al Pueblo*	.35
* 12	Nat'l. War Tax Resistance Coord. Comm. brochures	2.00
* 12	Eileen Sauvageau & Karl Meyer, speeches	.35
* 12	Weiss, interview with Brigham, *Life and Taxes #3*	.40
* 12	"Will Uncle Sam Remain an International Outlaw?"	.25
* 12	Irwin, Nonviolent Direct Law Enforcement	.95
* 12	Peace is Life Work of Scarsdale Man (Ferry)	.05
* 12	Kelly, New Forms of Power: Green Feminist View	.05
* 12	"Movement-Building" issue of *Peacework*	1.00
* 12	Alvarado, Don't Be Afraid, Gringo	.05
* 13	The Freeze Revisited (audio cassette)	4.00
* 13	Martin, The Individual	.45
* 13	Conn et al., *Keeping Us Going*	4.50
* 13	E. Boulding, Epilogue, *Building a Global Civic Culture*	.30

1. Cost for *Building a Peace System* $119.50
   (depends on group size; if ten copies:)

2. Subtotal for ExPro Papers   7-session   11.50
                                 15-session   13.00

3. Subtotal for other ExPro items 7-session   57.60
                                    15-session 102.20

4. TOTAL amount to send to ExPro for materials for
        7-session version   69.10
        plus for 10 copies of *Building a Peace System*   119.50
        plus postage/handling   <u>3.00</u>
                       TOTAL   191.60

   TOTAL amount to send to ExPro for materials for
        15-session version   115.20
        plus for 10 copies of *Building a Peace System*   119.50
        plus postage/handling   <u>4.00</u>
                       TOTAL   238.70

5. TOTAL amount to send to Food for Thought Books
        7-session version   69.55
        15-session version   144.85

6. GRAND TOTAL for 7-session study group (with 10 participants) $261.15

   GRAND TOTAL for 15-session study group (with 10 participants) $383.55

G: How to Do an "Imaging a World Without War" Workshop

People experienced with these workshops, originated by Warren Ziegler and Elise Boulding, recommend that you take a day or a weekend to do them, and arrange for an experienced facilitator to conduct one for you. We encourage you to do this. Start on this as early as possible to increase the chances of getting a facilitator before the study group is over. To find out the name of the facilitator nearest you, contact:

Mary Link, Coordinator
World Without Weapons Project
4722 Baltimore Avenue
Philadelphia, PA 19143
(215) 724-1464

If your group finds itself unable to arrange for a facilitator to come, another potentially rewarding possibility is to try doing a workshop for yourselves. The 1988 fifth edition of Warren Ziegler's "mindbook" for *Envisioning a World Without Weapons* has been designed to come as close as possible to being a do-it-yourself tool. Ziegler writes that his book "is no substitute for skilled facilitators. . . . [But] those persons will not always be available . . . and the envisioning cannot wait."[1] Ziegler's book is available for $11.95 (which includes postage and handling) from

The Futures-Invention Associates
2260 Fairfax Street
Denver, Colorado 80207
(303) 399-1077

We strongly recommend that you get either a facilitator or Ziegler's "mindbook." But since neither resource can be included in this book, the following can serve to give the flavor of the imaging workshops, and could be used by your group in place of them if necessary. These instructions for a three-hour workshop are taken from a design used by Sarah Pirtle, here modified slightly.[2]

1. **Enter a world without war.** Pick a date, say thirty years from the day, and ask the group to imagine that we are not gathered to prevent or stop a war, but to celebrate the fact that there is no longer a danger of war. "Let that in. How does your body feel? Is your breathing different? Your shoulders less tense? What are your plans now for the coming year?" By these and other questions the group is guided to enter this imagined future.

2. **Write headlines in small groups.** Groups of six are provided with newsprint and markers. Closing our eyes we move deeper into the chosen year. (E.g., "Where are you standing? What do you hear, touch, smell? Who do you see around you and what are they doing? What are the forms of transportation? the international agreements? . . . .") It is important that we place ourselves inside this new time rather than viewing it from afar.[3] After this silent period, the groups open their eyes, select a scribe, and begin to share images. Then we choose a type of newspaper appropriate to the kinds of images that emerged and proceed to create headlines. In the process we are often

surprised by our own inventiveness; a positive future becomes more concrete and believable. When finished, each set of headlines is presented to the whole gathering.

3. **Fill in the intervening history.** Moving backwards from the chosen date toward the present, we reflect on what needs to have happened for these developments to occur. A scribe can jot these events on a time-line; the key thing is that we are looking from a warless future backwards, rather than from our usual vantage point on *this* side of our present obstacles. We then are invited to think of work that is being done right now that fits into this backwards history, and to share good news from the present.

4. **Reflecting on our resistance.** To live toward a positive future we need to acknowledge what holds us back from working to create it. The group can brainstorm the question, "What fears do we have about being successful in eliminating war?"

5. **Closing.** Before ending with some songs expressing hope and determination, we can share what we have lived by going through this process and offer new images that have emerged (e.g., one participant said she felt like an amphibian in the process of evolving).

After doing this workshop, you may find you wish to do others. There are several good sources of workshop leaders, workshop outlines, and exercises out of which you can construct workshops yourself.[4]

Notes

1. Ziegler, *Envisioning a World Without Weapons,* p. ii.
2. Sarah Pirtle is the author of the award-winning novel *An Outbreak of Peace* (New Society Publishers, 1987). Pirtle's workshop instructions were published in Joanna Macy, *Despair and Personal Power in the Nuclear Age* (New Society Publishers, 1983), pp. 141-142. Pirtle spoke of "a world without weapons." This has been changed to "a world without war." (Given the possibility of defensive weapons systems, we do not want to prejudge the issue of whether achieving a world without war requires eliminating all weapons as well.) We have also substituted references to "war" for "nuclear war."
3. The details of the instructions are indeed important. A lively and fascinating presentation of the significance of variations in how people represent phenomena internally can be found in Richard Bandler's *Using Your Brain — for a Change* (Real People Press, 1985), one of several books about the powerful (and controversial) theory and technique called Neuro-Linguistic Programming.
4. In addition to the World Without Weapons Project, see Macy's book (note 2 above), which contains sample agendas and 47 exercises. See also *Resource Manual for a Living Revolution* (details in notes to "How to Organize a Peace System Study Group"), which contains dozens of exercises and several workshop outlines. Warren Ziegler's Futures-Invention Associates sells a half dozen other "mindbooks" for "citizen-leaders," "community envisioning," and the like. "Uses of the Imagination," Chapter Six of Elise Boulding's *Building a Global Civic Culture* (Teachers College Press, 1988), pp. 95-117, contains several remarkable exercises.

H: Evaluating Your
Study Group Experience

What was good about your peace system study group? What was bad? What could have been improved? We at ExPro would be very grateful if you mailed us your group's evaluative comments from your last meeting. (If you wish, you could mail us the folded-up flip charts or someone's legible hand-written notes, rather than type up the comments.) Individuals' evaluations are also welcomed, both from individual study group participants and from student or unaffiliated readers. To encourage responses, we offer the questions below (you can photocopy this so you don't have to tear it out), but feel free to respond however you wish. (Including your name and address is optional.) We want to know what you think of this book so we can improve it.

Name_____ Date_____

Address_____

When did your study group begin and end?_____

How did you hear about *Building a Peace System* or ExPro?

What was good or bad about the format?

What was good or bad about the readings?

What was the best thing about the study group?

What was the worst thing?

If you could go back and change one thing about the experience, what would it be?

What's the piece of advice you'd most like to give ExPro concerning how to revise this book?

What's the piece of advice you'd most like to give ExPro concerning anything else?

How do you assess using audio cassettes? Did they mesh well with the readings? Did they disrupt the sessions you used them in? Did they seem more expensive than their value for the group? In a revised version of this book should (circle one)   more   fewer · about the same number   of audio cassettes be included? Would you advise using videotapes?

In a revised version of this book should there be (circle one)   more   fewer   about the same number   of readings?

Does anyone from your group plan to organize another peace system study group?

Is there a way you would like ExPro to support you in your peace work?

Is there a way you can support our (ExPro's) work?

Use the space below or additional pages to say more if you wish.

Information
Resources

A: Recommended Periodicals
B: Audio, Video, and Computer Sources of News
and Commentary
C: Annotated Bibliography
D: Some Peace Organizations

A: Recommended Periodicals

"A recent long visit to California and New England [from Switzerland] reconfirmed for me how narrow a window on the world is provided by U.S. media. Newspaper and television coverage is wretched. Americans are really miserably informed about what's going on in the world." (Michele Burdet, *Whole Earth Review* #60 [Fall 1988], p. 35.)

"The U.S. is the 'information society.' No people on earth are at the receiving end of so much information, so much news. There are stations that broadcast nothing but news (and ads) twenty-four hours a day. Yet from the point of view of many people elsewhere in the world, Americans seem stunningly uninformed and misinformed." (Jim Forest, *Fellowship* [July/August 1984], p. 15.)

That people in the U.S. are ill informed about the rest of the world is an increasingly common observation. Yet the statement seems puzzling. We have newspapers, radio, and television in abundance, and experts on every world region.

Further, we are often told, we and the world's other democracies are fortunate to have a free press, unlike many Communist and Third World countries with government-controlled media. A Soviet dissident like Andrei Sakharov, for example, could not, until very recently, be published in his homeland. Such dissidents' views were known at home only through circulation of laboriously retyped manuscripts (known as "samizdat," or self-publishing). In contrast, his views were widely known and respected abroad.

In the United States, anyone who has the money can publish a book or distribute a newsletter, and thousands of people do circulate unorthodox ideas. Yet the contrast between the U.S. and more restrictive societies may be less sharp than most people in this country believe. Jim Forest, a U.S. pacifist now living in the Netherlands, has reported that dissenting U.S. figures like Dan Berrigan and Helen Caldicott may be more familiar to Dutch television viewers than to viewers in the U.S.[1] Noam Chomsky — who has been described as "the United States' leading dissident" — has said, in a statement reminiscent of Sakharov's former plight, that "although I am often asked to comment on international affairs or social issues by press, radio, or television in Canada, Western Europe, Japan, Australia, that is very rare in the United States."[2]

Virtually any opinion can be expressed in the U.S. But the publications in which fundamental criticisms of U.S. foreign policy and war-making are expressed often have circulations of twenty, ten, or five thousand, or less. They are dwarfed by *Time, Newsweek, Readers' Digest*, and the major dailies, which can boast circulations from a hundred to many thousand times greater.

Conveying a message more complicated than can fit on a sign to the mass public reached by the major radio and television networks is scarcely possible for those with dissident views. Perhaps at most a few hundred thousand out of 250 million citizens encounter with any regularity unorthodox viewpoints about their country and its world role. This image, if accurate, begins to bear a disquieting resemblance to other countries where control of the media is concentrated. But is that a problem?

Building a Peace System

If NBC (owned by RCA, which is owned by General Electric) can be trusted to do as tough an investigative reporting job as an independent journalist on General Electric's lobbying for policies using the nuclear components it manufactures; if the corporations that publish *Time* and *Newsweek* can be trusted to give incisive coverage of the domestic and foreign activities of those corporations whose advertising pays for each issue and whose directors eat lunch with the magazines' editors and sit on the same corporate boards; if, in short, a small, powerful group of corporations can be expected to serve the interests of the U.S. public, then there is little to concern oneself about.

An examination of the coverage produced, however, shatters this complacent picture, as a long series of exposes and analyses have shown.[3] Consequently, as communications scholar Herbert Schiller has written, along with Third World debt, the arms race, and other crises, an additional problem deserves attention: our information system. "What we know about . . . other problems — how they are defined and situated in our minds — is dependent entirely on our information/ cultural system. If the apparatus that informs us is itself out of alignment, providing an inadequate picture of reality, we are in deep trouble."[4]

What can we do about it? Visits to Nicaragua, the Soviet Union, and other official "enemies" have been eye-opening for many citizens, and sister city relations, the new "alternative tourism,"[5] and other international exchanges also give direct access to knowledge of other countries. Nevertheless, people who want to understand the world in order to work for peace more effectively need regular sources of news, information, and interpretation to supplement or substitute for what the media corporations choose to provide. Below is a list of periodicals that can help meet this need. (See also this book's section on audio and video sources of information.)

The mass media tend to demoralize and demobilize people in ways that only become evident as one reduces their presence in one's life. Anyone who begins subscribing to periodicals that aim to confront humankind's problems honestly and find solutions, rather than distract or sell to the reader, is likely to find the world becoming a more interesting and hopeful place. Sure, humanity's problems are quite serious. But the challenge of working to solve them, in the company of thousands and millions of others, is rewarding in many ways. By changing what you read, watch, and listen to, you can replace generalized worry and gloom with understanding of specific problems, knowledge of what people are doing about them, and awareness of how you can help. Try the media recommended below instead of *Time*, *Newsweek*, and the daily paper for 6 months, and see how your spirits improve.

Where to begin? Here is an annotated list of periodicals grouped according to levels of how much you might want to read or can afford to subscribe to, and including two clusters of more specialized periodicals on peace and alternative security. Don't be paralyzed by the length of the list; just choose to subscribe to something new. Even if you only start one new subscription, you'll be taking an important step for yourself (as well as supporting a worthy periodical). Perhaps you'll want to sample a range of items before subscribing; if so, send an estimated payment for a single copy. Pat yourself on the back when you've taken the steps you've chosen.

LEVEL ONE: Pick out three or four, like *Nuclear Times* (bimonthly), *Peacework* (monthly), *Breakthrough* (quarterly), and *New Options* (11/year). Read them carefully; you'll find plenty of news and ideas to sustain you plus information on organizations, books, and actions to get involved with.

Nuclear Times. Six times per year. $21. 1601 Connecticut Ave., NW, Washington, DC 20009; 202-332-9222. Forty glossy pages per issue plus "Deadline," a regular 12-page insert from the Center for War, Peace, and the News Media. Along with a range of well written, photo-illustrated articles on activities and ideas relevant to peace activism, each issue includes a "Network" section with short items by half a dozen peace groups which get the space in return for sending *Nuclear Times* to their members. Probably the best source for continuing coverage of the U.S. peace movement.

Peacework: A New England Peace and Social Justice Newsletter. 11 issues per year. $8 (3rd class) or $12 (first class). AFSC, 2161 Massachusetts Ave., Cambridge, MA 02140. Each 16 distinctly unglossy pages of this influential publication of the New England Regional Office of the American Friends Service Committee are filled with reports of action, reflections on what ought to be done, insightful analytic essays, and listings of published resources — all of interest beyond New England. Committed to raising unfashionable issues, new or old, *Peacework* has been praised as conveying "the authentic voice of the peace movement."

Breakthrough. Quarterly (with occasional double or triple issues; most recent issue 96 pp.). $15. C/o GEA, Suite 456, 475 Riverside Drive, New York, NY 10115. Edited by Patricia Mische and Melissa Merkling, *Breakthrough* is published by Global Education Associates. With members in more than 60 countries, GEA is one of the few groups that does not shrink from taking on the whole range of issues involved in building a peace system; it is strong on ethics as well as analysis. Its insightful, informative, sometimes inspiring articles are important education and nourishment for people working for peace.

New Options newsletter. Eleven eight-page issues a year. $25 (less if you can't afford it). P.O. Box 19324, Washington, DC 20036. Writer/editor Mark Satin, author of *New Age Politics* (1979), is often tough on the left and the peace movement to the point of unfairness. Yet the diligence of his coverage of current books, conferences, innovative ideas, and social change efforts (giving relevant addresses) conveys a message of hope and caring; and few if any publications pack so much fascinating information into so brief and easily readable a format. Satin's frankly evaluative reporting also sparks a lively letters column. *New Options* is an important tool for people seeking to create a new politics leading to peace.

Building a Peace System

LEVEL TWO: Ready for more than three or four? Here are suggestions for possible choices in five categories. The categories express the premise that making peace requires knowing what's happening in the world and attending to economics, ecology, science, and culture as well as politics more narrowly conceived. After descriptions of these additional recommended publications, there follow two clusters on alternative security and peace, further titles listed alphabetically, and information on a guide to periodicals. All these should enable you to begin experimenting in whatever way promises to suit you best.

A. One U.S. journal for news and commentary (a weekly or monthly): *The Nation; In These Times; The Progressive; Zeta Magazine.*

B. *Building Economic Alternatives.* For $15, you can become a member of Co-op America and not only receive periodic catalog mailings about products (many suitable for gift-giving) produced by socially responsible businesses, but also this informative quarterly that explores practical ways to bring our economic behavior into harmony with our ethics.

C. To provide non-U.S. viewpoints, a journal edited abroad (the U.S. addresses given for several of these below are for U.S. subscribers' convenience) or emphasizing foreign news and views: *Toward Freedom; New Internationalist; World Press Review; South; Third World Quarterly; IFDA Dossier; Third World Week* (listed in order of increasing cost).

D. *Greenpeace Magazine.* As with *Building Economic Alternatives,* your money ($20) supports an organization working to solve the problems covered as well as bringing you news. *Greenpeace Magazine* reports on ecological problems worldwide and on Greenpeace's efforts, from postcard campaigns to nonviolent direct action, to solve them; it is incisive, fast-paced, action-oriented (with color photos), and energizing.

E. A magazine that explores unorthodox ideas in a range of fields. (Many aspects of science and culture are relevant to building a peace system.) In addition to *New Options,* recommended above, three excellent ones are *Future Survey, Whole Earth Review,* and *Utne Reader.*

Here's how-to-get-it information on the magazines mentioned, listed alphabetically:

Building Economic Alternatives. Quarterly. $15. 28-40 pp. Co-op America, 2100 M St., NW, Suite 310, Washington, DC 20063. Described above.

Future Survey. Monthly plus *Annual* volume. $59.00. World Future Society, 4916 St. Elmo Ave., Bethesda, MD 20814. Edited by Michael Marien, this "monthly abstract of books, articles, and reports concerning forecasts, trends, and ideas about the future" has remarkable breadth — it has been called "the only generalist scanning service anywhere." Each 16-page issue summarizes 50-plus items from both mainstream and radical perspectives and highlights those deemed most important. Every large library should be urged to subscribe to this extraordinary resource. (See also the description of *Future Survey Annual* in this book's annotated bibliography.) A descriptive brochure and sample issue are free on request.

Greenpeace Magazine. 6 issues/year. $20. 1436 U Street, NW, Washington, DC 20009. Described above.

IFDA Dossier. 6 issues/year. $32. International Foundation for Development Alternatives, 4 place du Marche, 1260 Nyon, Switzerland. Highly recommended by Elise Boulding as "an important source of information about the South for Northerners."

In These Times. Weekly (41 issues/year). $34.95. 1300 W. Belmont, Chicago, IL 60657. A source of fine reporting and interpretation of what's happening both at home and abroad.

The Nation. Weekly (47 issues/year). $36. Box 1953, Marion, OH 43305. A leading journal of left and liberal opinion, its articles, columns, book reviews, and editorials often display style and wit. "On Project Censored's most recent list of the '10 most under-reported stories of the year,' chosen from all the news sources in the country, 5 of the stories — half the list — were from *The Nation*" (promotional letter, 11/88). Can be sampled in many public libraries.

New Internationalist. Monthly. $25.00. P.O. Box 1143, Lewiston, NY 14092. Well-known in Britain, Canada, and Australia and with a growing U.S. circulation, this colorfully designed and incisively written magazine focuses on world poverty and the relations between rich and poor.

The Progressive. Monthly. $27.50. P.O. Box 54615, Boulder, CO 80321-4615. A consistent source of solid articles, news shorts, columns, editorials, and book reviews. Stories from *The Progressive* have appeared each year on Project Censored's list of the "best censored" stories.

South: Business/Technology/Politics/Leisure. Monthly. $29.00. New Zealand House (13th floor), 80 Haymarket, London SW1Y 4TS, England. A thick (ca 128 pp.) business-oriented publication edited by persons of Third World background, offering a non-U.S. perspective on issues (and different corporate ads).

Third World Quarterly. Quarterly. $30. New Zealand House (13th floor), 80 Haymarket, London SW1Y 4TS, England. "Thorough coverage of fundamental issues concerning the Asia/Pacific region, Latin America and the Caribbean, Africa and the Middle East. Each issue devotes an entire section to literature and includes comprehensive book reviews." Free sample copy on request.

Third World Week. Weekly. $49.50/year. 4 West Wheelock St., Hanover, NH 03755. In the words of *Whole Earth Review #59*: " *Third World Week* has a two-part function: diffusion of grass-roots reporting from seldom-represented parts of the planet and an active sponsorship and training of local newspeople to perpetuate same." It's published by the South-North News Service, "a tax-exempt educational institution, dedicated to seeking out third-world writers with the potential of writing about their countries' events, issues and values for readers outside their societies" (SNNS subscription solicitation, 8/88). $34 of the $49.50 annual fee helps support the training program. Each 6-page issue of *Third World Week* supplies five articles (simultaneously marketed to 30 newspapers worldwide) plus a third-world children's tale. Free sample copy available.

Toward Freedom. 6 issues/year. $10. 64 North Street, Burlington, VT 05401. Ca 12 pages per issue reporting on "non-alignment and the developing countries."

Utne Reader. 6 issues/year. $24. Box 1974, Marion, OH 43305. Subtitled "The best of the alternative press," each issue of *Utne Reader* presents 100-plus pages of reprints (often grouped thematically), original articles, book notes, and news items culled from a myriad of other publications.

Whole Earth Review: Access to Tools and Ideas. Quarterly. $20. 27 Gate Five Road, Sausalito, CA 94965. An unpredictable, consistently stimulating journal founded by Stewart Brand, originator of the famous *Whole Earth Catalogs* (of which the latest, *The Essential Whole Earth Catalog* — 1986, 416 pp., $15 — also merits recommendation). *WER* may offer more directly usable information than any other periodical on this list; it's certainly among the most likely to provide something surprising and interesting on any conceivable subject.

World Press Review. Monthly. In U.S., $24.95/year; in Canada, $28.95. 230 Park Avenue, New York, NY 10169. Published by the Iowa-based Stanley Foundation, *WPR* "features excerpts from the press outside the United States and interviews with prominent international specialists on a wide range of issues." Free sample copy available from Stanley Foundation, 420 East Third St., Muscatine, Iowa 52761.

Zeta Magazine. Monthly. $24. 150 W. Canton St., Boston, MA 02118. Noam Chomsky, Dave Dellinger, Ynestra King, Bell Hooks, Howard Zinn, and a dozen other regular contributors on politics, movement debates, books, music, culture, and sports fill 112 ad-free pages per issue with a feast of ideas to inform and inspire efforts for a freer society.

Remember, don't be overwhelmed! Just choose one or more publications that might be right for you — enjoy starting a new subscription or sending for some sample issues.

Before listing the remaining titles in this section, we want to suggest two related clusters of periodicals specializing in a) peace and b) alternative security.

A) Peace. Peace research is a field only a few decades old. Two organizations (with newsletters), and several journals are of special importance for those wishing to keep up with it:

1) the Consortium on Peace Research, Education and Development (COPRED), publisher of the informative bi-monthly newsletter *COPRED Peace Chronicle* and of the scholarly quarterly *Peace and Change*. For information on joining COPRED, write COPRED, c/o Center for Conflict Resolution, George Mason University, 4400 University Drive, Fairfax, VA 22030; (703) 323-2806.

2) the International Peace Research Association (IPRA), publisher of *IPRA Newsletter*, an indispensable tool for learning of research-in-progress. For information on joining IPRA, write IPRA, Box 327, Conflict Resolution Consortium, University of Colorado, Boulder, CO 80309.

3) *Peace Research Abstracts Journal*. Provides comprehensive coverage of work in the field. Contact Peace Research Institute—Dundas, 25 Dundana Ave., Dundas, Ontario L9H 4E5, Canada concerning *PRAJ* and *Peace Research Reviews*.

4) *Peace Review*. Quarterly. $20.00. 2439 Birch St., Suite 8, Palo Alto, CA 94306; 415-328-5477. This new quarterly aims to make important current thinking on peace accessible to a general readership. Free sample issue available.

B) Alternative security. The following periodicals are useful for monitoring much of the latest alternative security thinking. All four can be obtained for a total of $43/year; they are listed here in approximate order of increasing cost per page. The first two and the fourth are described in the notes to Chapter 6.

Non-Offensive Defence, a survey of news and research, averages some fifty pages per issue (appearing three to four times per year) and is sent free on request from the Centre of Peace and Conflict Research at the University of Copenhagen, Vandkunsten 5, DK 1467 Copenhagen K., Denmark.

Civilian-Based Defense: News & Opinion. Bimonthly 8-page issues are obtainable for $8/year from the Civilian-Based Defense Association, Box 31616, Omaha, NE 68131.

Alternative Security. $10. Monthly. 1601 Connecticut Ave., NW, Rm 300, Washington, DC 20009; (202) 332-9222. Four pages per issue. Many short notices of books, journal articles, conferences, and events, plus address and phone information for all groups mentioned. From the publishers of *Nuclear Times*.

Defense & Disarmament Alternatives is available free for a year (12 issues; 4-12 pp. each) to Friends (donating $25 or more) of the Institute for Defense and Disarmament Studies, 2001 Beacon St., Brookline, MA 02146.

Some additional journals

Bulletin of Municipal Foreign Policy. Quarterly. $35.00 (includes membership in Center for Innovative Diplomacy). CID, 17931-F Sky Park Circle, Irvine, CA 92714. Autumn 1988 issue was 64 pp. Published by CID's Local Elected Officials Project, the *BMFP* prints many short items on "city involvement in international trade, cultural exchange, and global politics" and covers the growing awareness that it is the costs of an aggressive foreign policy that block the solution of the problems of U.S. cities. Editor Michael Shuman advocates democratization of foreign policy-making and gives specific suggestions as to how it could be, or in some cases, *is* being done by far-sighted mayors, city councillors, and citizens.

Daybreak: American Indian World Views. Quarterly. $12/year. P.O. Box 98, Highland, MD 20777-0098. "A vehicle of news, information, analysis and perception about the world as inhabited and as seen by Native Peoples . . . [emphasizing] ethnicity and land-based values, kinship and eco-systemic thinking and basic survival strategies for the 21st century." Write Box 71, Highland, MD 20777 to contact the related groups Indigenous Press Network (publisher of *IPN Weekly Report*, $12.50 for 3 months) and AICOM: The Fourth World Computer Network.

Extra!. 6 issues/year. $24.00. Sample issue free. FAIR, 130 West 25th St., NY, NY 10001. *Extra!* is the newsletter of Fairness and Accuracy In Reporting. According to an article in its June 1987 issue by Ben Bagdikian, author of *The Media Monopoly,* in 1982, 50 corporations controlled half or more of the U.S. media business; by 1987, that figure was around 26. *Extra!* provides hard-hitting analysis of media bias, advocating greater pluralism. The Jan./Feb. 1989 issue analyzed the male, white, elitist and pro-U.S.-government bias of ABC-TV's popular "Nightline" show.

Fellowship. Monthly. $12.00. Box 271, Nyack, NY 10960. Published by the pacifist Fellowship of Reconciliation, it features news, articles, and resource listings on a variety of peace-related issues and world trouble spots.

Green Letter. Several issues/year. No set subscription rate; contributions asked. PO Box 9242, Berkeley, CA 94709. August 1988 issue was 20 tabloid-sized pages. "Seeks to evolve a holistic Green politics appropriate to the unique political and cultural realities of our time." *Green Letter* also at present incorporates *Greener Times: The Newsletter of the Green Committees of Correspondence,* the principal organization of people in the U.S. interested in Green politics.

In Context: A Quarterly of Humane Sustainable Culture. Quarterly. $18/year. P.O. Box 11470, Bainbridge Island, WA 98110. Seeks "practical steps and useful insights" to aid in making the major cultural shifts our world needs to survive.

The Inter-Dependent. 6 issues/year. $10.00. 300 E. 42nd St., 8th floor, NY, NY 10017. Published by the United Nations Association of the USA, which seeks to build public support for the United Nations.

Listen Real Loud: News of Women's Liberation Worldwide. Quarterly. $5 or $10 donation requested. Nationwide Women's Program, American Friends Service Committee, 1501 Cherry Street, Philadelphia, PA 19102. A regular section on "Women and Global Corporations: Work / Roles / Resistance" adds to the value of this 16-page newsletter.

The Nonviolent Activist. 8 issues/year. $15 minimum contribution. 339 Lafayette St., NY, NY 10012. Published by the War Resisters League; focuses on militarism but covers many related issues in articles, letters, and reviews.

The Nuclear Resister. 8 issues/year. $15 ($10 low income). P.O. Box 43383, Tucson, AZ 85733. In addition to information about and support for imprisoned anti-nuclear activists, offers thorough coverage of nuclear resistance nationwide. 1988 statistics: 4,470 arrests during 160 actions at 65 sites.

off our backs. 11 issues/year. $15. 2423 18th St. NW, Washington, DC 20009. Detailed reports on women's conferences and excellent book reviews, plus interviews, news shorts, letters, cartoons, and consistent efforts at being multi-cultural and international in coverage, make *oob* one of the best feminist publications in the U.S. — and, at $15, a bargain.

RMI Newsletter. Quarterly. Free (donation requested). Rocky Mountain Institute, 1739 Snowmass Creek Road, Snowmass, CO 81654-9199. Ca. 12-16 pp. per issue of upbeat reporting on RMI's doings re energy efficiency, water conservation, economic renewal, and security. RMI's energy work, now influencing U.S. utility regulators and Soviet and Chinese policymakers, may have a major effect in slowing global warming. Its continually updated reprints list is a prime source on energy policy, including actions individuals can take to save money and energy.

The Women's Review of Books. 11 issues/year. $15. 828 Washington St., Wellesley, MA 02181. A first-rate source, through its reviews, advertisements, and lists of books received, for finding the latest feminist publications about anything.

Many other titles, arguably equally valuable, could have been added to this list; curtailing it is made easier by the existence of *The Progressive Periodicals Directory* (2nd ed., 1988), available from Progressive Education, P.O. Box 120574, Nashville, TN 37212 for $8.00 (five or more copies, $5 each). It packs short descriptions of approximately 600 national social concerns periodicals into 36 closely printed pages and can remedy most omissions here.

And finally, an alternative to all that reading: the Great Atlantic Radio Conspiracy offers a monthly 30-minute audio cassette (subscription $5/month) reviewing a selection of stories from 60 alternative media sources. (GARC, 2743 Maryland Ave., Baltimore, MD 21218; 301-243-6987).

NOTES

1. Jim Forest, "Tuning in on the World," *Fellowship* (July/August 1984), pp. 15-16. Forest recommends buying a Sony shortwave radio as the easiest way to correct U.S. media bias.

2. "The United States' leading dissident": Chomsky was so described by Britain's *Manchester Guardian Weekly* (quoted in Black Rose Books catalog, Fall 1988). Chomsky goes on to say that "The United States is unusual among the industrial democracies in the rigidity of the system of ideological control — 'indoctrination,' we might say — exercised through the mass media." (Noam Chomsky, *Language and Responsibility* [Pantheon, 1979], pp. 7-8.) Chomsky, an M.I.T. professor, became prominent as a critic of the Vietnam War by 1967, and is also world-famous as a linguistic theorist whose views have influenced philosophy and psychology and been the subject of many books. (He received a 1988 Kyoto Prize, newly established to honor achievement in fields not covered by Nobel Prizes.) His exclusion from the U.S. mass media is not a matter of obscurity; he is not equally excluded elsewhere. For example, Chomsky was invited to deliver the 1988 Massey Lectures, a prestigious annual series sponsored by the Canadian Broadcasting Corporation.

3. Here is a list of valuable studies, not presented as exhaustive, in reverse chronological order:

Edward S. Herman and Noam Chomsky, *Manufacturing Consent: The Political Economy of the Mass Media* (Pantheon, 1988);

Ben Bagdikian, *The Media Monopoly* (Beacon Press, 1983; 2nd ed., 1987);

Michael Parenti, *Inventing Reality: The Politics of the Mass Media* (St. Martin's Press, 1986);

Eleanor MacLean, *Between the Lines: How to Detect Bias and Propaganda in the News and Everyday Life* (Montreal: Black Rose Books, 1981);

Anthony Smith, *The Geopolitics of Information: How Western Culture Dominates the World* (Oxford University Press, 1980);

Herbert J. Gans, *Deciding What's News: A Study of CBS Evening News, NBC Nightly News, Newsweek, and Time* (Vintage, 1979);

Edward Jay Epstein, *News from Nowhere: Television and the News* (Random House, 1973);

Herbert I. Schiller, *The Mind Managers* (Beacon Press, 1973);

Robert Cirino, *Don't Blame the People* (Vintage, 1971). The back cover of this book is worth quoting: "The fact that we are a sick nation, with our priorities all out of order, should be blamed on the press and television, in Mr. Cirino's view, and not on the people. There is much validity in this thesis" (Harriet Van Horne). While oversimplified, this thesis is certainly much fairer than the oft-repeated, vicious saying that "people get the kind of government they deserve."

4. Herbert I. Schiller, "Information: Important Issue for '88," *The Nation* (July 4/11, 1987), p. 1.

5. For an introduction to the new "alternative tourism" designed to foster international understanding, and now sponsored by over 100 groups in the U.S., see Medea Benjamin, "Travel with a Purpose," in *Building Economic Alternatives* (Winter 1988), pp. 14-16. This article is accompanied by several pages of addresses of organizations conducting such tours, inexpensive directories to guide you to other ones, and ads for such tourism. Another option is SERVAS, a network of hosts and travelers concerned about peace and understanding that can be a low-cost, enjoyable way to meet people in another country (SERVAS, 11 John St., Suite 706, NY, NY 10038; 212-267-0252).

B: Audio, Video, and Computer Sources of News and Commentary

Audio and video programs at their best offer vividness and immediacy hard for printed sources to equal. Many of the following are excellent, and all are underutilized in relation to their value for counteracting the omissions and biases of the dominant news media. Many of the audio and video programs listed below are affordable for an individual or small group, yet can be used as focal points for public events and group discussions. (They do not require advance reading, but can be used along with it in ongoing groups or classes.) Some programs feature debates between different points of view and thus may be especially suitable for certain educational or public uses. Arranging for broadcast of programs and series on an occasional, or better, regular basis could be a valuable activity for an individual or group concerned to aid the long-term public education needed for building a peace system.

This list emphasizes sources of ongoing news and interpretation to supplement and correct corporate-owned and government-funded news media; it also includes some older materials of lasting value. At their best, these sources provide highly professional and timely commentary on events (i.e., within a month or two), while offering depth that is not soon outdated. For a list of 23 "Alternative Communications Organizations" compiled by Dr. Colleen Roach that includes both critics of the media and sources of alternative news, features, and commentary, contact ExPro.

AUDIO SOURCES

David Barsamian. Twenty tapes feature Noam Chomsky, including lectures, interviews, and question-and-answer sessions with audiences, on U.S. policies in Central America and the Middle East, the lessons of Vietnam, terrorism, and the threat of nuclear war. Speakers on more than three dozen other tapes include former CIA agents John Stockwell, David MacMichael, Ralph McGehee, and Arthur Macy Cox, and social critics James Petras, Edward Herman, Victor Navasky, Edward Said, and Michael Parenti. (More women would be good.) Among the offerings are the Rev. Dr. Martin Luther King, Jr.'s 1967 Canadian Massey Lectures, published in book form as *The Trumpet of Conscience*, but more powerful in oral form. Other tapes feature poetry and music. Each tape is $9; for three or more, $8; include 50 cents each for postage and handling. Transcripts of some are available. For a catalog, write: David Barsamian, 1415 Dellwood, Boulder, Colorado 80302; (303) 449-4885.

Citizens Network for Common Security. This organization, emphasizing "clear, easily understood" presentations, originally offered "Perspectives on the Arms Race" and "Fundamentalism and the New Right" by Joan Bokaer. Its new audiocassettes are: 1) a 60-minute how-to introduction to "Citizen Diplomacy" by Philip Bennett (tape plus detailed booklet, $10 + $1 p/h); and 2) a talk by Joan Bokaer on "Alternative Defense," based primarily on research by Randall Forsberg (tape with accompanying booklet, $10 + $1 p/h). The speaker's kit ($12 + $1 p/h), including speaking tips, transcript, charts, and bibliography, is designed to enable anyone to make a presentation on alternative defense. Contact: Citizens Network, Anabel Taylor Hall, Cornell University, Ithaca, NY

14853; (607) 255-8276 or 255-8270.

Common Ground. This weekly radio series on world affairs is produced by the Stanley Foundation. Autumn 1988 topics included the Philippine economy, the 1988 American-Soviet Peace Walk, "A United States of Europe?" (on the economic integration planned for 1992), cultural differences among Africans, and the Palestinian uprising on the West Bank. Earlier programs featured SANE/ Freeze president Rev. William Sloane Coffin, futurist Robert Theobald, Vietnam veterans discussing Central America, a Japanese consular official, and New Zealand's ambassador to the U.S. Lists of programs available on cassette ($6 each) and of local stations that broadcast Common Ground regularly can be obtained from The Stanley Foundation, 420 East Third Street, Muscatine, Iowa 52761; (319) 264-1500.

Consider the Alternatives. In addition to two six-tape series — "Mushroom: Nuclear War and the Imagination" and "War in Space" — CTA offers U.N. Disarmament Chairperson Inga Thorsson of Sweden (on the arms race), Rev. Herbert Daughtry of the Black United Front (on Star Wars), Cong. Patricia Schroeder (on the Comprehensive Test Ban), energy expert Amory Lovins (on nuclear power and nuclear weapon proliferation), a documentary on the Women's International League for Peace and Freedom's annual meeting offering women's perspectives on national security (#712, "Women and the Budget"), a series on the economic impact of military spending, and many more cassettes. $8.00 each ($36 for a six-tape series) including postage and handling. For further information, contact Consider the Alternatives, SANE Education Fund, 5808 Greene St., Philadelphia, PA 19144; (215) 848-4100.

Great Atlantic Radio Conspiracy. Produces new 30-minute programs, often quite timely, every month. Send $1.00 for a full catalog of several hundred programs priced at $5.00 per cassette (also available on open reels). GARC also offers (for $5.00 per month) a half-hour cassette reviewing stories selected from 60 "alternative periodicals." Contact Great Atlantic Radio Conspiracy, 2743 Maryland Avenue, Baltimore, MD 21218; (301) 243-6987.

The Riverside Church Disarmament Program sponsored on October 16-17, 1987 a "national teach-in on intervention in the Third World" entitled "Waging War in the Nuclear Age." Twenty-three 90-minute tapes make available lectures and workshop presentations by some 40 knowledgeable resource persons including Andrea Ayvazian, Sara Miles, Lyuba Zarsky, Susan George, Martha Honey, Carolyn Cottom, Eqbal Ahmad, Cherri Waters, Stoney Cooks, Michael Shuman, Larry Agran, Michael Klare, Gabriel Kolko, Noam Chomsky, and David Cortright. Several sessions discuss practical, specific how-to information for local foreign policy initiatives organizing. Most tapes are $5; some two-tape sessions are $7. For a brochure describing all the sessions, send a postcard to Riverside Church Disarmament Program, 490 Riverside Drive, NY, NY 10027 (or call 212-222-5900, x262).

VIDEO SOURCES

Alternative Views. Produced in Austin, Texas since 1978, Alternative Views each week offers "a segment of news stories from the alternative press, and an in-depth examination of one or two issues: corporate control of the economy, racism, alternative energy, government and media, and [other issues] getting little coverage in the mainstream news. The show is now also broadcast on 50 cable systems across the country from San Francisco to Fayetteville, Arkansas," and reportedly "gets a great deal of response, both locally and nationally." Sometimes progressive groups send their own tapes for broadcast, as did women at the Greenham Common peace encampment. All this is done on a budget of $10,000 per year, thanks to much volunteer labor. "If you would like to see 'Alternative Views' in your town, contact Frank Morrow at Alternative Information Network, P.O. Box 7279, Austin, TX 78713 or call (512) 474-2107. Morrow also encourages people to take advantage of public access television and produce their own local shows. For more information contact the National Federation of Local Cable Programmers at P.O. Box 27290, Washington, DC 20038-7290, (202) 829-7186." (Quotations from *Building Economic Alternatives*, Spring 1988, p. 26.)

Better World Society. The Better World Society, co-founded by Ted Turner with Jacques Cousteau, Russell Peterson, and Lester Brown, produces and distributes TV programs on nuclear and global environmental issues. "Already more than twenty Better World programs have been seen by millions of viewers on public television and Turner Broadcasting System (TBS) in the U.S., and on national networks abroad." (Russell Peterson, quoted in *Extra!*, May-June 1988, p. 11; this information courtesy of Colleen Roach.) Contact Better World Society, 1140 Connecticut Ave., NW, Suite 1006, Washington, DC 20036.

Educational Film and Video Project. The program "There Are Alternatives" (1987; 28:30 min.) is described as "a unique look at the growing international science of peace research," featuring Professor Johan Galtung summarizing "the results of peace research to date and his findings on East/West and North/South relationships, the conditions for a peaceful world, and alternative security policies and structures." Among other programs are "Toward a Governed World" (1988; 27 min.; on a democratic global federal government), "The Turning Point" (1987; 28:30 min.; a grandfather in 2007 shows his grandchild through photos and film how the world took its first major steps toward peace and the elimination of poverty and injustice), and "The Trial of the AVCO Ploughshares" (1987; 75 min.; courtroom footage of the defendants' personal stories plus testimony by Daniel Ellsberg, Admiral Gene LaRocque, Richard Falk, and a Hiroshima survivor). Available in VHS, Beta, or 3/4" formats. For rental and sale prices, contact Educational Film and Video Project, 1529 Josephine St., Berkeley, CA 94703; (415) 849-1649.

Paper Tiger. Since 1981 Paper Tiger TV has produced over 140 programs intended "to both dismantle and defuse the myths of mainstream media"; these are now available on videotape. Individuals, universities, and libraries can rent or buy the 30-minute programs on VHS and 3/4" formats. The programs appear live and are later re-cablecast in 25 cities across the U.S. Contact Paper Tiger TV at 339 Lafayette St., NY, NY 10012; 212-420-9045. (Information from *Building Economic Alternatives*, Summer 1988, pp. 4-5.)

COMPUTER NETWORK

Finally, to help you (if you have access to a computer and modem) to make news as well as learn about it, *PeaceNet* exists to facilitate communication among peace activists. For information on PeaceNet, "the first global computer network for peace," linking people in the U.S. and over 70 other countries, write or phone PeaceNet, 3228 Sacramento St., San Francisco, CA 94115; (415) 923-0900.

C: Annotated Bibliography

There are many works pertinent to building a peace system beyond those prescribed in this book for use by 7- or 15-session study groups. (Those so prescribed are listed in "How to Order the Materials," with cross-references to the chapters in which they are commented on; they are generally not annotated here.) Lengthy bibliographies exist on many of the topics we have touched on; accordingly, this short bibliography must be selective. It should, however, be of use to thoughtful activists and also to students doing research, faculty designing courses, and librarians wishing to strengthen collections in international relations, peace studies, future studies, and related areas.

This bibliography's main part emphasizes recent (1985-1989) and forthcoming books so as to alert readers to works they may not yet be acquainted with in a fast-developing field. The final titles and publication details of forthcoming books may differ from those given here; publisher's descriptions have been relied on for some annotations. A few older books are also included. The main bibliography is preceded by a listing of general guides to peace and related literature that, though mostly less up-to-date, are much more comprehensive and can be used along with this bibliography.

Most works cited in the extensive Notes to this volume are *not* included below; those interested should consider the Notes as supplementary to this bibliography.

Also included in the main bibliography are books whose authors and publishers kindly gave permission, often without fee, for single-copy reproduction of portions of their books for use by peace system study groups. The authors and editors referred to are: Alperovitz and Faux; Bennett; E. Boulding; Bradley et al.; Etheredge; Falk, Kim, and Mendlovitz; Foell and Nenneman (items by Fischer and Nagler); Glossop; Goodman; Gran; Greening (items by Marien and Ferguson); Kaldor and Falk; Martin; McAllister (item by Leghorn); Sharp; Singham and Hune; Vayrynen (item by E. Boulding). These permissions, which aid public education on issues of the highest importance, are hereby gratefully acknowledged.

I. General guides

Barnaby, Frank, ed. *The Gaia Peace Atlas: Survival into the Third Millennium.* Doubleday, 1988. 271 pp. $18.95. In three parts covering the lessons of the past, problems of the present, and solutions for the future, this ambitious work surveys UN peacekeeping, war, unequal distribution of wealth, population growth, international law, food, human rights, ecological sustainability, and dozens of other topics. With photos, drawings, or graphics (some in color) on nearly every page, the book is lively and inviting as well as comprehensive. Despite deficiencies difficult to avoid in so wide-ranging a work, this book draws attention to the right subjects, and should be welcomed both for itself and as a prototype for future works aiming to reach a broad public.

Boulding, Elise, J. Robert Passmore, and Robert Scott Gassler, compilers. *Bibliography on World Conflict and Peace.* Westview Press, 1979. xxx + 168 pp. $37.00. "More than 1,000 entries organized in 26 major categories . . . [including not only books but also] bibliographies, abstracts, collections, annuals, series, and periodicals" (Westview). Though in need of updating (it covers 1945-1978), still a valuable guide.

Forsberg, Randall, and Carl Conetta, eds. *Peace Resource Book 1988-89: A Comprehensive Guide to Issues, Groups, and Literature.* Ballinger, 1988. 440 pp. $14.95. This periodically updated book from the Institute for Defense and Disarmament Studies is primarily devoted to a directory of 7000 U.S. peace groups (cross-indexed by name, state, and zipcode) intended "to increase communication among groups and individuals working for a more peaceful world" (p. 35). The directory is preceded by a 28-page introduction to "Peace Issues and Strategies" surveying world military forces, arms control talks, and ideas including alternative security and alternative defense. Part III, a 65-page "Guide to Peace-Related Literature," describes "1,000 recent [mainly 1983-1987] books and articles on military policy, arms control, peace activism, and alternatives to the war system." A very worthwhile and usable reference.

Gran, Guy. *An Annotated Guide to Global Development: Capacity Building for Effective Social Change.* Resources for Development and Democracy (17119 Old Baltimore Road, Olney, MD 20832), 1987. 154 pp. $7.95 plus $1 postage/handling. This work annotates the author's choice of the 490 best books on development, broadly conceived — not defined as growth in GNP, but as a social change process involving equitable spread of benefits among participants, expansion of organizational effectiveness, and sustainability. "Democracy is an inherent part of the process" (p. vi). Coverage includes theoretical, practical, topical, and regional works, giving "an exceptionally broad overview of development literature" (Frances Moore Lappe) plus additional lists of journals, reference books, and computer-readable data bases. Gran asserts that "As a species, we have effective answers to all our socio-political and economic problems," a remarkable statement that merits serious attention, coming from so well informed a source. "But . . . these answers remain marginalized. By assembling them in one place, . . . I hope to expand the reader's vision of a better future and his or her ability and willingness to take part in its construction" (p. vii). More of us should become acquainted with these answers so they can be evaluated and, if sound, implemented. Gran's guide may be the best short introduction to the scope of the development field and, at $7.95, is a book no serious student or social change activist can afford to be without.

Marien, Michael. *Future Survey Annual* (1979-). World Future Society, 4916 St. Elmo Ave., Bethesda, MD 20814; (301) 656-8274. Descriptive brochure and sample issue of *Future Survey* free on request. Approx. 175 pp. each *Annual. Future Survey* is "a monthly abstract of books, articles, and reports concerning forecasts, trends, and ideas about the future." Each *Future Survey Annual* cumulates these, rearranging nearly 1,000 abstracts into precise categories, and adding regular or occasional special features such as a ranking of the principal global hopes and fears reflected in the literature reviewed. The 1986 annual contained "an annotated listing of 340 futures-relevant periodicals, including scholarly journals, magazines, and selected newsletters." Each *Future Survey Annual* is immensely valuable for anyone concerned to know what is happening worldwide, how people are interpreting it, and what is proposed to be done about it. There are few if any people whose thinking about peace and the multitude of factors working for and against it will not be deepened by a few hours' reading in any volume of *FSA*. *FSA*'s are available at $25 each, $20 each for three or more, or $129 for all eight Annuals — about $15 per volume for a total of nearly 9,000 abstracts, a remarkable bargain. Any college or city library should be encouraged to acquire this resource.

Marien, Michael. *Societal Directions and Alternatives: A Critical Guide to the Literature*. 1976. 400 pp. Out of print. Over one thousand books and articles summarized and evaluated, arranged in sixteen chapters, with an excellent general introduction (see especially pp. 17-19 on the virtual absence of genuine dialogue among thinkers, the fragmentation of knowledge, and the need for informed holistic thinking). *SD&A* provides concise accounts of both the best-known "futurist" works and many lesser-known, sometimes superior, works. Nine indexes aid access to the literature covered. A "civic curriculum" lists the fifteen and seventy-five items Marien recommends most highly. Though (sadly) out of print, the book may be obtainable through inter-library loan (ask a reference librarian). The pace of genuine intellectual progress means that *SD&A* is regrettably less outdated than one would wish; it remains unsurpassed.

Thomas, Daniel C., and Michael T. Klare, eds. *Peace and World Order Studies: A Curriculum Guide* (5th edition). Westview, forthcoming June 1989. Approx. 656 pp. $22.95. Each edition of this very comprehensive work has included numerous syllabi provided by teachers based in a variety of disciplines, as well as introductory essays. Extremely valuable for anyone wishing to study or teach about peace.

Woito, Robert S., ed. *To End War: A New Approach to International Conflict*. 1982. 755 pp. Contains a well-organized annotated bibliography of over 2,000 books plus interpretive material on nine "contexts" or perspectives concerning how to end war (pp. 461-503). Only one perspective is found "adequate": that of the World Without War Council, the book's sponsor. The WWWC's outlook contrasts in many respects with that of this book — perhaps most importantly concerning 1) the U.S.-Soviet power balance, 2) the meaning of "democracy" in the U.S. for world affairs, and 3) the legitimacy of nonviolent direct action to change U.S. policies.

Concerning 1), the WWWC view that the U.S. is "weak" (p. 477), see note 2 to "The Peace System Approach to Eliminating War" in this book. Concerning 2), the WWWC assumption seems to be that, because the United States is in some important respects democratic, it necessarily promotes democracy and peace in the world more than countries that are less internally democratic. The historical record is not so simple or comforting. Concerning 3), it is debatable whether citizens are relieved of their obligation to resist policies of criminal aggression by their government simply because it is an elected government — especially when government officials and mass media have concealed or misrepresented the policies. (For discussion of issues 2) and 3), see the readings by Cohen and Rogers, Bello [e.g., *Visions of a Warless World*, p. 46], Chomsky, Dellinger, and Irwin, among others, cited in this book.) Nevertheless, despite political bias that leads to substantial misrepresentation of some of the views with which its sponsors disagree, this book remains a valuable and thought-provoking work of impressive scope, well worth consulting.

World Encyclopedia of Peace. Honorary Editor-in-Chief, Linus Pauling. Executive editors, Ervin Laszlo and Jong Youl Yoo. Pergamon Press, 1986. Four volumes; 1,930 pp.; $375.00. Includes articles on major theories and philosophies of peace, contemporary peace issues and eminent peace theorists; a directory of institutes and organizations related to peace; a classified bibliography; a directory of journals; texts of 40 major peace treaties; and subject and author indexes. A useful reference work for libraries.

II. Main bibliography

Albert, Michael, and David Dellinger, eds. *Beyond Survival: New Directions for the Disarmament Movement.* South End Press, 1983. 365 pp. $8.00. See Chapter 11 for commentary on two essays from this book. The chapters by Albert (co-founder of South End Press and *Zeta Magazine*), Dellinger (a veteran theorist and practitioner of nonviolent action and an astute political commentator), and others also merit reading.

Alperovitz, Gar, and Jeff Faux. *Rebuilding America: A Blueprint for the New Economy.* Pantheon, 1984. 319 pp. $10.95. See commentary for Chapter 7.

Alvarado, Elvia. *Don't Be Afraid, Gringo: A Honduran Woman Speaks from the Heart.* Harper & Row, 1989. $7.95. Edited by Medea Benjamin. An eloquent peasant organizer discusses her experiences and the struggle for democratic change. See end of Chapter 12.

Beer, Jennifer E. *Peacemaking in Your Neighborhood: Reflections on an Experiment in Community Mediation.* New Society Publishers, 1986. 256 pp. $14.95. This provocative, unusually tough-minded assessment of a "Community Dispute Settlement" program outside Philadelphia explores ideas relevant to global as well as local peacemaking. "Leaves one with an overwhelming impression of hope, of dynamism, of having found the beginning of an exciting new road" (from the Foreword by Elise Boulding).

Bennett, Gordon C. *The New Abolitionists: The Story of Nuclear Free Zones.* Brethren Press, 1987. 269 pp. $9.95. See commentary in Chapter 10. A good survey of the NFZ movement, including a chapter on the (il)legality of nuclear weapons.

Boggs, Carl. *Social Movements and Political Power: Emerging Forms of Radicalism in the West.*

Temple University Press, 1986. 288 pp. Like Boggs's earlier books on Marxist strategist Antonio Gramsci, this volume grapples intelligently with the challenges of radically transforming social systems. Despite a lack of familiarity with nonviolent struggle (in particular, the possibility of nonviolent coercion) that invalidates some of his points, Boggs's sympathetic critique of West Germany's Greens is intelligent and thought-provoking.

Bookchin, Murray. *Remaking Society*. Montreal: Black Rose Books, 1989. 207 pp. $11.95. Murray Bookchin, originator of "social ecology," is an innovative U.S. thinker whose works have been translated into several languages. His pioneering classic, "Ecology and Revolutionary Thought" (1965), is available in *Post-Scarcity Anarchism* (1971; 2nd ed., Black Rose, 1986; 265 pp.; $14.95). *Toward an Ecological Society* (1980; Black Rose, 315 pp.; $14.95) collects additional important essays, as does *The Modern Crisis* (New Society Publishers, 1986, $7.95). *Remaking Society* is intended as a readable introduction to Bookchin's ideas, and expresses his view of issues facing the emerging U.S. Green movement. For information on the most recent writings by Bookchin and other "Left Greens," contact the Green Program Project, P.O. Box 111, Burlington, VT 05402. They publish the periodical "Green Perspectives."

Boulding, Elise. *Building a Global Civic Culture: Education for an Interdependent World.* Syracuse University Press, April 1990. 192 pp. $12.95. See Introduction to Part III (at note 14) and quotations and commentary in Chapters 10 and 13. In this uncommonly rich yet short and readable book, Boulding skillfully integrates an unusual set of topics ranging from the U.N., nongovernmental organizations, and ethnic, religious, and gender conflict to the processes of experience and learning in a high-technology culture, the social imagination and the shaping of the future, the creation by individuals of transnational links, and the skills of peacemaking.

The resulting book is visionary in the best sense of the term. It not only offers an appealing image of the future, but increases our awareness of neglected aspects of present reality, redirects our attention, and makes clear the need for diligent and intelligent efforts if the potential of the present is to flower into a better future. Not trapped in the warfare / competition paradigm pervading most male writing on global politics, Boulding's book offers a new perspective that outweighs in value whole libraries of the zero-sum mentality. It should be required reading in every course on international relations and global issues.

Other works of interest by Boulding include the chapter "The Coming of the Gentle Society" in her *Women in the Twentieth Century World* (Sage, 1977) and "Women's Visions of the Future" in Eleonora Masini, ed., *Visions of Desirable Societies* (Pergamon, 1983). A revised edition of her massive *The Underside of History: A View of Women through Time* (Westview, 1976), a survey of women from prehistoric times to the twentieth century that begins to correct the male-centered bias of most history and provide a more accurate image of what human experience has been, is to be published by Sage.

Boulding, Kenneth E. A co-founder of the peace research movement and a social philosopher whose breadth of knowledge and readability of style have few rivals, Boulding has authored many works relevant to building a peace system. *The Meaning of the Twentieth Century: The Great Transition* (1964) vividly outlined the imperatives posed by war and ecological change that many are still only beginning to face 25 years later. For an excellent overview of the fundamental ideas and themes in Boulding's earlier writings, see Cynthia Earl Kerman, *Creative Tension: The Life and Thought of Kenneth Boulding* (University of Michigan, 1974). Such works as *Stable Peace* (U. of Texas, 1978), *Ecodynamics* (Sage, 1978), *Human Betterment* (Sage, 1985), and *The World as a Total System* (Sage, 1985) represent his more recent thinking.

Boulding's conviction that gradual, evolutionary processes (especially learning) contribute much more to human betterment than struggle (even nonviolent struggle) contrasts provocatively with views popular in contemporary social movements. Even if Boulding overlooks the learning fostered by nonviolent struggle at its best and underrates the importance of injustice and exploitation, his views merit attention from anyone willing to learn from an unusually original mind. Few writers offer so many durable insights so entertainingly expressed. Johan Galtung's appreciative critique of the two most recent books cited above can be found in *Journal of Peace Research*, Vol. 24, No. 2 (1987).

Boyle, Francis Anthony. *Defending Civil Resistance Under International Law.* Dobbs Ferry, NY: Transnational Publishers, 1987. 379 pp. 1988 paperback edition $9.00 postpaid from The Center for Energy Research, 333 State St., Salem, OR 97301; (503) 371-8002. Boyle, a professor of international law at the University of Illinois, argues that, with neither the executive branch nor Congress keeping U.S. government policy within the bounds of law, civil (nonviolent) resistance by citizens to law violations is accordingly indispensable and constitutionally legitimate. Boyle's book includes materials that have been used, sometimes winning acquittal, at trials of civil resisters to criminal policies on nuclear weapons, Central America, and apartheid. Boyle recommends that civil resisters be represented by trial lawyers, but also offers his assistance (217-333-0931) to those who exercise their right to represent themselves. Excellent introductions by Richard A. Falk and the late Sean McBride add to the value of this powerfully argued work.

Bradley, Ben, et al., eds. *Por Amor Al Pueblo: Not Guilty! The Trial of the Winooski 44.* Front Porch Publishing (RR 2, Box 281, White River Junction, VT 05001), 1986. 176 pp. $10.00. See Chapter 12 for excerpts from the introduction by Dave Dellinger, one of the Winooski 44 who sat in at their Senator's office in an effort — ultimately successful — to end his support for U.S. aggression in Central America. This edited transcript provides the expert testimony and arguments that won acquittal by the jury.

Brock-Utne, Birgit. *Feminist Perspectives on Peace and Peace Education.* Pergamon, forthcoming August 1989. Approx. 256 pp., $14.95. "A milestone in the developing discipline of peace research. It is the first in-depth treatment of the field's core concepts, particularly the concepts of power and violence, using the tools of feminist analysis" (Elise Boulding). "She also has excellent ideas on 'what can be done about it' . . . . She gives us reasons to hope . . ." (Johan Galtung).

Brown, Seyom. *The Causes and Prevention of War.* St. Martin's Press, 1987. 274 pp. $9.00. This readable survey by an author of many books on U.S. foreign policy gives brief, respectful attention to the views of Falk, Sharp, and Galtung, but faults such approaches for "provid[ing] contemporary statesmen with no practical means for dealing with immediate threats of war" (p. 124). The book concludes with an array of reform proposals. For more on possible world futures and implications for enlightened policymakers, see chapters 11-15 of Brown's *New Forces, Old Forces, and the Future of World Politics* (Scott Foresman, 1988).

Bryan, Frank, and John McClaughry. *The Vermont Papers: Recreating Democracy on a Human Scale.* Chelsea Green Publishing (c/o AIDC, 64 Depot Rd., Colchester, VT 05446), 1989. 320 pp. $18.95. Makes "detailed, specific recommendations [for] a system of government through bio-regionally based shires — clusters of towns," through which Vermont could improve on its tradition of town meeting government and become a model of 21st century democracy. If more thorough-going democracy makes for citizens less prone to tolerate aggressive war, then improving democracy should aid the cause of peace.

Callenbach, Ernest. *Ecotopia Emerging.* Banyan Tree Books, 1981. 326 pp. $8.95. Callenbach's enchanting *Ecotopia* (Bantam, 1975; 213 pp.; $4.50) described the society resulting by 1999 from the 1980 secession from the U.S. of Oregon, Washington, and northern California to form an ecologically sound society. Inventive, insightful, gripping, and real enough to leave one homesick, it was rightly called "the finest utopian fiction in decades" (George Scialabba, *Village Voice*). *Ecotopia Emerging*, filling in the transition between present society and Ecotopia, is a rich source of ideas for Green activists of the 1990s, deserving to be widely read and discussed.

Capra, Fritjof, and Charlene Spretnak. *Green Politics: The Global Promise.* Dutton, 1984; 2nd ed., 1986. 262 pp. $8.95. A fine, readable introduction to the ideas and political activities of Green activists in many countries, emphasizing the West German Greens and the prospects for Green politics in the U.S. "An insightful and honest book that does not cover up the internal conflicts that must be solved when a movement is born" (Petra Kelly). Portrays Green politics as "neither left nor right"; for a contrasting view, see Hulsberg (below).

Chomsky, Noam. *Necessary Illusions: Thought Control in Democratic Societies.* South End Press, 1989. $16.00. In a book expanded from the Massey Lectures delivered in autumn 1988 over Canada's national CBC radio network, Chomsky "argues that the media operate in the service of powerful institutions rather than in opposition to them" (publisher's description). Chomsky's most recent books, which amount to a running commentary on U.S. foreign policy distinguished by its analytic power and attention to facts downplayed in the U.S. media, are: *Pirates and Emperors: International Terrorism in the Real World* (1986; from Claremont Research, 160 Claremont Ave., NY, NY 10027 or Amana Books, 802-257-0872); *On Power and Ideology* (South End, 1987); *The*

Culture of Terrorism (South End, 1988); and *Language and Politics*, 779 pages of interviews from 1968 to 1988 (Montreal: Black Rose Books, 1989; $24.95). See also Herman and Chomsky (1988), listed below. For Chomsky's earlier works, see notes to Chapter 3.

Collins, Sheila D. *The Rainbow Challenge: The Jackson Campaign and the Future of U.S. Politics.* Monthly Review, 1986. 386 pp. $11.00. Can a charismatic leader overcome the constraints of U.S. two-party politics and forge a winning multi-racial coalition of poor people, blacks, Hispanics, farmers, the elderly, peace activists, women, gays and lesbians, and other working and middle-class people? In contrast with many books focusing on the personality of the Reverend Jesse Jackson, Collins's book (based on her experience in Jackson's 1984 presidential campaign) explores the origins and potential of Rainbow politics, offering a sympathetic view of Jackson's candidacy as enabling the joining together of diverse constituencies with a common interest in "a transference of power from the military-industrial complex to the majority of the people" (p. 19).

Ehrlich, Paul R., and John P. Holdren, eds. *The Cassandra Conference: Resources and the Human Predicament.* Texas A&M University Press, 1988. 330 pp. $14.95. Among the noteworthy chapters in this interesting volume are two by Donella Meadows. The first discusses how the optimistic elements in *The Limits to Growth* (1972; co-authored by her) were downplayed and the book's message distorted, and seven lessons she learned. The second eloquently argues for the importance of communicating accurately, indicating obstacles honestly but conveying "hope, potential, and possibility," telling success stories people can copy, presenting "a clear image of a world to move toward," behaving with compassion, and projecting confidence and faith in our power to change the world.

Etheredge, Lloyd S. *Can Governments Learn? American Foreign Policy and Central American Revolutions.* Pergamon, 1985. 200 pp. $14.95. See Chapter 8's commentary. Etheredge has also written *A World of Men: The Private Sources of American Foreign Policy* (MIT Press, 1978; 178 pp.), a rigorous study supporting the hypothesis that "the fact that virtually all American and world political leaders have been male probably increases the likelihood of war" (p. xv). Among his findings: "Men I talked with were offended at being asked [when they 'had first begun to believe war was a legitimate instrument of national policy']. Some supported the Vietnam War but they did not believe 'war was a legitimate instrument of national policy.' Instead they felt that 'using force' was an unpleasant 'necessity'" (p. 34).

Everett, Melissa. *Breaking Ranks.* New Society Publishers, 1988. 256 pp. $12.95. This book, based on interviews, is an account of men who emerged from careers in the military-industrial complex to work for peace. Meet Daniel Cobos, ex-participant in spy flights over Nicaragua; former CIA analysts Ralph McGehee and David McMichael; former nuclear lab public relations director Bill Perry; Lou Raymond, former Trident sub builder and now member of Exodus, a support group for blue-collar workers who have quit jobs working for the military; and five others equally valuable as sources of insight into how people change. A provocative gift for military-industrial people in your life?

Falk, Richard, Samuel S. Kim, and Saul H. Mendlovitz, eds. *Toward a Just World Order.* Westview, 1982. 652 pp. $23.95. An ambitious and impressive anthology, the introductory volume of the series of which the next two books below are part.

Falk, Richard, Friedrich Kratochwil, and Saul H. Mendlovitz, eds. *International Law: A Contemporary Perspective.* Westview, 1985. 702 pp. $22.95. Thirty-eight essays examining the contributions and limitations of international law for dealing with issues of war, ecological protection, human rights, etc.

Falk, Richard, et al., eds. *The United Nations and a Just World Order.* Forthcoming, Westview Press. Approx. 500 pp.

Fischer, Dietrich, Wilhelm Nolte, and Jan Oberg. *Winning Peace: Strategies and Ethics for a Nuclear-Free World.* Crane Russak and Co., 1989. 270 pp. $25.00. A very readable, inviting, and wide-ranging book that advocates an "active peace policy" based on anticipating possible problems, cooperation, conflict resolution, and "protective defense." See also Tinbergen and Fischer, below.

Foell, Earl W., and Richard A. Nenneman, eds. *How Peace Came to the World.* MIT Press, 1987. 272 pp. $7.95. Essays from the *Christian Science Monitor*'s "Peace: 2010" contest. See Fischer's and Nagler's scenarios discussed in Chapters 9 and 12 respectively.

Friberg, Mats, and Bjorn Hettne, "The Greening of the World Economy," pp. 204-270 in Herb Addo et al., *Development as Social Transformation: Reflections on the Global Problematique.* Westview Press, 1985. 281 pp. $38.00. "The most systematic and politically sophisticated explanation of 'Green politics' that we have seen" (Mark Satin, *New Options*, 11/24/86). "Superb article on Green politics is followed by a trenchant [10-page] critique by Samir Amin" (Guy Gran, *An Annotated Guide to Global Development*, p. 8).

Fuglesang, Andreas, and Dale Chandler. *Participation as Process: What We Can Learn from Grameen Bank, Bangladesh.* NORAD, 1986. 234 pp. Free on request from Norwegian Ministry of Development Cooperation (NORAD), Information Unit, P.O.Box 8142-Dep, 0033 Oslo 1, Norway; allow 6-8 weeks. An inspiring analysis of a Third World development success story with implications for social change efforts elsewhere. The Grameen (village) Bank in Bangladesh loans money to the poorest of the poor (with a default rate less than 2%), while "in all thinkable ways it provides its loanees services which enhance their well-being, health and productivity" (p. 1). The bank enables its loanees (mostly women) to use their resourcefulness for mutual benefit in a brilliantly designed synergy of individual initiative and group solidarity combining the best ideals of capitalism and socialism. The result is concrete and immediate improvement of living conditions, benefiting whole families and communities, yet also promoting a profound gradual redistribution of power from men to women and from rich to poor. The Bank has expanded from a small pilot project to benefit over a million people in just ten years, with no slow-down in sight. The Grameen Bank approach is now being adopted in the U.S. and elsewhere (see n. 26 to Chapter 7). Anybody organizing anything is likely to gain inspiration and valuable ideas from this well-written book (in which photographs also tell the story). An effort is being made to get this book a U.S. distributor.

Galtung, Johan. *There Are Alternatives! Four Roads to Peace and Security.* Dufour Editions (Chester Springs, PA 19425 is the complete address), 1984. 221 pp. $11.95. A lively treatment of alternative security policies especially strong on what European countries have done or are doing, but with a global perspective. Galtung advocates "transarmament from offensive to defensive defense," non-alignment, and greater self-reliance. A co-founder of peace research, Galtung's work has been published in several languages. Many of his influential ideas are brought together in *The True Worlds: A Transnational Perspective* (Free Press, 1980). Nils Petter Gleditsch et al., eds., *Johan Galtung: A Bibliography of his Scholarly and Popular Writings 1951-1980* (Oslo: International Peace Research Institute; 286 pp.) includes three indexes and four essays on Galtung's intellectual development and influence, including a reprint (from *Journal of Peace Research*, XIV:1 [1977]) of Kenneth Boulding's thought-provoking "Twelve Friendly Quarrels with Johan Galtung." Those assembling new peace studies collections should note that Galtung's six volumes of *Essays in Peace Research*, including many often-cited articles, are available at an attractive discount for multi-volume orders. Details from Ejlers, Publishers, PO Box 2228, DK-1018, Copenhagen K, Denmark.

Glossop, Ronald J. *Confronting War: An Examination of Humanity's Most Pressing Problem.* McFarland & Co. (Box 611, Jefferson, NC 28640), 1987. 362 pp. $19.95 + 1.50 postage. Parts One through Three introduce the war problem, examine theories of its causes, and survey half a dozen aspects of the contemporary situation (ideological, military, economic, legal, etc.). Part Four considers solutions: reforming individual attitudes, national governments, government policies, or the nation system (of sovereign states). Glossop favors world federalism, but discusses varied viewpoints with admirable fair-mindedness. *Confronting War* surveys a sizable literature, gives many leads for further study, and urges the reader to action — all in a clear, readable style.

Goodman, Paul. In such books as *People or Personnel: Decentralizing and the Mixed System* (1965), *Like a Conquered Province: The Moral Ambiguity of America* (1967), *New Reformation* (1970), essays and interviews like "Confusion and Disorder" and "Our Standard of Living," and the extraordinary speech "A Causerie at the Military-Industrial" (these latter three are included in Taylor Stoehr, ed., *Drawing the Line*, 1977), Paul Goodman offered insights into the modern world, and the U.S. in particular, that still repay pondering.

Gran, Guy. *Development by People: Citizen Action for a Just World.* Praeger, 1983. 506 pp.

$14.95. See Chapter 7's commentary. A well-informed overview of development problems and how to remedy them, plus a lengthy bibliography.

Greening, Tom, ed. Rollo May, Carl Rogers, Abraham Maslow, et al., *Politics and Innocence: A Humanistic Debate.* Saybrook Publishers, 1986. 223 pp. $15.95. See Chapter 12's commentary. Articles primarily from members of the Association for Humanistic Psychology.

Harris, Adrienne, and Ynestra King, eds. *Rocking the Ship of State: Toward a Feminist Peace Politics.* Westview, 1989. 256 pp. $16.95. (not seen).

Harvey, Hal, Michael Shuman, and Daniel Arbess. *Reclaiming Security: Beyond the Controlled Arms Race.* Hill & Wang, forthcoming February 1990. A product of the Rocky Mountain Institute's Security Program, this book looks to "the economic and political *roots* of conflict. RMI's efforts are based on the premises that dominant concepts of security — based on offensive military threats — are making humankind poorer and less secure, that security can best be increased by making other nations more secure, not less, and that preventing conflict or other threats to U.S. security will work better and cost less" (RMI Security Program Update Report, 25 March 1988).

Herman, Edward S., and Noam Chomsky. *Manufacturing Consent: The Political Economy of the Mass Media.* Pantheon, 1988. 412 pp. $14.95. Explains how and why the U.S. mass media function as a propaganda system, offering powerful case studies of distortion of major aspects of U.S. foreign policy and international events, from Vietnam and Cambodia to Nicaragua, El Salvador, and "the plot to kill the Pope."

Hollins, Harry B., Averill L. Powers, and Mark Sommer. *The Conquest of War: Alternative Strategies for Global Security.* Westview, 1989. 250 pp. $9.95. "The authors explore the strengths and weaknesses of seven approaches to global security — the United Nations; a world peacekeeping federation (the Clark-Sohn plan); minimum deterrence; qualitative disarmament; nonprovocative defense; civilian-based defense; and strategic defense. . . . [T]hey consider . . . verification of disarmament, compliance with international law, and conversion from a war to a peace economy. Finally, [they] integrate the most promising elements from each approach into a proposal for a common security system" (publisher's description).

Hulsberg, Werner. *The German Greens: A Social and Political Profile.* Verso, 1988. 257 pp. $15.95. "The best, most thorough profile we yet have" (Robert Koehler, *Green Synthesis*).

Independent Commission on Disarmament and Security Issues (Palme Commission). *Common Security: A Blueprint for Survival.* Simon and Schuster, 1982. 202 pp. $5.95. This international commission's report made the concept of "common security" part of global peace thinking: "States can no longer seek security at each other's expense . . . . Security in the nuclear age means common security" (p. 139).

Kaldor, Mary, and Richard Falk, eds. *De-Alignment: A New Foreign Policy Perspective.* United Nations University, Basil Blackwell, 1987. 265 pp. $25.00. Ten papers from a 1983 conference in Amsterdam that explore alternatives to a Europe enmeshed in the Cold War.

Kehler, Randall, Andrea Ayvazian, and Ben Senturia. *Thinking Strategically: A Primer on Long-Range Strategic Planning for Grassroots Peace and Justice Organizations.* Exchange Project, Peace Development Fund (P.O. Box 270, Amherst, MA 01004), 1988. 40 pp. $7.50. The title says it all; a useful tool.

Kelly, Petra. *Fighting for Hope.* South End Press, 1984. This collection addressing ecology, nonviolence, and peace is so far her only book in English. A selection of recent speeches and articles on Kelly's activities can be obtained on request from her office in the West German parliament: Petra K. Kelly, MdB, Bundeshaus - HT 718, D 5300 Bonn, Federal Republic of Germany.

King, Martin Luther, Jr. *The Trumpet of Conscience.* Harper & Row, 1989 (originally 1968). 78 pp. $7.95. Foreword by Coretta Scott King. The speeches and corporate ads that annually praise an unspecified "dream" obscure the message Dr. King voiced in the last year of his life. He proclaimed the inadequacy of protest and the need to "organize a revolution" against "a cruelly unjust society" (p. 59). He urgently advocated — and began organizing for — "mass civil disobedience" that could "break" the "obstructive coalition" in Congress that complacently tolerated "not only the evils of racism but the scourge of poverty . . . and the horrors of war" (pp. 15, 61). King's call for an "international coalition of socially aware forces, operating outside governmental frameworks" to pressure through nonviolent struggle both "the capital and government power structures" (p. 63) remains a provocative conception worthy of consideration by peace and justice strategists.

Klare, Michael T., and Peter Kornbluh, eds. *Low Intensity Warfare.* Pantheon, 1988. 250 pp. $8.95. An introduction to major aspects of current U.S. military doctrine and practice, through which "the United States is at war throughout the world" (contrary to politicians' we-have-peace-and-prosperity election rhetoric), engaged in pro- or counter-insurgency or antiterrorism campaigns in Central America, the Middle East, Asia, and Africa. Nine authors "investigate the nature and future of American war-fighting capabilities" in Third World conflicts, including U.S. support for the Afghan resistance and the U.S.-guided war against New People's Army guerrillas in the Philippines.

Kull, Steven. *Minds at War: Nuclear Reality and the Inner Conflicts of Defense Policymakers.* Basic Books, 1988. 341 pp. $19.95. Kull, a clinical psychologist, interviewed 84 high-level U.S. defense policymakers (including Congresspeople and defense intellectuals as well as executive branch officials) "to learn how [they] rationalize . . . defense policies that seem inconsistent with nuclear reality" (p. 30). Alert to emotions as well as cognitive inconsistencies, Kull elicited candid comments ("Grenada was fun . . . but that part you can't admit to yourself"; p. 234) and revealing beliefs about human nature ("we live in a world in which you can't trust"; p. 244), and the prospects for peace ("wars are just going to go on"; p. 247). In his concluding chapter Kull finds that competitiveness and the desire to participate in a crusade for good against evil may be important motivations in the U.S.-Soviet antagonism; but nevertheless adaptation to reality sufficient to permit survival seems possible. A valuable source on the mentality of an elite.

McAllister, Pam, ed. *Reweaving the Web of Life: Feminism and Nonviolence.* New Society Publishers, 1982. 440 pp. $12.95. A pioneering anthology.

Mack, Andrew. *Peace Research in the 1980s.* Australian National University Press, 1985. 124 pp. After a brief history of peace research, this book is devoted to a survey of peace research in Europe, the U.S., and other countries, plus short discussions of bias in peace studies courses, of the relation of peace research to peace activism, and of feminist criticism of existing peace research. A 7-page bibliography and lists of periodicals, peace research centers, and organizations follow the 97-page text. "An expanded and more comprehensive second edition" is said to be planned.

Marien, Michael, and Lane Jennings, eds. *What I Have Learned: Thinking About the Future Then and Now.* Greenwood, 1987. 219 pp. $29.95. Seventeen futurists reconsider their views.

Martin, Brian. *Uprooting War.* London: Freedom Press, 1984; available from Libertarian Book Club, 339 Lafayette St., NY, NY 10012. 287 pp. Martin, a U.S. expatriate now settled in Australia, offers a sensible and unpretentious yet comprehensive and systematic discussion of different antiwar strategies. He favors grassroots mobilization and adoption of "social defense" (known in the U.S. as civilian-based defense). His book includes autobiographical sketches by activists explaining how they manage their peace work so as to maximize effectiveness and avoid "burn-out" (see Chapter 13 above); and also a good guide to further reading on social change strategy and democratization.

Meadows, Donella H., and J. M. Robinson, *The Electronic Oracle: Computer Models and Social Decisions.* John Wiley, 1985. 445 pp. Understanding complex social systems should help in changing the war system to a peace system. "Written from an insider's viewpoint, with an outsider's scepticism" (as the publisher rightly says), this volume describes with exceptional clarity and candor the state of the art of social-system modeling. Major improvement in modeling and its benefits to humankind, the authors conclude, requires that modelers transform themselves and their profession (p. 416). Computer models can be valuable because they surpass mental models in precision, comprehensiveness, logic, explicitness, and flexibility; but "these qualities cannot be realized unless modelers become compassionate, humble, open-minded, responsible, self-insightful, and committed" (p. 438). The book itself models combining technical competence and wisdom.

Mendlovitz, Saul H., and R.B.J. Walker, eds. *Towards a Just World Peace: Perspectives from Social Movements.* 1987. 403 pp. A special issue of the quarterly *Alternatives* containing fifteen essays, about half by members of the Committee for a Just World Peace (see Walker, below), including Elise Boulding, Richard Falk, Mary Kaldor, and Rajni Kothari. Topics include ecology activism in India, local development movements in Mexico, the challenge of linking grass-roots movements and initiatives in the U.S. to global tranformation, and how one can act as a citizen of the world as well as of a particular state.

Nixon, Richard M. *1999: Victory Without War.* Simon & Schuster, 1988. $8.95. "Perfect peace — a world without conflict — is an illusion. . . . Real peace is a process — a continuing process for managing and containing conflict . . . . It is . . . the only kind we can realistically hope to achieve" (pp. 27-28). On this much one can agree with Nixon. But he includes threatening mass murder (nuclear deterrence) and ruthless warfare as legitimate means for seeking peace — and "victory" — in a world whose essence he perceives as competition. When operating in the White House, this mentality of the perpetual candidate / competitor, ever insecure, produced a secret official "enemies list" of domestic opponents and, far more important, killed hundreds of thousands in the effort to dominate Indochina.

Norman, Liane Ellison. *Hammer of Justice: Molly Rush and the Plowshares Eight.* PPI Press, forthcoming September 1989. $12.95. In 1980 Molly Rush and seven others entered a General Electric facility and damaged nuclear components with hammer blows in the first of what has become a series of "Plowshares actions" combining sabotage of weaponry (in the spirit of "beating swords into plowshares") and nonviolence toward persons. Norman, co-director of the Pittsburgh Peace Institute, describes the trial of the Plowshares defendants and explores what led Rush, a working-class Catholic and mother of six, to undertake such an action. Norman shows intriguing connections between William Penn, who himself stood trial for acts of conscience and sought to establish Pennsylvania as an unarmed polity, and the contemporary imperatives of conscience and international law acted on by present-day Pennsylvanians.

Nye, Joseph S., Jr., Graham T. Allison, and Albert Carnesale, eds. *Fateful Visions: Avoiding Nuclear Catastrophe.* Ballinger, 1988. 280 pp. $14.95. This volume from the Avoiding Nuclear War Project at Harvard's Kennedy School of Government assesses (in separate chapters) ten publicly debated visions of a more desirable future. In addition to various superpower- and weapon-oriented scenarios there are chapters on "Nonprovocative and Civilian-Based Defenses" (see review of this chapter cited in note 13 to Chapter 6), internationalism, and world government.

The editors' concluding chapter rejects as illusory "'endpoint utopias' — conditions that once achieved would resolve the problem," and finds hope in "'process utopias': visions of a process for keeping the peace and reducing the risks of war, even if no ultimate solution is possible" (pp. 228-229). The editors' conclusion echoes that reached earlier by ExPro. Compare the essay (written in 1987) on "the peace system approach" at the beginning of this book, and Mark Sommer's *Beyond the Bomb* (published in January 1986), which endorsed the viewpoint (quoted from a 1983 article by Beverly Woodward) that peace "'should be seen mainly as a process rather than as an ultimate goal with static content'" (p. 93).

Raskin, Marcus G. *The Common Good: Its Politics, Policies and Philosophy.* Routledge & Kegan

Paul, 1986. 369 pp. $22.50. Praised by Jesse Jackson, George McGovern, and Noam Chomsky, this book contains a wealth of ideas on both foreign and domestic policy, including (pp. 230-254) a draft "Program Treaty for Security and General Disarmament" between the U.S. and U.S.S.R.

Roussopoulos, Dimitri I. *The Coming of World War Three. Volume 1: From Protest to Resistance / the International War System.* Black Rose Books, 1986. 299 pp. $14.95. The author argues that only an international social movement for peace can prevent World War Three. He surveys peace movement activity in many countries, including the non-official peace groups of Eastern Europe, and provides a detailed treatment of the first four conferences (1982-85) of European Nuclear Disarmament (END). A long-time advocate of non-alignment with either superpower, Roussopoulos provides documents on tensions between the Soviet-aligned World Peace Council and the non-aligned END in the years just prior to Gorbachev. This is a book useful for broadening U.S. activists' knowledge and sophistication. In Volume 2, *A New Agenda: From Resistance to Social Change* (forthcoming), the author promises exploration of the kind of "fundamental social change" needed to transform the war system.

Ruddick, Sara. *Maternal Thinking: Toward a Politics of Peace.* Beacon Press, 1989. $24.95. "A brilliant exploration of how mothering and maternal nonviolence can contribute to a new concept of peace" (publisher's description).

Schwartz, William A., and Charles Derber. *The Nuclear Seduction: Why the Arms Race Doesn't Matter— and What Does.* Forthcoming, University of California Press, 1989. An outgrowth of the Boston Nuclear Study Group, which consists of sociologists from Boston College and Brandeis University. See the Schwartz and Derber article described in Chapter 2.

Sharp, Gene. *Gandhi as a Political Strategist, with Essays on Ethics and Politics.* Porter Sargent Publishers, 1979. 357 pp. $7.95. Introduction by Coretta Scott King. See Chapter 6's commentary. For other writings by Sharp, see the notes to Chapter 6 and to the last parts of "The Peace System Approach to Eliminating War."

Shiva, Vandana. *Staying Alive: Women, Ecology and Development.* London: Zed Books, 1988. 224 pp. Shiva, a physicist, philosopher, and feminist, "links the violation of nature with the violation and marginalization of women, especially in the Third World." She identifies "the ecological path of harmony, sustainability, and diversity" as essential for "survival and liberation for nature, women and men," and seeks to show how the efforts of women in ecology movements "constitute a non-violent and humanly inclusive alternative to the dominant paradigm of contemporary scientific and development thought" (publisher's description).

Singham, A. W., and Shirley Hune. *Non-alignment in an Age of Alignments.* Lawrence Hill & Co., 1986. 420 pp. $14.95. See description in Chapter 10's commentary.

Solo, Pam. *From Protest to Policy: Beyond the Freeze to Common Security.* Ballinger, 1988. 240 pp. $19.95. A thoughtful insider's analysis of the Nuclear Freeze movement, its limitations, and its lessons for the future.

Smoker, P., R. Davies, and B. Munske, eds. *A Reader in Peace Studies.* Pergamon, forthcoming September 1989. Approx. 320 pp., $17.95. Among some three dozen selections are included B. Reardon on "Feminist Concepts of Peace and Security," B. Brock-Utne on "Feminist Perspectives on Peace," and four articles on "the alternative of nonviolence" by R. Ambler, G. Ostergaard, A. Carter, and N. Young.

Sojourners Magazine, The Editors of. *America's Original Sin: A Study Guide on White Racism.* Sojourners (Box 29272, Washington, DC 20017), 1988. 120 pp. $4.95 each for 1-9 copies, 10-99 copies $3.95 each, 100 or more $2.95 each. A challenging and enlightening collection of nearly three dozen short articles grouped into seven "study sessions" followed by "Questions for Reflection and Discussion."

Stableford, Brian, and David Langford. *The Third Millennium: A History of the World: AD 2000-3000.* Knopf, 1985. 224 pp. $13.95. (This summary abridged from Michael Marien, cited below.) Two British science fiction writers present a detailed, realistically written account of the human future. After The Period of Crisis (2000 to 2180), in which there are three nuclear explosions, a rise in sea levels resulting from the "greenhouse effect," and devastation of Japan by a major earthquake, comes The Period of Recovery (2180 to 2400), during which occur no major international conflicts or natural disasters. World population begins a slow decline. "Greens" vs. "greys" replaces the "left-right" distinction. The first space colony opens (on the moon), but few move there. During The Period of Transformation (2400 to 2650) life-extension technology increases life spans to 150 years; the first radically modified humans, amphibious "merpeople," are bioengineered. In the final centuries of the millennium, world population reaches an equilibrium at about 2.5 billion, with an average lifespan of 180 years. Motives are largely aesthetic, and there are four distinct human species: ordinary humans, merpeople, and two other bioengineered variants.

"One of the most stimulating futures-oriented efforts in many years . . . Skillfully combines plausible visions of technology, politics, and personalities. Well worth the price merely for its spectacular illustrations. . . This broad, sophisticated synthesis could possibly set a new standard for serious long-range thinking about the future." (Michael Marien, *Future Survey Annual 1986*, p. 1)

For all their merits, few of the works cited in this book look much beyond four decades into the future. In contrast Stableford and Langford, by narrating one scenario of how humanity might deal with the challenges of biotechnology and artificial intelligence — about which the authors cited in *Building a Peace System* (understandably preoccupied with insuring sheer survival) have been virtually silent — open out a longer future for minds that too often remain locked in the time horizon of a few decades. *The Third Millennium* is "food for thought" of the most nourishing and delectable kind.

Tinbergen, Jan, and Dietrich Fischer. *Warfare and Welfare: Integrating Security Policy into Socio-Economic Policy.* St. Martin's Press, 1987. 189 pp. Nobel economics laureate Tinbergen and ExPro member Fischer "presenting important economic data and sharing insights on the world order ramifications of current economic problems and processes, [plus] a treasury of difficult-to-obtain information on a wide range of documents, studies, international organizations, conferences and proposals" (Gerald F. Mische, *Breakthrough* 10:1, Summer/Fall 1988, p. 87).

Tokar, Brian. *The Green Alternative: Creating an Ecological Future.* R. & E. Miles (P.O. Box 1916, San Pedro, CA 90733), 1987. 174 pp. $7.95. A gracefully written primer on Green politics, followed by a valuable "Note on Sources" (pp. 151-167) guiding readers to other Green-oriented writings.

United States Institute of Peace. Title not yet available. Forthcoming, 1989 from USIP, 1550 M St., NW, Suite 700, Washington, DC 20005-1708. Papers and edited transcripts of seminar discussions from the Institute's first research project, the making of an "Intellectual Map of Approaches to International Peace" intended to delineate categories within the field of peace research to aid the Institute in carrying out its mandate. For more information see *USIP Journal*, I:4 (9/88), p. 1.

Vayrynen, Raimo, ed. *The Quest for Peace: Transcending Collective Violence and War among Societies, Cultures and States.* Sage, 1987. 356 pp. See description in Chapter 8. Twenty-one essays by a distinguished international cast of contributors.

Walker, R.B.J. *One World, Many Worlds: Struggles for a Just World Peace.* Lynne Rienner Publishers, 1988. 175 pp. $10.95. The Committee for a Just World Peace consists of twenty-two distinguished politicians, academics, Nobel Peace laureates (Adolfo Perez Esquivel and Archbishop Desmond Tutu), and others from around the world who meet periodically. This book presents one participant's "interpretation of the committee's overall understanding of the potential of critical social movements."

Waring, Marilyn. *If Women Counted: A New Feminist Economics.* Harper & Row, 1988. 386 pp. $19.95. The analyses of costs and benefits on which government policies are now based rely on statistics like Gross National Product (GNP) that portray as "objective" fact the judgment that turning a forest into lumber plus wasteland is economically positive, while unpaid childcare and other non-monetized work counts as nothing. Is it any wonder that the earth's ecology and humans' living conditions are being damaged? There are signs that this powerful book may strengthen efforts to change the anti-women, anti-nature "System of National Accounts" used around the world.

Watzlawick, Paul, John Weakland, and Richard Fisch. *Change: Principles of Problem Formation and Problem Resolution.* W. W. Norton, 1974. 172 pp. Paradoxical and counter-productive "solutions" (like arms build-ups to attain security) are major features of our time. This exploration and application of ideas from Gregory Bateson, Milton Erickson, and others might stimulate creative thinking about the problem of war and system change.

Wollman, Neil, ed. *Working for Peace: A Handbook of Practical Psychology and Other Tools.* Impact Publishers, 1985. 271 pp. $9.95. Thirty-five short, useful chapters on "getting yourself together," organizing a group, setting goals, avoiding burn-out, building coalitions, changing opinions, preparing for nonviolent confrontations, using humor and the arts, and more.

Women's Foreign Policy Council Directory. Women's Foreign Policy Council (Suite 923, 1133 Broadway, NY, NY 10010), 1987. 336 pp. $35.00. Are all foreign policy experts men? No. TV panels and presidential appointments just make it seem that way. This book describes 275 women who lecture or consult on foreign policy issues, with a full page describing each one's areas of expertise. Your public or college library should acquire this book to provide you access to them.

World Commission on Environment and Development. *Our Common Future.* Oxford University Press, 1987. 383 pp. $10.95. Known as the Brundtland Report (after the commission's chairperson, Norway's female prime minister Gro Harlem Brundtland) this UN-initiated document comprehensively examines the interrelation of environment and development problems. It concludes that "economics and ecology must be completely integrated in decisionmaking and lawmaking processes . . . [in order] to protect the environment [and] also to protect and promote development," a change "best secured by decentralizing the management of resources on which local communities depend and giving those communities an effective say over [their] use."

Addenda

Plant, Judith, ed. *Healing the Wounds: The Promise of Ecofeminism.* New Society Publishers, 1989. 262 pp. $12.95. Foreword by Petra Kelly. Contributions by Susan Griffin, Ursula LeGuin, Starhawk, Rachel Bagby, Sharon Howell, and nearly two dozen others combining ecological and feminist perspectives.

Sale, Kirkpatrick. *Dwellers in the Land: The Bioregional Vision.* 1985; distributed by New Society Publishers. 217 pp. $12.95 (hardback). An informative presentation of a vision of "community, economy, and governance consistent with the demands of a fragile ecological order" (publisher's description).

Theobald, Robert. *The Rapids of Change: Social Entrepreneurship in Turbulent Times.* Knowledge Systems, Inc. (7777 W. Morris St., Indianapolis, IN 46231; 317-241-0749), 1987. 252 pp. $9.95. Theobald seeks to persuade readers they can make a difference, and to help them find the roles they can play in solving humanity's problems. A 38-page study guide including two audio cassettes is available ($19.95) from KSI, as is an imaginatively arranged catalog of books designed to aid personal and social survival in the 1990s.

D: Some Peace Organizations

If you're just starting out in peace work, you could begin by contacting one or more of the organizations listed here, each working toward peace in some way. You'll find references to many of them in this book (see Index). These are not the only good groups, nor are they specially endorsed by ExPro, but each is worth becoming acquainted with. A much longer list of national and local groups is contained in Forsberg and Conetta, *Peace Resource Book* (see Annotated Bibliography).

American Friends Service Committee (AFSC), 1501 Cherry St., Philadelphia, PA 19102; (215) 241-7000.

Clergy and Laity Concerned (CALC), 198 Broadway, Room 302, New York, NY 10038; (212) 964-6730.

Center for Common Security, P.O. Box 275, 35 Spring Street, Williamstown, MA 01267; (413) 458-2159. Helps students become empowered citizen leaders; aids establishment of full-credit student-run courses on peace-related topics.

Center for Innovative Diplomacy, 17931 Sky Park Circle, Suite F, Irvine, CA 92714; (714) 250-1296.

Congressional Black Caucus, 344 House Office Building Annex #2, Washington, DC 20515; (202) 226-7790. The Congressional Black Caucus Foundation (1004 Pennsylvania Ave., S.E., Washington, DC 20003; 202-543-8767) is the Caucus's non-partisan research arm.

Exploratory Project on the Conditions of Peace (ExPro), 1601 Connecticut Ave., N.W., Washington, DC 20009; (202) 232-5477.

Fellowship of Reconciliation, P.O. Box 271, Nyack, NY 10960; (914) 358-4601.

Food First: Institute for Food and Development Policy, 145 Ninth St., San Francisco, CA 94103; (415) 864-8555.

Global Education Associates, Suite 456, 475 Riverside Dr., New York, NY 10115; (212) 870-3290.

Institute for Defense and Disarmament Studies, 2001 Beacon St., Brookline, MA 02146; (617) 734-4216.

Institute for Peace and International Security, 91 Harvey St., Cambridge, MA 02140-1718; (617) 547-3338.

Institute for Policy Studies, 1601 Connecticut Ave., N.W., Washington, DC 20009; (202) 234-9382.

SANE/Freeze: Campaign for Global Security, 711 G Street, S.E., Washington, DC 20003; (202) 546-7100.

TransAfrica, 545 8th St., S.E., Suite 200, Washington, DC 20003; (202) 547-2550.

War Resisters League, 339 Lafayette St., New York, NY 10012; (212) 228-0450.

WomanEarth Feminist Peace Institute, PO Box 2374, Stanford, CA 94305; (415) 237-2929.

Women's International League for Peace and Freedom (WILPF), 1213 Race St., Philadelphia, PA 19107; (215) 563-7110.

World Federalist Association of the USA, 418 7th St., S.E., Washington, DC 20003; (202) 546-3950.

World Order Models Project, World Policy Institute, 777 UN Plaza, New York, NY 10017; (212) 490-0010.

The Exploratory Project
on the Conditions of Peace

The Exploratory Project on the Conditions of Peace (ExPro) is a small group of activist citizens whose purpose is to catalyze thought and action adequate to bring peace with freedom, justice, and ecological sustainability to our world.

Many of ExPro's approximately two dozen members do public speaking or workshops. A list of speakers, topics, and contact information is available through the ExPro office:

ExPro
1601 Connecticut Ave., NW, 5th floor
Washington, DC 20009
(202) 232-5477

A brief summary of ExPro's origins, purpose, and history may be of interest. In the summer of 1983 farmer and writer Mark Sommer traveled through Western Europe visiting researchers on alternative security ideas. Sommer found much creative work being done, but little contact and cross-fertilization among the researchers. In Britain, however, he found an "Alternative Defence Commission" working to bring ideas on non-nuclear alternatives together into a coherent form that could influence public debate. In November 1983 Michael Randle of the ADC staff was invited to New York City to speak to a group of persons convened by long-time peace activist W.H. Ferry to consider the idea of establishing such a group in the U.S. This meeting and a subsequent one were inconclusive, but Ferry and Sommer persisted and managed in September 1984 to convene a group of some 25 activists, academics, and independent intellectuals for a weekend of discussion and planning on what could be done to engender a fruitful public discussion on why and how people concerned about nuclear war should go beyond arms control to a focus on the conditions necessary to create lasting peace.

The group adopted its present name and decided to hold three-day meetings three times a year to work through a two-year research agenda to identify "the conditions of peace." Under the chairmanship of M.I.T. political scientist George Rathjens (whose formulation of premises for ExPro's work, as summarized by Kirkpatrick Sale, is quoted at the end of Chapter 1 of this book), ExPro in January 1985 approved a research agenda developed by Charles Derber, Dietrich Fischer, Robert Irwin, Mark Sommer, Carolyn M. Stephenson, and Robert C. Tucker (and described in *ExPro Paper #7* by Stephenson).

Carrying out its research agenda through a series of internally commissioned papers and presentations by members and guests, ExPro began to develop a gradual consensus. Early efforts to formulate this in a comprehensive position paper (drafted by Kirkpatrick Sale) demonstrated, however, that when ExPro's membership had been chosen to represent a range of views that would afford lively debate, this goal had been met only too well! ExPro's members did not agree on pacifism, nonviolence, world government, the best scale at which to solve global problems, or the relation of increased economic justice to preventing nuclear holocaust.

Building a Peace System

While areas of consensus were indeed emerging — sizable majorities could have been forged on many points — in the absence of unanimity about the complex problems it was addressing, the group concluded that it was, for the time being at least, more valuable to continue inquiry and discussion than to risk losing the participation of those holding minority viewpoints by outvoting them in order to produce a document. In the meantime, ExPro was contributing to public debate through publication in January 1986 of Mark Sommer's *Beyond the Bomb: A Field Guide to Alternative Strategies for Building a Stable Peace* and of a series of eight *ExPro Papers* (beginning in January 1987) and, perhaps most importantly, through its influence on the speaking and writing of its members and thereby on their diverse audiences. In addition, the broad conception of "replacing the war system with a peace system," accepted within the group from early on, came to be recognized as in itself a substantive contribution to peace-oriented thinking.

As ExPro completed its initial research agenda in 1987, with former Nuclear Freeze national coordinator Randy Kehler having become chairperson of ExPro's executive committee, it sought ways to promote wider public discussion. First, it accepted a proposal from Robert Irwin to produce a book (now in your hands) that could be used to catalyze the organizing of grassroots discussion groups that could proliferate as far as public interest in new approaches to peace could be found. Second, W. H. Ferry proposed creation of a draft "Citizens Peace Treaty" involving pledges or commitments that could be signed onto by or between individuals and groups anywhere and used to stimulate local hearings, debate, and action.

As discussion of issues raised by the Citizens Peace Treaty (CPT) idea proceeded, it was decided to commission research that could lay the groundwork for treaty provisions. ExPro's board of directors, by 1988 headed by co-chairs sociologist Elise Boulding and Pittsburgh Peace Institute co-director Liane Norman, hired individuals to coordinate research on five research "tracks" addressing areas that would be covered by a comprehensive citizens peace treaty: Individual and Collective Defense; Information and Culture; Ecology and Technology; Political Participation and Dispute Settlement; and Economic Justice. Resource persons (coordinated by the Information and Culture track director) were also asked to assist track directors in strengthening their work's inclusion of awareness of racism and of feminist contributions.

As the track research proceeded in 1988-89, with periodic meetings to insure integration of the results and further efforts to refine the CPT project, ExPro recognized that no single form (such as "treaty") adequately encompassed all the action implications of the insights it had evolved, and the CPT work was renamed the "Peace System Project."

By mid-1989 the work undertaken in 1987-88 was beginning to bear fruit. ExPro's mission, as articulated in spring 1988, is to make the concept of the conditions of peace respectable, create an associated culture of peace, and help develop a new vocabulary, thereby changing the nature of the public conversation; and to point to specific action arenas and mobilize a variety of publics to generate actions that can advance us along the road to a world peace system. Three projects currently implement this mission.

1. The Peace System Project, with publications to become available in early 1990.

2. Encouragement of study groups and courses using *Building a Peace System*, so as to enable any group of people to study, discuss, and act on the ideas ExPro members and other activists have been developing.

3. The Soviet-American Initiative for a Citizens Ecological Treaty, initiated at an international meeting and coordinated in the U.S. by Patricia Mische of Global Education Associates' office in New York. ExPro is a founding sponsor and partial funder of the Initiative, which is an example of the citizen activity envisaged in its mission statement.

In 1989 the success of the first study group to use *Building a Peace System* provided encouragement that the ideas explored during ExPro's first years are equally exciting and inspiring to others. As study groups spring up elsewhere and additional ones are organized by enthusiasts from the first ones, we look forward to a great expansion of the numbers of people who can operate from a common basis of knowledge to bring their diverse perspectives to bear on the making of peace. This growing body of citizens will help to fulfill the vision held by ExPro's founders of a revitalized and empowered peace movement — a movement that has shifted from opposing feared futures to defining a goal of peace with justice and freedom and transforming present realities to achieve that peace.

We invite you to join in the work toward this goal.

Membership of ExPro (as of June 1989):

Andrea Ayvazian, Peace Development Fund *

Grace Boggs, Detroit, Michigan *

Robert Borosage, Institute for Policy Studies *

Elise Boulding, Boulder, Colorado *

DeAnne Butterfield, Boulder, Colorado **
        Political Participation and Dispute Settlement

Robert Chrisman, *The Black Scholar*

Carol Cohn, Center for Psychological Studies in the Nuclear Age *

W. H. Ferry, Scarsdale, N.Y. *

Building a Peace System

Dietrich Fischer, Pace University **
        Individual and Collective Defense

Sharon Howell, Detroit, Michigan *

Robert A. Irwin, Brandeis University *

Robert C. Johansen, University of Notre Dame

Randall Kehler, Colrain, Massachusetts *

Arjun Makhijani, Institute for Energy and Environmental Research *
        Economic Justice **

Gay McDougall, Lawyers' Committee for Civil Rights Under Law *

Liane E. Norman, Pittsburgh Peace Institute *

David Orr, Meadowcreek Project **
        Ecology and Technology

Elizabeth Richards, Toronto, Ontario

Colleen Roach, Fordham University **
        Information and Culture

Kirkpatrick Sale, Cold Spring, N.Y.

Michael Shuman, Center for Innovative Diplomacy *

A. W. Singham, Brooklyn College, CUNY *

Mark Sommer, Miranda, California

Carolyn M. Stephenson, University of Hawaii

(* denotes board members)
(** denotes track director)

In addition to the present members, the following former members attended two or more meetings, in many cases participating for more than two years: Gar Alperovitz, National Center for Economic Alternatives; Charles Derber, Boston College; Daniel Deudney, Princeton University; Johan Galtung, University of Hawaii; Robert R. Holt, New York University; Kermit D. Johnson, Center for Defense Information; Helen Kelley, Immaculate Heart Center; Eleanor M. LeCain, Executive Director of ExPro; Patricia Mische, Global Education Associates; Marcus Raskin, Institute for Policy Studies; George Rathjens, M.I.T.; Richard Smoke, Brown University; Pam Solo, Institute for Peace and International Security; Robert C. Tucker, Princeton University.

Robert A. Irwin studied philosophy at Princeton University and Antioch College (B.A., 1973) and lived and worked seven years at the Philadelphia Life Center (an international training center for nonviolent activists). He has lectured widely on nonviolent struggle and civilian-based defense, authored or co-authored study guides on ecological, economic, and social problems, political theory and strategy, and U.S. defense policy, and testified as an expert witness on the efficacy of nonviolent struggle. His article "Why Nonviolence?" (co-authored with Gordon Faison) has sold over 100,000 copies on three continents.

Currently pursuing a doctorate in sociology at Brandeis University, from 1980 to 1985 he assisted Dr. Gene Sharp in founding the Albert Einstein Institution and establishing the Program on Nonviolent Sanctions in Conflict and Defense at Harvard University's Center for International Affairs. He has served on the boards of Macro-Analysis Seminars, Inc., the Civilian-based Defense Association, and the Albert Einstein Institution. He has been a consultant to the Direct Action Task Force of the Nuclear Weapons Freeze Campaign and to the Security Program of Rocky Mountain Institute. He has been a member of the Exploratory Project on the Conditions of Peace (ExPro) since its beginning, and in 1989 chaired its board of directors.

He is interested in discussing with people the possibility that solutions are now known for many of humanity's most serious problems, and that we can put those solutions to work to make a better world. He can be contacted c/o Sociology Department, Brandeis University, P.O. Box 9110, Waltham, MA 02254-9110; (617) 736-2630.

Index of Names

Please note: most of this book is indexed, but not (with a few exceptions) the many names contained in the acknowledgments, the lists of readings, and the four Information Resources sections. (You are encouraged to consult those sections.)

A.J. Muste Memorial Institute 198
Abbott, Lawrence   47, 147, 174-175
Across Frontiers   194
Adams, Gordon   187
Adcock, Cynthia   81, 187
Afghanistan   49, 51, 59, 90-92, 98-99, 116, 200
AFL-CIO (American Federation of Labor–Congress of Industrial Organizations)   122, 187
Africa   100, 107, 110, 117, 124
Agency for International Development 182
Albert, Michael   122
Alcalay, Glen 194
Allison, Graham. See "Owls," Harvard.
Alperovitz, Gar   22, 71
Alternative Defence Commission 115, 195
Alternative Defense Network 199
Alternative Defense Project, The 177
Alternatives 199
Alvarado, Elvia 150
American Friends Service Committee 11, 117, 138, 149
American Revolution   201
American University 95
Amnesty International   61, 182
Andropov, Yuri   103
Angola   51, 116-117
Annual Review of Peace Activism 198
Argentina 91, 93, 110
Argyris, Chris 190
Arizmendi, Jose Maria   73
Art, Robert J.   164
Asia 112
Asia, East 91, 111-112
Asia, South   110
Asia, Southeast 110
Asian-Americans   112, 197
Association for Transarmament Studies. *See* Civilian-Based Defense Association.
Atlantic Ocean 111-112

Atlee, Tom   198
Auster, Bruce 138
Australia 58, 93, 102, 110, 146, 263
Austria   58, 67, 179-180
Awakening 171
Ayvazian, Andrea   139-140, 149, 201
Bagdikian, Ben 270
Bakan, David 82
Baldwin, J.   190
Bandler, Richard   258
Bangladesh   186
Barnet, Richard J.   138-139
Bateson, Gregory   295
Becker, Norma 11
Beer, Stafford 186
Bello, Walden 41, 81, 110, 112, 141, 199
Benhabib, Seyla   170
Bennett, Gordon   112, 193
Berlin Wall   112
Bernard, Jessie 192
Berrigan, Dan 263
Bertalanffy, Ludwig von   164
Bigelow, Albert   167
Birchard, Bruce   138-139
Bittner, Egon   90, 191
Blood-Patterson, Peter   229
Bloomfield, Lincoln P.   193
Bodner, Joan 181
Boguslaw, Robert   36, 172
Bok, Derek   15
Bondurant, Joan V. 187
Bookchin, Murray   170, 283
Borosage, Robert   165
Borsodi, Ralph 170
Boston Globe 95
Boston Nuclear Study Group   24, 50
Boston, Sandra. *See* deSylvia, Sandra Boston.
Boston Study Group 162
Botswana 117
Boulding, Elise 36-37, 41, 43, 75, 80-81, 84, 92, 111, 156, 165, 172, 174, 188, 192-193, 245, 257-258, 283

Boulding, Kenneth E.   35, 44, 163, 166, 172, 174, 190, 283-284
Boyle, Francis Anthony   191, 202
Brand, Stewart 172
Breakthrough 265
Brecher, Jeremy   74, 187
Brecht, Berthold   29
Brethren, Church of the 195
Brigham, Nancy   146
Britain   19, 58, 112
Brown, Lester R.   91, 176, 178, 191
Brown, Roger 165
Brown, Seyom 164
Browne, Robert S.   76
Brugmann, Jeb 125
Brundtland Commission 138
Buber, Martin 172
Buckley, William F., Jr.   188
Bulletin of Municipal Foreign Policy 126, 197
Bundy, McGeorge   17, 95
Burdet, Michele   263
Caldicott, Helen   11, 15, 263
California 112
Callenbach, Ernest 38, 173
Calvert Social Investment Fund 182-183
Cambridge (Mass.) Peace Commission 125
Campaign for Peace and Democracy/ East and West   194
Canada   61, 102, 111, 127, 263
Canadian Institute for International Peace and Security   79
Cantor, Daniel 197
Caribbean   92
Carlson, Don   17, 191, 199
Carlucci, Frank 105, 169
Carnesale, Albert . *See also* "Owls," Harvard.   15, 169, 188
Carothers, Andre   64, 108
Carson, Clayborne 168
Carter, Amy   129, 202
Castro, Fidel   85, 188
Cataldo, Mima 192

Center for Common Security   246, 297

Center for Defense Information 163

Center for Innovative Diplomacy 125-126, 197

Central America   12, 92, 94, 107, 114, 116-117, 125, 143-146, 148, 150, 154, 195, 200

Central Intelligence Agency (CIA) 117, 129, 148, 177, 186

Centre for the Study of Developing Societies   199

Chandler, Dale 186

Changeworks, The   203

Changing Work   183

Chernobyl   70, 112

Chicanos 197

Chile   99, 177, 186

China   65, 70, 91, 100, 133, 161

Chomsky, Noam   28-29, 98-99, 117, 162, 171, 184, 189, 192-193, 195-196, 263

Christian Science Monitor   103, 140

Christianity   80, 127

Civilian-Based Defense Association 59

Civilian-Based Defense: News and Opinion   59, 177

Clark, Grenville   137, 172

Co-op America   181, 183, 266

Cockburn, Alexander   179, 197

Cockburn, Andrew 163

Cohen, Joshua 93, 119, 122, 144, 168, 196

Cohen, Stephen F.   161

Cohen-Joppa, Felice and Jack 202

Cohn, Carol   81, 187

Coles, Robert 80

Collins, Carole 117

Comfort, Alex 170

Committee for Common Security 138

Committee for a Just World Peace 199

Committee in Solidarity with the People of El Salvador (CISPES) 195

Committees of Correspondence (U.S.Greens) 203

Commoner, Barry   178

Comprehensive Test Ban Treaty 126

Comstock, Craig   191, 199

Congo   99

Congress, United States   12, 24, 29, 77, 93, 117, 119, 145, 147, 196, 199

Congressional Black Caucus   75, 124, 196, 197

Conn, Sarah   152

Conser, Walter H., Jr.   201

Constitution, United States   47, 54, 119, 147

Cook, Alice   192

Cooney, Robert   167

Coover, Virginia   203, 220, 229

Cornell, Drucilla   170

Costello, Tim   74, 187

Council on Foreign Relations 37, 200

Covenants. *See* International covenants.

Cuba   116

Cuban Missile Crisis 85, 95

Czechoslovakia 58, 60, 90, 99, 177

Daly, Herman E.   68, 84, 180

Darnovsky, Marcy   125

Davidson, Mark   164

Dedring, Juergen   161

Defense & Disarmament Alternatives 177

Defense Monitor   163

Degranfenried, Mrs. 140, 199

Dellinger, David   144-145, 229

Dellums, Cong. Ronald V.   124, 197

Denmark 146, 191

Derber, Charles   19, 24, 195

deSylvia, Sandra Boston 203

Deudney, Daniel   30, 124-125

Deutsch, Karl W.   163

Disarmament 2000/Common Security Working Group   198

Discriminate Deterrence 105

Doble, John   22, 192, 196

Domestic Policy Association   140

Domhoff, G. William   196, 200

Dominican Republic   99

Doty, Paul   15, 188

Dower, John   113

Dragsdahl, Joergen 98, 103

Dresden   25

DuBois, W.E.B.   148, 202

Dubos, Rene   39

Dukakis, Michael   202

Dumanoski, Dianne 178

Dyson, Freeman   170

Eakins, David W.   189

East Germany 99

Ebert, Theodor 190

Ecotopia 173, 285

Edsall, Thomas Byrne   196

Effective Learning Systems   203

Ehrlich, Anne H.   68, 178, 181

Ehrlich, Paul R.   68, 178, 181, 185

Einstein, Albert   164, 189

El Salvador   74, 94, 99, 117, 193

Ellsberg, Daniel   28, 99, 129-130, 144, 161-162, 170, 198

Elshtain, Jean Bethke   188

Engels, Friedrich   36, 172, 189

Enloe, Cynthia 188

Erickson, Milton   203, 295

Etheredge, Lloyd S.   85, 171, 187-189

Ethiopians   25

Etzioni, Amitai 95, 97

Europe   21-22, 28, 58-59, 92-93, 98, 114-115, 143, 158

Europe, Eastern   194

Europe, Western   263

European Nuclear Disarmament 12, 114-115

European Parliament   111

Evans, Peter   72

Exchange Project   199, 203

Exploratory Project on the Conditions of Peace (ExPro) 1, 2, 7, 17, 45, 61, 115, 137, 148-149, 153, 157, 165, 182, 199, 207, 299-302

"Eyes on the Prize" 168

Falk, Richard A. 53-54, 89, 115, 137, 164-165, 171-172, 175-176, 187, 189, 192, 195, 199

Farren, Pat 149

Faux, Jeff 71

Feller, Gordon 192

Fellman, Gordon 24

Ferencz, Benjamin 49-50, 90, 147, 174-175

Ferguson, Marilyn 142, 200

Ferguson, Thomas 168, 184, 196

Ferree, Myra Marx 188

Ferry, W.H. 16, 148-149, 164

Feshbach, Seymour 161

Finland 58

Fischer, Dietrich 16, 45, 47, 54-57, 69, 104, 165, 174-175, 190

Five Continent Peace Initiative 110

Flanagan, Stephen 177

Foell, Earl 103, 165, 193

Food First Books 203

Foreign Policy Association 200

Forest, Jim 263

Forsberg, Randall 12, 15, 28, 133, 136, 138, 153, 162, 168, 198

Fourier, Charles 36

France 112, 127, 147

Fraser, Nancy 170

Freedman, David 116

Freeze. See Nuclear Weapons Freeze Campaign

French, Marilyn 81

Freud, Sigmund 81

Freundlich, Paul 183

Friends Committee on National Legislation 41

Fuglesang, Andreas 186

Fuller, John 167

Fund for Renewable Energy and the Environment 184

Future Survey 44, 142

Futures-Invention Associates, The 257-258

Galbraith, John Kenneth 175

Gall, John 190

Galtung, Johan 27, 119, 138, 161, 165, 170, 175-176, 190, 194-195

Gambrell, Leonard 177

Gamson, William 24

Gandhi, Mohandas K. 60, 170, 199, 201

Garrow, David J. 168

Garthoff, Raymond 102

General Electric 126, 181, 264

George, Alexander 191

George, Susan 179

Germany, East 149

Germany, West 119, 141, 149

Gerson, Joseph 27, 99, 149, 193

Gervasi, Tom 162

Gilligan, Carol 81

Gilman, Robert 73, 185

Gleick, James 190

Global Education Associates 54, 199

Glossop, Ronald J. 51, 174

Goldsmith, Edward 178

Goodman, Paul 128-129, 144, 151, 167, 170, 175, 179, 198, 203

Goodman, Percival 179

Gorbachev, Mikhail 19, 70, 94-95, 97, 101-103, 105, 162

Gorham, Deborah 78

Gowan, Susanne 191, 200

Grameen Bank 186

Gran, Guy 71-73, 185

Gray, Colin 16

Great Peace Journey 92, 192

Greece 93, 99, 110, 115, 193

Greenham Common 92, 192

Greening, Tom 142, 200

Greenleaf Books 170

Greenpeace 61, 112, 133, 182

Greens See also Committees of Correspondence (U.S.Greens) 119, 141, 149-150, 186, 202-203

Greenway, H.D.S. 193

Greider, William 199

Grenada 94, 200

Guatemala 52, 99

Guernica 25

Haig, Alexander 145, 163, 169, 193

Haldeman, Joe 187

Handbook of Organizational Design 38, 43, 173

Harford, Barbara 192

Harman, Willis 141-143, 193, 200

Harvard Nuclear Study Group 15, 21, 85, 99, 163, 188

Harvey, Hal 25, 27

Hatfield, Sen. Mark O. 168

Hawaii 112

Hayes, Peter 112

Healey, Richard 163

Hegel, G.W.F. 189

Hentoff, Nat 198

Herman, Edward S. 189, 192-193

Hersh, Seymour 60

Herz, John 176

Hess, Beth B. 188

Hildyard, Nicholas 179

Hirsch, Fred 181

Hiroshima 25, 112, 127, 148

Hitler, Adolf 25, 55, 57

Hockenberry, John 175

Hoffman, Abbie 129, 202

Hoffmann, Stanley 15, 188

Holdren, John P. 178

Holt, Robert R. 16, 82-83, 164-165, 190

Honduras 52, 117, 150

Hopkins, Sarah 192

Horvat, Branko 185

Howard, Michael 15, 17

Howell, Sharon 296

Hudgens, Tom A. 174

Hudson, Richard 52

Hülsberg, Werner 202

Hundredth Monkey, The 201

Hune, Shirley 107, 109, 115, 195

Hungary 90, 99

Hunt, Susan 181

Hunter, Allen 167

Huntington, Samuel P.   15, 116, 188

Iceland   111

"Imaging a World Without War" 209, 257-258

Independent Commission on Disarmament and Security Issues (Palme Commission)   138, 157

India   93, 110, 111, 199

Indian Ocean   110

Indonesia 99

Industrial Cooperative Association 183, 186

INF Treaty. *See* Intermediate Nuclear Forces (INF) Treaty.

INFACT   126, 198

Institute for Defense and Disarmament Studies133, 138, 195, 199

Institute for Peace and International Security   138

Institute for Policy Studies   138-139

Institute for World Order. *See* World Policy Institute.

Interhelp 140, 155, 171

Intermediate Nuclear Forces (INF) Treaty 19, 21, 94, 98, 102, 199

Internal Revenue Service 145-146

International Court of Justice   29, 49, 51, 94, 102, 104, 112, 141, 146-147

International covenants   185

International Federation of Chemical, Energy and General Workers' Unions (ICEF)   186

International Institute for Strategic Studies 161

International Labor Organization 51, 74

International Monetary Fund   182

International Social Science Council 84

Iran 51, 91, 99, 147

Iraq 51

Irwin, Robert A.   59-60, 62, 100, 144, 147-148, 165, 190-191

Islam   80

Israel   101

Jacobs, Paul   197

Jackson, Rev. Jesse 71, 93, 123, 148, 194, 202

Jahnkow, Rick 122

Jamaica   111

Jantsch, Erich   190, 193

Japan   67, 91, 93, 101, 107, 112-114, 127, 133, 179, 191, 194, 263

Jefferson, Thomas   197

Jensen, Ethel   27, 81-82

Jervis, Robert   164, 169, 171, 187

Jobs With Peace   123-124

Johansen, Robert C. 19, 24, 51, 102, 104, 165

Johnson, Kermit D.   41

Joint Chiefs of Staff 60

Jordan, Amos A.   193

Judaism 80, 127

Jung, Carl G.   81

K.G.B.   177

Kaldor, Mary   115, 171, 195

Kaufmann, Walter   171

Kehler, Randall12-13, 130, 148, 153-154, 168, 193, 202

Kelly, Petra K. 21, 149-150, 169, 202

Kennan, George F.   15, 17, 22, 58-59, 161, 163, 166, 171, 176

Kennedy, John F.   85, 95, 97, 139, 161, 188

Kennedy, Paul M.   191

Kennedy, Robert F. 85

Kennedy, Sen. Edward M.   168

Kenya   111

Kenyatta, Muhammad   149

Kerman, Cynthia Earl   174

Keyes, Ken, Jr. 50, 174-175, 201

Khan Abdul Ghaffar Khan   199

Khrushchev, Nikita S.   85

Kim, Samuel S. 89, 137, 164-165, 171-172, 187, 189

King, Rev. Dr. Martin Luther, Jr. 168, 290

Kirk, Gwyn   192

Kissinger, Henry   91

Klare, Michael 28, 104-105, 139-140, 162, 194

Knight, Damon   77

Kohler, Gernot   27

Kohn, Alfie   191

Kohn, Melvin L.   184

Kolko, Gabriel 175, 189, 192, 200

Korean Demilitarized Zone   112

Korean War   111

Kothari, Rajni 94, 138, 192

Kripke, Margaret   178

Kropotkin, Peter   170

Kull, Steven   77, 79, 81, 187

Kuttner, Robert180

Labor Notes   187

Labour Party   115, 130

Laffin, Arthur J.175

Lakey, George 29, 60-61, 129, 138, 164, 166, 180, 192, 198

Landau, Saul   197

Landauer, Gustav   170

Lange, David   131

Langford, David   173, 178

Latin America 92-93, 100

Law of the Sea Treaty   52, 94, 141

League of Nations   61

Leavitt, Robert 138-139, 163

Lebanon   102

LeCain, Eleanor M.   16

Leghorn, Lisa 74-75

Legvold, Robert   102

Lenin, Vladimir   101, 172

Lens, Sidney   11, 168

Lentz, T.F.   188

Lewin, Leonard C.   164

Libya   94, 191, 200

Lifton, Robert Jay   81, 175

Lincoln, Abraham   47

Linder, Benjamin   147

Link, Mary   257

Listen Real Loud: News of Women's Liberation Worldwide 187

Little, Paul   192

Loomis, Mildred   170

Lovins, Amory 25, 69, 184-185

Luard, Evan   188

Lutz, Mark A.   181

Lux, Kenneth   181

Lydenberg, Steven   183

Macy, Joanna Rogers   29, 81, 164, 171-172, 258

Magraw, K.   169

Makhijani, Arjun   75-76, 179

Marien, Michael   44, 53, 142-143, 176, 181, 193, 200-201, 266

Mars 124

Martin, Brian   60, 155, 177

Marx, Karl   36, 172, 189

Mayer, Jean   247

McAllister, Pam   187

McCarthy, Ronald M.   201

McCraw, Thomas K. 194

McNamara, Robert S.   17, 85

McPhee, John 57, 176-177

McVeigh, Kevin   149

Meadows, Donella H.   179

Meeker-Lowry, Susan   182

Meiklejohn Civil Liberties Institute   202

Meissner, Martin   184

Melko, Matthew   163

Melman, Seymour   187, 197

Mendlovitz, Saul H.   51-54, 89, 137, 165, 172, 189, 199

Mennonites   195

Merton, Thomas   149

Mexico   93, 110

Meyer, Karl   146

Michalowski, Helen 167

Middle East   28, 69, 100, 107, 110, 143, 154, 195

Miles, Sara   116-117, 195

Mill, John Stuart   197, 247

Minter, William   200

Mintzer, Irving 178

Mische, Gerald   29-30

Mische, Patricia M.   17, 19, 24, 29, 53-54, 82, 140, 165, 199

Mitrany, David   165

Mobilization for Survival   11-12

Moller, Bjorn   177

Mondragon   73-74, 185-186

Montgomery bus boycott   11

Montgomery, Anne 175

Morgan, Robin 192

Morris, Aldon D.   168

Morris, David 180

Morris, William   170

Morrison, Philip   162

Movement Action Plan   167, 201

Movement for a New Society   155

Moyer, William H.   143-144, 167, 201

Mozambique   117

Mumford, Lewis   170

Muste, A.J. *See also* A.J. Muste Memorial Institute   128-129, 198

Muwakkil, Salim   202

Myrdal, Alva   25, 170

Nagasaki 25

Nagler, Michael   140-141

Namibia   117

Nasser, Gamal Abdel   107

National Center for Economic Alternatives 71

National Guard   93

NATO   12, 22, 28, 58-59, 97, 115, 133, 149, 153, 158, 161-162, 191

National War Tax Resistance Coordinating Committee   202

Native Americans   197

NBC 264

Nehru, Jawaharlal   107

Neier, Aryeh   195

Nelson, Juanita 167

Nenneman, Richard 103, 165, 193

Neuro-Linguistic Programming 258

Nevada Nuclear Weapons Test Site   126

New England War Tax Resistance   202

New International Economic Order 75

New Options   83, 140, 142, 181, 265

New Society Publishers   203

New Zealand   58, 93, 111-112, 115, 130, 191

Newcombe, Alan   126-127, 174

Newcombe, Hanna   36, 43-44, 52-53, 61, 126-127, 161, 165, 174, 245

Nicaragua 49, 52, 92, 94, 100, 102, 116-117, 146, 195, 202

Nietzsche, Friedrich 171

Nigeria   111

Nixon, Richard M.   60, 101

Nkrumah, Kwame   107

Nobel Peace Prize   199

Non-aligned Movement   91, 93, 107, 109-110, 115, 141, 196

Non-Offensive Defence   177

Norman, Liane Ellison   59, 127-128

Norway   179

Nuclear Free America   126, 198

Nuclear Free and Independent Pacific Network   112

Nuclear Times 102-103, 138, 265

Nuclear Weapons Freeze Campaign   11-13, 21, 119, 133, 153-154, 168, 195-196, 198

Nunes-Schrag, Jim   224

Nuremberg   50, 128, 148, 175, 202

Nye, Joseph S., Jr. See also "Owls," Harvard   15, 169, 177, 188

Nystrom, Paul C.   173-174

O'Brien, James 167

O'Dell, Jack   123-124

Ochs, Phil 100

Ogilvy, Jay   172

Omang, Joanne   195

Operation MONGOOSE 85, 95

Operation PUSH   123

Ordway, Samuel H., Jr.   68, 181

Organization of African Unity 51

Organizing Macro-Analysis Seminars: A Manual 220, 223

Orwell, George 188

Osgood, Charles   95, 97

Other Economic Summit, The (TOES)   181

"Owls," Harvard   22-23, 169

Oxfam America   182

Pacific Ocean   100, 107, 111-113, 115

Palau   110, 115, 194

Palme Commission. *See* Independent Commission on Disarmament and Security Issues.

Panama Canal Zone 124

Parker, Katherine   74

Parliamentarians Global Action
110-111

Pateman, Carole   184, 197

Payne, Keith   16

Peace Brigades International   52,
141, 175, 199

Peace and Democracy News   194

Peace Development Fund   139,
154, 199

Peace Links   196

Peace Research Institute—Dundas
(Ontario)   43, 174

PeaceNet 25, 170, 197

Peacework   148-149, 265

Peck, James   171

Pell, Eve   197

Perkovitch, George   102

Perrow, Charles   179, 189

Philadelphia Macro-Analysis Collective
223-224

Philippines   74,91,99, 110, 124

Physicians for Social Responsibility
11, 195

Pirages, Dennis C.   178

Pirtle, Sarah   140, 257-258

Pittsburgh Peace Institute 59, 127, 177

Pledge of Resistance   92

Polak, Fred   174

Poland   91, 99, 141

Populist Caucus   196

Post-Reagan America   199

Program on Nonviolent Sanctions in
Conflict and Defense   57, 176

Public Agenda Foundation   196

Puerto Rico   124

Puget Sound Peace Camp   192

Putnam, Robert   190

Pyarelal   170

Quakers   195

Rainbow Coalition, National   71, 93,
109, 202

Rainbow Warrior   112

Rathjens, George   19, 23-24, 174

Rayman, Paula 122-123

RCA 264

Reader's Digest   50, 263

Reagan, Ronald   12-13, 16-17, 19,
24, 70, 91, 94, 97-98, 101-102, 117,
153, 162

Reardon, Betty 188

*Resistance, Politics, and the American
Struggle for Independence, 1765-
1775*   201

*Resource Manual for a Living
Revolution*   203, 220

Reves, Emery   50

Richards, Elizabeth   79

Richardson, Elliot   175

Ridley, Scott   184

Riles, Wilson, Jr.   126

Rise Up Singing   229

River City Nonviolent Resistance
Campaign   128

RMI. *See* Rocky Mountain Institute.

Roach, Colleen 275

Roberts, Adam 177

Robinson, J.M.   179

Rockwell International   127-128

Rocky Mountain Institute (RMI)
25, 69, 170, 185

Rogers, Joel   93, 119, 122, 144, 168,
196

Romania 115

Roosevelt, Franklin 121

Rosecrance, Richard 191

Roszak, Theodore   170, 181

Rousseau, Jean-Jacques   197

Rowland, F. Sherwood   178

Rubin, David M.   169

Ruddick, Sara   188

Ruina, Jack   23

Sagan, Scott   15, 188

Sakamoto, Yoshikazu   199

Sakharov, Andrei   263

Sale, Kirkpatrick   16-17, 25, 47

Sanday, Peggy Reeves   188

Sanders, Jerry W.   162

SANE   11, 13, 195, 198

San Francisco Study Group for Peace
and Disarmament 198

Satin, Mark   52, 140, 142-143, 181,
193, 201

Saudi Arabia   27

Sauvageau, Eileen   146

Scandinavia   67, 109, 115

Schaar, Stuart   26

Schell, Jonathan   81

Schiller, Herbert   264

Schlesinger, James   60, 193

Schmid, Alex P.   177

Schmookler, Andrew Bard   62

Schooler, Carmi   184

Schor, Juliet   197

Schroeder, Cong. Patricia 124

Schultz, Ted   201

Schumacher, E.F.   170, 181

Schumpeter, Joseph 197

Schwartz, Morris   24

Schwartz, Peter   172

Schwartz, William A.   19, 24

Scialabba, George   29

Seabrook 11

Seneca Falls (NY)   92

Senghaas, Dieter   161

SERVAS   273

Seventh Generation 183

Shalom, Stephen R.   202

Sharp, Gene   57-58, 60, 62, 80, 129,
165-167, 169, 176-177, 187, 198,
201

Shoup, Laurence H. 200

Shultz, George 98

Shuman, Michael   125

Silverstein, Ken   163

Singham, A.W. 107, 109, 115, 195

Sirianni, Carmen   173, 180

Sloan, Douglas 166

Small, Fred   199

Smith, Dan   162

Smith, Diana McLain   190

Smith, Gerard   17

Smoke, Richard   15, 21, 44, 54, 59,
69, 79, 141-142, 169, 200

Social Movement Empowerment
Project 167, 201

Soekarno, Achmed 107

Sohn, Louis B. 137, 172

Solo, Pam 138, 149, 168

Solon 77

Sommer, Mark 1, 16, 45, 54, 58, 79-80, 95, 97, 136, 138, 149, 163, 165, 167, 177, 189, 192

South Africa 27, 101, 117, 124-126, 149, 154, 165, 181-183, 195, 200

South Korea 112

South Pacific Forum 112

Soviet-American Initiative for a Citizens Ecological Treaty 199

Soviet Union *See* Union of Soviet Socialist Republics (U.S.S.R.)

Spain 73

Spanish Civil War 25

Stableford, Brian 173, 178

Stafford, Sen. Robert 144

Stalin, Joseph 101, 177

Stanley Foundation 58

Starbuck, William H. 173-174

Stauber, Leland 180

Stephenson, Carolyn M. 45, 112, 163, 165, 174, 176

Strauss, Anselm 188

Supreme Court, United States 47

Sweden 55, 58, 67, 69, 93, 102, 110, 179

Switzerland 55, 57-58, 67, 179, 263

Swomley, John M., Jr. 130

Syracuse Cultural Workers 192

Tajfel, Henri 165

Talloires Declaration 247

Tanzania 93, 110

Taylor, Maxwell 100, 193

Taylor, Richard K. 229

Taylor, Theodore B. 58, 177

Taylor, William J., Jr. 193

Thailand 147

The New Abolitionist 126

The Other Economic Summit (TOES) 181

The Progressive 11

The Third Millennium 63, 173, 178

Therborn, Goran 179

Thinkpeace 198

Third World 102-105, 107, 109-110, 116-117, 158, 199-200

Thompson, E.P. 15, 114-115, 162

Three Mile Island 167

Thucydides 3, 164

Tito, Josip Broz 107

Tokar, Brian 202

Tokyo 25

Tolstoy, Leo 170

Toscano, David J. 201

TransAfrica 195

Trebilcot, Joyce 188

Truman, Harry 47, 49

Tsurumi, Yoshi 194

Tucker, Robert C. 101, 103, 161

Turner, Stansfield 193

Twain, Mark 13

U.S.A.-Canada Institute 103

U.S.S.R. *See* Union of Soviet Socialist Republics.

UNESCO 77

Unger, Roberto Mangabeira 189

Union of Soviet Socialist Republics (U.S.S.R.) 1, 19, 24, 27-28, 70, 93, 100, 161

United Kingdom 111, 117, 147

United Nations 6, 49, 51-53, 61, 70, 74-75, 84, 91, 94, 98, 101-104, 107, 109-111, 127, 133, 137, 141, 192

United Nations Charter 146-147

United Nations Environment Program 70

United Nations Security Council 146

van Wolferen, Karel G. 113

Vanek, Jaroslav 73, 185-186

Vayrynen, Raimo 195

Vietnam War 11, 59, 90-92, 97, 116, 129, 178

Wachtel, Paul 83

Waldheim, Kurt 193

Walker, Paul 138, 162

Wall, Tom 149

Waller, Douglas C. 168

Waltz, Kenneth 3, 54, 164, 176

Walzer, Michael 181

War Resisters League 11

War Tax Resisters Penalty Fund 146, 202

Warsaw Pact 28, 60, 97, 115, 133, 153, 158

Waskow, Arthur 37, 172

Watzlawick, Paul 164

Weigel, Richard D. 163

Weinstein, James 189

Weiss, Lynne 135

Wertenbaker, William 175

Western Europe 107, 109

White, Ralph K. 161, 187

Whyte, Kathleen King 185

Whyte, William Foote 185

Williams College 246

Williamson, Janice 78

Winston Foundation for World Peace 198

Witness for Peace 52, 141, 175, 199

Witt, Matt 197

Wittner, Lawrence S. 167

Wohlstetter, Albert 164

Wolfe, Alan 161, 171

Women Strike for Peace 11

Women's Action for Nuclear Disarmament 196

Women's Budget 75

Women's International League for Peace and Freedom (WILPF) 75, 124, 192, 198

WOMP. *See* World Order Models Project.

Worker Owned Network 186

Working Assets 181, 183

Workplace Democracy 183

World Bank 182

World Commission on Environment and Development 138

World Court. *See* International Court of Justice.

World Federalist Association 48, 147

World Health Organization 51

World Order Models Project (WOMP) 37, 137, 140, 199

World Policy Institute (formerly
    Institute for World Order)   37, 51,
    53, 139, 199
World Policy Journal   111, 133
World War I   57
World War II   25, 28, 90, 94, 100-101,
    111

World Watch   176
Worldwatch Institute   63, 91, 178
World Without Weapons Project
    41, 257-258
Yankelovich, Daniel 22, 192, 196
Yazov, Dimitri 103

Yugoslavia   58
Zambia   117
Zarsky, Lyuba   112
Ziegler, Warren   190, 257-258
Zeta Magazine   117, 187